Neural Network Fundamentals

Neural Network Fundamentals

Dharamdas Kumhar
and Avanish Kumar

ARCLER
PRESS

www.arclerpress.com

Neural Network Fundamentals

Dharamdas Kumhar and Avanish Kumar

Arcler Press
4164 Lakeshore Road
Burlington, ON L7L 1A4
Canada
www.arclerpress.com
Email: orders@arclereducation.com

ISBN: 978-1-77956-965-3 (Hardcover)

ABOUT THE AUTHORS

Dharamdas Kumhar is Assistant Professor, Department of Mathematical Sciences and Computer Application, Bundelkhand University, Jhansi, U.P.-India of computer application. He has 22 years of teaching experience in the field of computer application. He has received his Doctor of Philosophy in Computer Science from Bundelkhand University, Jhansi U.P and Master of Philosophy in Computer Science from Madurai Kamaraj University, Madurai T.N. He completed his Master of Computer Application from Institute of Computer Science, Vikram University, Ujjain. He has attended many International Conferences, Seminars, FDPs and Workshops. He has published various research papers in International Journals and International Conferences. His areas of research are computer communication network, machine learning, computer graphics and theory of computation.

Avanish Kumar is Professor of mathematics, as well as Former Chairman, CSTT, and Former Director, CHD, Ministry Education, Government of India. He has completed his M. Sc., from Meerut University (presently CCS University), Meerut in 1989, M. Phil., from University of Roorkee (presently IIT), Roorkee in 1992 and Ph. D. in Mathematics, from Gurukula Kangri, University, Haridwar in 1999. He has awarded his 'University Medal' for standing First in First Class by University of Roorkee, Awarded Prof R C Mehrotra Best Teacher Award and Gold Medal for 'Outstanding contribution to the university services' by Bundel khand University Jhansi and Awarded 'Bharat Vikas Award' by Institute of Self Reliance, Bhubaneswar. He has 23 years of teaching and research experience in the field of RealAnalysis, Complex Analysis, Operations Research and Distributed Computing Systems. He is Vice President of VIJÑĀNA PARISHAD of INDIA, and Former Vice President of the OPERATIONAL RESEARCH SOCIETY OF INDIA. He has also a Copyright for "Questionnaire on CSTT/CHD" has filed with Department of Promotion of Industry and Internal Trade, Govt of India under class Literary/Dramatic; Current Status- Re-Scrutiny. He has a Patent on "Method for Optimization of Supply Chain Finance Management based on Big Data". He has more than 15 Ph D Student as guided and co guided. He has published more than 60 research papers in International Journals and more than 50 research papers in International Conferences. He has attended many International Conferences, Seminars, FDPs and Workshops.

TABLE OF CONTENTS

LIST OF FIGURES

PREFACE

Artificial intelligence has become one of the most revolutionary powers of modern science and technology, and neural networks are at the very heart of this revolution. They are the computational framework that enables machines to recognize images, understand speech, process natural language, and even forecast on the basis of enormous amounts of data. Compared to traditional rules-based algorithms, neural networks learn from examples and patterns, making them very powerful for solving challenging problems when direct solutions are not feasible. From healthcare diagnosis and self-driving cars to financial modeling and robotics, innovations driven by neural networks have impacted nearly every industry.

The history of neural networks is the convergence of mathematics, computer science, neuroscience, and engineering. While originating in the human mind, they are themselves computational models, composed of nested stacks of artificial neurons that process and transform information. Their success depends not only on architecture design but also on painstaking training, optimization, and fine-tuning to tasks. The field is growing at an increasingly rapid rate, incorporating new models and approaches that increase efficiency, accuracy, and generality. Familiarity with these fundamentals is important for students, researchers, and practitioners who need to apply neural networks to tackle actual problems.

Neural Network Fundamentals is authored to familiarize the reader with theoretical knowledge as well as working expertise in this fast-evolving field. The book presents the mathematics of neural networks systematically, discusses architectures, and elaborates on the training and optimization methods. Every chapter is a natural follow-up to the previous one, with unambiguous steps from initial concepts to advanced methods. Through explanation by example and well-structured discussions, the book enables readers to have the ability to understand, use, and evaluate neural network models.

Chapter 1 presents neural networks, their background, and the role they play in artificial intelligence. It begins with the subject by explaining how neural networks diverge from classic programming concepts and why they are suitable for pattern recognition and learning issues.

Chapter 2 addresses the mathematical fundamentals. Chapter 2 comprises linear algebra, probability, calculus, and other mathematical methods that form the basis of design and neural network training. It emphasizes how mathematical ideas are realized in computational models.

Chapter 3 deals with perceptrons and linear models. The chapter discusses the most basic neural network model—the perceptron—along with linear classifiers and their limitations. Readers get an insight into how these early models paved the way for how today's architectures have developed.

Chapter 4 deals with multilayer perceptrons (MLP). The chapter discusses the hidden layers, activation functions, and universal approximation theorem. It also briefly explains how MLPs are the foundation to more intricate architectures.

Chapter 5 discusses training and optimization techniques. Material covered includes loss functions, gradient descent, backpropagation, and methods to enhance convergence like momentum, regularization, and learning rate schedules. This chapter focuses on effective and stable training.

Chapter 6 presents convolutional neural networks (CNNs). It discusses their application in image processing, computer vision, and feature extraction. Readers are introduced to convolution layers, pooling layers, and contemporary applications of CNNs.

Chapter 7 covers recurrent neural networks (RNNs). Chapter 7 covers how sequential data, like speech and text, is dealt with by RNNs and includes key topics like vanishing gradients and solutions such as LSTMs and GRUs.

Chapter 8 covers more advanced structures, like generative adversarial networks (GANs), transformers, and hybrid models. Chapter 8 highlights recent advancements that push the boundaries of what can be achieved with neural networks.

Chapter 9 outlines architectures of neural networks. It explains mainstream software libraries such as TensorFlow, PyTorch, and Keras, and how they are employed to design, train, and deploy neural networks affordably.

Chapter 10 looks into the future with regard to trends in neural networks. It discusses ongoing research direction in the domains of explainability, energy-efficient models, neuromorphic computing, and ethical aspects of AI development.

This book is for a broad audience with interest in machine learning and artificial intelligence. It will be an instructed introduction for students explaining concepts step by step with the mathematical machinery sufficient for insight. Researchers, computer scientists, data scientists, and engineers can use it as a reference to make stronger connections between conventional and new models of neural networks. Practitioners applying neural networks in industry will welcome the balance of theory to practice, which can contribute to guiding implementation choices.

Brattle square of bringing conceptual foundations and applied knowledge together, *Neural Network Fundamentals* gives readers the tools and mastery to tackle one of the most dynamic and impactful areas of modern computing.

CHAPTER 1

INTRODUCTION TO NEURAL NETWORKS

Contents

INTRODUCTION

The timeline of neural networks has emerged as the wave of revolution in artificial intelligence (AI), reshaping the image of various industries with its capacity to represent and predict complex patterns. While teachers search for new means to teach the fundamental concepts of AI, the integration of machine learning ideas is gaining popularity. The integration is necessary because it enables the basic ideas to be understood in a clearer fashion and serves to attract students. The NSF-funded collaborative effort aims to enhance the learning experience in AI classes by presenting the material in flexible structures and hands-on lab projects. By bringing into relief the close relationship between computer science and AI, this project not only makes fundamental principles better understood but also sparks students interest in the field, pointing to the central place of neural networks in contemporary technology and science (Coleman et al., 2005). Under the overall umbrella of artificial intelligence is the intricate web of neural networks that has been instrumental in the creation of breakthroughs across domains from business to science. One of the most important strengths of neural networks is that they can learn from enormous amounts of information, which in turn makes them capable of tasks like image recognition and natural language processing. With these applications growing by the day, dynamic networks too have begun gaining ground in the ability to analyze changing relationships and interactions. This adaptability positions dynamic networks at the forefront of research fields such as epidemiology and social network analysis, showcasing their capacity to deal with intricate actual-world issues. However, merging concepts from various domains has a tendency to breed terminological inconsistency, and therefore the propagation of information regarding dynamic networks and their uses is particularly challenging (Gabrys et al., 2021).

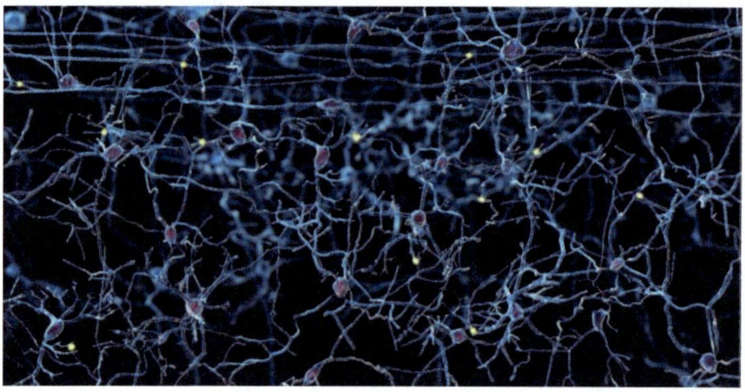

Figure 1.1. *Neural networks explained.*

Source: https://i0.wp.com/eastgate-software.com/wp-content/uploads/2024/10/Neural-Networks-Explained-.jpg?resize=1140%2C570&ssl=1.

While combining all these emerging paradigms, it is essential to establish a combined understanding of both dynamic network structures and neural networks. There is a need to comprehend the intricacies of graph neural networks (GNNs) because they are gaining prominence in link prediction and node classification in dynamic contexts. Nevertheless, with ongoing research, there remains an expansive gap in exploring GNNs tailored for dynamic networks specifically. Closing these gaps not only provides transparency in the academic literature surrounding neural networks but also lays the ground for later innovations in AI and machine learning. As the discipline further develops, it will become increasingly important to foster a learning community where theoretical concepts are merged with practice to prepare the next generation of AI engineers (Gabrys et al., 2021) (Figure 1.1).

Definition of Neural Networks

Neural networks, as one of the foundation blocks of artificial intelligence, can be defined as a collection of algorithms that mimic operations of the human brain. Neural networks are intended to detect patterns, classify data, and make decisions based on input data. Essentially, neural networks consist of nodes or neurons that are interconnected in layers and are intended to process input data and provide output to the succeeding layer. Each neuron receives numerous inputs, adds them up with weights, and returns the value using a nonlinear activation function. This structure allows neural networks to learn complex relationships in data and has rendered them a general-purpose tool in numerous fields such as computer vision, natural language processing, and stock prediction. In the area of deep learning, neural networks are typically defined by architecture, i.e., number of layers and interlayer connectivity. Deep neural networks have multiple hidden layers enabling derivation of highly abstract features from input. In image classification, for instance, early layers will recognize edges and textures, while deeper layers recognize particular objects or patterns. This hierarchical learning approach allows deep networks to effectively represent high-dimensional data. Furthermore, advancements in training algorithms such as backpropagation and stochastic gradient descent have also substantially increased the efficiency and effectiveness of neural networks in learning from large datasets, thus broadening their use in most real-world applications. Neural networks are applied innovatively in Case-Based Reasoning (CBR) systems. A major technique utilizes the strength of neural networks to enhance CBR by transforming problem situations and potential solutions into continuous characteristics, thereby enabling a process mapping that facilitates generalization among cases more easily. Specifically, RBF neural networks offer a multivariable input-output mapping and facilitate flexible adaptation to varied situations without relying solely on domain-specific techniques. This combination approach not only improves valuable similarity assessments like CBR's architecture but also provides local estimates of accuracy based on the probability distribution of available cases that can be extremely valuable in real-world applications such as sales advisory systems. Integrating neural networks and CBR, these advances illustrate the potential of neural networks to enhance and accommodate complex problem-solving cases (Murray-Smith et al., 1993) (Figure 1.2).

Figure 1.2. *Neural networks.*

Source: https://news.mit.edu/sites/default/files/styles/news_article__image_gallery/public/images/201704/MIT-DeepLearning_0.jpg?itok=9E_frNp0.

Historical Background

Historical development of neural networks is within the broad study of artificial intelligence and machine learning, evolving radically since their theoretical inception. The initial basis of neural networks was established in the 1940s with Warren McCulloch and Walter Pitts's creation of the first artificial neuron, which was a simple mathematical representation of biological neurons. This model presented the fundamental theory that neural networks would be capable of handling information by simulating the interlinked patterns of biological brain structures. Over the next few decades, scientists tried various architectures and algorithms, leading to the development of early models of neural networks, such as perceptrons. Although they did not enjoy much success during this period due to limited computational power and data availability, these early experiments served a vital role in propelling further research deeper into more advanced network architectures and learning mechanisms. As the computational technology advanced came also more developed methodologies within neural networks, particularly towards the latter part of the 20th century. The advent of backpropagation in the mid-1980s was a turning point with the ability to train deeper and more complex networks through effective computation of gradients. This opened up neural networks again, leading to a wave of research and applications across many fields as image and speech recognition came back into vogue. Above all, hardware advancements and the availability of big data enabled the exploration of complex architectures such as convolutional neural networks (CNNs) and recurrent neural networks (RNNs), which went on to become the backbone of today's deep learning. Momentum gained here was a portent of an emerging knowledge of the potential of neural networks to transform various fields and provide the basis for the many applications that exist today. Over the past few years, the history of neural networks has further developed, particularly with the advent of deep learning and its use in many technologies. The ability of neural networks to perform hierarchical feature extraction has made revolutionary strides in areas such as object detection, where recognition systems have achieved unprecedented accuracy. Research in this field indicates a clearly established trajectory of development; for example, a worldwide review of over 400 object detection articles highlights the game-changing role played by deep learning techniques in this significant computer vision field. Moreover, the technologies have been enhanced through visionary investigations of novel strategy and architecture, demonstrating the complimentary interactions between theoretical advance and practical innovation. As neural networks continue to advance, their historical origins are both a reminder of earlier setbacks and a master plan for developments to come, evidence that they have a long-term legacy in artificial intelligence (Cahill et al., 2001; Guo et al., 2019) (Figure 1.3).

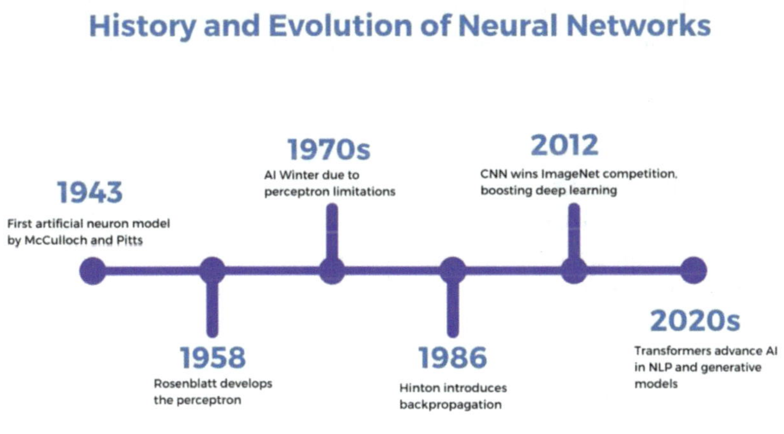

Figure 1.3. *History and evolution of neural networks.*

Source: https://i0.wp.com/eastgate-software.com/wp-content/uploads/2024/10/History-and-Evolution-of-Neural-Networks.jpg?resize=1536%2C865&ssl=1.

Importance in Modern Technology

Integration of neural networks into modern technology is the central foundation of innovation across various sectors, demonstrating their potential in the modern world. By leveraging the capacity of neural networks to process massive data, industries such as healthcare and finance have transformed the way information is processed and utilized. For instance, neural networks make it possible to identify patterns in complex data, leading to improved medical diagnostic tools and improved algorithms for identifying financial fraud. Moreover, as discussed in Doctor et al. (2020), combining Big Data with computational intelligence techniques holds potential in intelligent city buildings, encouraging innovation in planning and managing cities. Therefore, the reach of neural networks goes beyond academic research, finding its way into useful applications that tackle essential problems in society. The dependence on neural networks goes as far as AI, where their importance cannot be overstated. As organizations embrace AI technologies, the efficiency and impact of these systems depend on the underlying neural networks that give them their power. Most notably, the development of AI applications incites serious philosophic arguments about their ontology, including the nature of such systems and their manifest agency in society. As explained in Hawley et al. (2019), the evolving context of AI poses challenges to traditional definitions and forces stakeholders to rethink their position on technology's place in human life. Through the comprehension of neural networks as the key elements of AI, one can understand the far-reaching impact of neural networks on technology evolution, pinpointing the necessity of considering ethics in the wake of AI pervasiveness in day-to-day usage. Furthermore, the significance of neural networks in contemporary technology goes beyond industry-based applications, extending to social behaviors and personal experiences. In areas like machine learning, neural networks can provide more customized user experience, even more so in use cases like social media and web shopping. By virtue of these systems' utilization, users' preference and behavior drive algorithms that can learn and adapt, and there is a feedback loop that enhances users' engagement. This change, complemented by the effects of Big Data in Doctor et al. (2020), emphasized the way neural networks make smart, data-driven spaces that adapt to individual requirements. Thus, the significance of neural networks resonates to fostering connectivity, stimulating economic growth, and shaping societal norms through new technological advancements.

1.1. BASIC STRUCTURE OF NEURAL NETWORKS

The elementary structure of neural networks consists of several layers, which are primarily divided into input, hidden, and output layers. The input layer takes the raw information, which is the starting point of information processing. All the neurons in the layer pass its output to the neurons of subsequent hidden layers, where most of the calculation is performed. Hidden layers, the size and count of which varies with the complexity of the task, do the job of re-forming the input data through a network of neurons with learned weights and bias applied. Interconnectedness allows the network to learn intricate patterns and features in the data and lay the foundation for successful learning and generalization to a wide range of applications such as image classification and natural language processing. The adaptability of the architecture enables customization for specific tasks and ultimately determines the performance of the neural network. Activation functions form the core of neural networks since they introduce non-linearity into the model, allowing the model to learn intricate relationships between data. Sigmoid, hyperbolic tangent, and rectified linear unit (ReLU) are the most used activation functions that possess various benefits and characteristics.

For instance, the ReLU activation function has gained popularity since it assists in preventing the vanishing gradient problem, enabling deeper networks to be trained faster. Other breakthroughs such as batch normalization and dropout regularization are also used to learn best and prevent overfitting. These techniques stabilize the network and enhance its prediction power by normalizing the inputs and deactivating neurons at training time randomly, respectively. As neural networks are still in development, greater insight into these elements and how they interact with each other is increasingly necessary for researchers and practitioners seeking to tap into their full potential across a variety of fields, such as econometrics and biomedical engineering. The output layer of a neural network combines processed data from hidden layers to produce the end predictions or classifications. The structure of the output layer strongly depends on the nature of the task, for instance, regression, classification, or multi-class detection. For instance, for binary classification tasks, a single neuron with a sigmoid activation unit may suffice, while multi-class scenarios most often need more than one neuron organized under a softmax activation function to provide probabilities per class. This selection of architecture has immediate consequences for the interpretability and correctness of the networks. Also, the advancement in neural network architecture has introduced advanced architecture such as Convolutional Neural Networks (CNNs) and Recurrent Neural Networks (RNNs), which are tailored for some particular tasks such as image processing and time-series prediction, respectively. This continued enhancement highlights the dynamic character of neural networks, paving the way for even more intricate architectures that enhance artificial intelligence and machine learning technologies (Wu et al., 2024; Zhao et al., 2024) (Figure 1.4).

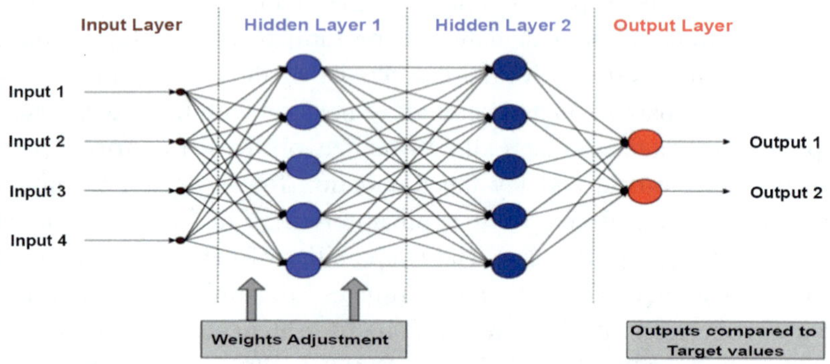

Figure 1.4. *Basic structure of neural network.*

Source: https://www.researchgate.net/publication/341716390/figure/fig1/AS:11431 281389372625@1745203944457/Basic-structure-of-neural-network.tif.

1.1.1. Neurons and Activation Functions

Neural network structure is constructed largely based on the behavior and interaction of neurons, which are the basic computational units. A neuron calculates the input data through weighted connections between the units, reflecting the strength of the relationship between units. The activation function specifies what a neuron output is, with the inclusion of non-linearity in the model computations. One of the most widely used activation functions is sigmoid, tanh, and ReLU (Rectified Linear Unit), each of which serves distinct purposes in network output. For instance, while sigmoid output is squeezed between 0 and 1—making it well suited to binary classification tasks—the ReLU function supports faster convergence by enabling layers to better respond to composite inputs. Such multivariate functionality enables neural networks to express complex patterns, which is required for tasks from image recognition to language handling. Activation functions also contribute significantly towards the effectiveness and interpretability of neural networks and raise significant questions about their inner workings. Feedforward neural networks' black-box nature limits our knowledge, making it difficult to ascertain the manner in which inputs map to outputs. For instance, while Kohonen's self-organizing feature maps (SOMs) offer a more transparent alternative in the form of storing knowledge in a form consonant with input data, standard neural networks do not. This transparency heightens the necessity for enhancing methods to explain the functional roles of neurons, particularly when addressing the complexities of activation functions. As researchers try to extract understanding of neural network behaviors, the development of procedures which transform standard networks mathematically into more interpretable forms can be pivotal, allowing more observation of the knowledge embedded in such systems (Slump et al., 2003). How activation functions play a role in the overall robustness of neural networks is also of critical concern, especially in safety-critical applications. Recent research has shown that the output error due to neuron failures is limited by network characteristics, for example, the Lipschitz constant of activation functions. This result indicates the influence of activation functions on the networks tolerance of errors in the face of disturbances, which is of increasing importance as neuromorphic hardware progresses. By experimentally establishing robustness without the need for total failure testing or existence of training sets, researchers achieve crucial information about neural network resilience and practical applications. Therefore, comprehending neurons and activation functions not only enhances the theoretical elements of neural network feasibility but also becomes a gateway to applied innovations in the topic (Guerraoui et al., 2017) (Figure 1.5).

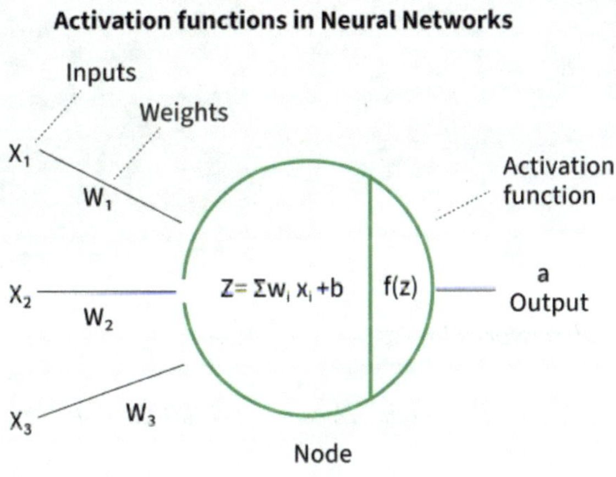

Figure 1.5. *Activation functions in neural networks.*

Source: https://media.geeksforgeeks.org/wp-content/uploads/ 2025052 8125143 444422/A ctivation-functions-in-Neural-Networks.webp.

1.1.2. Layers: Input, Hidden, and Output

The architecture of a neural network basically consists of three primary layers, namely input, hidden, and output. The input layer serves as the data entry point, consuming raw input data and converting it into a state to which the neural network can operate. Each neuron in this layer is mapping to a specific feature or attribute of the input data and, in essence, is acting as a filter that helps set the stage for more complex interpretations. The initial process is significant because it establishes the fundamental framework upon which the remaining hidden layers will operate. How information is communicated and projected in the input layer can play a significant role in the networks overall performance, necessitating stern focus in the neural network design process. The real thinking in the neural network occurs within the hidden layers, allowing a sophisticated level of understanding of the intrinsic patterns within the information. These layers consist of numerous interlinked neurons that work on and refine the input data through nonlinear mappings. Increasing the number of hidden layers increases the networks classification ability, but diminishing returns come into play; deeper networks do not necessarily exhibit proportionally increased accuracy.

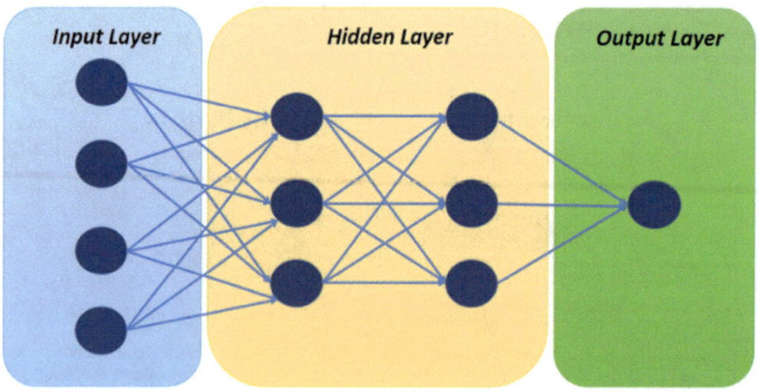

Figure 1.6. *Neural networks layers.*

Source: https://miro.medium.com/v2/resize:fit:4800/format: webp/1 LFJ3O-4vgRF6jBi1k_ej14w.png.*

As seen in most studies, such as the process described through layers that differ with respect to classification confidence, some data is typically needed to be further processed in depth, enhancing efficiency and reducing computational cost (Bohez et al., 2015). This indicates the necessity of optimizing layer structure for some tasks and preserving depth and complexity. The role of the output layer is central as it receives the previously processed data in the hidden layers and converts it into a final output, which could either be a classification or prediction. Every neuron in this layer is assigned to a single class or outcome and provides a real-world interpretation of the neural networks calculation. In the majority of cases, techniques such as dropout are employed during training to prevent overfitting so that the network still generalizes to new examples. The significance of dropout is that it causes resiliency by preventing complex co-adaptation among neurons, which allows all neurons to learn features valuable in a large number of contexts, as evidenced in benchmark tasks in speech and object recognition (Hinton et al., 2012). Therefore, input, hidden, and output layers interact in order to create a solid and adaptable neural network with the ability to solve many problems (Figure 1.6).

1.1.3. Weights and Biases

Weights and biases are a core idea in neural networks' operation as fundamental parameters the model adjusts with training. Weights govern the strength of the interaction between neurons and dictate the mapping of input to output. Biases, similarly, allow the model to shift the activation function by adding a certain amount of flexibility that helps the model learn complex patterns more efficiently. With increasingly complex and deeper neural networks, control over these parameters is crucial for best model performance. Algorithms which fail to learn to initialize their weights and biases properly may struggle to converge, leading to suboptimal performance and inefficient computation. Hence, understanding and managing these parameters does not only enhance the learnability of the networks but also impacts resource allocation and training time efficiency. Constraints in training neural networks have necessitated the requirement of robust algorithms for weight and bias optimization. Traditional methods such as gradient descent are the basis for these optimization procedures, enabling the gradual adjustment of biases and weights in the direction to minimize error. More advanced methods, including adaptive learning rate methods, offer some advance with dynamically adapting the learning rate during training to ensure that the model is able to navigate more in difficult loss landscapes. For example, the use of local decoders via convolutional neural networks indicates the value of optimizing weights in high-dimensional spaces, as is the case in quantum error correction applications. Such techniques need to follow an adaptive strategy toward weights and biases to ensure continued efficiency and accuracy despite the growing dimensionality of the data (Breuckmann et al., 2017). In examining how weights affect biases, and architecture of the model, one will observe the way design choices emerge in the functioning of neural networks. The activation function choice, regularization strategies, and even layer setup significantly influence not only the initialization of the weights and biases, but also how they evolve in training. Research has indicated the potential for reduced qubits required and gate operations in quantum-based neural network computation, which has been explored in ongoing research (Daskin et al., 2018). Application of new computational paradigms highlights how redesigning weight and bias strategies can lead to significant processing speed gains as well as model performance. As these developments progress, the debate about weights and biases will continue to be at the center of conversations about innovation and best practices in developing neural networks, effectively pushing the field forward (Figure 1.7).

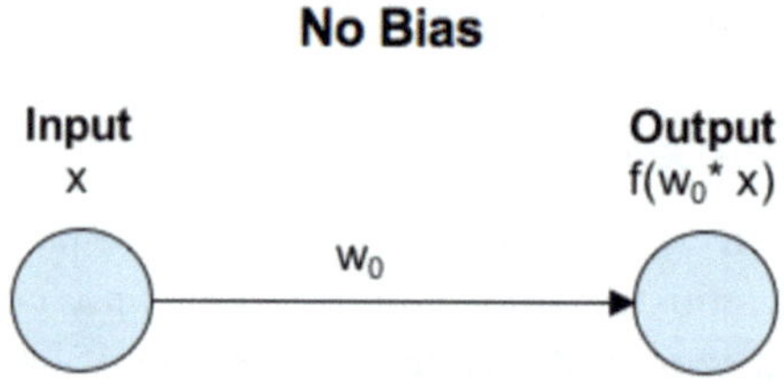

Figure 1.7. *The role of bias in neural networks.*

Source: https://www.pico.net/assets/kb/13-the-role-of-bias-in-neural-networks/no-bias.png.

1.2. TYPES OF NEURAL NETWORKS

Variability of architectures is the hallmark of the discipline of neural networks, each being for specific tasks and applications. Among the most remarkable architectures is the Convolutional Neural Network (CNN), which works best with grid-structured data, particularly images. CNNs utilize convolutional layers to learn and detect spatial hierarchies of features automatically, making them particularly well-suited to visual recognition tasks. This capability is beyond the capability of ordinary computer vision techniques, enabling CNNs to outperform conventional models for object detection and image classification, among other tasks. Recent developments have also boosted their application in domains such as medical imaging and autonomous vehicles. Consequently, CNN optimization and growth have been key topics to research, as is the application in this instance making use of a mixture of such networks coupled with reinforcement learning methods in order to gain better performance in intricate settings, as has been seen in Chebotar et al. (2017). Another key classification of neural networks is the Recurrent Neural Network (RNN), which is particularly well-suited for sequence data. RNNs are characterized by their ability to maintain memory over sequences, and therefore they are well suited for tasks such as natural language processing and time series prediction. RNNs are distinct from the traditional feedforward networks in that they use feedback loops that enable them to pass information from one step in a sequence to the next step. This structure makes them capable of maintaining temporal dependencies and learning dynamically. However, standard RNNs are susceptible to issues like vanishing gradients that complicate learning for long sequences. To address these shortcomings, alternatives like Long Short-Term Memory (LSTM) and Gated Recurrent Units (GRU) have been developed, basically resolving these shortcomings by incorporating mechanisms that manage information flow. These improvements have made RNNs crucial across applications ranging from language translation to speech recognition. Besides, Generative Adversarial Networks (GANs) are an innovative method in the field of neural networks, most notably for its ability to generate novel synthetic data. Two adversarial neural networks form a GAN: a generator, which produces candidate outputs, and a discriminator, which makes decisions on them. The two-way architecture allows GANs to achieve such spectacular results in areas like image synthesis, where the synthesized images are nearly impossible to distinguish from real ones. Applications range from mere visual generation; they encompass applications such as art generation, data augmentation, and image super-resolution from low-resolution images. The collaboration between the generator and discriminator provides a new learning platform driven by adversarial dynamics. With increasing complexity of GANs, their usage finds its place in different industries as a representation of the significance of their application in present research on neural networks, as is reflected in articles discussing optimization and applications in machine learning (N/A, 2022) (Figure 1.8).

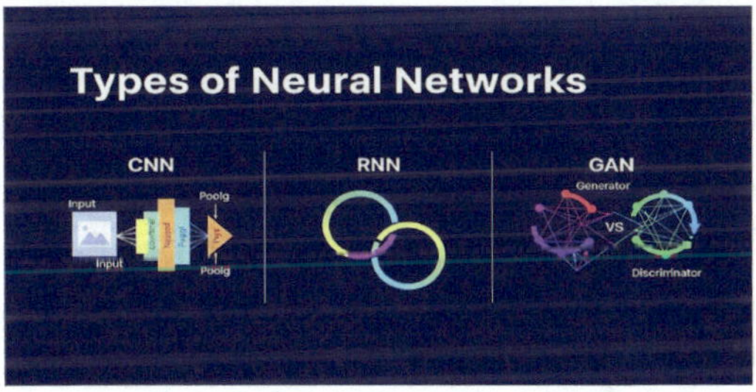

Figure 1.8. *Types of neural networks.*

Source: https://i.ytimg.com/vi/M15JQuwyENo/hq720.jpg?sqp=-oaymwEhCK-4FEIIDSFryq4qpAxMIARUAAAAAGAElAADIQj0AgKJD&rs=AOn4CLA6fuLGMP7XIwpZvdY44UzKoBTTjA.

1.2.1. Feedforward Neural Networks

Feedforward Neural Networks (FNNs) are one of the simplest architectures in the case of neural networks, characterized by its straightforward flow of information. Unlike their periodic equivalents, FNNs have no cycles or feedback loops, so it is simple to possess a clear and unobstructed way from input to output. This simplicity renders them simple to implement across a broad spectrum of applications, e.g., image and speech recognition, in which they excel at function approximation and classification. Parallel processing by FNNs renders them computationally efficient, rendering them perfect for real-time systems. Also, algorithmic advancements such as the Levenberg-Marquardt have enhanced training effectiveness to enable FNNs to achieve high-quality solutions in constrained computational environments, particularly when dealing with complex data sets or large networks as cited in recent studies (Grando et al., 2018). The structure of a Feedforward Neural Network, typically having an input layer, one or more hidden layers, and an output layer, determines its performance significantly.

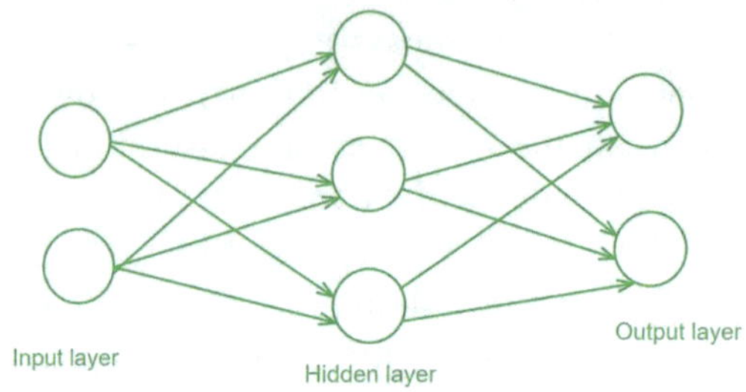

Figure 1.9. *Feedforward neural network (FNNs).*

Source: https://media.geeksforgeeks.org/wp-content/uploads/20240601001059/FNN-768.jpg.

Each neuron in the layers projects input signals through weighted connections and activation functions, which are important in bringing non-linearity into the model. The choice of the activation function has a significant influence on the networks learning power and expressiveness. For instance, ReLU (Rectified Linear Unit) has become popular due to its effectiveness in taming the vanishing gradient problem and therefore allowing deeper networks to be trained in an efficient manner. The importance of activation function selection is brought out by how it influences the rate of convergence as well as overall prediction ability. Thus, much effort is spent extending the capabilities of FNNs with advances in architectures and schemes of activation. Aside from this, Feedforward Neural Networks are applied further in other fields including healthcare, finance, and natural language processing. In the field of medicine, for example, FNNs have been employed for predicting clinical patterns in patient information to aid in diagnosis and treatment planning. In finance, they are employed in the evaluation of risk and for detection of fraud, illustrating their potential to be applied to vast amounts of transactional data. In addition, novel brain-computer interface applications focus on the network's capability to unravel complex signals, such as EEG, to improve human-machine collaboration. Such plasticity affirms the long-term applicability of FNNs as they improve existing methods while providing avenues for novel artificial intelligence breakthroughs as discovered through the comparison of various neural network applications under BCI technology (al-Ketbi et al., 2013) (Figure 1.9).

1.2.2. Convolutional Neural Networks (CNNs)

CNNs have gained a central role in the area of neural networks due to their excellent ability to process and analyze graphical data. Compared to traditional neural networks, CNNs are designed specifically for detecting patterns in images through hierarchical feature learning. With convolutions, pooling, and activation handled in layers, CNNs can efficiently reduce dimensions from input data without compromising on essential features needed in classification problems. This structure not only minimizes the risk of overfitting but also eases training such that these models are more likely to be better with greater precision in use in image classification and object detection. The design uniqueness of CNNs has made them the pillars for computer vision applications, ranging from autonomous vehicles to face detection. Facial expression recognition is one of the significant applications of CNNs that is an emerging industry that will enhance human-computer interaction. In the recent past, researchers have come up with hybrid models that integrate image pre-processing techniques with various CNN architectures to improve both accuracy and training speed in classifying simple human emotions such as sadness, happiness, anger, and surprise. These developments are exemplified by a model that attained a high accuracy of 89.58% on JAFFE dataset and 100% on KDEF dataset, exhibiting CNNs capacity to pick up fine emotional cues amidst complex contexts. By employing multiple databases and face orientations in their test environments, scientists have established the flexibility and stability of CNN models in processing complex visual inputs, establishing their pivotal role in modern affective computing (Puthanidam et al., 2017). In addition to face recognition, CNNs are found to be versatile for most NLP tasks, resulting in revolutionizing how text-based information is processed. By converting the temporal convolution operation into word embeddings and using low-rank n-gram tensors, CNNs can learn subtle word interactions even between non-consecutive words. This allows the model to identify and recognize patterns better, enabling performance improvements in sentiment classification and news classification tasks. Impressively, this architecture achieved state-of-the-art accuracy levels, including a notable 51.2% on fine-grained sentiment classification tasks. Such advancements reflect the interdisciplinary use of CNNs, both within vision domains and linguistic use, demonstrating their revolutionizing significance to other fields of inquiry (Barzilay et al., 2015).

1.2.3. Recurrent Neural Networks (RNNs)

RNNs are among the key advancements in the neural network field, more particularly designed to handle sequential data. As opposed to traditional feedforward neural networks, RNNs possess a unique architecture where they can have some form of memory via connection loops, which enables them to be applied to tasks involving time-series data, such as language modeling and speech recognition sequences. This enables RNNs to remember previous inputs and provide an evolving context for the information they handle. This is particularly valuable when the complexity of natural language is also considered, where words can have extremely differing meaning depending on the context they're being used in, thereby putting high value on a model that can learn and make predictions on sequences over time. A significant evolution of the baseline RNN architecture has been the inclusion of gated mechanisms, namely Long Short-Term Memory (LSTM) and Gated Recurrent Units (GRUs). These variants overcome the inherent shortfalls of standard RNNs, namely their vulnerability to issues like vanishing and exploding gradients, which can significantly impair their operation during training. LSTMs possess forget gates and input/output gates, enabling them to selectively ignore or recall knowledge on long sequences. This makes LSTMs and GRUs particularly well-suited for applications that involve both short- and long-term dependencies, such as machine translation and sentiment analysis. Their implementation in various fields demonstrates the flexibility and robustness of RNNs, validating their relevance in the ever-evolving environment of neural network study and application (Heidemann et al., 2018). The configuration and training of RNNs, or more explicitly, the hyper-parameter optimization, is one of the problems of applying RNNs. The naturally high sensitivity of RNNs to configurations renders the process tedious, most commonly leading to suboptimal performance if not properly managed. Despite the development of automated hyper-parameter optimization software as a potential solution, their computational cost has mitigated their implementation. Recent attempts have been made to optimize the methods of optimization, such as adapting the MAE random sampling method for use with multi-hidden layer networks, which could provide an economic method of comparing the performance of networks without leading to outrageous computational costs. Such successes are vital in facilitating further research on deep RNN models and their application across various disciplines, especially as researchers strive to overcome existing barriers and optimize the effectiveness of these highly impactful models (Litjens et al., 2018) (Figure 1.10).

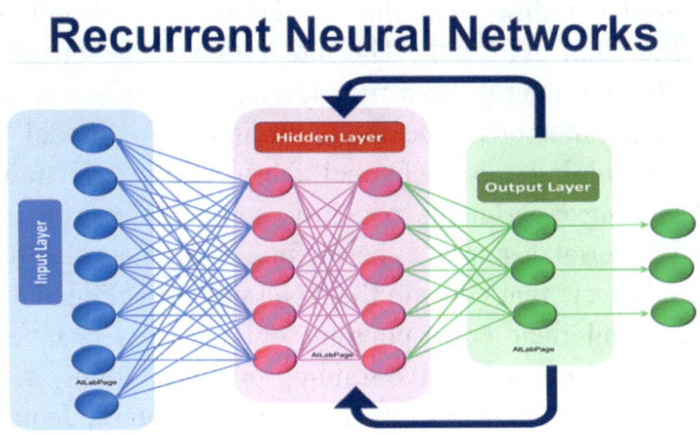

Figure 1.10. *Recurrent neural network (RNN).*

*Source: https://miro.medium.com/v2/resize:fit:1100/format:webp/1*5bjD7kmtaJl-n3qztBC2Ig.png.*

1.3. TRAINING NEURAL NETWORKS

Training neural networks is a complex yet fundamental aspect of developing effective artificial intelligence models. As it learns, a neural network develops the capacity to recognize patterns and make predictions from given input data by adjusting its internal parameters, or weights and biases. Training typically consists of using labeled data sets, for which the network minimizes the difference between its predicted outputs and true results by backpropagation. Performance of training also relies heavily on the architecture selection, training data volume and quality, and the optimization algorithms employed. Moreover, activation function choice is critical because it determines the ability of the network to learn non-linear relationships in the data, which in turn determines the performance of the learned model. In an application context, the neural network training often encounters difficulties which can affect the accuracy and efficiency of the learning process. For instance, the computation cost of executing training algorithms may become prohibitive for large data sets or more complex models. In order to seek means to overcome this, researchers have begun studying other methods, such as approximation techniques, which maintain solution quality at reduced computational needs. One such promising technique is the use of neural network learning algorithms to approximate vertex centrality measures in large networks. Surprisingly, a study showed that utilization of regression models produced by feedforward neural networks can offer more superior results in computational efficiency and accuracy of solutions compared to traditional methods and thus is a viable option for diverse applications (Grando et al., 2018). The integration of design of experiments (DOE) with artificial neural networks (ANN) demonstrates another new approach for training methods to be applied to improving model performance. In laser micro-machining micro-channel fabrication, ANN training can be enhanced by designing experiments to identify optimal laser process parameters. By employing a factorial design of experiments, researchers are able to develop diverse training datasets that educate the ANN on interactions between varied input parameters and their corresponding outputs, i.e., channel width and production cost. This comprehensive training process not only accelerates the development process but also optimizes the use of resources, demonstrating the practical benefit of integrating experimental designs and sophisticated neural network techniques (Brabazon et al., 2011).

1.3.1. The Role of Data in Training

The role played by data in the training of neural networks is better since the performance of such networks is heavily reliant on the data used to learn, being either quality, quantity, or diversity. In practice, neural networks work on recognizing patterns and making predictions based on the data they ingest. Hence, bad or skewed data can lead to underperforming models generating biases or inaccuracies that may adversely affect outcomes. The requirement of big data is not merely about numbers; the data must cover a wide variety of situations with which the network will have to contend so that it may generalize best to new, unseen instances. Without diversity of this kind, the model becomes prone to overfitting, where it learns to remember the training data instead of learning to make accurate predictions from underlying patterns. Furthermore, new approaches for enhancing neural network training have been opened up by the emergence of data generation approaches. As noted by recent research works, statistical behavior of complex systems can be used to produce large datasets useful for training neural networks. For instance, spin network models illustrate how physical systems with stochastic fluctuations can yield raw information available to neural networks to construct a model. While such fluctuations offer important information, they will obliterate the disparity among separate states of a system so that learning is not possible. This second role emphasizes the importance of optimization in data usage in that researchers must attempt to balance between the random noise embedded in the data and the meaningful data to enhance inference efficiency and improved model performance (Huang et al., 2018). In robotics, the marriage of deep learning with physical systems has further depicted the significance of data in training neural networks. As can be seen through a review of recent literature, the convergence of robotics and deep learning has exploded with several papers considering the mutualism between the two. In this context, not only does training data inform the neural networks but also informs the operation of robotic systems, both how they move and how they learn to reshape themselves in dynamic environments. The achievement of these programs demonstrates explicitly the relationship of neural network complexity with available training data, pointing to advances in both as necessarily interdependent. Continued research into data-driven methods will necessarily enhance our understanding of neural networks, allowing increased innovation in robot systems (Gashler et al., 2017).

1.3.2. Backpropagation Algorithm

The Backpropagation Algorithm is a critical process in training neural networks, particularly in gradient descent weight optimization. In short, the algorithm uses the chain rule of calculus to compute the gradient of the loss function with respect to each weight by propagating errors back through the network. This effective computation process allows network weights to be adjusted so as to reduce prediction error, making it crucial for modern deep learning applications. Although it is broadly utilized, backpropagation's classical formulation faces challenges when used with networks that have recurrent connections. All of these demands call for modifications to excel beyond its application as it is in traditional feedforward designs, ultimately paving the way for broader applications in complicated scenarios like control systems and temporal dynamics of data processing (Pineda et al., 1989). Aside from its initial application for traditional neural network training, backpropagation forms a basis for automatic evolutionary algorithms that optimize network designs. A major innovation in this field can be found in the EXACT algorithm, which improves the architecture of convolutional neural networks (CNNs) by incorporating neuroevolutionary processes. The results of the EXACT model illustrate the manner in which backpropagation can be blended with new computational processes to improve network performance without too much human design input. With long trials, the inclusion of rudimentary backpropagation strategies resulted in CNNs achieving superb correctness rates, proving that major performance gains can be achieved even from basic training protocols (Krizhevsky et al., 2017). When researchers move to hybrid methods, they identify the necessity to adjust the hyperparameters of backpropagations to yield optimal results. Moreover, the emergence of training strategies also illustrates the ways in which new technologies can augment current backpropagation for the purpose of fine-tuning artificial neural networks. With increasingly complex neural networks, synergy between backpropagation and evolutionary strategies reveals new paradigms for searching neural architectures. This breakthrough also necessitates reevaluation of traditional training paradigms that promote adaptive strategies for taking advantage of the complex landscape of modern neural network architectures. Future research into the optimization of backpropagation through mechanisms such as dropout, pretraining, and the utilization of elastic distortions promises to free new levels of potential for gains in performance as well as efficiency. The continuous development of algorithms like EXACT works to highlight that the pursuit to expand neural network performance remains, with backpropagation as a fundamental pivot point in the chain of computation (Krizhevsky et al., 2017).

1.3.3. Overfitting and Regularization Techniques

Overfitting is perhaps the most serious problem with neural network training, whereby a model can well fit the training data but generalize poorly to novel data. Overfitting often occurs when the model is too flexible, learning noise and idiosyncratic patterns that are not generalizable to the entire dataset. This causes validation or test set performance to degrade even as training becomes lucrative. Efficient action must be undertaken to combat overfitting and make the model more resilient. Incorporating regularization mechanisms is essential in this regard to provide a means of limiting the models' complexity and improve generalization without compromising predictive capability for diverse datasets. Out of all methods employed for regularization, dropout is one of the most effective ways to utilize against overfitting of neural networks. By dropping a subset of neurons at random during training, dropout forces the model to learn features that are more robust and independent of the specific neuron or subset of features. The probabilistic nature of dropout forces a form of ensemble learning, as the network can be viewed as an ensemble of many different subnetworks acting in tandem when being trained. Implementing this practice has been proven to significantly improve model generalization capabilities. Batch normalization and noise injection are also methods that coexist with dropout by activating normalization or adding randomness in training, which results in further model performance improvements as noted by several studies (Jiang, 2023). Pooling techniques, such as those used in Convolutional Neural Networks (CNNs), are also significant through minimizing overfitting risk. These techniques, e.g., max-min difference pooling, are an abstraction process allowing models to focus on important features and disregard less informative variations in the input. Beyond traditional pooling strategies, novel schemes have been introduced to meet specific datasets, e.g., sound classification tasks in which temporal sequences contribute a significant role in classification accuracy. It has been revealed in studies that employing advanced pooling methods in conjunction with CNNs can lead to improved performance, particularly in challenging tasks involving environmental sounds (Rashmi et al., 2025). Lastly, the integration of various regularization techniques strengthens the neural network model such that predictions become more accurate across numerous applications.

1.4. APPLICATIONS OF NEURAL NETWORKS

The advent of neural networks has revolutionized many areas, particularly in web applications concerning user interaction prediction. Traditional statistical models find it challenging to deal with the richness of categorical data, especially when transformed into high-dimensional sparse representations by techniques like one-hot encoding. Product-based Neural Networks (PNNs) step in here as a potential candidate that effectively utilizes an embedding layer to obtain distributed representations. This method allows the identification of patterns of interaction between categorical features, which is required for applications such as recommendation systems and online advertising. Experimental results demonstrate that PNNs not only enhance predictive accuracy but also outperform well-known models by many measures, a radical improvement in applying neural networks to real-world problems within web environments (Cai et al., 2016). And yet another principal use of neural networks lies in the intersection of computer vision and natural language processing, i.e., automated image captioning. This usage has paramount practical relevance as it enables machines to caption visual material naturally. Techniques in this field can be classified as top-down, which generate descriptions from a broad subject of the image, or bottom-up, which generate words by first identifying individual entities in the image. There is a new algorithm that is a blend of the two directions using a semantic attention mechanism, and it has produced promising results. Through its enabling of concentrated attention over disparate semantic concepts, the algorithm bridges both perspectives' knowledge as well as enhances recurrent neural networks' descriptive accuracy. The effectiveness of the method has been evaluated across eminent benchmarks, outperforming earlier approaches consistently and heralding the strengths of neural networks in data type bridging (Fang et al., 2016). Beyond the fields of web applications and image captioning, neural networks have far-reaching applications across other sectors such as healthcare, finance, and manufacturing. In healthcare, for instance, predictive analytics using neural networks is applied to forecast the outcome of patients or detect diseases, enabling timely intervention. In finance, they are applied for fraud detection and for crediting scores and making extensive use of transactions' data to identify anomalies and quantify risks. Besides, the production sector applies neural networks in predictive maintenance, anticipating machine failure before it happens. The broad spectrum of applications has revealed the universality and effectiveness of neural networks in decision-making as well as process optimization across diverse industries. As technology expands, the future for innovation and efficiency propelled by neural networks expands, emphasizing their importance in modern society (Figure 1.11).

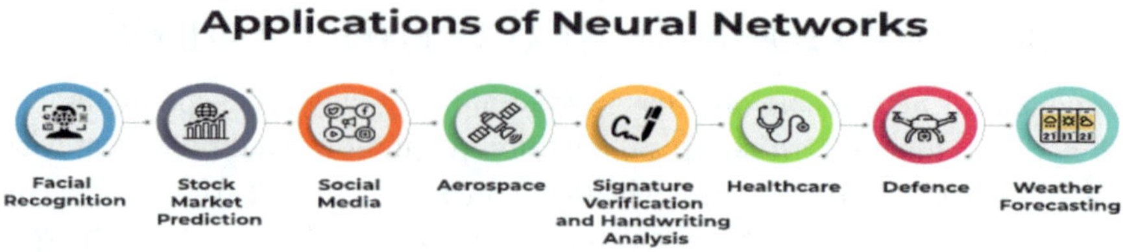

Figure 1.11. *Applications of neural networks.*

Source: https://lh7-rt.googleusercontent.com/docsz/AD_4nXfDB9R9V6ozZ7SM_IzPSp-H2qptLS_ApCGopYIGzTAlBPputQ-flXIA0R37Ubm5a1y4BEvA-Mwmst-aDE2y4pK14JUIRTnpGSnJiCLM2lpVBWpue7mDhYOtjzqto1ltPCe1286yL-3Xe-KQhR-tUQRAMxsFE?key=t44fzT5QFvN1UaxQYnN6Ew.

1.4.1. Image and Speech Recognition

The progress in the neural network has transformed image and speech recognition enormously, enabling systems to process and understand data to tremendous levels of accuracy. Techniques of image recognition, particularly involving convolutional neural networks (CNNs), employ hierarchical layers to establish patterns and characteristics of visible data. These models excel at object discrimination between objects in pictures, a requirement of numerous applications, including social network automatic tagging and advanced surveillance. The ability of neural networks to learn features directly from data without feature engineering manually greatly assists their performance. For instance, neural networks perform exceptionally well in benchmark datasets, which demonstrate their ability in tasks of image classification, which are crucial in the development of intelligent systems that require visual perception (Berdichevsky et al., 2018). Speech recognition has also been improved through recurrent neural networks (RNNs) and even more recently through transformers that excel in tasks involving sequential data. Such architectures enable machines to improve understanding of spoken words through capturing speech contextual dependencies. Virtual assistants, real-time transcription software, and voice-controlled devices are some of the applications of neural networks in speech recognition. The technology relies on models being trained on large sets of data so they can recognize and interpret several accents, dialects, and speaking styles. However, despite such developments, there remain issues regarding understanding the mathematical foundations and behaviors of neural networks in such environments. Further research is focused on elucidating the functioning of such models while improving robustness and interpretability (Sirignano et al., 2019). With further developments in neural networks, their applications in image and speech recognition are spreading to numerous industries like healthcare, cars, and entertainment. In medicine, for instance, neural networks have been employed to diagnose illness from medical images and therefore offer immediate analysis that can lead to improved patient outcomes. In transport technology, speech recognition systems make it possible to operate hands-free, enhancing the convenience and safety of drivers. Also, interposing neural networks in conjunction with other technologies such as augmented reality and natural language processing promises even more visionary capabilities. As these systems continue to mature, concern for ethical dilemmas involving privacy and data protection will gain growing importance. Overcoming such dilemmas will make possible the full power of neural networks in speech and image recognition to be harnessed responsibly and justly (Berdichevsky et al., 2018; Sirignano et al., 2019) (Figure 1.12).

Figure 1.12. *Speech recognition.*

Source: https://specials-images.forbesimg.com/imageserve/61c4dab3dcce70ad2cd f606a/960x0.jpg.

1.4.2. Natural Language Processing (NLP)

NLP is an imperative area of artificial intelligence that addresses human-computer interaction in the natural language. Its significance has grown with tremendous power as the revolution of the digital era continually impregnates all facets of life and enterprise. NLP by definition involves the employment of computer-based techniques for interpreting and manipulating human language in a semantically useful way so that machines can interpret speech and text. The addition of neural networks has enhanced the functionality of NLP to a great degree, allowing models to learn complex patterns and nuances in language data. This varies from operations such as sentiment analysis to machine translation, demonstrating how deep learning architectures can make human-machine communication more efficient. Current trends in NLP leverage advanced models based on the deep learning paradigm. For instance, text processing by convolutional neural networks (CNNs) is a paradigm shift for the analysis of language data. Scientists have developed methods through the re-definition of temporal convolution operation in CNNs that allow words to interact even if there is text between them in a sentence.

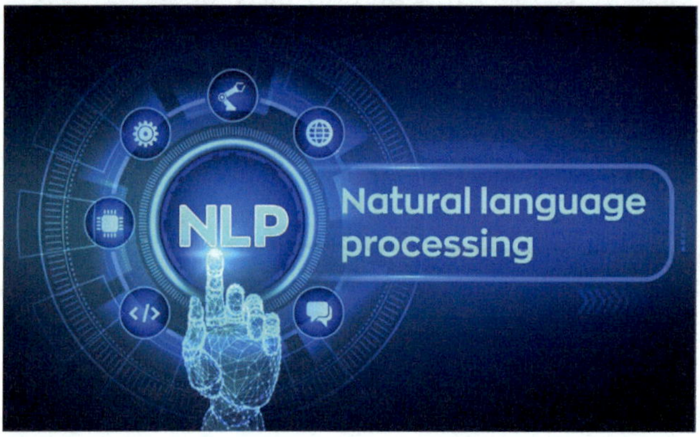

Figure 1.13. *Natural language processing (NLP).*

Source: https://www.shaip.com/wp-content/uploads/2022/10/Blog-What-is-NLP.jpg.

This new strategy yields a more intense context and meaning concept because it captures patterns directly accountable for sentiment categorization and classification tasks. A recent paper reports the use of low-rank n-gram tensors significantly improving performance measures, with state-of-the-art results for accuracy and training efficiency, as evidenced through outcomes that mirror 51.2% accuracy in such hard sentiment tasks (Barzilay et al., 2015). Also, the creation of machine learning techniques applied to graph structures has opened new fronts for improving NLP applications. Sentence-level graph representations assisted researchers in accurately extracting semantic and term relationships that are least addressed by conventional methods. The graph model facilitates more explicit examination of semantic relations within text, and this corresponds to improved performance in sentiment analysis and other text mining tasks. The ability to incorporate stop words in these representations further improves the context knowledge of language, resulting in more robust feature extraction processes. Employing deep neural networks on these learned features not only enhances the classification accuracy but also demonstrates the models flexibility across various datasets without applying pre-trained embeddings (Bijari et al., 2019). Thus, graph-based approaches to NLP represent a key shift in the ongoing evolution of natural language understanding (Figure 1.13).

1.4.3. Autonomous Systems and Robotics

The intersection of autonomous systems and neural networks represents one of the key innovations in robotics, given that it enables machines to execute tasks that were previously contingent on human cognition and emotional processing. By incorporating neurobiologically realistic mechanisms in robotic systems, scientists are able to create behaviors and responses that reflect human emotions. This is in line with day and night cycles of mammalian existence, where robots can be active in real-time while performing intricate data processing during downtime. Such dual-phase operation not only makes decision-making easier but also enhances autonomous systems' resilience and adaptability, allowing them to react to multifarious environments with a level of sophistication similar to living entities (Mazzara et al., 2016).

The application of continuous-time recurrent neural networks (CTRNNs) in robot systems is another instance of the innovation of intelligent autonomy. CTRNNs can generate adaptive behaviors that are critical in maneuvering dynamic environments. Yet, problems like node saturation can hinder responsiveness, similar to the hyper-excitability in biological neural systems. Through the application of homeostatic plasticity mechanisms in such networks, scientists have overcome issues in signal propagation, thus improving the networks sensitivity to input signals. This capacity is essential for robots because the usefulness of autonomous agents in practical applications depends on their ability to sense and respond appropriately to a range of stimuli (Noble et al., 2007). The recent breakthrough in the joining of neural networks and robotics is a sign that forthcoming autonomous systems will not only work well but also reach emotional intelligence. With technological advancement, the integration of affective computing into robots will revolutionize all industries from healthcare to manufacturing. Robots that can sense and respond to emotional cues will enhance human-robot interaction, pushing collaboration and social approval. The potential of systems to give context-specific answers by virtue of emotional intelligence can result in more empathetic care, therapy, and learning, thus making robots not just machines but kind companions in all aspects of human life (Mazzara et al., 2016) (Figure 1.14).

Figure 1.14. *Autonomous systems.*

Source: https://user-images.githubusercontent.com/45159366/133000541-3da7a795-00e5-4287-b644-917f5644c610.png.

1.5. CHALLENGES IN NEURAL NETWORK DEVELOPMENT

The emergence of neural networks, while a remarkable achievement in artificial intelligence, is fraught with serious issues that researchers and practitioners must address. The most serious is the demand for high-quality and large datasets for training the models extensively. Primarily, neural networks are trained from patterns and prediction on data but gathering a sufficient amount of labeled data can be extremely challenging where data is scarce or expensive to obtain. Moreover, obtaining data typically involves intense preprocessing for quality and usability. Consequently, a lack of robust datasets can cause overfitting, where models learn extremely well from training data but are unable to generalize to other data, thus eliminating the actual world applicability of neural networks. Besides data-related problems, another prominent barrier in building neural networks is that they are architecturally intricate. Designing the architecture of a neural network, including number of layers, types of activation functions, and connectivity, is an art and science. Its intricacies call for experimentation along with intuition. In addition, as networks become deeper, they are also more susceptible to vanishing and exploding gradients, thus making them hard to train and may lead to wasteful learning. Solving these issues takes advanced methods, such as residual connections or special training algorithms, that can bring sophistication levels to both model architecture and implementation. Importantly, advancements in the use of neural networks for advanced control applications, such as in particle accelerator systems, underscore the need to address these architectural issues to achieve successful results in specialist fields

(Biedron et al., 2016). Finally, the computational cost of neural networks is another huge challenge to their building. Training deep neural networks involves processing vast amounts of data and performing numerous calculations that demand a lot of computational resources. Big resources of high-performance hardware such as GPUs or tensor processing units may sometimes be needed to accelerate training and inference times. However, reliance on such technology is a matter of access and sustainability, particularly for lesser research institutions or developing countries that lack the necessary infrastructure. Further, as neural networks become more sophisticated, the energy required to train such models becomes a rising environmental concern. The use of new techniques, such as coherence-based networks that optimize learning with distributed intelligence, can offer solutions that optimize not only efficiency but also reduce the overall computational cost and energy needs (Grazia et al., 2015).

1.5.1. Computational Resource Requirements

Greater complexity in neural networks, particularly in fields like image and speech recognition, calls for large computational resources. This is brought about by the large amount of parameters that deep learning models are trained with, which requires a lot of computational capability and memory. The more complex and deeper neural networks are, the more computationally intensive forward passes and backward passes during training are, hence requiring an increasing demand for high-end hardware. The application of central processing units (CPUs) was always conventional, but their ineffectiveness in handling parallel calculation paved the way for the application of stronger architectures. The addition of advanced processors like graphics processing units (GPUs) has therefore revolutionized the field to enable improved model training and prediction. The balance between processing efficiency and resource management remains a central concern for researchers in this rapidly evolving discipline. In addition to hardware choice, architecture and neural network implementation must consider the environment in which they will be deployed. For example, for wireless sensor networks, efficiency is desirable while having the ability to adapt to a dynamic environment. As per current literature, machine learning techniques can be utilized to optimize the use of resources in these networks, ensuring their lifetimes are extended and extraneous computational costs are reduced (Alsheikh et al., 2014). By optimizing system performance with intelligent control of computational needs associated with learning procedures, system efficiency can be optimized while not significantly increasing resource consumption. This balance is required because sensor networks are likely to be applied to resource-constrained environments, so an urge for solutions that not only perform well but also do so economically in terms of computational resource usage. Advances in neural networks have also uncovered the potential of upcoming technology, including field-programmable gate arrays (FPGAs), to transcend resource limitations. These reconfigurable hardware platforms offer a flexible means for deep learning tasks to attain a balance between the performance and power costs (Bouganis et al., 2018). With their capability to accommodate varying neural network architectures and provide flexibilities in terms of design space exploration, FPGAs are an exciting means to reduce the computational resource requirements. Such versatility is particularly beneficial in the therapy of the diverse needs of today's applications, where the researcher can tailor their approach to meet specific performance goals. The challenge brought by the complexity of CNNs and computational needs demands ongoing hardware innovation, as researchers not only call for performance but resource-frugal and environmentally friendly solutions in the field of neural networks.

1.5.2. Interpretability and Transparency Issues

Greater application of neural networks to decision-making points to significant interpretability and transparency issues that need examination. With these sorts of algorithms increasingly controlling significant aspects of daily life, from lending to hiring decisions, the uncertainty regarding their operation creates ethical concerns. Specifically, the decisions made by such models can inadvertently reinforce biases that unfairly burden marginalized groups along race or gender lines. Enforcement of laws like the General Data Protection Regulation (GDPR) has increased awareness towards such biases, and now greater emphasis is given to a closer inspection of machine learning processes. It is essential that the computer scientists concentrate on these matters of transparency and that algorithms improve fairness and do not assist in developing systemic discrimination so that one may have trust in technology systems that shape the outcomes of society (Baumann et al., 2018). In discussing interpretability, one should note that most typical neural network models are black boxes. Their inherent complexity and non-linearity hide decision routes and users find it challenging to understand how conclusions are arrived at. Such transparency limitation inhibits accountability and raises significant ethical issues. Consequently, scientists have been urging models that not only make predictive performance a priority but also provide explanations of their internal workings. One such potential avenue is through the creation of network architectures that inherently support explanations in addition to predictions. The models possess mechanisms that give feedback through visualizations and interpretations of the relationships underlying predictions, thus maximizing user comprehension and trust in the process (Chen et al., 2017). Progress in neural network architecture, including that which addresses interpretability, can bridge the gap between the intricate algorithmic computation and human understanding. Some architectures, for instance, incorporate prototype layers that link output classes with some of the input features, thereby de-mystifying decision-making. By employing latent space comparisons and reinforcement between encoded inputs and prototypes, such models provide a clearer explanation of their outputs. The alignment of computation and explanation guarantees that users are not left in the dark about decision-making. With growing calls for explainable AI, such innovations will be needed to counteract the dangers of discriminatory outputs and forge a more equitable technological world (Chen et al., 2017).

1.5.3. Ethical Considerations and Bias

The use of neural networks across various industries necessitates vigilant examination of the ethical issues and bias that are most probable to occur. One of the most prevalent is the algorithmic bias, a recognized mechanism by which present stereotypes and structural biases are perpetuated. If neural networks are trained on data sets representative of society's bias, they will most likely yield discriminatory outcomes. For instance, if a dataset that is used to develop an AI hiring tool is biased towards some groups, the system that it produces can discriminate in favor of qualified individuals from underrepresented groups. Thus, avoiding these biases while designing and deploying neural networks will render applications fair and equitable and will instill confidence among users and stakeholders. Additionally, in artificial intelligence, there has to be security interventions to ensure compliance with ethical standards and regulations rules. The High-Level Expert Group (HLEG) on AI Ethics Guidelines notes accountability and transparency when dealing with AI systems, particularly as technologies begin to intersect with sensitive issues such as cybersecurity. The Task Force established by the Centre for European Policy Studies identifies the precise dangers related to AI technologies and appeals to the development of instruments to prevent risks related to skewed decision-making. This cross-disciplinary effort not only tries to improve the performance of neural networks but also to establish a moral foundation for their use so that advances in AI technology are not made at the expense of ethical soundness. There also arises a pressing need to examine the social implications of AI systems using neural networks. The rising prevalence of sizeism, as evidenced by increasing concern over fat shaming, indicates the dangers of uncontrolled use of data within machine learning algorithms. Researchers have sought ways to use computer vision to infer an individual's body mass index from social media pictures, raising significant ethical questions regarding privacy and consent. Although this technology could give feedback regarding attitudes toward body weight in society, it also has the potential to stigmatize and discriminate further. Ethical considerations should be to maintain the dignity and well-being of people so that the use of neural networks is for broader social benefit and not part of causing harm or segmenting society.

1.6. FUTURE TRENDS IN NEURAL NETWORKS

With the evolving face of technology, the future of neural networks appears to be marked by increasing computational efficiency and novel architectures. In particular, the transition from traditional methods to deep learning architectures has noted the central role that developments in computational paradigms such as quantum computing will play in designing and implementing neural networks. This shift might make possible a drastic decrease in processing time, allowing for the analysis of larger data sets and more complex models. The synergy anticipated between quantum computing and neural networks promises a revolutionary advance in the field, as evident in the increasing reliance upon sophisticated algorithms able to refine predictions recursively and optimize accuracy in numerous applications, including finance and medicine. This highlights a promising direction for the future application of neural networks in sophisticated, real-world problem-solving. Another fascinating trend is the growing relevance of unsupervised and semi-supervised learning approaches to the design of future neural networks. With the data-greedy nature of supervised learning, there is a pressing need for more efficient approaches that can be learned from fewer labeled instances.

Technologies like self-supervised learning platforms are arising to meet this need, making the most out of unlabeled data. They improve model performance but also lower the expensive prices charged for data labeling. As can be seen in many studies, for example, a broad classification of the AI techniques applied in operations management, these will tend to promote neural network development in many industries literally changing their use for better performance in accuracy and overall efficiency (Kobbacy et al., 2007). Apart from this, integration of ethical considerations and explainability in neural network systems will become a defining hallmark of future developments. Since these models increasingly influence high-stakes decisions, such as legal and medical ones, the need for compliance and transparency also scales.

The future generation of neural networks will need mechanisms that not only offer up performance metrics but also provide insight into their decision-making. There has already been a shift in research to achieve equilibrium between model interpretability and intricate model structure, anticipating that the future of neural networks will be constructed upon responsibility as much as on efficiency. This is to be essential to users' reliance on these systems, particularly in high-stakes areas such as bankruptcy forecasting and medical diagnosis, and therefore laying a foundation for responsible practice in AI (Akers et al., 2007).

1.6.1. Advancements in Deep Learning

The landscape of deep learning has witnessed radical transformations in recent years with the dominance of neural networks as key tools for numerous applications. One such high-profile advance is the application of convolutional neural networks (CNNs) that have revolutionized image processing operations. CNNs employ hierarchical feature extraction, making them able to identify intricate patterns in visual data. This development has not only boosted image classification performance but also led the way toward breakthroughs in such fields as self-driving cars and medical imaging. Supported by the developments in CNNs, their operation is further supplemented by techniques such as transfer learning and model pruning, where efficiency is optimized with the reduction of computational needs. The ability to port pre-trained models to new tasks with minimal data showcases the remarkable malleability of modern deep learning methods. In addition to advances in image processing, deep learning has enabled substantial enhancements in speech recognition systems, demonstrating its versatility across multiple modalities. The development of Convolutional Recurrent Neural Networks (CRNNs) marks a new era for audio signal processing and classification. By treating speech activity detection as a two-dimensional multilabel image classification problem, researchers have been able to leverage techniques initially applied to visual data in order to solve the task in the audio domain. An interesting breakthrough in this area is the application of CRNNs to reach a decision cost function (DCF) that was significantly better than the state of the art. This exceptional growth indicates that deep learning platforms might exceed their traditional spaces, shattering the paradigm in various fields like telecommunications and speech recognition, thereby enhancing user experiences in daily technology. The combination of deep learning with precision agriculture is a typical instance of such a critical development, revealing how neural networks are disrupting outside of normal areas of technology. Recent advancements have introduced autonomous systems to advance farming processes so that maximum efficiency and minimum usage of resources are ensured. One such instance is the application of RGB-D cameras in motion planning, which illustrates how deep learning enables complex navigation in a complex agricultural environment to be feasible. These systems combine localization, mapping, and path planning techniques to enable the machine to operate more autonomously in diverse environments. The significance of such innovations lies not only in the fact that they can reduce labor costs but also because they offer sustainability benefits. With increasing use of agriculture with such smart technologies, the complementarities between advanced machine learning algorithms and real-world applications underline the paradigmatic nature of deep learning in essential industries, emphasizing its broad applicability in contemporary society (Aghi et al., 2020) (Figure 1.15).

Figure 1.15. *Deep learning.*

Source: https://stepmediasoftware.com/wp-content/uploads/2025/04/deep-learning.webp.

1.6.2. Integration with Other Technologies (e.g., IoT)

The integration of neural networks with other emerging technologies such as the Internet of Things (IoT) has immense potential for innovation, particularly in areas such as energy management and sustainability. As the world's energy demand continues to rise and the planet faces growing environmental issues, their integration becomes increasingly important. For instance, research offers an integrative model that employs IoT and Artificial Neural Networks (ANNs) in smart monitoring systems to optimize energy consumption in household settings. Through the utilization of real-time information from IoT sensors, the ANNs have been able to predict patterns of consumption and provide personalized suggestions to the users, completely transforming the manner in which homes consume their energy resources. The flexibility of the neural network and the predictive capability in this configuration not only accelerates productivity but also elicits consumers toward sustainable practices, which highlights the utilitarian benefit of such technological convergence (Mohamed et al., 2025). The combination of neural networks and IoT also opens up unprecedented scope for enhancing cyber-security configurations. Wireless sensor networks (WSNs) are a part of IoT infrastructure and are vulnerable to growing sophistication and complexity in cyber-attacks. By integrating neural networks into the security protocols of the networks, one can develop high-end classification models to identify and eliminate threats more effectively. For instance, models that utilize data sets like CICIDS2017 and UNSW-NB15 draw upon neural network architectures that improve cyber-attack detection rates through the use of sophisticated feature extraction techniques. These unions not only improve the security of IoT infrastructures but also demonstrate the versatility of neural networks in addressing contemporary problems across disciplines (Cherukuri, 2025). In addition to cyber-security and energy management, the integration of neural networks with IoT technologies is very important for healthcare as well. The smart health monitoring system is a new field that demonstrates the potential of this convergence to enable real-time patient care along with data analysis. Wearable health devices collect vital biometric data, which can be analyzed through neural networks to predict health events and provide personal suggestions. This not only enhances patient engagement but also enables pro-active health interventions, ultimately enhancing health outcomes. With the use of neural networks in conjunction with IoT infrastructures, medical practitioners are able to achieve more accurate diagnoses and tailored treatment plans, ultimately revolutionizing paradigms of patient care. Symphonic coexistence of these technologies is the basis for innovative solutions to critical health challenges, showcasing the diversified benefits of integration in the digital economy (Mohamed et al., 2025).

1.6.3. Potential Impact on Various Industries

The innovative power of neural networks will transform various industries, especially the health industry. The use of these advanced algorithms could enhance diagnostic accuracy and automate procedures by analyzing vast amounts of data better than conventional techniques. For instance, neural networks can be employed to assist in the detection of healthcare fraud billing, a significant issue given that the US system loses between $600 billion and $850 billion annually to fraud, waste, and abuse. As this issue continues to escalate, incorporating sophisticated fraud detection features based on neural networks might not only reduce the cost of financial losses but also ensure that resources will be more efficiently managed, thereby improving patient care outcomes. Drawing out the applicability of existing electronic fraud detection techniques to particular sectors can draw valuable lessons regarding future developments in healthcare, illustrating the immense potential of neural networks in addressing long-term issues in the industry (Hillegersberg et al., 2011). Financial services sectors also stand to benefit immensely from the forecasting ability of neural networks, particularly in areas of risk management and customer dealing. These algorithms can monitor customer behavior in real-time, reacting to changing market conditions and adapting services. This adaptation enhances customer experience, ultimately driving loyalty and sales. As markets reach maturity, the ability to predict trends and model future circumstances becomes increasingly critical. Neural networks can analyze complex relationships in the data so that businesses can make decisions based on the data that can predict not just the needs of the customers but also the intricacies of the competition. Moreover, the application of neural networks in financial fraud detection gives a preventive approach to combat illegal transactions. This use is key in an industry whose compliance and regulation keep evolving and where it shows the enormous capability neural networks have to improve efficiency and security in the financial sector (Nijkamp et al., 2025). Finally, the industrial manufacturing sector can benefit a great deal by incorporating neural networks, especially automation and supply chain optimization. With such Python-driven intelligent systems, producers can make use of predictive maintenance, reducing downtime and optimalizing productivity in general. Neural networks can analyze sensor readings from machines, uncovering patterns that predict impending failure prior to failure happening, thus leading to timely interventions. These systems can even optimize inventory management and production schedules by predicting variations in demand, thus optimalizing operation efficiency further. In a competitive landscape where reducing costs and improving quality are the key, the ability to leverage neural networks can play significant roles. In the context of globalization and technological revolution transforming the manufacturing sector, the introduction of such advanced systems will be crucial for firms that wish to maintain their market positions and respond quickly to global trends (Hillegersberg et al., 2011; Nijkamp et al., 2025).

SUMMARY

The study of neural networks portrays their extensive scope and versatility in numerous applications. Be it image recognition from visual images or understanding natural language, deep learning models, particularly Deep Neural Networks (DNNs), have demonstrated previously unseen performance when compared to traditional machine learning approaches. Though computationally intensive, as seen in the performance comparison between DNNs and Random Forest algorithms in identifying malware, DNNs are more likely to be more effective for complicated tasks. However, one should be appreciative of the fact that traditional methods sometimes have more accuracy, and therefore the need to select between the methods should be based on context and necessity, and not due to a strict inclination towards the newest technology (Rathore et al., 2018). Such appreciation enables one to seek an equilibrium approach towards neural networks being means that can both challenge and supplement standard computational methods. Besides, neural networks are not only used for creating applications but also for answering serious security problems, particularly for web applications. With the evolution of threats, e.g., SQLi attacks, there is a need for efficient techniques to detect vulnerabilities. In light of this, the development of new tools like DeepSQLi, utilizing deep learning to enhance SQLi vulnerability analysis, is an indication of the potential of neural networks in cybersecurity. DeepSQL's ability to create sophisticated test cases based on semantic knowledge from possible attacks highlights the revolutionary capability of DNNs in advancing security levels. Experimental results demonstrating the efficacy of DeepSQLi compared to traditional automation tools such as SQLmap strengthen the case that neural networks hold tremendous potential to surpass traditional methods, highlighting their capabilities to revolutionize a plethora of areas (Cheng-Zhi et al., 2020). Briefly put, the use of neural networks transcends technology itself; it is a shift in the approach we take to problem-solving across all areas. The twofold capability of neural networks to enhance performance as they work on critical problems, such as security vulnerabilities, dictates that they play the core part of contemporary computational designs. The recognition of equilibrium between new and old methods highlights the need to make informed decisions when adopting these technologies. With continued research development, neural networks will play a more and more central role in addressing not only existing but also future challenges, solidifying their position as fundamental components of future artificial intelligence and machine learning systems. That equilibrium is what renders ongoing research and investment in both deep learning and traditional techniques so crucial as we move toward an increasingly complex technological future.

Advances in neural networks have transformed several fields, particularly in the context of image and video processing. One of them is the development of an end-to-end online video style transfer network that generates stylized video streams with temporal coherence. Traditional methods of processing each frame of a video separately have a tendency to introduce flickering artifacts that deteriorate visual quality. But the network proposed contains short-term coherence such that consistency is not only local but preserved over larger time scales. This approach definitively outperforms previous per-frame baselines with quantifiable gains in visual and computational efficiency and thus marks a significant contribution in the field of dynamic content generation (Chen et al., 2017). In mobile security, neural networks have also served as invaluable tools for enhancing system reliability and privacy. Detection of communication links between software programs in the Android system is one of the significant challenges where classical static analyses are likely to generate an excess of false positives that render useful data extraction cumbersome. Static analysis augmented with a trained neural network has been shown to be effective in solving the issue. The architecture proposed in the chapter utilizes type-directed encoders (TDE), which methodically construct encoders for composite data types. Through experiments on a range of Android applications, it has great prediction accuracy when detecting the existence of communication links, therefore allowing space for a more effective mechanism of security through higher precision (Martín et al., 2018). These two examples together demonstrate the malleability and power of neural networks in different applications. From enhancing video quality to enhancing security components in mobile applications, neural networks have proven to be effective and dynamic in solving complex problems. With the technology growing even more, the efficacy and precision of information processing will continue to improve, leading to further innovations in areas considered side lines to artificial intelligence. The ongoing research into the potential of neural networks can reveal new uses and methods, ensuring continued relevancy in an increasingly digital and networked world. The future of research into this subject is full of the promise to address emerging challenges and extend the boundaries of modern technological paradigms.

REFERENCES

1. Abadi, M., Allamanis, M., Elish, K. O., Kim, Y., Kremenek, T., et al. (2018). Neural-augmented static analysis of Android communication. http://arxiv.org/abs/1809.04059 (accessed on 25th September 2025).
2. Aghi, D., Chiaberge, M., & Mazzia, V. (2020). Local motion planner for autonomous navigation in vineyards with a RGB-D camera-based algorithm and deep learning synergy. https://core.ac.uk/download/pdf/327177639.pdf (accessed on 25th September 2025).
3. Akers, M. D., Giacomino, D., & Gissel, J. L. (2007). A review of bankruptcy prediction studies: 1930–present. https://core.ac.uk/download/67756673.pdf (accessed on 25th September 2025).
4. al-Ketbi, O., & Conrad, M. (2013). Supervised ANN vs. unsupervised SOM to classify EEG data for BCI: Why can GMDH do better? https://core.ac.uk/download/29821899.pdf (accessed on 25th September 2025).
5. Alsheikh, M. A., Lin, S., Niyato, D., Tan, H. P., et al. (2014). Machine learning in wireless sensor networks: Algorithms, strategies, and applications. https://core.ac.uk/download/35456291.pdf (accessed on 25th September 2025).
6. Aytar, Y., Camurcu, M., Kocabey, E., Marin, J., et al. (2017). Face-to-BMI: Using computer vision to infer body mass index on social media. http://arxiv.org/abs/1703.03156 (accessed on 25th September 2025).
7. Barzilay, R., Jaakkola, T., & Lei, T. (2015). Molding CNNs for text: Non-linear, non-consecutive convolutions. http://arxiv.org/abs/1508.04112 (accessed on 25th September 2025).
8. Baumann, E., & Rumberger, J. L. (2018). State of the art in fair ML: From moral philosophy and legislation to fair classifiers. http://arxiv.org/abs/1811.09539 (accessed on 25th September 2025).
9. Berdichevsky, Y., Devincentis, K., Ferdous, Z. I., Guo, H., et al. (2018). A supervised STDP-based training algorithm for living neural networks. http://arxiv.org/abs/1710.10944 (accessed on 25th September 2025).
10. Biedron, S. G., Chase, B. E., Edelen, A. L., Edstrom, D., et al. (2016). Neural networks for modeling and control of particle accelerators. http://arxiv.org/abs/1610.06151 (accessed on 25th September 2025).
11. Bijari, K., Kebriaei, E., Veisi, H., Zare, H., et al. (2019). Leveraging deep graph-based text representation for sentiment polarity applications. http://arxiv.org/abs/1902.10247 (accessed on 25th September 2025).
12. Bohez, S., Dhoedt, B., Leroux, S., Simoens, P., et al. (2015). Resource-constrained classification using a cascade of neural network layers. https://

core.ac.uk/download/55825884.pdf (accessed on 25th September 2025).

13. Bouganis, C. S., Kouris, A., & Venieris, S. I. (2018). Tool flows for mapping convolutional neural networks on FPGAs: A survey and future directions. https://core.ac.uk/download/189837587.pdf (accessed on 25th September 2025).
14. Brabazon, D., & Karazi, S. (2011). An artificial neural network for dimensions and cost modelling of internal micro-channels fabricated in PMMA using Nd:YVO_4 laser. https://core.ac.uk/download/11310459.pdf (accessed on 25th September 2025).
15. Breuckmann, N. P., & Ni, X. (2017). Scalable neural network decoders for higher dimensional quantum codes. https://core.ac.uk/download/210963943.pdf (accessed on 25th September 2025).
16. Cahill, R. T. (2001). Smart nanostructures and synthetic quantum systems. https://core.ac.uk/download/25324183.pdf (accessed on 25th September 2025).
17. Cai, H., Qu, Y., Ren, K., Wang, W., et al. (2016). Product-based neural networks for user response prediction. http://arxiv.org/abs/1611.00144 (accessed on 25th September 2025).
18. Chebotar, Y., Hausman, K., Levine, S., Schaal, S., et al. (2017). Combining model-based and model-free updates for trajectory-centric reinforcement learning. http://arxiv.org/abs/1703.03078 (accessed on 25th September 2025).
19. Chen, C., Li, O., Liu, H., Rudin, C., et al. (2017). Deep learning for case-based reasoning through prototypes: A neural network that explains its predictions. http://arxiv.org/abs/1710.04806 (accessed on 25th September 2025).
20. Chen, D., Hua, G., Liao, J., Yu, N., et al. (2017). Coherent online video style transfer. http://arxiv.org/abs/1703.09211 (accessed on 25th September 2025).
21. Chen, K., Eksombatchai, P., Hamilton, W. L., He, X., et al. (2018). Graph convolutional neural networks for web-scale recommender systems. http://arxiv.org/abs/1806.01973 (accessed on 25th September 2025).
22. Chen, L., Fanioudakis, E., Giakoumis, D., Hamzaoui, R., et al. (2019). Two-dimensional convolutional recurrent neural networks for speech activity detection. https://core.ac.uk/download/228189775.pdf (accessed on 25th September 2025).
23. Cherukuri, B. R. (2025). Advanced multi-class cyber security attack classification in IoT-based wireless sensor networks using context-aware

depth wise separable convolutional neural network. Journal of Machine and Computing. https://www.semanticscholar.org/paper/34b20a9a5972f9bf9c04eef44f538aa8bd3413a8 (accessed on 25th September 2025).

24. Coleman, S., Georgiopoulos, M., Markov, Z., Neller, T., et al. (2005). Unifying an introduction to artificial intelligence course through machine learning laboratory experiences. https://cupola.gettysburg.edu/cgi/viewcontent.cgi?article=1007&context=csfac (accessed on 25th September 2025).
25. Das, A., Nandy, S., & Sarkar, P. P. (2012). Training a feed-forward neural network with artificial bee colony-based backpropagation method. http://arxiv.org/abs/1209.2548 (accessed on 25th September 2025).
26. Daskin, A. (2018). A simple quantum neural net with a periodic activation function. http://arxiv.org/abs/1804.07633 (accessed on 25th September 2025).
27. De Filippo De Grazia, M., Testolin, A., Zanella, A., Zorzi, M., et al. (2015). Cognition-based networks: A new perspective on network optimization using learning and distributed intelligence. https://core.ac.uk/download/53523614.pdf (accessed on 25th September 2025).
28. Doctor, F., Iqbal, R., Mahmud, S., More, B., et al. (2020). Big data analytics: Computational intelligence techniques and application areas. https://core.ac.uk/download/228156656.pdf (accessed on 25th September 2025).
29. Fang, C., Jin, H., Luo, J., Wang, W., et al. (2016). Image captioning with semantic attention. http://arxiv.org/abs/1603.03925 (accessed on 25th September 2025).
30. Fantin, S., Ferreira, A., & Pupillo, L. (2020). CEPS Task Force on Artificial Intelligence and Cybersecurity: Technology, Governance and Policy Challenges. Task Force Evaluation of the HLEG Trustworthy AI Assessment List (Pilot Version). CEPS Task Force Report, 22 January 2020. https://core.ac.uk/download/287647893.pdf (accessed on 25th September 2025).
31. Gabrys, B., Musial, K., & Skarding, J. (2021). Foundations and modelling of dynamic networks using dynamic graph neural networks: A survey. http://arxiv.org/abs/2005.07496 (accessed on 25th September 2025).
32. Gashler, M. S., & Pierson, H. A. (2017). Deep learning in robotics: A review of recent research. http://arxiv.org/abs/1707.07217 (accessed on 25th September 2025).
33. Grando, F., & Lamb, L. C. (2018). Computing vertex centrality measures in massive real networks with a neural learning model. http://arxiv.org/abs/1811.12809 (accessed on 25th September 2025).

34. Guerraoui, R., Mhamdi, E. M. E., & Rouault, S. (2017). On the robustness of a neural network. https://core.ac.uk/download/148032019.pdf (accessed on 25th September 2025).

35. Guo, Y., Shi, Z., Ye, J., Zou, J., et al. (2019). Object detection in 20 years: A survey. http://arxiv.org/abs/1905.05055 (accessed on 25th September 2025).

36. Hawley, S. H. (2019). Challenges for an ontology of artificial intelligence. https://core.ac.uk/download/187718197.pdf (accessed on 25th September 2025).

37. Heidemann, G., & Tanisaro, P. (2018). An empirical study on bidirectional recurrent neural networks for human motion recognition. https://core.ac.uk/download/161589401.pdf (accessed on 25th September 2025).

38. Hinton, G. E., Krizhevsky, A., Salakhutdinov, R. R., Srivastava, N., et al. (2012). Improving neural networks by preventing co-adaptation of feature detectors. http://arxiv.org/abs/1207.0580 (accessed on 25th September 2025).

39. Huang, A., Sheldan, B., Sivak, D. A., Thomson, M., et al. (2018). Physically optimizing inference. https://core.ac.uk/download/211384193.pdf (accessed on 25th September 2025).

40. Huang, C. Z. A., Appelt, D., Ariu, D., Choudhary, W. G. J., Diederik, D., Dong, L., Doshi, R., et al. (2020). DeepSQLi: Deep semantic learning for testing SQL injection. http://arxiv.org/abs/2005.11728 (accessed on 25th September 2025).

41. Jiang, L. (2023). Spoken digit classification through neural networks with combined regularization. 2023 8th International Conference on Frontiers of Signal Processing (ICFSP). https://www.semanticscholar.org/paper/fed7f121f1db3454be58830676eef51a27f9e5ab (accessed on 25th September 2025).

42. Kamilaris, A. (2018). A review on the application of natural computing in environmental informatics. https://core.ac.uk/download/572206900.pdf (accessed on 25th September 2025).

43. Kobbacy, K. A. H., Rasmy, M. H., & Vadera, S. (2007). AI and OR in management of operations: History and trends. https://core.ac.uk/download/104325.pdf (accessed on 25th September 2025).

44. Krizhevsky, A., & Krizhevsky, A. (2017). Large scale evolution of convolutional neural networks using volunteer computing. http://arxiv.org/abs/1703.05422 (accessed on 25th September 2025).

45. Litjens, G., Bracewell, R. N., Albelwi, S., Haykin, S., Hochreiter, S.,

Min, S., Ojha, V. K., et al. (2018). Comparing deep recurrent networks based on the MAE random sampling, a first approach. https://core.ac.uk/download/214846286.pdf (accessed on 25th September 2025).

46. Mazzara, M., Safina, L., Talanov, M., Tchitchigin, A., et al. (2016). Robot Dream. http://arxiv.org/abs/1603.03007 (accessed on 25th September 2025).

47. Mohamed, A., Ismail, I., & AlDaraawi, M. (2025). IoT-driven intelligent energy management: Leveraging smart monitoring applications and artificial neural networks (ANN) for sustainable practices. Computers. https://www.semanticscholar.org/paper/b182324e395cead4e61fe17d7af2ca6b8c2ad2a9 (accessed on 25th September 2025).

48. Murray-Smith, R., & Thakar, S. (1993). Combining case-based reasoning with neural networks. https://core.ac.uk/download/pdf/295999721.pdf (accessed on 25th September 2025).

49. N/A. (2022). Computational optimizations for machine learning. https://core.ac.uk/download/520258758.pdf (accessed on 25th September 2025).

50. Nijkamp, P., & Wang, S. (2025). Winners and losers in the European Monetary Union: A neural network analysis of spatial industrial shifts. https://core.ac.uk/download/pdf/7036327.pdf (accessed on 25th September 2025).

51. Noble, J., & Williams, H. (2007). Homeostatic plasticity improves signal propagation in continuous time recurrent neural networks. https://core.ac.uk/download/22879825.pdf (accessed on 25th September 2025).

52. Pineda, F. J. (1989). Recurrent backpropagation and the dynamical approach to adaptive neural computation. https://core.ac.uk/download/4881017.pdf (accessed on 25th September 2025).

53. Puthanidam, R. V. (2017). Time-efficient hybrid approach for facial expression recognition. https://core.ac.uk/download/153450594.pdf (accessed on 25th September 2025).

54. Rashmi, P., & Singh, M. P. (2025). Performance analysis of convolutional neural networks with different optimizers and hybrid pooling methods for sound classification. International Journal of Advances in Soft Computing and its Applications. https://www.semanticscholar.org/paper/f69f3bf35a0c120610840da719bd6c1926b9f87f (accessed on 25th September 2025).

55. Rathore, H., Sahay, S. K., & Sewak, M. (2018). Comparison of deep learning and the classical machine learning algorithm for the malware

detection. http://arxiv.org/abs/1809.05889 (accessed on 25th September 2025).

56. Sirignano, J., & Spiliopoulos, K. (2019). Mean field analysis of neural networks: A law of large numbers. http://arxiv.org/abs/1805.01053 (accessed on 25th September 2025).
57. Slump, K., Spaanenburg, L., & van der Zwaag, B. J. (2003). Translating feedforward neural nets to SOM-like maps. https://core.ac.uk/download/pdf/11458434.pdf (accessed on 25th September 2025).
58. van Hillegersberg, J., Müller, R. M., Thornton, D., Travaille, A., et al. (2011). Electronic fraud detection in the U.S. Medicaid healthcare program: Lessons learned from other industries. https://core.ac.uk/download/pdf/11481166.pdf (accessed on 25th September 2025).
59. Wu, J., He, X., Niu, Y., Huang, T., & Yu, J. (2024). Circuit implementation of proximal projection neural networks for composite optimization problems. IEEE Transactions on Industrial Electronics, 71, 1948–1957. https://www.semanticscholar.org/paper/8f554743f42d9ef42f9323941ea405b11ee8f595 (accessed on 25th September 2025).
60. Zhao, X., Wang, L., Zhang, Y., Han, X., Deveci, M., & Parmar, M. (2024). A review of convolutional neural networks in computer vision. Artificial Intelligence Review, 57, 99. https://www.semanticscholar.org/paper/ad06c8a5fd292af518f878c7ced132b61739cdd8 (accessed on 25th September 2025).

CHAPTER 2

MATHEMATICAL FOUNDATIONS

Contents

INTRODUCTION

The journey of discovery in neural networks has essentially revolutionized our concept of artificial intelligence and machine learning, unearthing the complex mathematical structures at the basis of their operations. These biological-inspired networks are based on mathematical constructs like linear algebra, calculus, and probability theory. Through the breaking down of data into layers of interconnected nodes, neural networks learn patterns and make smart predictions. This initial discussion highlights the importance of mathematics as the foundation of neural networks because, in addition to being the doorway to the structure of algorithms, it also enhances the efficiency and precision of algorithms in solving problems. By systematically investigating these mathematical ideas, one can gain a better understanding of the potential and limits of neural networks in applications such as image recognition and natural language processing. To include an understanding of the mathematics underlying neural networks is to allow for more detailed investigation into the design and optimization of neural networks. Mathematical equations play a significant role in governing the interaction between neurons, weights, and activation functions, which govern data processing and decision-making. With the expansion of neural networks, new optimization strategies and architectures have emerged, including those based on gradient descent and backpropagation, mathematical methods pivotal in optimizing network performance.

Figure 2.1. *Mathematics behind neural networks.*

*Source: https://miro.medium.com/v2/resize:fit:750/format:webp/1 *qG1qexW-2PrbR-Jj7w9m_TQ.jpeg.*

Furthermore, the incorporation of advanced notions such as convolutional and recurrent layers raises the level of mathematical complexity, emphasizing the importance of a rigorous mathematical foundation. Identification of these components is paramount to practitioners and researchers in as much as they handle problems of training neural networks effectively, which eventually culminate in computational advancements. Beyond theoretical insight, the significance of mathematical underpinnings pertains to developing usable neural network applications. For instance, projects that involve the application of machine learning principles, motivated by some unifying theme, can rely on solid mathematical foundations in order to incorporate primary artificial intelligence concepts. Such integrative approaches enhance students' interest and comprehension as seen in classrooms where experiential projects give life to mathematics. As investigated in a number of studies, including those funded by the National Science Foundation, creating adaptable frameworks for teaching advanced material illustrates the worth of math in facilitating learning. By providing students with a deep level of understanding regarding the mathematical foundations, educators empower future innovators to solve complex real-world issues (Coleman et al., 2005; Florian et al., 2002). Briefly, the connection between mathematics and neural networks is essential, enabling breakthroughs within the field and guiding the course of upcoming evolution (Figure 2.1).

Definition of Neural Networks

Neural networks are theoretical models derived from the biological neural networks forming animal brains. They are trained to recognize patterns and make decisions based on input data, basically replicating human cognitive functions. The architecture of a neural network includes layers of interconnected nodes, or artificial neurons, which execute information in a manner akin to the synaptic links in biological brains. Every node performs a mathematical operation on input data, and then it is passed through an activation function in order to introduce non-linearity into the model. This architecture allows neural networks to learn complex patterns within datasets, in accordance with the rudimentary mathematical principles behind their function. Neural network learning relies heavily on the optimization of the weights assigned to connections between neurons. Through training, typically performed by way of algorithms such as backpropagation, the network optimizes the weights to minimize the difference between predicted and actual outputs. This iterative loop is strongly rooted in calculus and linear algebra, whereby gradients are computed to guide weight updates optimally. Furthermore, cybernetics governs the comprehension of the dynamics of such networks. Predecessors of the discipline, including John von Neumann and Warren McCulloch, laid the foundation for modeling complex systems with artificial neural networks, leading into an abstract knowledge of algorithmic processes defining high-level computing (Christen et al., 2019). In addition to their foundational structures, neural networks have multiple types and architectures specific to specific applications. These are feedforward networks, convolutional neural networks (CNNs), and recurrent neural networks (RNNs), all of which are capable of handling different kinds of data and tasks efficiently. For example, CNNs are particularly well suited for image recognition tasks, using layers that maintain spatial hierarchies, while

RNNs are well suited for sequential handling of data, essential for tasks such as natural language processing. The uses of neural networks extend beyond the conventional applications, to overlap with fields such as finite element analysis (FEA), whereby artificial intelligence techniques enhance reliability and safety in engineering designs (Sharif et al., 1997). Such diversity reflects the contribution of neural networks in the mathematical foundations of contemporary artificial intelligence and machine learning paradigms (Figure 2.2).

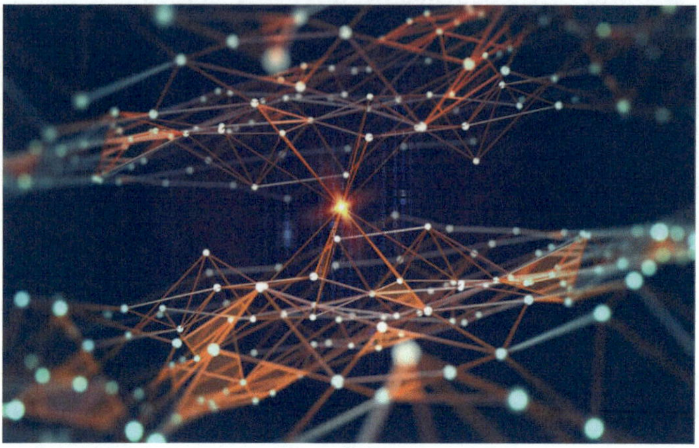

Figure 2.2. *Definition of neural networks.*

Source: https://www.mygreatlearning.com/blog/wp-content/uploads/2019/11/shutterstock_1061069282.jpg.webp.

Importance of Mathematics in Neural Networks

In artificial intelligence, the neural network has emerged as one of the most significant frameworks to solve complex problems, and mathematics is the underlying foundation for how they work. Center to this assumption is the use of linear algebra, which enables the representation and manipulation of data in neural networks. These operations like matrix multiplication and vector addition are crucial in the adjustment of connection weights between neurons to eventually enable the network to learn from input data. It is on the shoulders of these mathematical principles that the intricate structures that constitute the architecture of a neural network would otherwise lack the formality necessary in processing and analyzing vast amounts of input information. As neural networks continue to discover new uses in today's times, it is clear that mathematical skills to create robust models are a must in order to make meaningful findings in areas as diverse as identifying pictures and natural language processing. Calculus also comes into critical play in the optimization methods that are the cornerstone of neural networks. Neural network training is generally parameter-tuning to minimize error, something accomplished with techniques based on differential calculus. Backpropagation algorithm, a landmark technique for neural network training, relies on computation of gradients employed to modify weights stepwise, guiding the learning towards a solution. This repeated refinement is important in optimizing model performance since it converges to a solution that models the patterns in the data. Secondly, awareness of activation function characteristics and their derivatives is necessary to apply neural networks efficiently. This mathematical insight enables the selection and development of activation functions, which are vital to the convergence behavior and learning capability of models employed in practical applications. Linear algebra and calculus aside, probability and statistics provide neural networks with critical tools to boost their performance, particularly in the estimation of uncertainty and model evaluation. Probabilistic-based methods allow for incorporating randomness within learning procedures, leading to stronger generalization capabilities. For instance, Bayesian approaches enable neural networks to update their beliefs in model parameters adaptively given observed data, capturing inherent uncertainties without overfitting. Secondly, statistical techniques are required to verify the model's accuracy and reliability utilizing validation techniques such as cross-validation and confusion matrices. As the demand for advanced computational models is escalating in various areas, the integration of mathematical sophistication through probability and statistics will definitely be a cornerstone in designing effective neural network systems that still suit and are realistic in actual scenarios (Florian et al., 2002; Markova et al., 2018).

2.1. BASIC CONCEPTS OF NEURAL NETWORKS

Neural networks, being a mathematical representation, define the spirit of pattern recognition and decision-making like human cognition. Essentially, the systems consist of interconnected nodes or neurons organized in layers like input, hidden, and output layers. The neuron works by processing signals from the connections through a weighted sum of inputs and an activation function that provides non-linearity to the model. This composition of layers allows neural networks to learn and generalize from examples and learn complex inherent relationships present in data and significantly improve their generalizability. In learning settings, as discussed in Markova et al. (2018), the use of neural network modeling helps to establish a connection between theoretical computer science and practical usage and illustrate basic ideas behind these powerful mathematical constructs.

The training process of neural networks, learning, is based on the adjustment of weights through numerous optimization methods. Backpropagation is the most used process and efficiently calculates gradients to optimize error between predictions and outputs to its optimal point. Through incremental updates of the weights using gradients, the network becomes capable of making improved predictions with the passage of time. One of the key elements of this training is selecting the right activation functions like sigmoid or tanh functions to decide how the input signals contribute to the neuron output. This design aspect plays a crucial role as it influences the rate of convergence during training, as well as the overall performance of the neural network. The discovery of these techniques, as well as platforms such as CoCalc, highlights their position in computational learning as noted by Markova et al. (2018), providing practical experience while learning fundamental concepts. Furthermore, architecture in a neural network depends on mathematical concepts that serve as the foundation of their building and application. A good example of such a theory is the Kolmogorov-Arnold representation theorem that provides explanations on how neural networks can approximate any continuous function by means of some structures, including multilayer networks. This is a mathematical rationale justifying the use of neural networks in the solution of complex problems in various domains. As discussed in, the emerging field of neurocognitive informatics is essentially devoted to the task of enhancing the harmony between artificial systems and human cognition. Not only does this multidisciplinary area trigger the development of new computational algorithms, but also advances research toward effectively merging natural and artificial information-processing systems, demonstrating how fundamental principles of neural networks are much more than just applicable within traditional frameworks, but also inform future ways of computing (Figure 2.3).

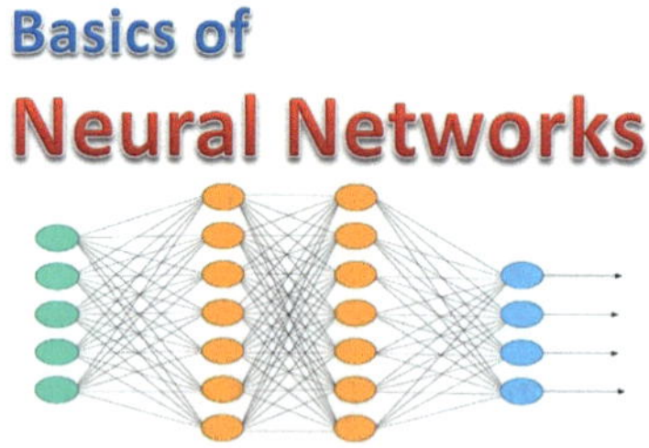

Figure 2.3. *Basics of neural networks.*

Source: https://2.bp.blogspot.com/-OyGhUE1OkqY/WjbiAfLLliI/AAAAAAAAAhQ/u78Y8lZfcfQNenTaO4bMj8YwsIJwJBV_gCLcBGAs/s1600/Basics-of-Neural-Networks.jpg.

2.1.1. Neurons and Activation Functions

The neurons are the elementary building blocks of a neural network, and they function much like neurons in the brain by accepting inputs, generating outputs, and enabling communication across the network. A neuron has a mathematical model that accepts multiple inputs, performs a linear transformation specified by weights and biases, and then passes the output through a non-linear function referred to as an activation function. This mathematical framework is required to detect implicit patterns within data. A choice of activation function is important—popular functions like sigmoid, tanh, and ReLU (Rectified Linear Unit) differ significantly in the way they introduce non-linearity and influence the learning dynamics while being trained. For instance, the piecewise linear ReLU is gaining prominence in virtually all deep learning applications due to its computational efficiency and suitability for eliminating the vanishing gradient issue. Activation functions perform an extremely crucial role in enabling neural networks to learn sophisticated relationships by introducing non-linearities that make them expressive. The non-linear mappings ensure that each output of a neuron is not only a linear combination of the inputs, but allow the network to learn complex input-output mappings. Sigmoid functions, for instance, are helpful in binary classification tasks since they can squish the outputs within the range 0–1, and can also be used as probability estimators. Nevertheless, their tendency to saturate while learning makes learning harder, especially in deep networks. In other cases, activation functions like softmax are used for multi-class classification problems where outputs are scaled to produce a probability distribution.

The development from basic functions to sophisticated activations indicates the fine nuances involved in designing neural architectures that can generalize effectively over a large set of problem spaces. The connection between neurons and activation functions is more than computation; it has a strong bearing on the learning dynamics and generalization capability of neural networks. Current developments in optimization methods, especially in over-parameterized models, have brought to the forefront the impact of activation functions on the dynamics of gradient descent through networks such as the neural tangent kernel. The kernel, which occurs at the time of initialization of the networks, is essential in explaining the behavior of neural networks in arriving at solutions and the stability and approximation properties of functions represented within their structure. Examination of such kernels reveals inherent learning biases in paths, as in convolutional networks where stability to image deformations becomes important. Thus, comprehension of the mathematical foundation of neurons and activation functions is important not only to include neural networks but also to encourage research in neurocognitive informatics and enhance the coordination of artificial and natural information systems, as reflected in advancing research (Bietti et al., 2019; Duch et al., 2009) (Figure 2.4).

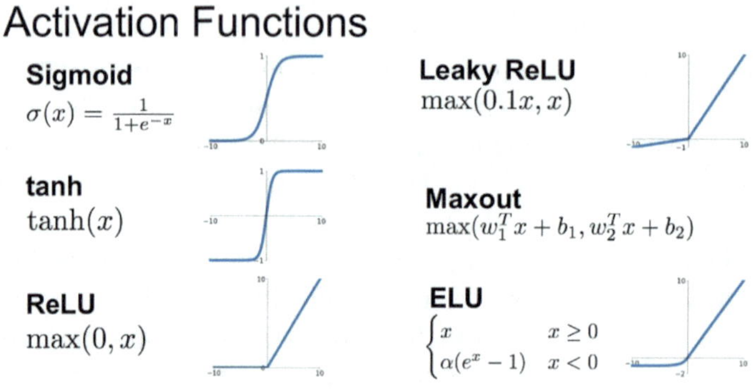

Figure 2.4. *Activation functions.*

Source: https://global.discourse-cdn.com/dlai/original/3X/c/d/cd5ed325f38ed-ba1755ebfdd06009ee58b8ba1bd.jpeg.

2.1.2. Layers in Neural Networks

In neural network studies, the layer arrangement between various layers plays a significant role in establishing the networks ability to learn and generalize data. Neural networks are typically constructed utilizing several layers, i.e., the input layer, one or more hidden layers, and the output layer. Each layer contains numerous neurons, which are computation units that perform specific mathematical operations on input data. The synapses in between neurons, having synaptic weights, allow for the transfer of information in the network. Intrinsic modifications through successive layers allow the network to build representations of growing sophistication in the input, a phenomenon greatly reliant on the multilayer network's structure as described under the Kolmogorov-Arnold representation theorem. This theorem suggests that multilayered neural networks are capable of approximating any continuous function, and this emphasizes the importance of layered structures in approximating functions and the capacity to learn (Markova et al., 2018). The specific functions carried out by various layers also explain the diverse abilities exhibited by neural networks in addressing various tasks. In particular, lower levels of a neural network are assigned to abstract higher-order features from input data, on which the more fundamental patterns seen in earlier layers are founded. This hierarchical approach is an exemplification of biological neural operations; for instance, in the case of the visual cortex, specific pathways specialize in specific functionalities like action and perception. Multi-task deep neural network research has shed light on the specialization of layers for varying goals such that task-specific layer configurations result in shared representations while unrelated tasks are assigned more segregated features (Bohte et al., 2017). How the layers interact and make contributions to overall function is central to improving neural network design and deployment across domains. The layer examination of neural networks extends past the straightforward structure and functionality; it also includes the impact on computation capabilities and learning efficiency. The depth of a neural network, in terms of how many hidden layers it possesses, directly impacts its ability to learn sophisticated data distributions. However, as networks increase in depth, they come with problems like overfitting and increased training time. Methods like dropout, batch normalization, and optimization methods are employed to overcome these issues so that deeper networks do not lose their efficacy. Additionally, the specific selection of layer types, such as convolutional layers for spatial data or recurrent layers for sequential data, also assists in enabling specialized functionality in networks. Understanding these interactions provides a sound basis for innovation in the application of neural networks, illustrating the profound worth of layers in the mathematical foundations of neural networks (Markova et al., 2018).

2.1.3. Architecture of Neural Networks

Neural network structure is essentially driven by mathematical ideas that define how neural systems treat information. The design of a neural network—constituent layers of interconnected nodes or neurons—is meant to mimic biological processes, but it is rooted deeply in mathematical equations. The network's layers are characterized by their activation functions, which introduce non-linearity, allowing the model to learn complex patterns in data. Also, the layer type decisions, e.g., convolutional or recurrent layers, make a significant impact on the networks ability. This is comparable to work in invertible neural networks (INNs), where a mathematical explanation of feedforward networks helps to explain their behavior. Having these architectures mathematized not only helps train them effectively but also enhances performance in many tasks, such as image classification and generative modeling, as seen in the i-ResNets explanation in Behrmann et al. (2019). Besides structural design, the integration of domain knowledge into neural network architectures is also significant to optimize their performance. Integration of specific domain information can guide the design of custom architectures designed for specific data types or tasks. For instance, the training of neural networks to process imaging mass spectrometry (IMS) data makes use of information regarding principles underneath the surface of the discipline in a bid to maximize classification accuracy (Behrmann et al., 2019). Such well-designed architectures are capable of overcoming limitations unique to high-dimensional spaces and can generalize more by moving the model closer into line with the nature of data it observes.

This synergy of domain knowledge and neural architecture not only continues the practical application of neural networks but also shows the broader context of the mathematical foundations that go into constructing successful machine learning strategies. Moreover, the confluence of symbolic reasoning and neural networks suggests that artificial intelligence could be implemented more harmoniously. Neural-symbolic integration, as proposed in the literature, aims to integrate the robust learning of the neural networks with the representational reasoning of the classical symbolic systems. Dual paradigmic approach eliminates the limitation of the application of a single paradigm by itself, capitalizing on advancements in areas such as automated reasoning and multi-agent systems. By designing an architectural framework that encompasses both neural and symbolic elements, researchers can more effectively tackle uncertainties and complexities in data interpretation. As such, these architectural developments reveal an enhanced understanding of the neural networks, emphasizing their adaptability and the capacity for nuanced mental functions, finally leading artificial intelligence research towards its future path (Figure 2.5).

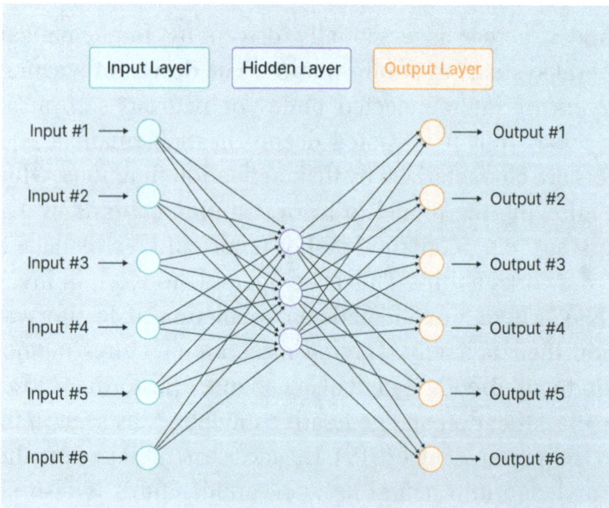

Figure 2.5. *Neural network architectures.*

Source: https://framerusercontent.com/images/aZW0MrFDu8LFrU2iSYHOIpI8E.png?scale-down-to=1024.

2.2. LINEAR ALGEBRA IN NEURAL NETWORKS

The relationship between neural networks and linear algebra is a key background of how such complicated systems function. Neural networks employ matrix computations in order to handle and change information across various layers. Linear transformations are done by nodes or neurons in each layer on input vectors, which are themselves matrices. Through operations such as matrix multiplication, addition, and activation functions, the neural network is able to learn data patterns. Through this linear algebraic form, besides facilitating computation at high speeds, the interpretability of affine transformations used is also enhanced. Through representing transformation at every layer in algebraic form, researchers can interrogate underlying structures of information flow and decision-making in the network. Thus, linear algebra is a simple tool for modeling that describes biological processes as the theoretical models imply in individual control models of biological systems (Aguilar et al., 2016). Besides, mathematical principles underlying linear algebra make optimization methods imperative when training networks. Neural networks update their weights employing algorithms like gradient descent, which rely on vector calculus and matrix derivatives rooted in linear algebra. This process of optimization becomes essential in minimization of the loss function, leading to the improved performance of the network on a task. What makes these training processes work is the manner in which gradients can be represented concisely in terms of matrix notations. Therefore, advanced methods in linear algebra, including singular value decomposition and eigendecomposition, are involved in dimensionality reduction and principal component analysis. Not only does this capability power computation, but it enables deeper understanding of the underlying structures of high-dimensional data, and in the process, enhances the effectiveness of neural networks in practical use (Wallace et al., 2006). Other than optimization and data processing, representation and manipulation of relationship among variables are intrinsic to the working of neural networks. Linear algebras' contribution to defining relationships through vector spaces, norms, and inner products enables one to comprehend relationships within the network more effectively at the interconnectivity level of information. By various linear transformations, each neuron can classify and transform input data in geometric space and give rich meaning to the problem space. The application of linear algebra in dimension reduction techniques not only simplifies complex data but also retains significant features that aid the networks learning process. This mathematical accuracy helps to specify the boundaries of model generalizability, influencing the degree of accuracy by which neural networks are able to generalize over unseen data. The unity of these linear algebra concepts with the theory of neural networks eventually enhances both domains and indicates their utility in addressing challenging problems across multiple domains (Aguilar et al., 2016) (Figure 2.6).

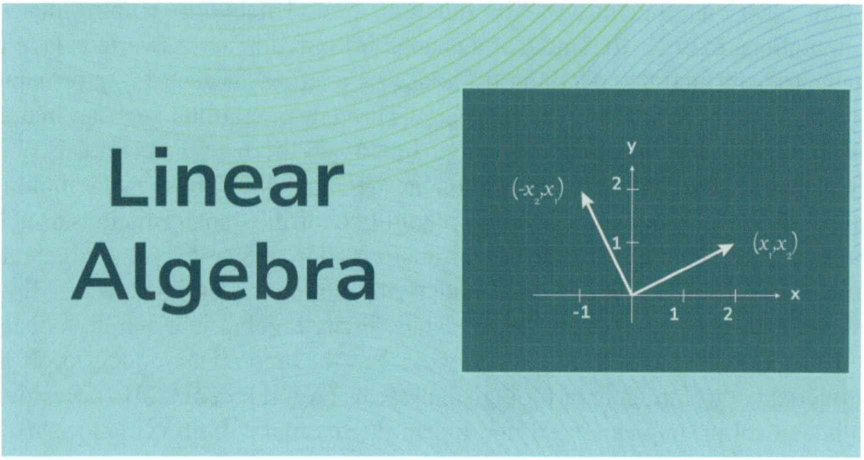

Figure 2.6. *Linear algebra.*

Source: https://media.geeksforgeeks.org/wp-content/uploads/20240502180026/Linear-Algebra.png.

2.2.1. Vectors and Matrices

Vectors and matrices are basic entities in neural networks that serve as the foundation for the mathematical processes that are needed to represent data and change it. A vector is a list of ordered numbers which can be used to represent various forms of data such as inputs and outputs for a neural network. When these vectors are organized as matrices, they facilitate complex data manipulations, and multiple data points may be arranged within a coherent framework. Matrices are extensively applied in operations like transformations and linear mappings, which are fundamental to the functioning of neural networks. They are involved in the way the networks learn from data and provide a mathematical framework on which algorithms are created and optimized for performance and precision. At a more basic level, the abilities of neural networks to perform operations such as classification and regression rely on matrix manipulation. For instance, training a neural network involves the tuning of weights in matrix format, which indicate the strength of connections between neurons. One part of this process involves operations such as matrix addition and matrix multiplication that allow the inputs to be summed to calculate the outputs for neurons. Additionally, newer techniques, such as the employment of density matrices in models such as Quantum Language Models, demonstrate how matrices can be utilized to portray complex semantic content. These representations facilitate the incorporation of multi-dimensional attributes into learning, significantly increasing the ability of the model to generate and comprehend contextual relations in data (Ma et al., 2018). The mathematical issue of low-rank matrix completion is of vital relevance in applications involving neural networks, particularly in dealing with incomplete or sparse data sets. Matrix completion technique, as investigated through avenues of algorithms like MaCBetH, indicates the importance of matrix structure in recovering underlying data representations from sparse entries. By utilizing spectral methods to discover the rank of matrices, the approach relates directly to the capacity of neural networks to reconstruct and learn sparse information. Such performance is a demonstration of the capacity of networks to generalize from sparse data, thereby making prediction more accurate. Thus, the resolution of rank detection and reconstruction error problems by sophisticated matrix manipulation can help bring neural network training and application in the real world to greater efficiency (Krzakala et al., 2015) (Figure 2.7).

Figure 2.7. *Vector.*

Source: https://www.oxfordwebstudio.com/user/pages/06.da-li-znate/sta-je-vektor/sta-je-vektor.jpg.

2.2.2. Matrix Operations and Their Applications

Matrix operations are at the heart of numerous applications in neural networks, with the mathematical framework engaged in data manipulation and transformation. Matrix multiplication, addition, and transposition are all significant operations in deep learning that find application in computations that neural networks carry out. For instance, input data coming in the form of vectors can be transformed by weight matrices that contain learned patterns. Various layers carry out some operations to produce output that assists in optimizing models performance.

Efficiency of these matrix operations is essential as it has a direct bearing on the training speed and quality of neural network models, especially when handling large data or complex structures, and thus it's important to grasp these basis mathematical principles in everyday applications. Apart from basic applications, matrix operations provide advanced functionalities such as backpropagation and gradient descent, which are required to train neural networks. Backpropagation usage computes the gradients of loss functions with weights using chain rule applications based on matrix calculus in nature. The procedure helps the model in making its parameters operate iteratively to lower errors, hence improving its accuracy. Furthermore, recent machine learning breakthroughs mark a shift towards optimizing such operations through extensive ranges of techniques and hardware accelerations. While researchers pursue efficient implementations of matrix computations, they are striving to reduce the computational cost, thus facilitating the utilization of deep neural networks in environments with limited resources, such as in developments like those addressed in Becking et al. (2020). In the evolving paradigm of machine learning, the integration of quantum computing is associated with challenges and opportunities for matrix computations. Quantum algorithms are restricted by their reliance on traditional computing hardware; hence, researchers are increasingly curious about how quantum algorithms could complement these primitive operations. Certain matrix multiplications, for example, would be executed more quickly on a quantum device, and this could be mirrored in sensational reductions in time for neural network training. On top of that, quantum techniques can handle noisy big data better, so the scope of applications for machine learning is expanded. The intersection of matrix operations and quantum computation is a hopeful frontier that may redefine efficiency expectations during neural network training, as depicted in visions of research frontiers in the future (Ben-David et al., 2018) (Figure 2.8).

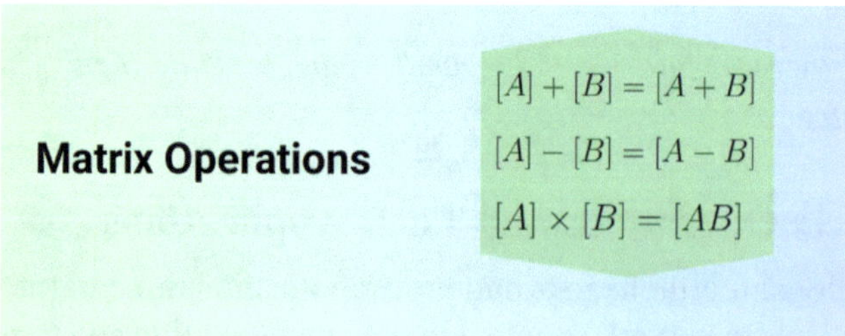

Figure 2.8. *Matrix operations.*

Source: https://cache.careers360.mobi/media/article_images/2024/10/10/Complex_numbers_59.png.

2.2.3. Eigenvalues and Eigenvectors

Eigenvectors and eigenvalues are fundamental principles in the understanding of different mathematical frameworks, which are of paramount relevance in neural network development and operation. In such a context, eigenvalues capture the proportion of variance captured by one of a dataset's principal components, while eigenvectors are the directions along which the variance exists. Such an identification becomes central to dimensionality reduction techniques, such as Principal Component Analysis (PCA), that reduce a dataset without compromising the most significant features. By compressing high-dimensional spaces into lower dimensions, eigenvalues and eigenvectors enable neural networks to generalize and learn patterns more effectively. The research on eigenvalues and eigenvectors thus forms the basis for enhanced performance of neural networks in classification and regression tasks.

Eigenvalues and eigenvectors do more than perform basic dimensionality reduction; they are crucial in demystifying the properties of data structures represented by matrices. Particularly, matrix completion techniques utilize the spectral properties of matrices, in which eigenvalue analysis is vital. For example, in MaCBetH, matrix rank is estimated as a function of the number of negative eigenvalues in the Bethe Hessian matrix. The estimation enables better matrix reconstruction with reduced root-mean-square error compared to the traditional methods. These developments underscore the significance of spectral analysis in simplifying neural network frameworks so that they can handle incomplete data inputs in the best possible manner. Current work on these mathematical foundations strengthens our understanding of the efficiency and accuracy of algorithms for neural network function (Krzakala et al., 2015). Spectral analysis finds broader uses, like in the modeling of complex networks with the assistance of eigenvalues and eigenvectors. Spectral graph theory, the study of graph structure, reveals a connection between the architecture of these networks and their functionality.

A look at the overall distribution of eigenvalues provides researchers with information about other centralities measures that claim how central or significant the nodes are within a graph. These interpretations are significant in social network studies applications through to biology modeling. By borrowing methods from condensed matter physics, researchers can compute spectral densities efficiently even in huge networks, thereby enabling better comprehension of their structure (Benson et al., 2019). Finally, the intricate relationship between eigenvalues, eigenvectors, and neural networks is a testimony of the richness of mathematical underpinnings that drive new solutions in machine learning and artificial intelligence (Figure 2.9).

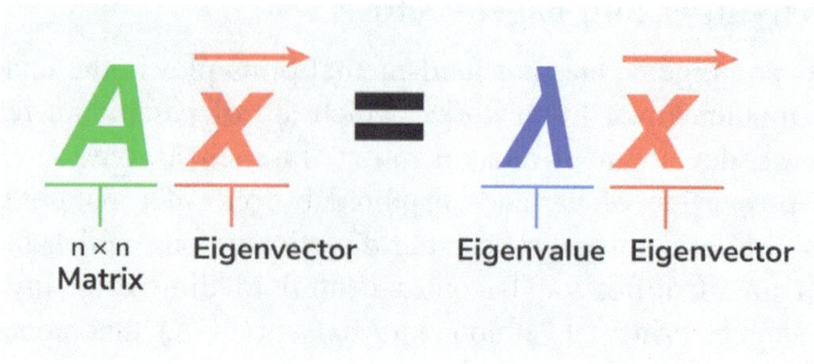

Figure 2.9. *Eigen value and Eigen vector.*

Source: https://media.geeksforgeeks.org/wp-content/uploads/ 2025070 4123843 108020/Eigenvalues.webp.

2.3. CALCULUS AND OPTIMIZATION

The relationship between optimization and calculus is the heart of the design and training of neural networks, where the minimization of a loss function is most often the primary goal. The practitioner needs to have strong foundations in both differential calculus and optimization techniques. Using derivatives, practitioners are able to understand in what direction the parameters of a model should be adjusted in order to obtain steepest descent toward optimal solutions. The principle is shown in the gradient descent method, where the calculated gradients through calculus are used to iteratively make adjustments to the neural network's weights. The efficacy of this optimization process is extremely important, particularly in high-dimensional spaces, a common characteristic of neural networks. Therefore, having a solid understanding of calculus not only helps in comprehending the intrinsic mechanics of neural networks but also makes it possible to create more advanced optimization algorithms specifically designed for particular neural network topologies. In more sophisticated applications, particularly those with constraints formulated by partial differential equations (PDEs), the standard optimization procedures might prove inadequate. As explained in current studies, when one deals with high-dimensional models, the weakness of traditional optimizers is revealed. To name just one, nonlinear model predictive control (NMPC) requires real-time optimization solution in problems that may not be addressed by typical black-box approaches. In such a scenario, the integration of tailored solvers, sequential quadratic programming (SQP), and neural networks can go a long way in improving computational efficiency for solving PDE-constrained optimization problems. This hybrid approach allows efficient offline phase that, though long, contributes significant speed-up to the online evaluation phase. Such new optimization methods illustrate the necessity of calculus for developing advanced strategies for specific problems of neural networks and thus allowing more advanced applications and researches. In addition, understanding the relationship between optimization frameworks and probabilistic modeling also facilitates advancement of neural networks functionality. For example, factor graph application gives a robust way of succinctly summarizing complex probability distributions ubiquitously employed in machine learning. Bethe approximation, an optimization-based paradigm, has been promising for partition function computation related to factor graphs. Empirical success with belief propagation is there though its theoretical foundations are involved and sometimes obscure. Therefore, reformulating the Bethe approximation as a polynomial optimization problem provides new insights into its efficacy and duality with belief propagation. This explanatory conversion illustrates how calculus and optimization can unveil secret knowledgc of probabilistic models employed with neural networks, which ultimately make them more advanced and efficient to use in various arenas of research (Figure 2.10).

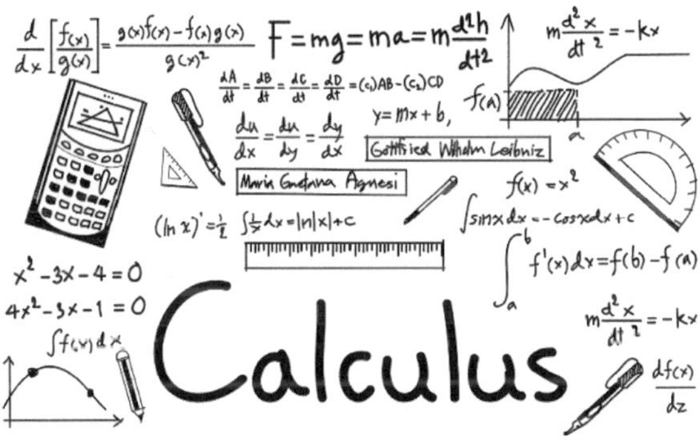

Figure 2.10. *How calculus and optimization power neural networks.*

*Source: https://miro.medium.com/v2/resize:fit:640/format:webp/1*baBiOm0CJvB xCK2Qg33Zkg.jpeg.*

2.3.1. Derivatives and Gradients

Derivatives and gradients form a fundamental building block in the realm of neural networks, particularly within the optimization process used on model training. Derivatives provide the data required regarding the sensitivity of a neural network's output to a parameter change. This is significant because the process of training involves changing these parameters—weights and biases—in order to optimize the difference between outputs predicted and target actually desired. The power of gradients, as being partial derivative vectors, unfolds in the usage of optimization algorithms like gradient descent. They effectively steer the direction and magnitude by which the parameters are to be tweaked so the learning can be optimized. As we move toward learning the mathematics behind neural networks, the role of automatic differentiation (AD) becomes increasingly prominent. AD facilitates precise and fast calculation of derivatives of complex functions expressed in terms of computer programs, an important aspect in machine learning frameworks. AD is more precise and efficient compared to traditional methods of numerical differentiation, which are error-prone and inefficient. AD calculates gradients in an accurate fashion that can be executed very rapidly. This talent is particularly crucial given the over-parameterization of contemporary neural networks, in which the optimization methods must overcome extremely complex loss surfaces. By integrating AD into the training of neural networks, practitioners can better understand the optimization landscape, leading to more robust learning mechanisms (Baydin et al., 2018). Also, advances in the theory of neural networks, more particularly the exploration of the neural tangent kernel, accentuate the intricate interaction between gradients and the learning dynamics of the models. The gradient descent dynamics in an over-parameterized setting are greatly influenced by this kernel, which captures the shape in which learning emerges during parameter initialization. Analyzing the properties of this kernel—i.e., smoothness and stability—provides hints regarding the inductive biases that are embedded within the model parameters. Such analyses prove that learning dynamics not only control convergence but also exert influence on the models generalization behavior, particularly in the event of data perturbations (Bietti et al., 2019). Thus, gradient and derivative analysis extends beyond sheer theoretical computational aids, influencing critical decisions at each stage of neural network construction.

2.3.2. Gradient Descent Algorithm

The Gradient Descent Algorithm forms the heart of the optimization methods applied to training neural networks. Essentially, the algorithm repeatedly updates model parameters in order to minimize some cost function, which quantifies the error of predictions with respect to actual outcomes. Every iteration involves calculating the gradient, or partial derivatives vector, of the cost function with regard to the parameters. This direction is towards the steepest descent, and consequently, the algorithm goes in the reverse direction, hence gradient descent. As this iteration is repeated many times, it tries to converge to a minimum point in the parameter space. Notably, the convergence of the algorithm can be regulated by various parameters, including the learning rate, which determines the size of the steps in the direction of the minimum.

This recursive nature is indicative of a lot of the optimization terrain in neural network training. Another significant aspect of the Gradient Descent Algorithm is that it is able to accommodate a variety of optimization problems in neural networks, particularly in non-convex terrain. The objective functions in most real-world use cases, particularly deep learning use cases, are typically non-convex and possess multiple local minima and saddle points. Recent work has proposed methods that generalize the use of gradient descent to issues beyond strictly convex issues. For instance, some convex optimization algorithms can now be applied successfully to non-convex targets with convergence guarantees to stationary points in some cases.

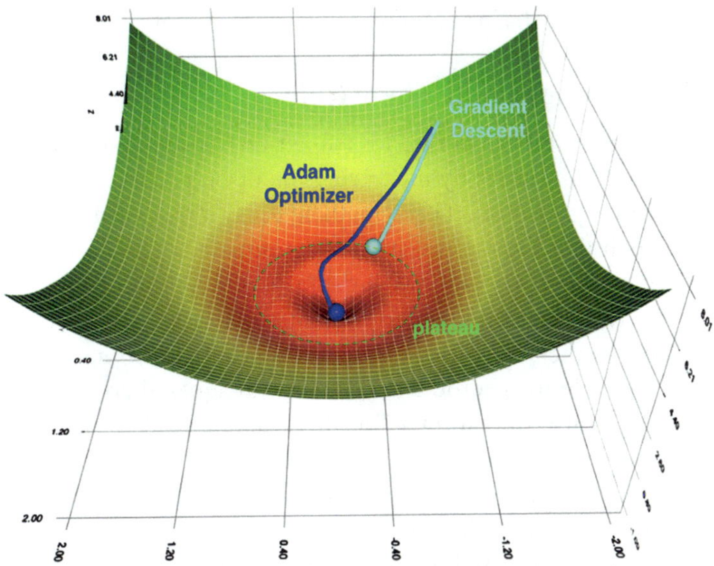

Figure 2.11. *Optimization and gradient descent: The learning process.*

*Source: https://miro.medium.com/v2/resize:fit:4800/format: webp/0*1 PjB003ND-GDtZjbn.png.*

This versatility is crucial since it allows practitioners to use gradient descent not only for classical issues but also for the sophisticated optimization issues common in modern-day machine learning designs. Such advancements improve mathematical foundations behind neural network algorithms and leave room for additional exploration within optimization theory (Drusvyatskiy et al., 2017). In addition, the integration of gradient descent with adaptive control system principles has opened new avenues for understanding and boosting convergence properties of learning algorithms. Historic control systems and modern machine learning both have analogues in goals: both aim for stability, performance, and efficiency in learning data. By discovering analogues in these aspects, scientists discovered potential in applying insight in adaptive control to boost gradient descent algorithms. For instance, controlling update rules in manners that borrow from the fundamentals of control theory can sharpen stability in learning, particularly when it is used in complex neural network architectures. Not only does this interaction create deeper theory, but it also suggests algorithmic improvements relevant to existing algorithms. By examining these intersections, the mathematical foundations of neural networks are strengthened but also innovative, paving the way for algorithm design and deployment breakthroughs in the future (Annaswamy et al., 2019) (Figure 2.11).

2.3.3. Loss Functions and Their Role

In the context of neural networks, loss functions are also very important in directing the training process by measuring the discrepancy between predicted values and true target values. These mathematical models act as measures of performance such that the optimization algorithms can update the weights of the network iteratively. By minimizing the loss function, a neural network is able to effectively learn the underlying patterns of the data it is trained on and develop its predictability. There are several loss functions that are used, each being applicable to specific tasks, like mean squared error for regression tasks and categorical cross-entropy for classification tasks. These operations influence not only the models learning trajectory but also the models capacity for generalization to novel data, making this an important consideration in the architecture of neural networks. Theoretically, the choice of loss function can influence both performance and stability, and as such, it is a critical model design choice. As discussed in the literature today, intersections of optimization methods and adaptive control give rise to similar formulations of loss, which support improved analysis of algorithms (Annaswamy et al., 2019). Understanding the intersection allows researchers to develop more robust learning procedures that go beyond typical neural network structures. This information improves convergence aspects of the training process, allowing more freedom and efficacy in model optimization. Thus, the intrinsic relationship between loss functions and convergence behavior is essential in an effort to create neural networks that are not only trustworthy but also computationally efficient. Recent advancements in machine learning methodologies have shown the significance of exploring how loss functions can be adapted so as to embrace novel computational paradigms such as quantum computing. The ability of quantum algorithms to enhance learning processes is particularly fascinating, especially in cases where there are limitations for traditional algorithms (Ben-David et al., 2018). From the perspective of quantum machine learning, scientists can identify new approaches for solving complex problems, like learning under noisy environments. This renewed interest in the leveraging of quantum resources risks undermining established methods and opening up new avenues for algorithm development that will provide significant advantages in speed and efficiency. Loss functions are thus at the forefront of investigation, inspiring the orientation of neural network application in an ever-evolving technology landscape (Figure 2.12).

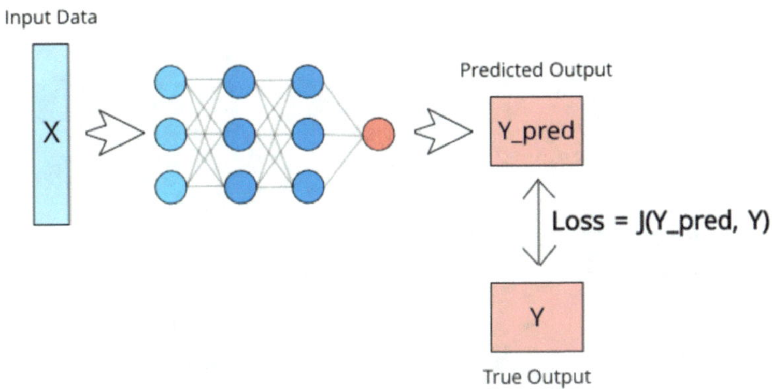

Figure 2.12. *Neural network loss visualization.*

*Source: https://miro.medium.com/v2/resize:fit:786/format:webp/1*N1PyOYeog-vyytRbwEwQCQ.png.*

2.4. PROBABILITY AND STATISTICS

It is crucial to comprehend probability and statistics in the creation of stable neural networks because these establish the logic behind which techniques are utilized in training as well as model validation. Probability is the framework within which data as well as model prediction uncertainties are measurable. By probabilistic modeling, neural networks are able to make predictions about the probability of outcomes from observed inputs, a detail that is crucial in making the right decisions. Statistical methods support this by offering methods for analyzing data distributions, estimating central tendencies, and assessing variability. By combining all these, neural networks can be optimized so that their predictive performances are maximized while accounting for the inherent variability in real-world data. Probabilistic analysis of neural network outputs also allows for decision-making based on risk estimates, providing direct links between statistical foundations and real-world applications in domains ranging from medicine to finance. As it is applied to larger and more complex datasets, new optimization algorithms, such as Adaptive Simulated Annealing (ASA), have proven superior to traditional modeling approaches. ASAs adaptability to the high-dimensional nature of large data is particularly beneficial in cases where standard regression methods will most likely break down. The algorithm is also skilled at navigating the massive search spaces normally involved in training neural networks, allowing one to select the optimal parameters that improve prediction ability.

Figure 2.13. *Probability and statistics.*

Source: https://media.licdn.com/dms/image/v2/C4E12AQG2gC7jJXOvjQ/article-cover_image-shrink_600_2000/article-cover_image-shrink_600_2000/0/1604310994662?e=2147483647&v=beta&t=eavuGAU0Wwu8ZxwwAa8abZC_FYD6B-k0dXLR-uA5I5Tw.

The comparative analysis illustrates that conventional methodologies are largely effective in limited data but ASA provides an appropriate framework for large population analysis. Such adaptability affirms the fundamental contribution of statistical procedures to optimize neural network performance irrespective of data sizes, and that illustrates the intricate relationship between statistical procedures and enhancements in machine learning (Goldstein et al., 2003). Besides, how CI relates to AI brings the two into the intersection of neural network topology in its more general probabilistic frame. CI comprises neural, fuzzy, and evolutionary techniques to solve complex, algorithm-impossible problems, while AI is a sub-discipline that addresses higher-order cognition. This delineation highlights probabilistic and statistical models' crucial role in enabling CI techniques to facilitate intelligent accommodations within data that are inherently uncertain. The change in focus from algorithmic approaches toward problem-solving frameworks generates a required debate about challenges faced by real-world applications, thus making mathematical foundations more applicable to neural networks. Through the analysis of these relationships, we reveal the key roles of probability and statistics to CI and AI, ultimately establishing the powers and acumen of neural networks in sophisticated problem-solving environments (Duch et al., 2007) (Figure 2.13).

2.4.1. Probability Distributions in Neural Networks

Probability distributions are central to the functioning of neural networks, that is, in data modeling and interpretation. In a neural network configuration, input information is often represented as probabilistic, allowing the network to learn pattern bottom-up from uncertainties and variations of real-world information. The probability distribution concept gives the network capability to make intelligent predictions based on estimating the probabilities of different outcomes. Such distributions have the effect of naturally adding strength to the model, making it possible for the model to generalize appropriately with unseen data. Thus, probabilistic techniques combined with integration enable the neural networks to broaden their ability to perform complex tasks such as classification and regression, particularly in conditions of noise and uncertainty. Based on this premise, methodology using specific probability distributions can be selectively chosen based on the nature of the neural network architecture as well as the problem domain. For instance, Gaussian distributions can be employed in models with the assumption that normal distribution is followed by errors and categorical distributions may be employed in classification problems where the results are discrete. Besides, recent developments in machine learning accommodate twin-framework consisting of classic methods and quantum methods aiming at leveraging special quantum features to optimize classical learning algorithms. In this case, scientists underscore the acknowledgment of the weakness of these quantum algorithms in attempting to achieve their advantages within learning problems, particularly in scenarios that entail noise and computational complexity (Ben-David et al., 2018). Beyond that, there is one extra level of complexity in understanding the way in which neural networks can learn and automatically select best data representations from probability distributions. This representation learning autonomy is most crucial as it allows models to be capable of learning from various representations of data and maintaining selectivity in distinguishing between relevant features. From this understanding, the performance of neural networks is significantly enhanced, enabling them to generate stable representations closely associated with actual occurrences. Such representations ought to encapsulate the rich interplay between input data and outputs, with two points being assignable the same representation only if and only if they can be transformed into one another (Anselmi et al., 2015). This postulate not only identifies the central position of probability distributions in neural network architecture but also illustrates their key role in extending our understanding of data-driven learning mechanisms (Figure 2.14).

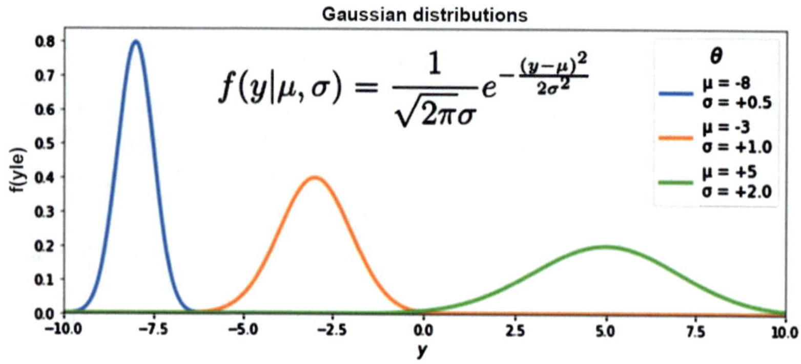

Figure 2.14. *Gaussian distribution.*

*Source: https://miro.medium.com/v2/resize:fit:828/format:webp/1*Fj60gbMk6p54VWAyhsqmSg.png.*

2.4.2. Bayesian Inference

Bayesian inference is a dominant statistical approach that enables neural networks to incorporate prior knowledge as well as revise beliefs when presented with new evidence. By applying Bayes theorem, practitioners are able to quantify uncertainty and arrive at probabilistic conclusions, which are crucial to many machine learning applications. For neural networks, this translates into more evidence-based decision-making, particularly under the presence of limited data or noisy data. In particular, Bayesian models can learn parameters based on observed outcomes, encouraging models that are not only resilient but also capable of expressing basic uncertainties about predictions. These are attractive properties in high-risk domains like medicine and finance, where mistakes can be exorbitantly expensive. The addition of Bayesian concepts further enhances the interpretability of neural networks so that users will understand how prior assumptions influence results and decision paths. Mathematical formulations characteristic of Bayesian inference, including prior, likelihood, and posterior distributions, form the basis for interpreting model behaviors in neural networks. The capacity of a neural network to learn from data can be understood with a

Bayesian approach, with the parameters being considered distributions rather than fixed values. This enables the computation of the posterior distribution of the parameters given the observed data, thus enabling a more richer learning process. Further, techniques such as Markov Chain Monte Carlo (MCMC) and variational inference provide efficient ways to approximate these distributions, making Bayesian approaches scale to large-scale neural network applications. As the complexity of data increases and model complexity increases, Bayesian approaches become essential, enabling neural networks to deal with uncertainty in a correct way and improve performance in an uncertain world without sacrificing the theoretical basis that unifies statistics and machine learning. The confluence of Bayesian inference and neural networks remains complemented by advances in neural-symbolic integration that strives to marry the strengths of neural computation with symbolic reasoning. The merging produces a more comprehensive cognitive computational model consistent with the tenets of Bayesian methods that supports a dual learning and reasoning under uncertainty. Researchers here illustrate how bringing together neural networks and symbolic structures can model effective learning and express sophisticated reasoning abilities. Crucially, this pairing has significant implications on many applications, including natural language processing and autonomous systems, where vague information processing and understanding is central. With machine learning, research into such interdisciplinarity is an intriguing research direction for the future, resulting in intelligent systems that combine statistical techniques and logical reasoning frameworks, as postulated in the challenges of Ben-David et al. (2018) and Garcez et al. (2010).

2.4.3. Overfitting and Regularization Techniques

One of the most fundamental issues in training and developing neural networks is overfitting, characterized by the models' overlearning from the training set at the expense of its generalizability. Overfitting is the scenario where a model learns not only the underlying patterns but also the noise and outliers in the training set, leading to generalization poorly on novel data. Consequently, practitioners must apply specific techniques to minimize overfitting and thereby realize a compromise between model complexity and prediction performance. Overfitting detection requires rigorous validation procedures, such as cross-validation or the use of independent validation sets, to ensure that a model exhibits reasonable performance under several circumstances, representing its true predictive capability. Regularization techniques are at the core of combating overfitting by imposing complexity restraint on the model. L1 and L2 are among the most widely used techniques applied, whereby terms of penalty are incorporated into the loss function based on the magnitude of the model parameters. L1 regularization encourages sparsity, favoring simpler models in the form of enforcing weights towards zero for some, whereas L2 regularization penalizes large weights to produce smoother models with superior generalization to unseen data. Both of these approaches not only reduce overfitting risk but also assist in enhancing model performance by guiding optimization towards solutions with retained essential prediction capabilities but diminished complexity. The use of these regularization methods is important in situations where the data dimensionality is high or when the size of training data is relatively small. The importance of both overfitting and regularization methods carries over to other areas of use, such as game data science, where predicting player behavior is crucial. Just as with the case of training neural networks, modeling player behavior and monetization both rely on avoiding overfitting to capture dynamic user behavior in the game environment. Regularization can be used to enhance predictability in models in this context to ensure consistent performance while simulating in-game events and maximizing player retention. By employing advanced techniques, such as those created through the development of adaptive control and optimization methods, researchers highlight that a balanced approach to designing algorithms eventually contributes to better prediction outcomes in complex systems, such as games and elsewhere (Annaswamy et al., 2019; Natekin et al., 2017) (Figure 2.15).

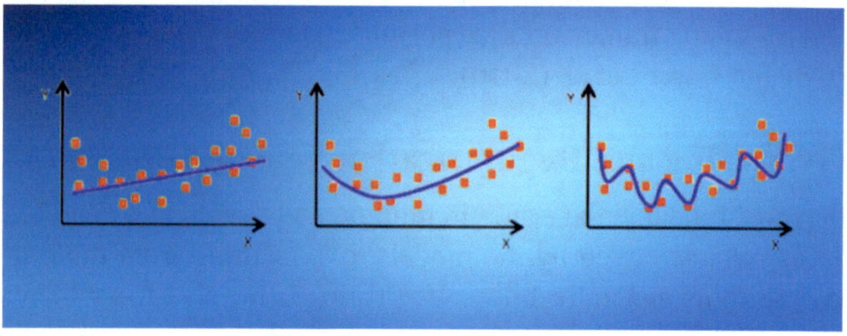

Figure 2.15. *Regularization techniques in neural networks.*

Source: https://teksands.ai/resources/images/blogs/various-regularization-techniques-in-nn/Regularization-Techniques-in-Neural-Networks.png.

2.5. INFORMATION THEORY

Information Theory, the theory developed by Claude Shannon, provides essential information regarding the measurement and regulation of information, which is central to the design and function of neural networks. In the broadest sense,

Information Theory is the study of communication, processing, and storage of information within various systems. This theoretical background becomes especially crucial when one reflects on the most optimal manner in which neural networks can acquire information from data. By measurement of entropy, the measure of randomness or uncertainty in information, neural networks can learn to adjust their weights and biases to minimize loss of information, thereby improving their performance. Mastering these terms is essential to developing the mathematical building blocks of neural networks, as it links the abstractions of information quantification to concrete applications in computing and artificial intelligence, stressing the importance of strict mathematical concepts in designing efficient learning algorithms. The connection between Information Theory and neural networks also occurs in error correction and data compression, both of which are essential to optimizing model performance. As the neural networks become more complex, there are greater chances of overfitting, and precautions are needed to balance between accuracy and generalizability. Information Theory provides statistical techniques that help determine the best network architecture by knowing the distribution of the input data and enabling the formation of noise-invariant models. Techniques adapted from this field, such as rate-distortion theory, can assist researchers in selecting appropriate levels of complexity for their networks so that they can maintain proper representational capacity without too much burden of computation.

Figure 2.16. *Left: An equation form Shannon (1948), the paper that launched information theory. Right: Claude Shannon (1916–2001).*

Source: https://thatsmaths.com/wp-content/uploads/2014/12/claudeshannoninfo.jpg.

This theoretical perspective lends substantiation to the broad account that the mathematical foundations of neural networks have tight interconnections with information management and representation concepts. Furthermore, the emerging field of neurocognitive informatics is the syncretization of Information Theory principles and cognitive science to support mutual support among artificial and natural information systems. According to human cognition knowledge, researchers will be able to engineer more effectively neural network designs that can exhibit enhanced robust and flexible behavior. This multi-disciplinary approach not only inspires novel computational algorithms for intricate comprehension and problem-solving endeavors but also inspires a reconsideration of existing neural network models within the framework of cognitive efficiency. As covered by recent reviews, there is massive potential for artificial systems to surpass their present limitation through the amalgamation of knowledge from neurocognitive studies into the mathematical frameworks that support neural networks, paving the way for smarter, more intuitive devices (Duch et al., 2009; Markova et al., 2018) (Figure 2.16).

2.5.1. Entropy and Information Gain

Entropy and information gain are fundamental ideas in understanding the mathematical concepts of neural networks. Entropy, as a concept in information theory, is a measure of randomness or uncertainty within a system and is a critical metric for information processing and storage. It allows for a theoretical framework to ascertain the proficiency with which a neural network can encode and decode information. Through verifying input data entropy, researchers can ascertain the level of unpredictability that is present and this can significantly influence the performance of neural forms. This basic understanding of entropy is not only required for the development of neural networks but also for the understanding of the optimal configurations that facilitate learning and generalization to various applications in order to facilitate robust data analysis and significant output to various fields of study (Effenberger et al., 2013). Increase in information, which is the same as entropy, is a degree of uncertainty decrease achieved through the addition of new data or features. Information gain can be quantified in neural networks, and it aids practitioners in measuring the effectiveness of different connections between neurons as well as feature selection within the model. By measuring the amount of information the network loses or gains when certain variables are revealed or the neural parameters are modified, model interpretability and performance are enhanced. That knowledge aids in developing adaptive algorithms that can respond to varying levels of data complexity, and it is therefore important in application domains such as deep learning and reinforcement learning. The proper quantification of information gain enables the growth of networks that not only learn from experience but also adapt strategically to achieve optimum performance (Boonstra et al., 2019). The dynamic interaction of entropy and information gain is pivotal in evolving the description of neural connectivity and function. Multivariate approaches employed in explaining interactions between different neural pathways underscore the relevance of such concepts, unveiling intricate patterns that control neural activity and synchronization.

For example, approaches based on concepts like transfer entropy can uncover directed interactions between different components of neural systems, which aids in enhanced understanding of how information moves within neural circuits. Such knowledge has profound implications for fields as diverse as neuroscience and artificial intelligence, as it inspires the creation of algorithms modeling biological learning systems. Consequently, research into entropy and information gain within the framework of neural networks adds depth to theoretical debate as well as benefits functional applications in technology and medicine (Effenberger et al., 2013).

2.5.2. Cross-Entropy Loss

As a key component in the topography of neural networks, Cross-Entropy Loss provides a robust basis for quantifying the performance of classification models. Cross-Entropy Loss quantifies the proximity of the true probability distribution of the labels to that of the model's predicted distribution. By measuring how close the predicted probabilities of the model are to the actual labels, Cross-Entropy Loss forces the model not only to make correct predictions, but also to have confidence in its predictions. In supervised learning, in the case of multi-class classification, making Cross-Entropy Loss to be minimized guides fine-tuning the weights in the neural network, and hence, it is guiding the process of learning towards higher accuracy. The connection of cross-entropy to predicted probabilities and conditions of truth is made through its capacity to effectively penalize labeling mistakes such that it can act as the foundation for updating complex models. Secondly, the mathematical basis of Cross-Entropy Loss lies in its relation to information theory as a quantifier of the quantity of average bits required for encoding the information within the prediction. This abstraction is directly connected to the concept of entropy, in the sense that smaller Cross-Entropy Loss values are reflective of better representations. Its applicability increases in applications involving deep learning, wherein neural networks have millions of parameters. Through the application of Cross-Entropy Loss while training, the function of the optimizer becomes pivotal in utilizing gradients computed based on this loss function so as to make iterative weight adjustments for the network. Thus, this recursive process is necessary to enhance the model's predictive quality so that it converges to an optimal solution that optimizes classification certainty while keeping misclassification to a minimum. While widespread in use, Cross-Entropy Loss is not flawless, particularly when used in special cases such as semantic segmentation. In some tasks, measures like the Jaccard index might outperform Cross-Entropy Loss in capturing model performance. The Jaccard index revolves around the intersection-over-union score, which can potentially serve as a more accurate measure of precision in the scenario of pixel-wise classification, such as in image segmentation tasks. It has been shown by researchers that optimization for the Jaccard index can potentially be better than the conventional Cross-Entropy Loss because it takes into account the geometry-based nature of the problem. These recognitions identify the necessity of advanced approaches to loss function selection, particularly in high-dimensional spaces where models want to find manifold structures or complex object relationships, as in applications with frameworks like the Gromov-Wasserstein distance for generative model adaptation across diverse spaces (Alvarez-Melis et al., 2019) and highlighting relative strengths in optimization approaches (Berman et al., 2018).

2.5.3. Mutual Information in Neural Networks

Mutual information in neural networks is fundamental to an understanding of how such systems process and represent information. Mutual information quantifies information that one random variable contains concerning another, and it is a significant method of quantifying the input-output dependencies of neural networks. In neural networks, mutual information can be used to indicate how well a network learns to represent the data's underlying structure. By studying such dependencies, researchers can determine contributing layers and parameters to performance to enable more informed model designs. This is not only important for network optimization but is also revealing about learning mechanisms, offering an explanation of how information is transmitted along the complex architecture of neural models. Mutual information has a role greater than mere performance analysis, influencing theoretical accounts of learning procedures within neural networks. With ever-improving brain architectures, researchers adopt concepts like those in Baars Global Workspace model to investigate how the network processes and exploits information. The model provides us with a framework for understanding how distributed representations can lead to coherent output, just like conscious processing in biological organisms. With information measures, we can examine modular structures in networks, dissecting how layers communicate and learn to establish useful connections. Such analyses not only enhance our comprehension of machine learning but also bridge the gap between computational models and theories of cognition, stimulating inter-disciplinary debate on intelligence in biological and artificial systems. Moreover, the understanding obtained from studying mutual information in neural networks can fuel progress in design in artificial intelligence. As highlighted by Brooks' call for new mathematics in AI, an additional investigation of information dynamics might reveal new paths toward developing systems not just to mimic but potentially instantiate consciousness or higher-level cognitive processes. By extrapolating these principles to machine design, researchers can develop models that more closely approach human cognition, particularly in how they can understand psychological processes. Such a trajectory places the design of neural networks into the framework of empirical research in cognitive science and studies of consciousness, ultimately towards more robust and effective artificial systems. Tackling the mathematical foundations behind these computations pushes the discussion between technology and the philosophical implications of intelligence to further underscore the importance of understanding mutual information in this emerging area (Wallace et al., 2006a, 2006b).

2.6. ADVANCED MATHEMATICAL CONCEPTS

Their interaction with deeper mathematical abstractions is more profound, particularly in the area of learning algorithms and optimization. Neural networks as universal approximators survive on mathematical foundations laid down in linear algebra and statistics. At the heart of training them is the optimization process, where techniques such as gradient descent are used for the optimization of error functions. By interpreting the biases and weights of a neural network as parameters to be optimized, mathematicians have developed powerful tools for customizing these models. Furthermore, application of regularization methods prevents overfitting by constraining model complexity at training time such that advanced mathematical techniques are underlying improved neural network performance. The underlying mathematical theories of such optimization techniques, thus, are not detached theoretical constructs but are integral to the practical efficiencies of applications of neural networks. Moreover, research into symbolic learning within machine learning paradigms has the effect of reinforcing the significance of advanced mathematical concepts. Symbolic learning, alongside neural networks, entails imitating learning processes through human-like thought. By categorizing the different forms of learning—such as rote learning and analogue learning—we can see a direct use of mathematical modeling to improve machine comprehension of data. The symbiosis between symbolic and sub-symbolic approaches (e.g., neural networks) makes clear the imperative need for a robust mathematical framework to investigate and improve on reliability analysis tools. As researchers advance these models further, the implementation of mathematical theory into practice continues to surface in higher emphasis, confirming its sheer necessity in advancing machine learning paradigms, especially in Reliability Analysis systems (Hong et al., 1994). Finally, artificial perception is a fine example of how advanced mathematics widens our understanding of neural networks. By relating the artificial learning process to the process of human perception, scientists have employed mathematical models to study the intricacy of cognitive activity. In this case, perceptrons are employed as simple but effective devices to project difficult sets of data onto a numerical space. The similarity between human perception and its artificial counterpart serves to depict the mathematical principles that direct the design and operation of neural networks. For instance, Optical Character Recognition and Iris Recognition software demonstrate how advanced mathematical models can bridge the artificial-perception/human-perception divide, with desired outcomes varying according to the complexity of their mathematical foundations (Turing et al., 2012). Such a marriage of mathematics and machine learning not only enhances algorithmic advances but also drives the broader agenda of artificial intelligence.

2.6.1. Differential Equations in Neural Networks

Differential equations give a fundamental framework for the formulation of neural networks, particularly in the description of dynamic processes that control neural activity. Through the use of differential equations, scientists can properly model how signals propagate through networks of neurons over time. This mathematical rigor allows more profound understanding of complex interactions within neural systems and allows for the simulation and prediction of behavior of neural networks under various conditions. The employment of these equations facilitates the creation of neural architectures that can learn from inputs and adapt over time, demonstrating the importance of mathematics in enhancing artificial intelligence systems. Furthermore, the application of differential equations also results in effective neural network training methods, bridging the gap between theory and applications of neural computation (Markova et al., 2018). In explaining how differential equations impact neural networks, it is evident that some forms, such as integro-differential equations, provide a sophisticated manner of representing the complexity of neural dynamics. These equations take into account time delays and spatial interactions that are typical in actual biological systems, particularly for neural fields. The employment of these mathematically advanced models contributes to a more accurate model of how neurons talk to one another in various areas of the brain. Particularly, the study of mean-field equations, products of averaging various interactions, yields critical information on the population activity at a large scale. For this purpose, differential equations enhance the neural network modeling ability as well as contribute to the field of neuroscience by identifying underlying dynamics in neural computations (Touboul et al., 2014). Furthermore, the pedagogical implications of making differential equations a part of neural network study cannot be overstated. As mathematical informatics classes evolve, the emphasis on modeling neural networks with the assistance of such equations is an essential link between theoretical education and practical experience for future practitioners. Using tools like CoCalc, students can experiment with various network configurations, making them appreciate how differential equations drive neural dynamics. This practice-led approach encourages critical thinking and problem-solving to equip students for real-world challenges in machine learning and artificial intelligence. The emphasis on differential equations in this learning can provide an educational environment where the mathematical foundations of neural networks are appreciated and utilized effectively in contemporary research and industrial settings (Markova et al., 2018).

2.6.2. Convex Optimization

The use of convex optimization in neural networks cannot be overstressed. Convex optimization is minimizing a convex function over a convex set, which is particularly ideal for attaining global optima with optimality. This corresponds to most machine learning optimization problems whose objective functions have the ability to be convex and thereby permit the application of robust algorithms such as gradient descent. With the help of these algorithms, neural networks are able to learn fine-tuning weights and biases to minimize errors, thereby increasing the performance of a model. Further, convex optimization helps ensure that solutions derived through these techniques are not only computationally viable but also stable, thereby providing a sound mathematical framework for learning in neural networks. Convex optimization works as a bridge between theoretical principles and practical applications in the case of neural networks. Convergence behavior rules and stability behind effective model training are based on convex analysis. By identifying and specifying the loss function as convex, researchers can design neural network architectures with improved convergence rate and computational efficiency. The interaction between convexity and optimization constraints also typically results in more interpretable models and improved generalization performance. As various machine learning tasks grow more demanding, leveraging the advantage of convex optimization becomes essential in a bid to maintain neural networks in an efficient state as much as possible while tackling more complex tasks. Greater incorporation of convex optimization into machine learning and particularly in neural networks underscores the potential for enhancing algorithmic performance and efficiency. New advances in quantum computation suggest new avenues for enhancing these processes, as they hold the promise of outperforming classical algorithms in some cases. This new field of quantum machine learning, while in its initial phases, suggests some appealing methods for tackling difficult optimization problems in neural networks. With scientists studying the synergies between quantum and classical computing and their learning approaches, it is important to look at what these synergies hold in terms of implications for performance outcomes and stability in machine learning. With these new intersections, we can aim towards the design of future-proof algorithms that maximize the training protocols of neural networks while preserving their own capacity for learning and adaptation (Annaswamy et al., 2019; Ben-David et al., 2018).

2.6.3. The Role of Topology

Topology is a hidden structure in the mathematical foundations of neural networks that controls what they do and how they look. At its core, topology is the study of space properties that are invariant under continuous change and is therefore highly applicable to the study of network performance under varying conditions. Topology is utilized in neural networks to establish relationships between neurons such that they can represent complex data patterns. Several topological structures can be employed within neural network architecture, providing a platform for exploring how differences in architecture influence learning and generalization ability. This becomes relevant because the topology of a neural network could influence its ability to navigate the high-dimensional spaces that are typically present in data analysis and pattern recognition, thereby deciding the networks effectiveness and efficiency in applications involving problem-solving. The use of topological concepts, such as continuity and compactness, in designing neural networks can enhance algorithmic efficiency in practical applications. Specifically, the Kolmogorov-Arnold representation theorem demonstrates topologys capability by offering insights into the structure of multilayer neural networks. By applying the theorem, continuous functions may be approximated by arrangements of neural networks that put abstract mathematical topology into practical network design. As explained in current education programs on neural network modeling, systems like CoCalc have been instrumental in the teaching of these topics. By making students of mathematics and computer science observe connections between theory and practice, topological ideas are made accessible with a comprehension that bridges the gap between theoretic abstractions and real engineering solutions (Markova et al., 2018). Moreover, the maturation of neural networks into complex systems needs a strong mathematical foundation, with topology being central to it. The nuances of neural communications and their implications for cognitive processes only add to the necessity of having a new mathematics of artificial intelligence. Following Rodney Brooks's suggestion, there is a critical need for a new mathematics to illuminate the complexities of machine cognition. Topology, in describing the connection and architecture between neural networks, can provide the insight that is necessary to understand how networks can mimic cognitive function, particularly in psychopathology models. Thus, the application of topological principles not only enriches our theoretical formulation of neural network design but also encourages investigation of the cognitive processes that artificial systems attempt to replicate, putting topology at the leading edge of new development in the mathematics of neural networks (Wallace et al., 2006).

SUMMARY

In conclusion, mathematical essentials of neural networks play a critical role in promoting theoretical and practical application in the field of artificial intelligence. These foundations, encompassing linear algebra techniques, calculus, and advanced mathematical informatics, form the foundation of developing robust neural models for addressing complex problems. Notably, incorporation of tools such as CoCalc enhances learning through the provision of technical support in understanding neural network modeling and what lies behind it. This approach stresses the importance of relating theoretical concepts to pragmatic applications, such as in the special course Foundations of Mathematical Informatics, which is aimed at equipping future IT practitioners for applied work in computing and systems engineering (Markova et al., 2018). Furthermore, the use of advanced mathematical concepts, including the Kolmogorov-Arnold representation theorem, becomes the pivotal element in determining the structure of multilayer neural networks. This theorem enables the comprehension of how neural networks can approximate any function well. Experiments' simulations have revealed the limitations and sufficiency's of the intended networks, demonstrating not only their viability but also ways in which they can improve. Such are required to guide future artificial neural network research and guarantee they keep up with developing needs in technology. As developments in the area progress, further research of how the mathematical theory interacts with the practical application of neural networks will be important to ensure ongoing development and efficiency in information technology (Markova et al., 2018). Lastly, the study of fractional-order derivatives in neural networks raises questions concerning periodic solutions and system dynamics. The quantitative distinction in the integer-order and fractional-order derivatives means that many existing models may have to be re-examined so that they incorporate the special character exhibited by fractional systems. As highlighted in research, the absence of exact periodic solutions for fractional-order dynamics means that there is a requirement to alter the way such neural networks are addressed. The implications of such findings would be to develop more accurate and sophisticated models that better capture the nuances of natural processes. Ultimately, an understanding of these mathematical nuances will see us better grasp the strengths and weaknesses of neural networks, thus making way for further theory and applications development.

The fundamental mathematical concepts integral to understanding neural networks are essentially rooted in linear algebra, calculus, and probability theory. Linear algebra provides the mathematics to define and manipulate data in such networks in terms of vectors and matrices representing the relationships between different layers of neurons. The mathematical formulation allows for the application of operations such as matrix multiplication, which is essential to compute network layer outputs. Calculus is also required to minimize neural network performance using gradient descent. Through the computation of derivatives, practitioners can efficiently optimize error functions during training, adjusting the weights applied for each connection in the network to increase accuracy. Good knowledge of these mathematical ideas is thus central to both the theoretical exploration and practical application of neural networks, much of the technology that powers modern artificial intelligence. Within the context of neural networks, application of the Kolmogorov-Arnold representation theorem illustrates the significant role played by sophisticated mathematical concepts in the determination of neural network architecture. The theorem stipulates that multi-dimensional continuous functions can be represented as superpositions of continuous functions of a finite number of variables. This is the basis of multilayer neural networks, whereby there are layers of neurons that can approximate complex functions so that the network will be capable of learning complex data patterns. The success of neural networks relies not only on their architecture but also on the mathematical principles that control their behavior. By application of this theorem, practitioners can better understand the limits and potentialities of network architectures and build efficient systems for learning from masses of information and generalizing to novel, unseen environments. In addition, the intersection of computational theory and information science reveals the ongoing evolution of neural network techniques, namely in the context of neurocognitive informatics. This emerging research focuses on enhancing alignment of artificial systems with the complexities of human cognition towards enhancing computational algorithms for practical use. As recent controversies have brought to focus, greater attention is needed towards bridging the gaps in knowledge between theory and practice in artificial intelligence. Neurocognitive informatics will drive the innovation of how neural networks are created, mirroring the complexity of human information processing. Thus, integrating these new concepts makes it possible to construct more sophisticated neural models that not only simulate but also go beyond the workings of natural systems and, therefore, expand the frontiers of applications of neural networks towards the solution of computational problems (Duch et al., 2009; Markova et al., 2018).

REFERENCES

1. Aguilar, B., Laubenbacher, R., Murrugarra, D., Veliz-Cuba, A., et al. (2016). Identification of control targets in Boolean molecular network models via computational algebra. https://core.ac.uk/download/pdf/81203199.pdf (accessed on 25th September 2025).
2. Alvarez-Melis, D., Bunne, C., Jegelka, S., Krause, A., et al. (2019). Learning generative models across incomparable spaces. http://arxiv.org/abs/1905.05461 (accessed on 25th September 2025).
3. Annaswamy, A. M., Bolender, M. A., Gaudio, J. E., Gibson, S., et al. (2019). Connections between adaptive control and optimization in machine learning. http://arxiv.org/abs/1904.05856 (accessed on 25th September 2025).
4. Anselmi, F., Poggio, T., & Rosasco, L. (2015). On invariance and selectivity in representation learning. https://core.ac.uk/download/78065933.pdf (accessed on 25th September 2025).
5. Baydin, A. G., Pearlmutter, B. A., Radul, A. A., Siskind, J. M., et al. (2018). Automatic differentiation in machine learning: A survey. https://core.ac.uk/download/297029995.pdf (accessed on 25th September 2025).
6. Becking, D., Marban, A., Samek, W., Wiedemann, S., et al. (2020). Learning sparse & ternary neural networks with entropy-constrained trained ternarization (EC2T). http://arxiv.org/abs/2004.01077 (accessed on 25th September 2025).
7. Behrmann, J. (2019). Principles of neural network architecture design–Invertibility and domain knowledge. https://core.ac.uk/download/286540221.pdf (accessed on 25th September 2025).
8. Ben-David, S., Bishop, C. M., Bottou, L., Breuer, H. P., Chiang, C. F., Getoor, L., Golub, G. H., et al. (2018). Quantum machine learning: A classical perspective. https://core.ac.uk/download/154747677.pdf (accessed on 25th September 2025).
9. Benson, A. R., Bindel, D., & Dong, K. (2019). Network density of states. http://arxiv.org/abs/1905.09758 (accessed on 25th September 2025).
10. Berman, M., Blaschko, M. B., & Rannen Triki, A. (2018). The Lovász-Softmax loss: A tractable surrogate for the optimization of the intersection-over-union measure in neural networks. http://arxiv.org/abs/1705.08790 (accessed on 25th September 2025).
11. Bietti, A., & Mairal, J. (2019). On the inductive bias of neural tangent kernels. https://core.ac.uk/download/266928303.pdf (accessed on 25th September 2025).

12. Bohte, S. M., de Haan, E. H. F., Losch, M. M., Ramakrishnan, K., et al. (2017). Visual pathways from the perspective of cost functions and multi-task deep neural networks. https://core.ac.uk/download/301642592.pdf (accessed on 25th September 2025).
13. Boonstra, T. W., Faes, L., Kerkman, J. N., Marinazzo, D., et al. (2019). Information decomposition of multichannel EMG to map functional interactions in the distributed motor system. https://core.ac.uk/download/225020486.pdf (accessed on 25th September 2025).
14. Christen, P., & Del Fabbro, O. (2019). Cybernetical concepts for cellular automaton and artificial neural network modelling and implementation. http://arxiv.org/abs/2001.02037 (accessed on 25th September 2025).
15. Christiansen, L. H., Jørgensen, J. B., Karup-Engsig, A. P., et al. (2019). Reduced order modeling for nonlinear PDE-constrained optimization using neural networks. http://arxiv.org/abs/1904.06965 (accessed on 25th September 2025).
16. Coleman, S., Markov, Z., Neller, T. W., et al. (2005). Enhancing undergraduate AI courses through machine learning projects. https://cupola.gettysburg.edu/cgi/viewcontent.cgi?article=1002&context=csfac (accessed on 25th September 2025).
17. Drusvyatskiy, D., Harchaoui, Z., Lin, H., et al. (2017). Catalyst acceleration for gradient-based non-convex optimization. https://core.ac.uk/download/84965348.pdf (accessed on 25th September 2025).
18. Duch, W. (2007). What is computational intelligence and where is it going? https://core.ac.uk/download/pdf/86765.pdf (accessed on 25th September 2025).
19. Duch, W. (2009). Neurocognitive informatics manifesto. https://core.ac.uk/download/pdf/87330.pdf (accessed on 25th September 2025).
20. Effenberger, F. (2013). A primer on information theory, with applications to neuroscience. http://arxiv.org/abs/1304.2333 (accessed on 25th September 2025).
21. Florian, R. V. (2002). Why it is important to build robots capable of doing science. https://core.ac.uk/download/pdf/85249.pdf (accessed on 25th September 2025).
22. Garcez, A. (2010). Neurons and symbols: A manifesto. https://core.ac.uk/download/2707716.pdf (accessed on 25th September 2025).
23. Goldstein, D., Murray, W., & Yang, B. (2003). Using artificial intelligence for model selection. http://arxiv.org/abs/cs/0310005 (accessed on 25th September 2025).

24. Hong, H. L. (1994). Machine learning and its applications in reliability analysis systems. https://core.ac.uk/download/9640661.pdf (accessed on 25th September 2025).
25. Kaslik, E., & Sivasundaram, S. (2011). Non-existence of periodic solutions in fractional-order dynamical systems and a remarkable difference between integer and fractional-order derivatives of periodic functions. http://arxiv.org/abs/1108.2825 (accessed on 25th September 2025).
26. Krzakala, F., Saade, A., & Zdeborová, L. (2015). Matrix completion from fewer entries: Spectral detectability and rank estimation. http://arxiv.org/abs/1506.03498 (accessed on 25th September 2025).
27. Ma, L., Niu, J., Song, D., et al. (2018). End-to-end quantum-like language models with application to question answering. https://core.ac.uk/download/146487378.pdf (accessed on 25th September 2025).
28. Markova, O., Popel, M., & Semerikov, S. (2018). CoCalc as a learning tool for neural network simulation in the special course "Foundations of Mathematic Informatics." http://arxiv.org/abs/1807.00795 (accessed on 25th September 2025).
29. Natekin, A., Fox, A. J., Bauckhage, C., Chen, C., Ackley, D. H., Ridgeway, G., Schwarz, G., et al. (2017). Forecasting player behavioral data and simulating in-game events. http://arxiv.org/abs/1710.01931 (accessed on 25th September 2025).
30. Sharif, A. M. (1997). The management of intelligence-assisted finite element analysis technology. https://core.ac.uk/download/336716.pdf (accessed on 25th September 2025).
31. Straszak, D., & Vishnoi, N. K. (2017). Belief propagation, Bethe approximation and polynomials. http://arxiv.org/abs/1708.02581 (accessed on 25th September 2025).
32. Touboul, J. (2014). Propagation of chaos in neural fields. http://arxiv.org/abs/1108.2414 (accessed on 25th September 2025).
33. Turing, A. M., Bhattacharjee, D., Zadeh, L. A., Sugeno, M., Kohonen, T., Balas, V. E., & McCullock, W. (2012). Examples of artificial perceptions in optical character recognition and iris recognition. http://arxiv.org/abs/1209.6195 (accessed on 25th September 2025).
34. Wallace, R. (2006). Generalized inattentional blindness from a Global Workspace perspective. https://core.ac.uk/download/pdf/86486.pdf (accessed on 25th September 2025).

CHAPTER 3

PERCEPTRON AND LINEAR MODELS

Contents

INTRODUCTION

The invention of the neural network, particularly in the context of perceptrons and linear models, is a unique point of convergence between machine learning and mathematics. In order to enjoy the root elements of neural networks, there must be an appreciation for their mathematical roots, which include linear transformations and the activation function. The perceptron, invented by Frank Rosenblatt during the late 1950s, is a fundamental building block of current-day neural network models. Its simplicity and binary classification draw attention as an element leading towards more sophisticated systems from basic linear models. The perceptron thus not only symbolizes part of the original artificial intelligence endeavors but also sets the stage for improved understanding of more complex neural network schemes. Further analysis of linear models works to illustrate their pivotal role in contemporary machine learning initiatives.

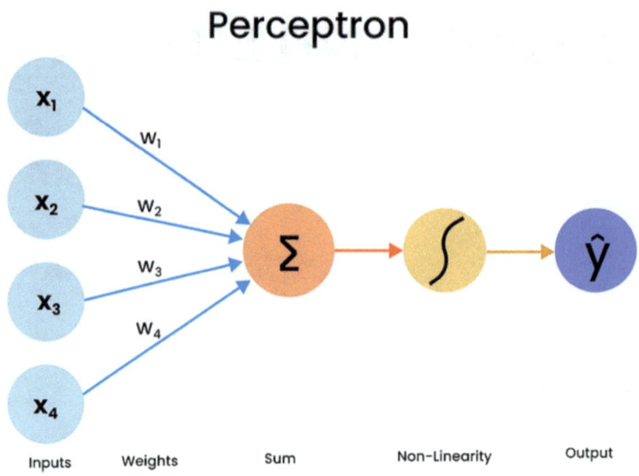

Figure 3.1. *The perceptron.*

Source: https://miro.medium.com/v2/resize:fit:4800/format: webp/1 IXkOgW-WYg0HqHu-wi-R8YA.png.*

These models are most appreciated for their interpretability and efficiency and are a great place to begin when it comes to solving data classification issues. Compared to more sophisticated neural structures, linear models allow for straightforward understanding of feature significance via coefficient values. This property continues to be important in domains like finance and healthcare, where model transparency is essential for making decisions. But it is striking that linear models do have their weaknesses, primarily their inability to explain non-linear relationships in complex data sets. Overcoming this weakness has spurred the creation of non-linear models, like multi-layer perceptrons, thereby broadening the applicability and horizon of neural network systems. The ongoing development in the research of neural networks emphasizes not only researching the theoretical aspects of the models but also their usefulness. Recent papers reflect a growing tendency to research complex-valued neural networks despite the traditionally used real-valued counterparts due to limitations in training and performance measurement. As put forward by Manandhar et al. (2018), real-valued and complex-valued networks are often compared in a manner that ignores the fine variation in their structure, leading to inappropriate conclusions about their possible potential. This debate further engages the argument on neural network models and encourages researchers to compare various architectures based on the constraints of tasks. In summary, the study of perceptrons and linear models gives a basic foundation to enter the diversified and dynamic field of neural networks (Figure 3.1).

Definition of Perceptron

The perceptron is a basic concept in the field of neural networks, representing the simplest type of artificial neuron used for binary classification. Created by Frank Rosenblatt during the latter half of the 1950s, the perceptron algorithm processes input signals through a series of weighted links, with an activation function applied to produce an output. Functionally, the perceptron is best thought of as a linear classifier, determining which of two possible classes an input belongs to by drawing a decision boundary. However, the perceptron is known not only for its discriminative capability but also for the basis of more complex models such as the multilayer perceptrons and other deep learning models, thereby reflecting its ubiquity within the arena of artificial intelligence. The architecture of the perceptron consists of input nodes with weights assigned to each, a function of summation, and an output activation function. The perceptron computes a weighted sum of the inputs and afterwards uses the sum to activate a non-linear activation function, typically a step function. This characteristic enables the perceptron to classify the inputs into multiple classes based on their linear combinations. While a single-layer perceptron efficiently classifies linearly separable data, its failure to classify non-linearly separable data is revealed. This seminal characteristic points to the necessity of more capable neural network architecture that is able to break away from such confines, hence necessitating further deeper architecture development that is based on a series of perceptron layers combined in operation. The comparative significance of perceptrons remains vindicated by research, particularly in their extension to multi-layered architectures, where their fundamental principles are used and expanded to achieve more complexity and problem-solving capacity. For instance, studies demonstrate that multilayer perceptrons (MLPs) can approximate continuous functions to any level of precision desired, demonstrating their universal approximation property. Further, advancements in the field demonstrate how these principles are developed further to handle more sophisticated inputs so that the generalization ability of neural networks is improved across a wide range of applications. Thus, the significance of understanding the perceptron goes beyond its past; it makes sense of the contemporary approaches and innovations in neural network design, stressing its significance for machine learning paradigms, especially as emphasized in current research on the convergence of functional inputs towards perceptron-like architectures (Abraham et al., 2003) and computer-aided safety verification for giant systems (Xiang et al., 2004) (Figure 3.2).

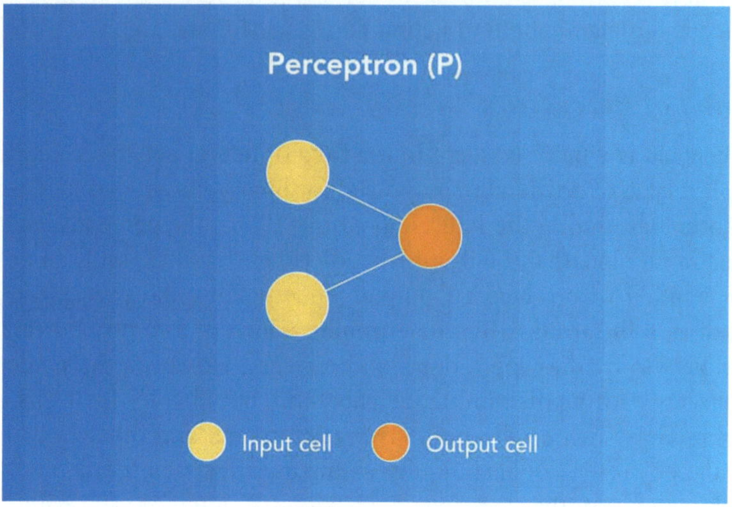

Figure 3.2. *Definition of perceptron.*

Source: https://www.mygreatlearning.com/blog/wp-content/uploads/2020/05/Blog-images_21_5_2020-01-1536x1024.jpg.webp.

Overview of Linear Models in Neural Networks

The perceptron and discussion of linear models in neural networks is a logical stepping stone to more advanced architecture. A perceptron is basically a simplified model of a neural network that is designed to transfer binary classifications based on linear separability of the input. The perceptron accepts weighted inputs, which are learned in training, and feeds them through a function of activation to produce an output. This simple structure highlights the key interaction between input features and their corresponding weights, its mathematical makeup that is central to the model. With the advancements of neural networks, the principles of linear models like the perceptron still remained relevant, guiding the design of deeper and more complex networks for optimal processing of non-linear data distributions. Linear models are also essential tools in numerous applications of neural networks, extending beyond traditional boundaries for classification tasks. For instance, recent works have demonstrated structured perceptron training to be extremely powerful for parsing tasks, shedding light on how the model can differentiate very subtle linguistic structures. This is observable in recent research, where by incorporating core neural representations along with large datasets, parsing accuracy can be pushed to unprecedented levels, like 94.26% unlabeled and 92.41% labeled attachment accuracy achieved by employing structured perceptron methods on the Penn Treebank. This is proof that although simple models linear are, they can be further advanced to provide industry-benchmark results in niches, where they show flexibility and ongoing relevance in modern applications of neural networks (Alberti et al., 2015). Linear models have also been used more and more across various applications beyond traditional domains, such as air quality sensing through machine learning methods. In this case, inexpensive sensors paired with artificial neural networks are capable of significantly improving environmental reading accuracy. The requirement for calibration processes to reconcile sensor data with reliable outputs encapsulates the difficulties that arise when employing linear models in real-world applications. By utilizing neural network frameworks for model training, practitioners are able to leverage the benefits of linear relationships among multi-sensor parameters that make up intricate datasets. This indicates not just how flexible linear models are but also their essential position in developing intelligent systems capable of solving critical environmental challenges, highlighting their applicability in theoretical and applied machine learning environments in equal measure (Malagón Fernández et al., 2018).

Importance of Studying Perceptrons

The significance of studying perceptrons is not only their applicability to their role as one of the very first forms of artificial neural networks but also in their foundational concepts that are used in machine learning today. Originally developed during the 1950s, perceptrons provided a simple yet powerful way to understand the dynamics of supervised learning. They work essentially as inverse linear classifiers, an understanding needed to grasp higher neural network models. By dissecting the perceptron model, students are able to grasp concepts such as weights, activation functions, and training—a turning point in learning that sets them up for a good grasp of derivative algorithms in deeper networks. Furthermore, the simplicity of perceptrons facilitates experimentation and visualization, hence a good instructional tool for illustrating concepts of computational intelligence. Research into new perceptron designs shows their adaptability and flexibility in executing complex tasks. Advances over the last few years in neural network architectures exemplify further refinements of the classical perceptron design by incorporating more sophisticated structures, such as multiple dendritic branches as in biological neurons. For instance, network rewiring techniques brought forth, e.g., those used in high-level liquid state machine models, demonstrate the pursuit of efficiency in the use of synapses that can yield improved measures of performance compared to that for the classical single-layer perceptron. Such innovations bear witness to the fundamental impact of perceptron research towards advancing current techniques in artificial intelligence and spurring the development of new paradigms that introduce complexity without sacrificing efficiency. In addition, the applicability of perceptrons is not limited to binary classification problems but extends to more advanced uses like image denoising. Recent studies have shown that multilayer perceptrons (MLPs), upon being trained heavily on large datasets, can significantly outperform conventional denoising algorithms, thereby making it easier to map noisy inputs to high-fidelity outputs. This use of perceptrons proves their capacity for solving real-world problems, which forms the core for why an in-depth understanding of their structure and operation is crucial. With linear models still defining the direction of research in artificial intelligence, comprehending perceptrons' intricacies and capabilities provides researchers and practitioners with the foundation to innovate where theory and practical application meet, extending the merit of learning about such models (Figure 3.3).

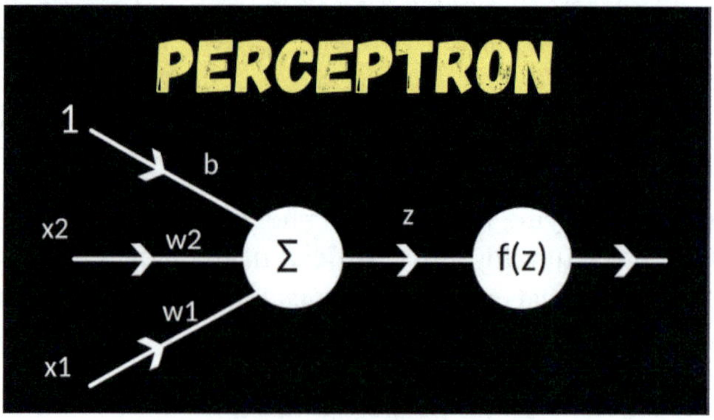

Figure 3.3. *The image illustrates the design of the simplest neural network known as perceptron.*

*Source: https://miro.medium.com/v2/resize:fit:4800/format:webp/1*ptYdDzN2t26oKzV2DqUesQ.png.*

3.1. HISTORICAL BACKGROUND

The origin, both historically, of the neural networks, and the perceptron and linear models in particular, is the foundation for the field of artificial intelligence and computational learning. The discovery of the perceptron stems as far back as Frank Rosenblatt's efforts in the late 1950s, who dreamed up a machine which had the ability to learn through experience through trial and error. This early work demonstrated the capability of a simple unit, the perceptron, to carry out binary classification by learning its weights from input. Rosenblatt's contribution not only laid the groundwork for future improvements in neural network architecture but also catalyzed a new wave of artificial intelligence research, encouraging further study into algorithmic learning. However, the initial hype surrounding the perceptron was later confronted with challenges as its computational limitations were realized, and artificial neural networks fell out of favor in the 1970s. It was in the 1980s that the landscape for neural networks had altered with the discovery of backpropagation, an innovation critical to the revival of interest in multi-layered networks.

This algorithm addressed the limitations of the single-layer perceptron in the sense that it accommodated the training of deeper structures capable of expressing more complex functions. This re-emergence of the study of neural networks coincided with the improvement in computing technology and the availability of larger datasets, allowing researchers to implement these models successfully across different areas. Furthermore, the new ability of neural networks to approximate non-linear functions brought about a paradigm shift in the understanding of machine learning. Growing popularity of linear models in the context stemmed from the favorability of these simpler systems in problems such as regression analysis and classification problems and offered useful applications in a variety of fields, from finance to engineering. Despite the groundbreaking advancements in neural network science, issues persisted in demanding the development of linear models to become more efficient and practical.

In certain uses, the explainability of linear models was advantageous, especially where explainability of predictability is most important, such as in creating regulatory regulations or predict models for cost estimates. More recent studies have discovered methods like the methods employed in regression analysis to be more comprehensible than complex neural networks, highlighting the sustained relevance of linear models in current studies. Further, the flexibility of neural networks, as revealed in the study of expert systems in cost modeling, illustrates how such models can be adjusted and refreshed from time to time to accommodate new information and maintain their forecasting role. Thus, the evolution of perceptron and linear models creates a fundamental background to understand their present development and impact on machine learning practices today (Amusan et al., 2013; Ibrahim et al., 2018) (Figure 3.4).

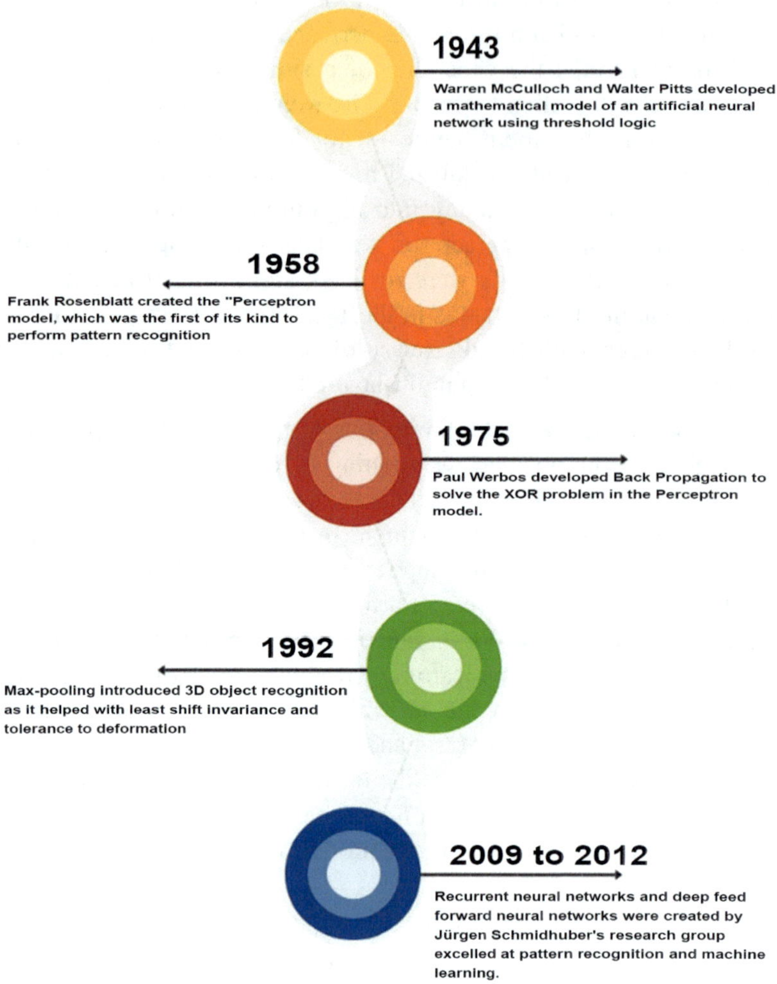

Figure 3.4. *The history of neural networks.*

Source: https://www.allerin.com/wp-blog/wp-content/uploads/2018/12/The-evolution-of-neural-networks.png.

3.1.1. Development of the Perceptron by Frank Rosenblatt

The Perceptron, developed by Frank Rosenblatt during the second half of the 1950s, was a milestone in the history of artificial intelligence and neural networks. As a simple simulation of biological neurons, the Perceptron demonstrated the power of machine learning by supervised learning. By adjusting the weights to input signals through learning from error feedback, Rosenblatts model was able to classify linearly separable data into separate classes. This simple principle laid the groundwork for more complex neural networks, informing the rest of artificial intelligence and cognitive science work. The Perceptron was not only a computational model, but also an actualization of the hope of simulating human cognition in machines, establishing a benchmark for subsequent work in neural-like architecture in computational models. Rosenblatts Perceptron attracted a lot of attention since it was a new technique and it showed so much promise in solving many real-world problems.

Figure 3.5. *Frank Rosenblatt '50, Ph.D. '56, works on the "electronic profile analyzing computer" – a precursor to the perceptron.*

Source: https://news.cornell.edu/sites/default/files/styles/story thumbnail_xlarge/public/2019-09/0925_rosenblatt_main.jpg?itok=SE0aS7ds.

The original design was able to handle binary classification, which was really significant in the time when most computational systems were not that powerful. As more researchers became aware of the Perceptrons potential, they conducted experiments exploring its application in different fields, from pattern recognition to image processing. The constraints of the Perceptrons were established, though, when it was unable to deal with non-linearly separable patterns, triggering waves of criticism and controversy within the scientific community. The constraints created more research on more complex architectures and birthed multi-layer networks and backpropagation algorithms that could tackle more complex tasks outside the Perceptron's single-layer scope. Though overshadowed by superior neural network architectures, the Perceptron remains a fundamental principle of artificial intelligence. Its simplicity gave rise to an initial testing ground for neural computing, illustrating how iterative operations of model training lead to increased performance. The Perceptron has been reinterpreted and reassigned within the broader machine learning arena in recent years, particularly with researchers aiming to assimilate deeper learning paradigms. Development of the Perceptrons is an exercise that rings true today, pointing towards the necessity for adaptive learning systems. Writers cite ongoing advancements in sensor technology and machine learning technologies and the intrinsic foundation of models like the Perceptron in ongoing research efforts (Malagón Fernández et al., 2018). With advancing technology, the legacy of Rosenblatts original design remains firmly in place, cementing its position in computational intelligences history (Gordleeva et al., 2016) (Figure 3.5).

3.1.2. Evolution of Neural Network Models

The history of neural network models is characterized by enormous advances that have transformed artificial intelligence and machine learning. At the center of all such development is the perceptron, a linear classifier designed in the 1950s that provided the starting point for subsequent advances in neural networks. By applying a linear approach to classification, the perceptron was possible that artificial neurons might be employed to capture decision-making operations. It was limited, however, to linearly separable problems alone. That limited it, which led to more research and development in the guise of multilayer perceptrons and the backpropagation algorithm in the 1980s, which called for deeper networks to provide solutions to more complicated problems. Multilayer perceptrons were a breakthrough that set the trajectory for neural networks. This configuration allowed for the simulation of non-linear decision boundaries, significantly improving the simulation of intricate relationships in data. Backpropagation particularly allowed for the effective training of deeper architectures through weight updates based on error gradients in a systematic manner. This approach simplified the training computation in large networks and situated machine learning on a new paradigm. As a result, there were some applications written, ranging from image recognition to natural language processing, which showed the superior performance of neural network models compared to linear models. Researchers then shifted to explore not only the theoretical aspects of neural networks but also their pragmatic uses in real-world scenarios. While perceptron and multilayer network success was realized, the challenge remained to scale such models to handle large and complex sets of data. Overfitting and vanishing gradients became more apparent as architectures deepened and evolved. Regularization techniques and other network architectures, such as convolutional and recurrent neural networks, were therefore used to address these issues. These developments were meant to optimize learning processes and make models more generalizable. Furthermore, increasing availability of large data sets and high-computational power facilitated the development of deep learning, which has gone on to revolutionize numerous fields of study, including healthcare and ecology, to highlight the relevance of neural network models to the conduct of the day. The continuous evolution and adaptation of such models promise a promising prospect for artificial intelligence application in various disciplines, which justifies the significance of knowing their past evolution and revolutionary potential.

3.1.3. Key Milestones in Neural Network Research

Development of neural networks, particularly where the perceptron is involved, is a key milestone in artificial intelligence study. Originally formulated by Frank Rosenblatt in 1958, the perceptron provided a simple model for binary decision making through a linear classifier. The design allowed for the solving of those problems that could be solved using linearly separable functions, upon which more complex neural network designs were subsequently built. Despite its shortcomings, most notably not being capable of learning non-linear relationships such as the XOR function, the perceptron opened up extensive research and set the stage for subsequent developments in neural network theory. Initial enthusiasm with perceptrons saw greater investigation into artificial intelligence, influencing design of algorithms and following neural architectures, establishing a stream of research that would ultimately give rise to the creation of deep learning technologies. Throughout the following decades, the evolution of neural network research saw many milestone moments that characterized machine learning. Yet another milestone came through the discovery of backpropagation during the 1980s that made multilayer perceptrons capable of learning by adapting weights in proportion to the error gradient over several layers. This breakthrough made it possible to train more complex models and significantly improved the efficiency of neural networks on a range of tasks. Scientists like Geoffrey Hinton and David Rumelhart were responsible for popularizing this method, illustrating its efficiency across a wide range of uses. With hardware's growing capability for computation and access to large data sets, the backpropagation algorithm helped to bring neural networks to the fore, opening up innovations across a range of fields including vision and natural language processing. These advances served to underscore the growing importance of neural networks in theoretical research and practical applications. In comparatively recent years, renewed interest in neural networks has resulted from the advent of deep learning, which is characterized by architectures with numerous hidden layers. Deep neural networks have proved spectacularly effective for complex tasks, including image recognition and natural language processing. Studies during this period have been facilitated by spectacular growth in computational power and available data, which have allowed the application of more sophisticated models. Moreover, the use of techniques, such as dropout and batch normalization, assisted in limiting issues like overfitting and boosting training rates of convergence. Particularly, uses of neural networks have also had unforeseen use in healthcare and autonomous vehicles and systems, expressing versatility and potential for radical transformation. As the research has gone on to evolve, learning about these turning points, such as the ones in Compton et al. (2025) and Kumar et al. (2016), puts into perspective how early concepts have evolved into advanced frameworks currently employed.

3.2. STRUCTURE OF THE PERCEPTRON

Perceptron structure operates essentially as a binary classifier in the context of neural networks and is the minimal building block for more complex structures. In essence, a perceptron is a single input node layer connected to an output node, which eventually classifies into a class. Every input dimension is given a weight, allowing the perceptron to weight the contribution of the individual inputs with the weights. The weighted sum is passed through an activation function, often a step function, where the output node gives a binary output depending on a particular threshold. The linear aspect of this structure renders it effective in addressing linearly separable data, showing its applicability in simple machine learning operations, yet laying grounds for greater neural constructs. Scaling perceptrons to address issues of complexity gives rise to the perceptron's organization in a multilayer capacity, departing from the conventional single-layer limitations.

This innovation weaves the perceptron with the concepts of non-linear decision boundaries, which are key to addressing complexity within datasets. By introducing hidden layers, the multilayer perceptron is introduced, which maintains the root architecture of the perceptron but permits multiple layers of transformations. Each layer works on the outputs of the previous layer and passes them to the next, using non-linear activation functions. This setup enables the multilayer perceptron to make representations of complex relationships among data, making it better perform a range of tasks such as classification and regression issues. Interestingly, such an improvement is not only structural but conceptual, pushing the boundaries of what is possible through learning from data.

The relationship between the structure of the perceptron and how it learns, particularly in the context of training, further defines its limits. In more advanced implementations, structured perceptron training can optimize the process of learning, significantly improving results in performance. For instance, as has been demonstrated in recent research, structured perceptrons can efficiently employ beam-search decoding in tiered architectures with good accuracy in difficult tasks such as dependency parsing (Alberti et al., 2015). Accuracy does not end at lowly binary classification but extends to high-order multi-class problems and structured output spaces. The incorporation of statistical physics concepts reveals the competitive dynamics between training error and the generalization ability of the models, establishing the perceptrons evolving function within neural network paradigms (Biehl et al., 1997). These advancements cement the perceptrons place not only as a linear player but also as an integral member of the nascent field of neural networks (Figure 3.6).

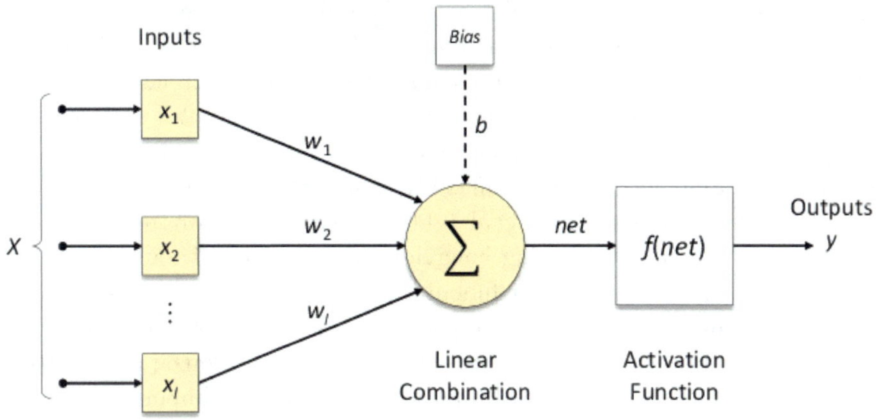

Figure 3.6. *Structure of perceptron.*

Source: https://www.researchgate.net/profile/Antonio-Parmezan/publication/330742498/figure/fig2/AS:721823524200448@1549107547175/Structure-of Perceptron.png.

3.2.1. Components of a Perceptron

The perceptron model, which is the foundation of neural networks, has some of the important elements that work in tandem to perform learning and decision-making tasks. Perceptron itself has input nodes, where each node will map to a feature in the data. The input values are multiplied by corresponding weights, which play a crucial role in determining the effect of every feature on the final output. The weighted sum of these inputs is then provided as an input to an activation function, usually a step function in case of binary classification tasks. Activation introduces non-linearity to the model, enabling the perceptron to differentiate the classes well. The last factor that provides the perceptron with the ability to minimize prediction errors is the flexibility to change weights during training, symbolizing the dynamic operation of the same in linear models of neural networks. The other essential component of a perceptron is the bias term, which helps ensure the model is capable of shifting the decision boundary regardless of the inputs. With the addition of the bias, the perceptron can learn to be able to fit to various distributions of data, enhancing its performance on classifying inputs correctly even if they are not from a zero-centered distribution. This modification is especially significant if the data cannot be linearly separated without additional transformations. Finally, the learning rule utilized for weight and bias adjustments is also important. Techniques such as gradient descent enable the model to minimize the difference between the output predictions and actual labels, highlighting the importance of this feature towards achieving high performance. Understanding these features is critical in exploring how perceptrons function within larger neural network settings, where they are applied as the basis for more complex systems. The perceptron's effectiveness transcends its simple implementation; it has also triggered research into more advanced systems based on its concepts. For example, as mentioned in Kanter et al. (2000), generalized forms of perceptrons are adaptable to generate varying behaviors like creating chaotic time series data with non-monotonic transfer functions. This reflects the versatility of the perceptron architecture in solving complex problems. Also, its application in the area of chemical process optimization, as described in Amghizar et al. (2019), shows its potential to forecast real-time data, showing the important role that perceptron-like models may have in industrial applications. This adaptability and functionality emphasize the significance of understanding the perceptron's elements, as they form the basis upon which modern theoretical studies and practical implementations exist in the frame of neural network platforms (Figure 3.7).

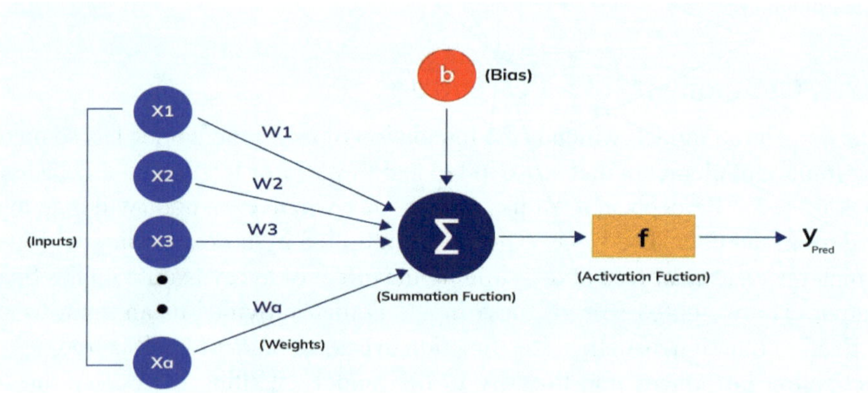

Figure 3.7. *Components of a perceptron.*

Source: https://www.analytixlabs.co.in/wp-content/uploads/2022/07/04.jpg.

3.2.2. Activation Function and Its Role

The function of the activation function in artificial neural networks is to decide what a neuron produces as output, affecting the capacity of a network to learn and generalize knowledge from data. Activation functions create non-linearity in models, enabling networks to map complex functions that would otherwise not be possible. As far as perceptrons and linear models are concerned, activation functions take unprocessed input signals and convert them into an activation signal for the neuron, merely mimicking the decision-making process of biological neurons. The simple threshold activation of the perceptron restricts its capability to linear separability, illustrating the necessity of non-linear activation functions in more intricate architectures, e.g., multilayer perceptrons. Different activation functions serve different purposes depending on the architecture and requirements of the neural network. For example, ReLU (Rectified Linear Unit) is becoming increasingly important as it is computationally cheap and prevents the vanishing gradient problem so that deeper networks can learn.

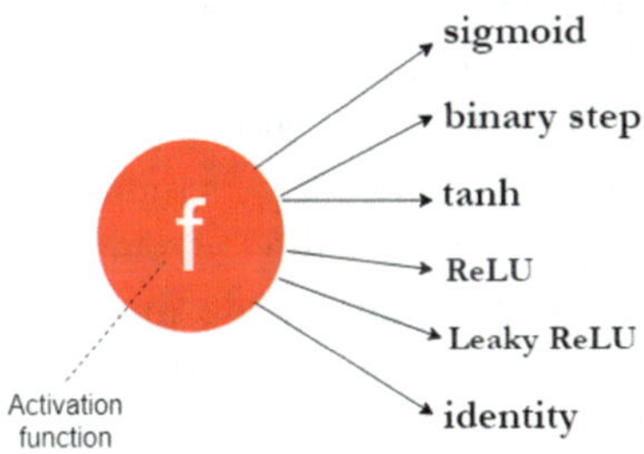

Figure 3.8. *Type of activation functions.*

Source: https://towardsdatascience.com/wp-content/uploads/2021/ 12/14RkikPcO-z3L8H-qj6Cfm1w.png.

On the other hand, sigmoid and tanh functions are of historical significance in neural network architecture but generally are less desirable in more contemporary applications based on limitations in comparison to saturation and convergence. The selection of an activation function has a direct impact on model behavior and performance and must therefore be carefully considered in designing neural architectures, particularly in task-specific application where various output needs are present. The consequences of activation functions extend beyond mere output transformation, affecting the optimization during training very significantly. A well-chosen activation function can enhance convergence rates, allowing a network to quickly determine optimal weights through backpropagation. Additionally, certain activation functions, e.g., the softmax function in classification problems, make output interpretation possible, scaling raw scores into probability distributions. Modern studies have also focused on theoretical fundamentals of activation functions, linking their characteristics to network performance and stability. For instance, the concept of maximum sensitivity of activation functions has helped advance understanding and methods for output attainable sets of multilayer perceptrons, identifying that effective activation mechanisms are necessary in both performance and reliability in neural networks (Gordleeva et al., 2016; Xiang et al., 2004) (Figure 3.8).

3.2.3. Learning Algorithm for Perceptrons

The perceptron learning algorithm is the key to understanding how the linear model of perceptrons relates to the broader picture of neural networks. Effectively, the perceptron learning algorithm involves adjusting the weights for every input on the basis of predictive error. This process is most commonly carried out by an algorithm known as stochastic gradient descent, which continuously updates the weights in the direction that minimizes the prediction error. The generality of this algorithm provides a useful point of departure for more complex neural network training algorithms. Yet, as data gets more complex, the perceptron's limitations come into view, specifically the fact that it cannot handle non-linear problems, so further developments are made in more complex models, e.g., multilayer perceptrons (MLPs) which can learn complex relationships among data. In real-world applications, the effectiveness of the perceptron learning algorithm may actually be greatly impacted by the dataset used for training, i.e., its quality and type. For instance, handling imbalanced datasets poses unique challenges to perceptron models in the sense that they produce biased predictions leaning towards the majority class. This is particularly important in use cases like fraud detection, where real cases outnumber fraudulent ones. To tackle these issues, numerous optimization techniques have been attempted by researchers, including resampling techniques that enhance the training process by demonstrating a better class-balanced representation of classes in the data set. By merging these approaches, the perceptron can be enhanced to tackle more complex tasks, ultimately leading to more efficient and more accurate models for use in real-world applications. Moreover, recent advancements in the tuning of the perceptron learning algorithm indicate the promise of improved performance in a wide variety of prediction and forecasting situations. One of these studies employed a multilayer perceptron and utilized a specialized learning algorithm for the optimization of database distribution in successfully predicting relative humidity in Tangier, Morocco. This study emphasized how an optimized model performed at 0.983 R and MSE = 0.00295, signifying a significant improvement compared to the conventional approach like multiple linear regression. These developments not only confirm the necessity of streamlining perceptron learning algorithms, but also emphasize their applicability in different domains, spanning meteorology to financial data analysis, where accurate forecasting can have immense real-world implications, exactly in line with the persistent progress of neural network technology (de Zarzà et al., 2023; Yahia et al., 2025) (Figure 3.9).

Figure 3.9. *Perceptron learning algorithm.*

Source: https://www.mygreatlearning.com/blog/wp-content/uploads/2020/07/iStock-974104916.jpg.

3.3. FUNCTIONALITY OF LINEAR MODELS

The functionality of linear models is a fundamental concept in the field of neural networks, particularly the perceptron. Linear models try to predict high-dimensional functions based on linear combinations of the input features. The perceptron, which is the simplest form of a neural network, uses a linear function to separate data points into various groups. By redistributing the weights corresponding to each attribute and introducing an activation function, the perceptron can effectively separate datasets. Linear separation is of utmost importance, as it is what dictates classification task accuracy. Linear models do strong work with linearly separable data presented to them; however, they are unable to deal with more complex datasets that call for non-linear transformations. This limitation proves the requirement of complex architectures with increasing data complexity, exemplifying the importance and limitation of linear base models in neural network architecture. As they are limitations in nature, linear models have promoted computational design innovations, particularly for neuromorphic computing. Memristive threshold logic circuits, mimicking synaptic behaviors in living organisms, are an innovation over linear modeling. These circuits exploit memristive devices to mimic the delivery of neurotransmitters, enabling the execution of operations with greater efficiency and speed on nanoscale devices. Their ability to generalize and minimize physical space without signal loss offers significant advantages across a broad array of applications such as pattern recognition and programmable logic. Recent materials technology advances, such as the use of TiO_2 and ferroelectrics, have stimulated activity on these architectures toward more sophisticated edge computing platforms. This advance highlights the long-lasting relevance of linear frameworks, since they present the opportunity for further research into alternatives that retain some linear characteristics but aim to expand functionality in order to facilitate complex tasks (Chua et al., 2018). Moreover, the integration of linear models with neuromorphic systems provides the potential for optimizing computational efficiency across several domains. With a discussion of the merit and disadvantage of having memristive circuits integrated into linear models, scientists are beginning to redefine neural architectures' functionality. The combination of velocity, low-power consumption, and high-density application capacity promises performance gains in edge computing systems, addressing erstwhile inhibitive energy and scalability issues. For instance, the ability to undertake calculations reminiscent of biological processes not only increases its efficiency but also the creation of autonomous systems capable of making decisions in real-time. Thus, linear models' functionality is dynamical and not static and represents a dynamic foundation on which more advanced and efficient systems can be developed, as evidenced by their indispensable role in the ongoing evolution of neural networks and artificial intelligence (James et al., 2016).

3.3.1. Mathematical Representation of Linear Models

The mathematical description of linear models is a core concept toward understanding how they function in neural networks, particularly the perceptron. Essentially, a linear model strives to establish a relationship between input variables and an output variable through a linear equation. This equation is typically expressed as the equation \(y = wx + b \), with \(w \) being the weight vector, \(x \) being utilized to denote input features, and \(b \) being the bias. This equation is really an excellent description of how linear combinations of input features can be employed to generate output, and this makes the frequently complicated relations utilized with real-world data more comprehensible. By optimization of weights and bias in training, linear models can be tuned to reduce prediction error so that neural networks like perceptrons can classify and predict by regression with some measure of accuracy based on data structure. Additionally, the mathematical formulation of linear models extends to the nature of complex interactions found in algorithms like those involving graphical structures. For instance, neurocomputational models like HyperSAT employ hypergraph representations to capture not only variable dependencies but also their weighted implications in logical structures. These models illustrate how linear equations have often the potential to become more complex systems capable of coping with non-linearities and structural complexities. Example. Specifically, the use of a hypergraph structure allows for the advanced representations that reflect the degree of complexity in Weighted MaxSAT problems and thereby expands the model's ability to deal with varying weights for various clauses in data. The incorporation of such mathematical models shows an advancement towards developing more profound relations in data beyond ordinary linear models but with foundations drawn from them (Chen et al., 2025). Neural architecture advancements, in the form of Kolmogorov-Arnold Networks (KANs), continue to further our understanding of linearity in mathematical abstraction. Through deviation from Multi-Layer Perceptrons (MLPs), KANs introduce learnability to the activation function over edges rather than pre-specified node weights. This new approach facilitates more profound data representation and the ability of the network to learn even complex relationships adaptively without sacrificing interpretability and accuracy. Theoretically grounded in the Kolmogorov-Arnold representation theorem, the paradigm shift of linear model representation enhances predictive capability and consistency with a broad range of scientific and engineering applications. The implications of such model structural changes mean the destiny of deep learning, where advanced mathematical representations allow neural networks to more effectively capture and describe the dynamic nature of real-world behaviors (Liu et al., 2024).

3.3.2. Comparison with Non-linear Models

The difference between simple linear models such as the perceptron and the advanced non-linear ones opens up a drastic change of paradigm for neural networks. Linear models rely on a simple correspondence between input data and their corresponding outputs. But subsequently this linearity is typically at the cost of flexibility and capacity since only linear decision boundaries can be approximated by these models. In contrast, non-linear models like multilayer perceptrons (MLPs) employ many layers and non-linear activation functions in order to learn intricate patterns of data. This property makes them particularly suitable for use in applications where feature-to-feature relationships are non-linear, as witnessed in a host of applications where MLPs surpass classical linear models. Including non-linearity allows for increased complexity in mappings between inputs and outputs, ultimately leading to enhanced prediction performance and robustness of the model (Iqbal et al., 2018). The advantages brought by employing non-linear models are greater than the capacity to enhance accuracy; they signify a shift towards acceptance of indigenous complexities in real-world data. For instance, popular recommendation systems typically exploit matrix factorization-based methods, which may conceive of linear dependence between items and users. These assumptions restrict the models capacity to find fine user preferences. Therefore, recent advancement proposed deep learning models capable of learning both non-linear interactions and complex patterns in user-item interactions. These models not only enhance the performance of recommendation systems but also have more general implications of non-linear modeling on other domains (Kong et al., 2019). Consequently, the ability to model complex relationships places non-linear neural networks on the forefront of fixing complex problems that cannot be solved by linear models. Despite being useful, non-linear models also have their own set of problems. Increased model complexity will usually need more computational resources, necessitating more training data as well as longer training time. Moreover, as a risk of overfitting, getting the right balance between model capacity and generalization is essential. The development of sophisticated techniques, such as functional augmentations and other algorithmic innovations, attempts to mitigate these issues by reducing model complexity without sacrificing or even enhancing prediction ability. The innovation of more sophisticated architectures, for instance, the Chebyshev Wavelets Functional Link Neural Network (CWFLNN), is one such example of efforts towards this balance between complexity and computability. These developments seek not only to maintain the advantage of non-linear modeling but also to solve the embedded problems, setting the course for the future development of neural network applications and their practical application in different fields (Iqbal et al., 2018).

3.3.3. Applications of Linear Models in Machine Learning

Linear models are a foundation of machine learning, playing a fundamental role in their analysis and interpretation of relations among complex datasets. These models, though simple but effective, quantify how independent variables influence a dependent variable by calculating linear equations that express these relationships. In neural networks, the perceptron model is a practical implementation of this principle through being a linear classifier which makes input data classification dependent on linear separability. Application of perceptrons is extended to other fields like finance, marketing, and healthcare, where it helps in the prediction of outcomes given the history. By enabling fast decision-making and possessing clear interpretability, linear models enable practitioners across these fields to extract actionable insights from their data. One of the major applications of linear models is in the context of real estate markets, where they assist in their estimates of prices given numerous characteristics specific to properties. For instance, a machine learning application for the purpose of locating undervalued properties utilizes linear regression to predict housing prices with numerous online listings serving as a source of information. This model of regression fully examines such parameters as location, plot size, and trends in the market to generate timely reports for investors. By developing a predictive model, practitioners use linear models to make strategic investment opportunities possible in volatile markets, thus enhancing profit margins on real estate ventures. These uses show how linear models bridge the theoretical-practical gap between economic theory and real-world decision-making practice (Afonso et al., 2018). Moreover, linear models play a key role in improving predictive analytics in industries like energy forecasting and maintenance, more so in the area of solar power production. Through the application of intelligent optimization modeling techniques, linear models take massive datasets constructed by energy monitoring systems and turn them into actionable intelligence. In predictive analytics, stakeholders are able to forecast energy output and calculate maintenance needs, hence minimizing operating downtimes and return on investment. The ability to condense complex operational data into future insights significantly enhances analytical capabilities and enhances decision-making processes in energy management. This usage demonstrates the wide range and immense impact linear models exhibit across disciplines, thereby showcasing their relevance and suitability in contemporary machine learning applications (Crespo Márquez et al., 2019).

3.4. LIMITATIONS OF THE PERCEPTRON

Although the perceptron has been a significant stepping stone in the development of neural networks, its weaknesses are revealed when attempting to solve complex classification issues. One of its fundamental weaknesses is that it can't process linearly inseparable data. The canonical example, the XOR problem, illustrating this flaw is that the perceptron can only make a linear decision boundary and therefore can't accommodate non-linear relationships in the data. Thus, the perceptron does not work well under most real-world situations where class distributions are very dependent on each other. This is a shortcoming necessitating the employment of more robust architectures, such as the multi-layer perceptrons, which utilize additional layers for identifying strong patterns and, in the process, evading boundary conditions of the perceptron framework. Besides, the perceptron learning rule is limited to the use of simple binary outputs, which can render it inadequate for accepting probability distributions as inputs into making decisions. Despite the simpleness of computation being permissible under this model, the binary output creates problems in cases demanding complex classification outputs. Such are encountered in instances of brain-computer interface (BCI) technology, where noise tolerance and accuracy are crucial. According to comparative analyses, research suggests that techniques like Group Methods of Data Handling (GMDH) are able to classify BCI data more efficiently than perceptrons and thereby exhibit significant accuracy in handling multifaceted signal interpretation functions, as discussed in al-Ketbi et al. (2013). This necessitates going beyond perceptron towards more superior neural network models that have improved performance capability. Beyond its theoretical shortcoming, perceptron has deeper practical challenges, particularly in terms of training efficacy and scalability. The simple gradient descent algorithm used in weight updates is slow to converge, particularly in high-dimensional space. This inefficiency is further exacerbated by the perceptron's fundamental failure to deploy advanced optimization techniques, which are beneficial in large sets of data. As an illustration, recent advances in deep learning underscore the need for biologically plausible training regimes that enable network behavior superior to perceptron-like performance, such as outlined in work on spiking neural networks and local learning rules capable of achieving high accuracy on benchmark datasets like MNIST, as witnessed in Brea et al. (2019). With continuous developments in real-world complexities of data, the perceptron limitation raises such basic questions about its application in modern neural network frameworks and significance of seeking alternative, more adaptable options (Figure 3.10).

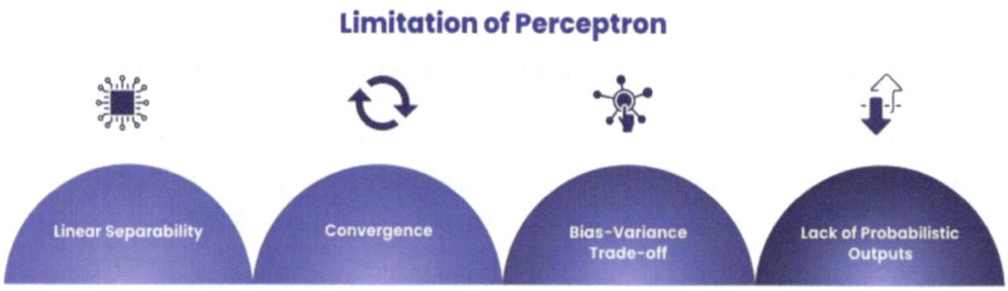

Figure 3.10. *Limitations of perceptron.*

Source: https://intellipaat.com/blog/wp-content/uploads/2023/07/Limitations-of-Perceptron.png.

3.4.1. Inability to Solve Non-linearly Separable Problems

The perceptron idea, a foundation of linear neural networks, is basically limited when applied to solving non-linearly separable problems. This limitation is due to the fact that a linear decision boundary is employed by perceptrons in classifying input data. Where the pattern cannot be easily separated by a linear line, the perceptron fails to converge on an optimal solution and typically results in misclassification. Its practical uses in complex real-world problems—that typically entail complex patterns and multidimensional interactions—are therefore highly restricted. This restriction is typical of broader issues to which linear models are open in the neural network paradigm, and underscores the necessity for richer architecture in dealing with effective non-linear separability. The exploration of other structures for neural networks has been an essential counter-reaction to the perceptron failures. Multi-layer perceptrons (MLPs), to illustrate, incorporate hidden layers capable of learning non-linear mappings of the input space. By virtue of activation functions like sigmoid or ReLU, these networks of deeper layers are able to model more complicated functions and distinguish between points in data that are not collinear. This shift from a single-layer framework, only capable of drawing linear boundaries, to a more complex design is a major leap in the field of machine learning. This advancement highlights not only the technological limitation of early models like the perceptron but also the revolutionary advancements in addressing the flaws built into linear separability (Azzollini et al., 2025). Furthermore, the modern artificial intelligence landscape more and more depends on neuromorphic designs, which seek to replicate the effectiveness of biological neural networks while being able to solve non-linear problems well. By integration of features such as memristors and parallel processing, these kinds of architectures can process huge quantities of data with decreased power requirements (Chua et al., 2018). This indicates how solving non-linear separability becomes increasingly important with data complexity growing and with operations being multi-dimensional in nature that need to be performed. Hence, the failure of linear models, as seen through the perceptron, is a significant impetus for technological innovation in neural network design and, ultimately, for enhancing the discipline to cope with the complexity of contemporary data problems.

3.4.2. Issues with Convergence and Learning Rate

Convergence and learning rate problems are paramount in the determination of the efficacy of training algorithms under the perceptron perception of neural networks and the linear neural network models. Convergence is the term used for the potential of algorithms to converge to a stable solution with reduced error through iterations. A common problem arises when the learning rate, that decides the size of steps in the solution direction in the weight space, is not properly set. If the learning rate is too high, the model will diverge or oscillate, failing to converge to an optimal solution; conversely, a low learning rate will equate to lengthy training times, confining the model to local minima. Thus, for achieving an optimal convergence, balancing the learning rate becomes necessary. This not only impacts the training time but also the accuracy of the model at convergence. Moreover, the characteristics of real-world data sets also worsen convergence issues in the training of neural networks. Missing values that occur in real data sets can seriously impair the functionality of basic learning algorithms. Insufficiency of models in adequately handling these lacunae can lead to less-than-ideal convergence outcomes and reduced accuracy levels. Techniques such as imputation, which replaces missing values with estimates, represent one measure to address this issue. For instance, the Unsupervised Backpropagation (UBP) algorithm has proven to have potential for missing value prediction with less error rates than traditional algorithms. Effectively addressing the complexity of data sparsity, UBP enhances neural network convergence behavior and thus overall classification performance as defined in research studies (Gashler et al., 2013). In addition to updates in learning rate and manipulation of data issues, convergence dynamics also arise from the structure of neural networks. Multi-layered networks can provide better learning capabilities but complicate training procedures. For example, while perceptrons are acceptable for linearly separable data, multi-layer neural assemblies must be employed in order to recognize non-linearly separable patterns. This need increases the delicacy of convergence, as deeper networks will be more sensitive to the accurate adjustment of learning rates and other hyperparameters. Well-trained algorithms must embrace this complexity in order not to stifle convergence with advancements in neural architecture. Furthermore, simulations confirm that well-designed multi-layer systems can outperform simpler architectures significantly, as long as the learning environment is well-tuned to forestall convergence issues (Hampson et al., 1982).

3.4.3. Comparison with Multi-layer Perceptrons (MLPs)

The evolution of neural networks has also brought into question the contrast between single-layer perceptrons and MLPs. While single-layer perceptrons are restricted to dealing with linearly separable data, MLPs, with the inclusion of hidden layers, introduce nonlinear mappings that improve the models capability to approximate complex functions. This aspect is important while tackling problems dealing with complex relationships, e.g., applications in image processing. One of the most significant advantages that MLPs have over perceptrons is that they can learn and pick out patterns in hierarchical representations of the input data, and thus are best suited for application where deep learning architectures are prevalent. The layered structure of MLPs allows features to be learned at various levels of abstraction, making MLPs more generalizable compared to simpler linear models. MLPs thus become an even better model for most of the machine learning issues. In addition, MLP stability and performance can be inconsistent depending on architecture and training approach. Of especial attention is the multiplicative factor whereby multi-layered networks can impose instability in training, particularly through the use of techniques such as Q-learning approximation for reinforcement learning purposes. The globalized updates that are typical of neural networks can be accountable for unstable performance unless properly configured. Research has demonstrated that modifications to MLP structure can counteract such instabilities to achieve improved learning performance. This aspect emphasizes the need for accurate design in using MLPs on dynamic systems where performance consistency is a requirement, but one more reason MLPs are distinct from linear models of lower complexity but reduced predictability in terms of performance. So, the architecture of the MLP captures the balance between complexity and stability required for their success across various applications. In the context of practical applications, the outperformance of MLPs is illustrated through image denoising, where they outperform traditional denoising procedures in learning a noisy-to-clean image mapping from large-scale training based on databases of images. The quality achieved by MLPs not only surpasses existing denoising algorithms but also indicates their ability to handle different kinds of noises, like mixed Poisson-Gaussian noise and JPEG artifacts. These applications verify the scalability and optimality of MLPs in major areas of application. This versatility is compared to the comparatively more static behavior of single-layer perceptrons, which lack the sophistication required to handle such heterogeneous data. The gains in performance that accompany MLPs, particularly in high-risk settings, render them central components of contemporary neural network models, considering the role that their function plays in theory-pushing and practice-pushing in machine learning (Burger et al., 2012; Grzes et al., 2018).

3.5. ADVANCES IN NEURAL NETWORK MODELS

Neural network model development has significantly influenced numerous fields, particularly in the handling of complex data patterns. Traditional models like perceptron and linear regression are likely to be unsuitable in modeling the complexity with real-world scenarios, where variable relationships can naturally be non-linear. For instance, while most recommenders have traditionally been linear-based, shortcomings in these models in capturing the user-item interaction complexities have come to increasingly show. Innovations in recent years have witnessed models like the Signed Distance-based Deep Memory Recommender, which has been able to successfully identify non-linear patterns. By employing deep learning, the innovative model outperforms several state-of-the-art recommenders by identifying latent patterns which certain other approaches might not be able to identify, thus resulting in enhanced accuracy and relevancy of recommendation in diverse settings (Kong et al., 2019). The other key advancement for the neural network models is multi-modal integration of data, particularly for applications concerning delicate comprehension in different contexts. In active speaker detection in social interaction, for example, taking acoustic information alone may be deceptive, particularly in noisy scenarios. Pioneering proposals demonstrate the importance of combining auditory and visual modalities to increase detection resilience. Through the application of self-supervised learning techniques, the systems have managed to separate active speakers from mere visual input using auditory cues to enhance the learning process. The techniques make it possible to detect overlapping voices and further enhance cognitive systems' performance in social situations, emphasizing the importance of leveraging diverse data sources for robust outcomes (Beskow et al., 2019). This paradigm shift demands that the core function that neural networks provide in designing more sophisticated, adaptable systems that can handle effectively dynamic real-world situations. The groundbreaking impact of newer neural network models is not confined to theory in the classroom but firmly roots them in industrial applications. As researchers continue to improve these models, the union of neural networks and deep learning not only enhances making predictions stronger but also drives innovation in fields such as natural language processing, image recognition, and robotics. The ability to process large sets of data while figuring out complicated patterns enables these models to get better and adjust their actions as time passes, displaying a learning curve comparable to that of human understanding. Such flexibility is essential in handling problems inherent in the data-driven world of today, allowing for the development of systems capable of learning through experience and making logical choices. The developments in models of the neural network demonstrate their potential not only in executing a specific task, but also in mapping out the future of artificial intelligence and cognitive systems, providing avenues to more accessible and responsive technology.

3.5.1. Introduction of Multi-layer Perceptrons (MLPs)

The emergence of MLPs is a milestone in the evolution of neural networks, which overcame the limitations of single-layer perceptrons. MLPs possess one or more hidden layers, along with an input layer and an output layer, making them theoretically capable of representing data with complex relationships. Such a multi-layered organization enhances the networks ability to learn nonlinear mappings, a critical breakthrough for numerous applications, including image recognition and natural language processing. The MLP architecture enables improved feature extraction because each layer learns successively higher-level abstractions from the input data. The hierarchical approach enables MLPs to discover intricate patterns, thus enhancing their representational capability compared to traditional linear models. Arguably the most famous characteristic of MLPs is that they possess a universal approximation property, that is, they can be employed to approximate any continuous function given sufficient neurons and training data.

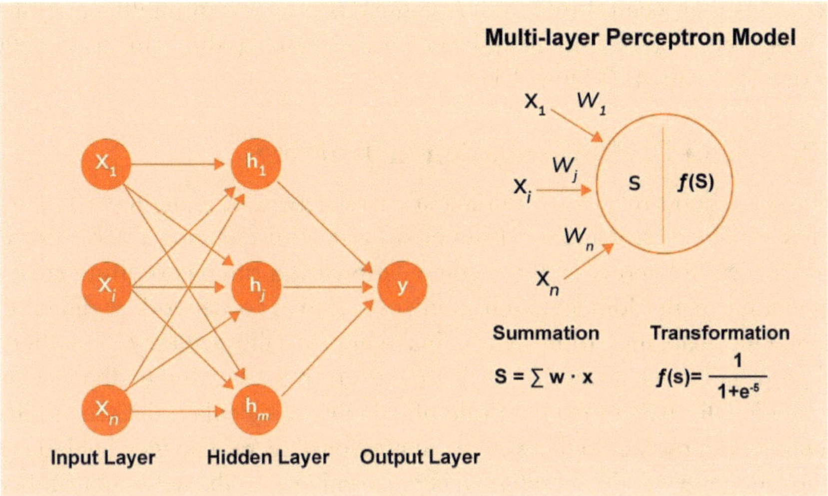

Figure 3.11. *Multilayer perceptron (MLPs) model.*

Source: https://www.analytixlabs.co.in/wp-content/uploads/2022/07/014.jpg.

This is supported by some of the first results which have been generalized from standard MLPs to functional MLPs and established that the expressiveness of such networks remains true irrespective of the form of input. Specifically, this principle has been vindicated empirically in recent work, showing that MLPs are capable of modeling real and simulated data. As they are theoretically well-founded, not only are MLPs theoretically interesting, but they are also pragmatically beneficial, expanding the scope of problems that can be dealt with on the basis of neural networks. The meeting of theoretical elegance and operational performance puts MLPs at the forefront of present-day paradigms of machine learning that extend opportunities for innovation in a wide range of disciplines. In addition, advancements in hardware have also promoted the popularity and adaptability of MLPs. For instance, novel techniques based on biologically inspired neural networks such as dendritically enhanced readout architectures have been proposed. These improvements increase learning efficiency and reduce resource consumption, thus making MLPs more attractive for their use in neuromorphic systems. Implementations that facilitate network rewiring and adaptive learning emulate biological processes, which enhance the flexibility and functionality of MLPs in dynamic environments. These improvements not only advance the performance of MLPs but also achieve dramatic error rate reductions from traditional perceptron architectures. The continuous development of MLPs, in addition to novel hardware methods, underscores their central role in the continuous progress of intelligent systems and reasserts their role in neural network research (Abraham et al., 2003; Banerjee et al., 2014) (Figure 3.11).

3.5.2. Role of Backpropagation in Training

Backpropagation's role in the training of neural networks, including perceptrons and linear networks, is the most important aspect of reducing error efficiently during the learning process. It is a computational algorithm permitting effective computation of the loss function gradients relative to network weights, thus directing the adaptation of these weights to improve the accuracy of prediction. Backpropagation operates by pushing the error back through the network, computationally using the chain rule of calculus to calculate the sensitivity of the output with respect to the weights in previous layers. The idea behind is not just updating the weights iteratively, but also enhancing the networks' ability to generalize from training data to new cases, hence enhancing its utility in real-world situations. This learning process is critical to enhance the measures of performance, particularly where precision matters most, such as in meteorology and environmental observation. The uses of backpropagation also emphasize its significance in numerous fields, as demonstrated by applications of neural networks to predict mean summer-monsoon rainfall over India. Scientists constructed multilayer networks with varying amounts of hidden neurons to test the effectiveness of backpropagation in learning complex patterns from the data. Especially, models using backpropagation have superior predictive performance by tuning their parameters in order to find minute relationships in the training set so that there is enhanced accuracy in rain prediction. As illustrated in studies, a well-tuned network design can dramatically outperform existing models, giving valuable insights into water resource management and agricultural planning. Here, backpropagation not only affects short-term computational efficiency but also pays long-term dividends by means of heightened model dependability and efficiency. Further, machine learning's interface with backpropagation extends to emerging technologies, such as air quality monitoring, where low-cost sensors are tuned with neural networks. In such instances, sensor measurements can be significantly improved by training artificial neural networks using backpropagation, correlating reported measurements with actual readings of air quality. While public administration struggles with the exceedingly high costs associated with advanced monitoring technology, backpropagation is one realistic solution for enhancing the accuracy of sensors and thus enabling more accurate environmental health assessments. The process in repeating this training method conditions networks to systematically eradicate variance in output so that more credible analyses of pollution can be made. Thus, the use of backpropagation in this context not only aids real-time monitoring but also has a significant role to play in public health interventions and environmental policy (Malagón Fernández et al., 2018; Matthews et al., 2006) (Figure 3.12).

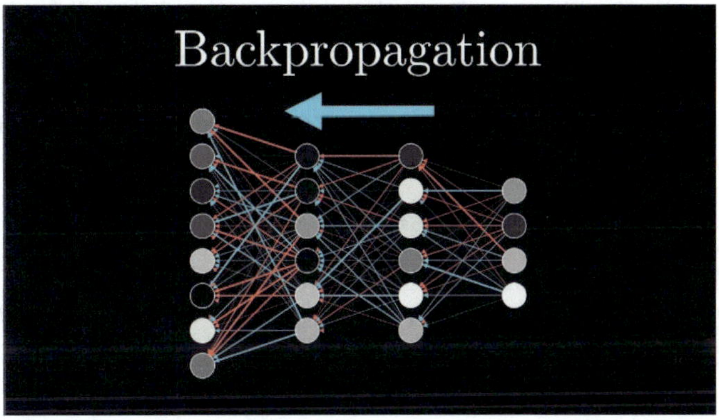

Figure 3.12. *Backpropagation.*

Source: https://lh4.googleusercontent.com/z3FZq_1u4UgY XyrtHZF GpcndAsEzsh_y-KPYB-SQfZkPvsuOz-M3CgvXraVKUU39Yim1gO9Tmel-8K0e8N3kl8KD-3eeGLE8gxebnWX20Mmb5yP6o90pCZUGTORYZQXuY-56im6YX-.

3.5.3. Impact of Deep Learning on Neural Networks

Deep learning propelled a revolutionary change in the performance and capability of neural networks. Neural networks have mostly relied on basic architectures such as perceptrons and linear models that could not address more sophisticated problems such as image recognition and natural language processing. Notwithstanding this, the development of multilayered networks in deep learning has enabled the development of sophisticated models capable of learning hierarchical feature representations. This has enabled neural networks to automatically learn subtle patterns from vast amounts of data, which is extremely useful in many applications across sectors. For instance, deep learning has revolutionized real estate predictive analytics to allow investors to employ machine learning algorithms to identify undervalued properties through real-time market analysis (Afonso et al., 2018). Improving performance is a true reflection of how deep networks are important today in the world of artificial intelligence. In addition, the impact of deep learning is not just in increasing accuracy but also in changing the way data gets preprocessed and analyzed. In previous linear models, features would typically consume a lot of engineering, but deep learning works with raw data better using automatic feature extraction. That saves data scientists' workload so that they can work on higher-level implementation and strategy. For example, sophisticated optimization techniques in deep learning enhance condition-based maintenance (CBM) approaches in energy generation based on predictive analytics. With the utilization of large volumes of operational data gleaned from legacy assets, deep learning algorithms have the capacity to develop actionable intelligence that guides decision-making and optimizes efficiency (Crespo Márquez et al., 2019). This capacity has revolutionized predictive maintenance technologies as being more reliable, as well as cost-effective, by preventing potential losses. While there are numerous advantages of deep learning, it has some disadvantages as well, like a need for a lot of computational resources and access to large amounts of labeled training data. These needs can be barriers to smaller organizations and resource-constrained researchers, possibly widening the gap between people who are able to reasonably benefit from such technologies and those who are not. Also, as neural networks become more complex, interpretability and transparency are issues, hence deployment of such models in mission-critical environments is an issue. Thus, existing research attempts to address such limitations through the development of methods for simplifying model complexity while enhancing interpretability without compromising on predictive accuracy. As deep learning continues to advance, the way that it impacts traditional neural networks needs to be understood in order to tap its potential in many fields and to ensure appropriate ethical application in society.

3.6. APPLICATIONS OF PERCEPTRONS AND LINEAR MODELS

Applications of perceptrons and linear models are crucial to appreciating modern machine learning systems. Originally conceived in the middle of the 20th century, perceptrons were originally used for problems of binary classification as the basic building blocks for more complex neural network architectures. Due to their simplicity, they can solve images recognition issues efficiently where they can recognize simple visual patterns. This application remains relevant in the majority of scenarios, particularly when dealing with large datasets where interpretability and performance are critical. With the evolution of algorithms, the underlying theory of perceptrons continues to exist in designing modern deep learning architectures, demonstrating their lifespan of use in theoretical and real contexts alike. Linear models, including perceptrons, have also been used widely in a variety of domains ranging from finance to medicine. One example is the prediction of wind energy output, wherein a neural network realization of the measure correlate predict algorithm uses linear transformations to attain optimal performance in energy output forecasting (Addison et al., 2000). By adding these traditional models with perceptron designs, scientists can leverage linearity's potency without sacrificing the nuances inherent in dense datasets. The introduction of perceptrons in predictive models helps to reduce computation and enhance convergence rates, thereby creating such applications efficient and effective in resolving real-world issues. Additionally, work on generalized discrimination values (GDV) is evidence of the sophistication of comprehension that is achieved through thorough study of perceptrons and linear models. The GDV quantifies the dissimilarity among classes of data being separated in varying layers within a neural network and provides a way to optimize the hyper-parameters depending on the architecture and network depth (Gerum et al., 2019). This capacity to quantify class separability supplies the essential information to enhance model performance, particularly when dealing with intricate data structures. Secondly, the discovering's of class separability and energy barriers demonstrate an inner complexity in the training of neural networks, again emphasizing that gaining insight into the operation of simpler systems can be a recipe for dramatic breakthroughs in advanced learning systems. As such, the legacy of perceptrons continues to have an impact on research and applications across many fields.

3.6.1. Use in Pattern Recognition

In artificial intelligence, pattern detection is a fundamental process that reflects the functional abilities of perceptrons and linear models of neural networks. These models are skilled at labeling sophisticated data by mapping input features onto corresponding labels through learned weights. This capability is applicable to numerous applications with different environments, such as image and voice identification, in which detection of minute patterns proves to be vital. The learning process is that of adjusting the weights by various algorithms to minimize the classification errors and thereby maximizing the accuracy of the model. While dealing with linearly separable data, perceptrons are a formal method which not only addresses simple classification problems but also forms the foundation for more complex hierarchical learning systems within neural networks. Lastly, pattern recognition is an integral component in creating automated systems that efficiently decode massive volumes of information. The use of perceptrons for pattern recognition is extensive beyond minimalist applications and also serves as a stepping stone to advanced models. For instance, the combination of multiple perceptrons leads to the formation of multilayer perceptrons (MLPs) and enables the recognition of intricate patterns through hidden layers. Every layer learns different hierarchies of features, making the models more capable of handling non-linear relationships. The sequence reflects a radical change in addressing intricate real-world issues. As a matter of fact, these intricate neural network models can distinguish objects in photographs, understand voice commands, and even process emotional tone from text, reflecting their broad applications. The efficacy of such models is based on how they learn from massive datasets and adaptively adjust their parameters, thus enhancing their predictive powers in real-world conditions. With improving technology, the emphasis on developing computationally savvy algorithms for edge computing has increased, particularly where pattern recognition models are concerned. With the immense volumes of data generated from cognitive devices and sensors, information-processing frameworks that can execute functions locally with minimal latency are badly needed. Innovatively, neuromorphic computing technologies offer an attractive alternative. By emulating the functioning of biological systems in processing information, neuromorphic architectures have the potential to enhance the ability of edge devices without demanding a lot of power usage. These advances are in accordance with the demand for scalable and sustainable computation models, as noted in Chua et al. (2018). The advances will not only speed up computing the pattern recognition processes but also support a smarter and responsive digital world, hence underpinning the importance of perceptrons and linear models in modern and future applications (Figure 3.13).

Figure 3.13. *Pattern recognition.*

Source: https://cdn.educba.com/academy/wp-content/uploads/2020/01/Pattern-Recognition.jpg.

3.6.2. Applications in Natural Language Processing (NLP)

For NLP, linear neural networks and Perceptrons are the fundamental building blocks that are the backbone of many sophisticated applications. They are easy, cost-effective, and most suitable for linear separability problems. For text classification, sentiment analysis, and information retrieval applications, linear models can process heavy data within a fraction of a second and can give output in real-time, making them best for high-speed processing applications. For instance, their utilization in chatbots and virtual assistants enhances their ability to quickly recognize user intent, thus improving the overall user experience. As businesses shift towards automation, the demand for efficient NLP solutions is ever on the rise, justifying the role of linear models in the current digital age. Another significant innovation of NLP applications facilitated by neural network models is the emergence of Semantic Hashing. This approach enables the embedding of text data for applications such as Intent Classification, which evades word embedding limitations. Where small datasets dominate environments such as chatbot development, out-of-vocabulary tokens and spelling errors become hindrances to performance. With Semantic Hashing, dependence on huge vocabulary lists is significantly reduced, allowing for more flexible processing of user input by models, which is truly required in real-world applications.

Figure 3.14. *Understanding natural language processing (NLP).*

*Source: https://miro.medium.com/v2/resize:fit:1400/1*3Au5DTaJO7wv8Mtq6D47ag.png.*

It is said that with this revolutionary approach, state-of-the-art performance is achieved over a variety of datasets, highlighting its effectiveness and usability in the ever-changing world of NLP applications (Alonso et al., 2019). Besides, the use of deep learning artificial neural networks (DL ANNs) has revolutionized process control and optimization processes in chemical and industrial processes. The application of such sophisticated models in the prediction of effluent composition, such as in steam cracking, is a testament to their usability in many other fields beyond the traditional NLP. The capacity to rapidly and precisely describe complex data sets, in a way that reduces computational efforts, is a reflection of the natural flexibility of neural networks. Not only does this flexibility accelerate processes but also enhances efficiency in tracking and enhancing production parameters. It is imperative, however, to consider issues of absent foundational comprehension, which deep learning engulfs, and question the reliability of knowledge capture in engineering applications. Nevertheless, the profound implications of such technologies are reconfiguring industries, mirroring the expanding potential of neural networks within contemporary applications (Amghizar et al., 2019) (Figure 3.14).

3.6.3. Role in Image Classification

The perceptrons and linear models role in image classification provide the foundation for the development of neural networks and machine learning algorithms. Image categorization is the process of classifying images into pre-existing categories based on their visual information, a problem that has attracted a lot of attention with the advent of deep learning techniques. The perceptron model, being a linear classifier, is an abstraction of how neurons process information in biological systems. Perceptrons can classify between classes through a decision boundary by employing a linear transformation of input data. This becomes a characteristic that is fundamental to operations such as discriminating between different kinds of images. Such a simple mechanism is not only applicable in binary classification tasks but also serves as the foundation for other, more complex architectures that effectively handle multi-class classification problems, thereby its far-reaching influence in the image classification domain. Improvements over perceptron-based architectures have led to the adoption of sophisticated architectures such as multi-layer perceptrons (MLPs), which are an upgrade from simple linear classifiers. With multiple layers of perceptrons, MLPs introduce non-linearity into decision-making, so that the models can learn sophisticated patterns in imaging data. For instance, in medicine, brain tumor classification has been deeply investigated from numerous models, including multi-layer perceptrons, to improve the accuracy and reliability of diagnoses. Recent studies indicate that while traditional classifiers will be incapable of functioning optimally, MLPs are capable of distinguishing fine distinctions among different types of brain tumors in MRI images. Therefore, it is evident that such state-of-the-art models derived from the perceptron concept are a major player in the changing landscape of image classification, particularly when high stakes are in play and precision is the determining factor (Oh et al., 2024). Furthermore, the integration of linear models and perceptrons with contemporary techniques such as convolutional neural networks (CNNs) has ushered in a watershed in the field of image classification. CNNs, which utilize hierarchical feature extraction, surpass classical linear models through their capacity for learning from large datasets without human feature engineering. The interaction between linear transformations and deep learning architectures underscores how underlying principles endure in combined systems, endowing them with robustness and efficiency for classifying intricate image datasets. This combination is most evident in modern innovations, with the diffractive deep neural networks-based optical neural networks being explored for increased computational effectiveness for classification (Feng et al., 2024). As image classification continues to evolve, understanding the functionality of perceptrons and linear models remains fundamental, as the underpinning concepts that drive progress in neural network designs.

SUMMARY

In bringing forth the analysis of perceptrons and linear models of neural networks, it is evident that these early architectures are essential to understanding the more complicated neural mechanisms. The perceptron is effective under linear separability conditions, which align with specific tasks where data can be separated clearly. However, as data science evolves, the limitations of linear models become apparent. They do not catch up on complex patterns that are inherent in non-linear data distributions. This suggests a need for future development and incorporation of more sophisticated neural networks in an ability to manage these complexities, thus enhancing predictive power and generalization capacity. The dynamic nature of perceptrons also enables it to have extensive uses beyond just classification tasks. For instance, research has established that the use of a non-monotonic transfer function in a perceptron can yield robust chaos, accounting for such intricate systems common in real-world systems. This versatility thus validates the ability of perceptrons to represent not just fundamental associations, but intricate dynamics present in data, and thereby validating its application in high-level computational paradigms. These features encourage scientists to explore the diverse applicability, making perceptrons a valuable topic for further investigation in machine learning, particularly in understanding time-series behaviors (Kanter et al., 2000). Moreover, the efficiency of perceptrons is supported in empirical research, such as mean monthly total ozone concentration models, where artificial neural networks exhibit spectacular predictive power. The outcomes of such research show that, while multi-layer perceptrons are more complex and better performing, knowing the basic architecture is still critical. Single-layer and two-layer perceptron relative performance highlights that basic knowledge can direct the design of more complicated models. It is towards the future of research involving neural networks that the lessons from perceptrons and linear models will definitely shape the course of more sophisticated algorithms to fit into an even wider array of applications (Acharya et al., 2006).

The invention of perceptrons and linear models for use in neural networks remains significant in the learning of the fundamental building blocks of machine learning. In principle, perceptrons are binary classifiers that decide on the basis of linear combinations of input features. This can be effectively calculated and programmed in algorithms, making perceptrons a reasonable choice for first-level machine learning exercises. The constraint of the models is starkly apparent when operating on non-linearly separable data. In doing so, perceptrons are unable to properly classify points that don't extend linearly along a boundary, echoing the call for more sophisticated models. This initial understanding of perceptrons lays the groundwork for understanding the more nuanced aspects of neural networks and their ever more sophisticated models, which can handle a broader range of data characteristics. Building upon the ideas of perceptrons, linear models are a precursor to more advanced neural networks by linking many perceptron units together. Coupling these units together gives rise to multi-layer perceptrons (MLPs), paving the way for greater data representation with non-linear mappings. Each layer within an MLP specializes in feature extraction and enhancement to provide greater learning capabilities. Moreover, the use of activation functions introduces some level of non-linearity that eliminates the imperfections that are inherent in a single perceptron model. The use of such mathematical techniques enables the combination of various factors of input, such as distance, mean speed, and number of bus stops in the travel time predictions as shown from empirical investigations based on Statistical Neural Network (SNN) software (Kamaruddin et al., 2010). Thus, such advances seal the place of linear models in the history of neural network architecture. An understanding of the difference and relationship between perceptrons and linear models helps in understanding how the modern neural networks evolved. By boosting the complexity and adaptability level through linear models, scientists can apply advanced methods to predict outcomes with numerous variables. For instance, a neural network-based measure can make precise estimations of parameters influencing wind energy generation by correlating various environmental parameters (Addison et al., 2000). The ability to utilize linear models in conjunction with perceptrons is an indication of how understanding fundamental algorithms can guide the future research direction within the subject area. With advances in machine learning continuing, the integration of such fundamental concepts will remain pivotal to addressing complex real-world problems as well as driving predictive analytics and artificial intelligence developments.

REFERENCES

1. Abraham, A., Besse, P., Breiman, L., et al. (2003). Functional multi-layer perceptron: A nonlinear tool for functional data analysis. https://core.ac.uk/download/50360245.pdf (accessed on 25th September 2025).
2. Acharya, U. R., Bronnimann, S., Comrie, A. C., Dorling, S., Gardner, M., Bandyopadhyay, G., Kartalopoulos, S. V., et al. (2006). Artificial neural network to predict mean monthly total ozone in Arosa, Switzerland. http://arxiv.org/abs/nlin/0608043 (accessed on 25th September 2025).
3. Addison, J. F. D., Bass, J., Hunter, A., et al. (2000). A neural network version of the measure correlate predict algorithm for estimating wind energy yield. https://core.ac.uk/download/53912.pdf (accessed on 25th September 2025).
4. Afonso, C., Baldominos, A., Bernárdez, Ó., et al. (2018). Identifying real estate opportunities using machine learning. http://arxiv.org/abs/1809.04933 (accessed on 25th September 2025).
5. Alberti, C., Collins, M., Petrov, S., et al. (2015). Structured training for neural network transition-based parsing. http://arxiv.org/abs/1506.06158 (accessed on 25th September 2025).
6. al-Ketbi, O., & Conrad, M. (2013). Supervised ANN vs. unsupervised SOM to classify EEG data for BCI: Why can GMDH do better? https://core.ac.uk/download/29821899.pdf (accessed on 25th September 2025).
7. Alonso, P., Dash, A., Kovacs, G., et al. (2019). Subword semantic hashing for intent classification on small datasets. http://arxiv.org/abs/1810.07150 (accessed on 25th September 2025).
8. Amghizar, I., Marin, G., Plehiers, P., et al. (2019). Artificial intelligence in steam cracking modeling: A deep learning algorithm for detailed effluent prediction. https://core.ac.uk/download/286549694.pdf (accessed on 25th September 2025).
9. Amusan, L. M., Anosike, N. M., Joshua, O., et al. (2013). Expert system-based exploratory approach to cost modeling of reinforced concrete office building. https://core.ac.uk/download/18294887.pdf (accessed on 25th September 2025).
10. Azzollini, M., & Pacelli, V. (2025). An artificial neural network approach for credit risk management. https://core.ac.uk/download/pdf/24060757.pdf (accessed on 25th September 2025).
11. Banerjee, A., Basu, A., & Roy, S. (2014). Liquid state machine with dendritically enhanced readout for low-power, neuromorphic VLSI

implementations. http://arxiv.org/abs/1411.5458 (accessed on 25th September 2025).

12. Ben Yahia, A., Kadir, I., Abdallaoui, A., & Elazhari, K. (2025). Architectural optimization of a multilayer perceptron (MLP) neural network enhanced by the Levenberg–Marquardt algorithm for predicting relative humidity: Application to Tangier, Morocco. Water SA. https://www.semanticscholar.org/paper/0606718846be7ebf33bb4adbe0795ff89cddee6c (accessed on 25th September 2025).
13. Beskow, J., Salvi, G., & Stefanov, K. (2019). Self-supervised vision-based detection of the active speaker as support for socially-aware language acquisition. https://core.ac.uk/download/646180255.pdf (accessed on 25th September 2025).
14. Biehl, M., Opper, M., Kinzel, W., & Yeomans, J. (1997). Phase transitions of neural networks. http://arxiv.org/abs/cond-mat/9704098 (accessed on 25th September 2025).
15. Brea, J., Gerstner, W., & Illing, B. (2019). Biologically plausible deep learning – but how far can we go with shallow networks? https://core.ac.uk/download/211996163.pdf (accessed on 25th September 2025).
16. Burger, H. C., Harmeling, S., & Schuler, C. J. (2012). Image denoising with multi-layer perceptron's, part 1: Comparison with existing algorithms and with bounds. http://arxiv.org/abs/1211.1544 (accessed on 25th September 2025).
17. Chen, Q., Tan, S., Gao, S., Lu, J., et al. (2025). HyperSAT: Unsupervised hypergraph neural networks for weighted MaxSAT problems. https://www.semanticscholar.org/paper/eb76c0260fda31e83779c3db3c789c039f772b1f (accessed on 25th September 2025).
18. Chua, L. O., James, A. P., & Krestinskaya, O. (2018). Neuro-memristive circuits for edge computing: A review. http://arxiv.org/abs/1807.00962 (accessed on 25th September 2025).
19. Compton, M., Friedland, P., & Zweben, M. (2025). The 1990 progress report and future plans. https://core.ac.uk/download/pdf/42812208.pdf (accessed on 25th September 2025).
20. Crespo Márquez, A., Ferrero Bermejo, J., Guillén López, A. J., et al. (2019). Review and comparison of intelligent optimization modelling techniques for energy forecasting and condition-based maintenance in PV plants. https://core.ac.uk/download/288003394.pdf (accessed on 25th September 2025).

21. de Zarzà, I., de Curtò, J., & Calafate, C. (2023). Optimizing neural networks for imbalanced data. Electronics. https://www.semanticscholar.org/paper/fedcf7fef31cd3fadab5b08086ba7db36ff25702 (accessed on 25th September 2025).

22. Érdi, P. (2015). Teaching computational neuroscience. http://arxiv.org/abs/1412.5909 (accessed on 25th September 2025).

23. Feng, P., Zhang, Z., Chong, M., & Tan, Y. (2024). AE-D2NN: Autoencoder in diffractive neural network form. 2024 Photonics & Electromagnetics Research Symposium (PIERS). https://www.semanticscholar.org/paper/db08334d18193a56e8dc2a37b1e886140d715a06 (accessed on 25th September 2025).

24. Gashler, M. S., Martinez, T., Morris, R., et al. (2013). Missing value imputation with unsupervised backpropagation. http://arxiv.org/abs/1312.5394 (accessed on 25th September 2025).

25. Gerum, R., Krauss, P., Metzner, C., et al. (2019). How deep is deep enough? –Quantifying class separability in the hidden layers of deep neural networks. http://arxiv.org/abs/1811.01753 (accessed on 25th September 2025).

26. Gordleeva, S., Ivanchenko, M., Kazantsev, V., et al. (2016). Mammalian brain as a network of networks. https://core.ac.uk/download/42130432.pdf (accessed on 25th September 2025).

27. Grzes, M., & Shannon, J. (2018). Reinforcement learning using augmented neural networks. http://arxiv.org/abs/1806.07692 (accessed on 25th September 2025).

28. Hampson, S., & Kibler, D. (1982). A Boolean complete neural model of adaptive behavior. https://core.ac.uk/download/287623564.pdf (accessed on 25th September 2025).

29. Ibrahim, N., Noh, M. Z., Razali, S. A., et al. (2018). Observation of charge ordering signal in monovalent doped $Nd_{0.75}Na_{0.25-x}K_xMn_1O_3$ ($0 \leq x \leq 0.10$) manganites. https://core.ac.uk/download/17194331.pdf (accessed on 25th September 2025).

30. Iqbal, U. (2018). An improved functional link neural network for data classification. https://core.ac.uk/download/12005635.pdf (accessed on 25th September 2025).

31. James, A. P., Jayadevi, D. A., & Maan, A. K. (2016). A survey of memristive threshold logic circuits. http://arxiv.org/abs/1604.07121 (accessed on 25th September 2025).

32. Kamaruddin, I., Napiah, M., Suwardo, S., et al. (2010). Bus travel time

in the mixed traffic based on statistical neural network. https://media.neliti.com/media/publications/142968-EN-bus-travel-time-in-the-mixed-traffic-bas.pdf (accessed on 25th September 2025).

33. Kanter, I., & Priel, A. (2000). Robust chaos generation by a perceptron. http://arxiv.org/abs/cond-mat/0007074 (accessed on 25th September 2025).

34. Khatipov, R., Mazzara, M., Negimatzhanov, A., et al. (2018). Hikester–The event management application. http://arxiv.org/abs/1801.06400 (accessed on 25th September 2025).

35. Kong, X., Lee, K., Liu, X., et al. (2019). Signed distance-based deep memory recommender. http://arxiv.org/abs/1905.00453 (accessed on 25th September 2025).

36. Kumar, N., Peesapati, R., & Yadav, V. K. (2016). Assessment of temporary overvoltage's during network lines re-energization. https://core.ac.uk/download/84396466.pdf (accessed on 25th September 2025).

37. Liu, Z., Wang, Y., Vaidya, S., Ruehle, F., Halverson, J., Soljačić, M., Hou, T. Y., et al. (2024). KAN: Kolmogorov-Arnold networks. https://www.semanticscholar.org/paper/14fdab35cc6288083a38a92392af3f1da0b95a90 (accessed on 25th September 2025).

38. Malagón Fernández, S. (2018). Artificial neural networks applied to improve low-cost air quality monitoring precision. https://core.ac.uk/download/187264846.pdf (accessed on 25th September 2025).

39. Manandhar, S., & Mönning, N. (2018). Evaluation of complex-valued neural networks on real-valued classification tasks. http://arxiv.org/abs/1811.12351 (accessed on 25th September 2025).

40. Matthews, A. J., Men, B., Sivakumar, B., Widrow, B., Brown, B. G., et al. (2006). Multilayered feed forward artificial neural network model to predict the average summer-monsoon rainfall in India. http://arxiv.org/abs/nlin/0609014 (accessed on 25th September 2025).

41. Oh, A., Noh, I., Choo, J., Lee, J., Park, J., Hwang, K., Kim, S., et al. (2024). Machine learning approach to brain tumor detection and classification. https://www.semanticscholar.org/paper/76dabb7f76d1cf0ad932fc44297df90a3a9415b5 (accessed on 25th September 2025).

42. Xiang, W., Tran, H. D., & Johnson, T. T. (2004). Output reachable set estimation and verification for multi-layer neural networks. https://core.ac.uk/download/147889057.pdf (accessed on 25th September 2025).

CHAPTER 4

MULTILAYER PERCEPTRONS (MLP)

Contents

INTRODUCTION

Multilayer Perceptrons (MLPs) are a fundamental neural network building block in the field of artificial intelligence, and their uses have been the focus of most learning problems. An MLP contains a number of layers of nodes, e.g., an input layer, some number of hidden layers, and an output layer. Each node, often referred to as a neuron, has a weighted sum of inputs and subsequently an activation function that introduces non-linearity to the model. This structure allows MLPs to be able to learn complex functions, and therefore they are applied across many domains ranging from image classification to money prediction. The design and evolution in MLPs have been a key driving factor in developing machine learning abilities, and they play a central role in the examination of deeper neural architectures. The native adaptability of MLPs is highlighted through advances in algorithmic training, especially the use of gradient descent methods. Conventional gradient descent tends to be handicapped when dealing with the multimodal mappings of high-dimensional parameter spaces. Yet as pointed out in recent literature, algorithms like natural gradient descent boost learning efficiency by taking into account the parameter space's geometric layout.

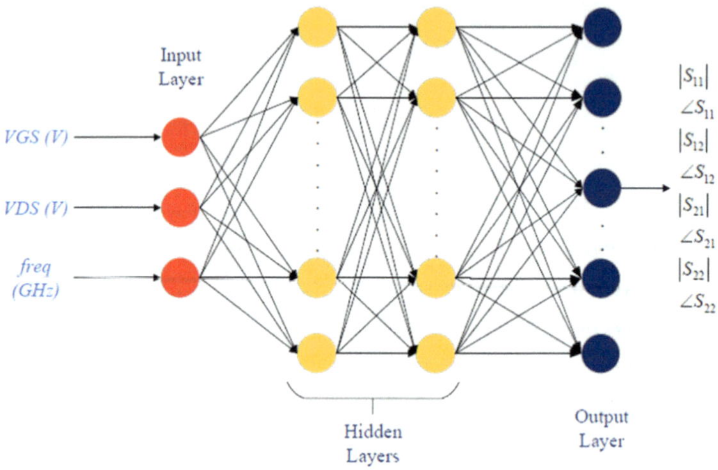

Figure 4.1. *Multilayer perceptron (MLP) neural network architecture.*

Source: https://www.researchgate.net/publication/338213708/figure/fig4/AS:11431281176256308@1690086036451/Multilayer-perceptron-MLP-neural-network-architecture.png.

This is achieved by maximizing updates in a manner that is compatible with the natural curvature of the loss surface, thus accelerating convergence rates. Specifically, the use of methods such as Bidirectional whitened neural networks, which involve whitening procedures in feed-forward as well as back-propagation steps, realizes impressive enhancement on task performance such as handwritten character recognition, as introduced by the MNIST dataset (Park et al., 2017). Moreover, the behavior of MLPs can be optimized further by studying their synchronization properties, which shed new light on collaborative machine learning contexts. It has been shown through research that two neural networks, which are trained on each other's output bits, turn out to be synchronized, and hence, end up having the same time-dependent weights. Such behavior not only demonstrates the robustness of training neural networks but also promises novel applications, such as secure communication based on secret key exchanges through public channels. As neural network development continues, identification of these rich behaviors in MLPs will be critical in designing more robust and effective AI systems (Kanter et al., 2002). Through continuous experimentation and research, MLPs are at the forefront of creating machine learning abilities, resulting in the better understanding of theoretical as well as practical aspects of artificial intelligence (Figure 4.1).

Definition of Multilayer Perceptrons (MLPs)

MLPs represent a simple architecture within the subset of neural networks, distinguished by more than one layer of nodes (or neurons) arranged systematically. An MLP is typically composed of an input layer, a number of hidden layers, and an output layer. Each neuron in each layer applies a transformation to the input data with the help of weighted connections such that the network is able to learn complex patterns. Every neuron applies an activation function to introduce nonlinearities in the model so that it can map any continuous function. This capacity for non-linear transformation is fundamental in applications such as image and speech recognition, where relationships in the data are intrinsically multidimensional and complicated, and hence advanced and multi-layered approaches to successful inspection are required. MLP training usually relies on backpropagation, an algorithm that modifies the weights assigned to the connections based on the error encountered on the output layer. This optimization process gradually closes the gap between the estimated outputs and actual targets using optimization techniques such as gradient descent. Optimizations in the process like natural gradient descent have surprisingly been developed to improve the efficiency of training. These approaches apply principles of information geometry to search the weight space more effectively, allowing them to realize faster convergence and improved performance on difficult tasks, such as handwritten character recognition (Park et al., 2017). The subtleties of training need to be understood in order to best realize the potential of MLPs in practical applications. MLPs also possess special characteristics that contribute towards determining their learning dynamics as well as stability. Among them is the invariant set of weights, which defines the interval range within which the entire network may work effectively. The invariant sets have been explained by research, an observation that hints at conditions on which the stability and injectiveness of the forward dynamics of perceptrons are assured (Ho et al., 2010). This aspect is particularly prominent in the context of complex patterns of data, where the ability to guarantee stability while fine-tuning for new data can determine the success of the learning process. Hence, comprehending these aspects of MLPs not only advances theoretical knowledge but also enhances practical applications to varied machine learning issues, which makes them a fundamental topic in the study of neural networks (Figure 4.2).

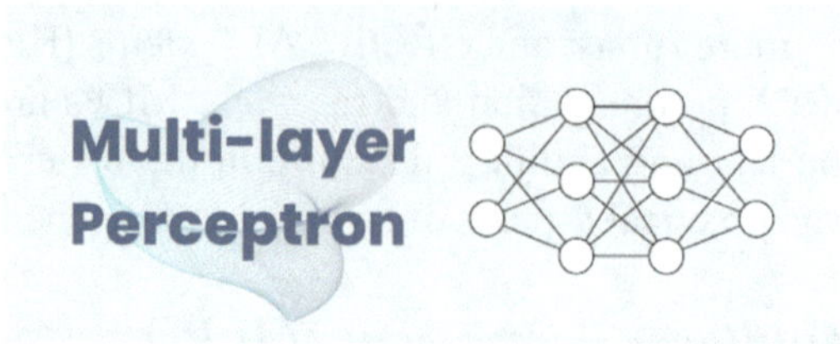

Figure 4.2. *Multilayer perceptron (MLP).*

Source: https://blogger.googleusercontent.com/img/b/R29vZ2xl/AVvXsE-jH2GbE1DXODQ8tnCVkn8S7F4KiCfaC0RvFt3I2L8d6YQplfHbKWG-kaU20EwY7zWj9TjLxn1WdKey8kpqnox_KAKmS3qn0fN2kRLht9tr1bGNkcLgNiK3IUKJiAYd1bP5IXsaKc5s__4H0nLkLw2m2kNLoOU7R_hMpBXfDES-NxIFPPY_RBOpUkoUt-aQ/w613-h345-rw/Multi-layer%20perceptron%20intro%20image.png.

Historical Context and Development

Historical development of MLP can trace its roots back to the first experiments with neural networks during the mid-20th century. The early research of psychologists and mathematicians like Frank Rosenblatt with his development of the Perceptron model in 1958 laid the ground for what would eventually become more advanced structures. This initial model was designed to mimic human learning on the basis of simple binary discriminations, and this encouraged later academic enthusiasm for the capabilities and limitations of artificial neural networks. As computing power exploded in the following decades, researchers could do away with a number of these initial limitations and thereby build more sophisticated multilayer architectures that could deal with non-linear interactions among input data, something that was an intractable problem with classical linear models. Thus, MLPs began to take shape at this initial phase, making way for their later widespread application in diverse disciplines. The 1980s marked a turning point for MLP development, prompted by the introduction of the backpropagation algorithm. This algorithm enabled effective training of multilayer networks through the application of gradient descent methods in the minimization of error in the output predictions. The revived interest in neural networks during this decade, also referred to as the AI Winter, was in part created by the marvelous success stories being reported in various areas, such as pattern recognition and speech processing. Backpropagation not only enhanced the capacity of MLPs to generalize more complex patterns but also provided a theoretical framework that justified their use in an enormous variety of practical problems. As a result, the platform was laid for MLPs to become real entities from theoretical curiosities and become an essential component of artificial intelligence research, providing incentives for increased academic and industrial investment in neural network technologies. By the end of the 1990s, MLPs continued to advance and expand in capability and function. The introduction of MLPs into fields such as image processing, natural language processing, and even finance modeling stressed their practicality. Advances in computing capacity and data availability enabled the training of larger and more profound networks that, in turn, profoundly enhanced their predictive capabilities. The focus moved towards improving architectures and studying hybrid models that merged MLPs with other machine learning techniques. For instance, studies began to demonstrate how MLPs could handle complex tasks in Traffic Engineering, where they recognized nonlinear patterns on network data in training processes (Chicaiza et al., 2008). Apart from that, economic impact studies, for instance, sustainability of Greece's current account deficit, applied neural networks to perform higher-order analytics, thus testifying to the flexibility of MLPs and their force in theoretical and practical applications (Andreou et al., 2025).

Importance in the Field of Artificial Intelligence

The relevance of MLP within the realm of artificial intelligence is brought out by their ability to provide complex relationships among data. MLPs, with their nested arrangement composed of input, hidden, and output layers, enable the processing of non-linear relationships, which are endemic in real-world data sets. It is a critical characteristic, especially in applications such as image recognition, natural language, and predictive analytics, where linear models are typically not sufficient. Additionally, the ability of MLPs to learn flexibility through processes like backpropagation and gradient descent allows for continuous optimization as new data becomes available, hence growing in effectiveness over time. Such adaptability allows MLPs to become a cornerstone of modern AI solutions, facilitating them to cope with increasingly intricate issues that are pivotal towards driving intelligent systems in different industries. Furthermore, MLPs are used beyond mere task automation, evolving into advanced structures that support multi-agent operations—such as in collaborative robotics systems. As noted in contemporary research, concurrent operations of several robots working together are central in executing intricate jobs that cannot be performed by one unit, hence assigning significance to coordinated uses of MLP in robotics

(Mansour et al., 2011). The form and operation of MLPs in this context facilitate enhanced information communication and processing, propelling the efficiency and effectiveness of collaborative robots. Through the application of MLP structures, autonomous robots are able to learn from collective experiences, updating action in real time to achieve maximum task performance as they move through difficult, dynamic environments. This is an example of how MLPs play a crucial role in facilitating innovation across sectors via artificial intelligence. Moreover, the integration of MLPs with symbolic reasoning mechanisms is a significant domain in AI research. Current tradition isolates connectionist systems, i.e., MLPs, from the traditional logical approaches, which lessens the prospects of developing uniform intelligent systems with sophisticated reasoning powers. Effort in the direction of integration of these paradigms is necessary, since symbolic knowledge representation renders neural networks interpretable, hence permitting tasks that not only require decision-making but also decision justification. As seen in the neural-symbolic integration literature, overcoming symbolic knowledge encoding into MLPs is a problem that can open new avenues to artificial intelligence applications, leading to more powerful knowledge extraction algorithms and a better understanding of data interpretation (Bader et al., 2004). The integration of such methods will definitely encourage development, bringing about a new generation of hybrid systems that take advantage of the strengths of both neural networks and symbolic reasoning.

4.1. STRUCTURE OF MULTILAYER PERCEPTRONS (MLPS)

The MLP structure is essential to understanding how they work and are flexible in neural networks. An MLP contains an input layer, multiple hidden layers, and an output layer, all consisting of interconnected neurons. The structure allows every layer to transform the input data successively, abstracting features with each increasing level. Neurons within a layer are linked to the subsequent layer's neurons through weighted edges that get tuned at training time. The layering gives rich decision-making capability, where every neuron has a non-linear activation function on its output, enabling the network to encode rich patterns in the data. Complexity is required in use cases from image and speech recognition to medical diagnosis, where linear models would not succeed. The performance of MLPs can be tightly regulated by the depth of the architecture. Both parameters control the ability of the network in learning patterns from data, striking an underfitting and overfitting balance. Deeper architecture, where there are many hidden layers, can learn more complicated relationships but also has problems, e.g., increased computational cost and vanishing gradient susceptibility. Consequently, scientists often use techniques like dropout or batch normalization to make training more efficient as well as the performance of the network. In addition, the interaction amongst the neurons gives rise to a statistical complexity in which competition between model complexity and training error can cause interesting phenomena such as discontinuous properties in the behavior of neural networks, as shown in various studies (Biehl et al., 1997). Moreover, the multilayer topology of the perceptron is a basis for most advanced algorithms. For instance, an understanding of MLP topology has improved techniques like measure correlate predict algorithm, which best predicts, in this case, wind energy production (Addison et al., 2000). These advancements underscore the versatility of MLPs as well as their foundation in more advanced network architectures, e.g., convolutional and recurrent networks. As machine learning keeps accelerating, the structural principles of MLPs continue to influence researchers on how architecture, learning algorithms, and application-specific performance relate to each other. Thus, the multilayer architecture serves not only as a point of reference for basic MLP processes but also as a stepping stone for future advancements in neural network architecture (Figure 4.3).

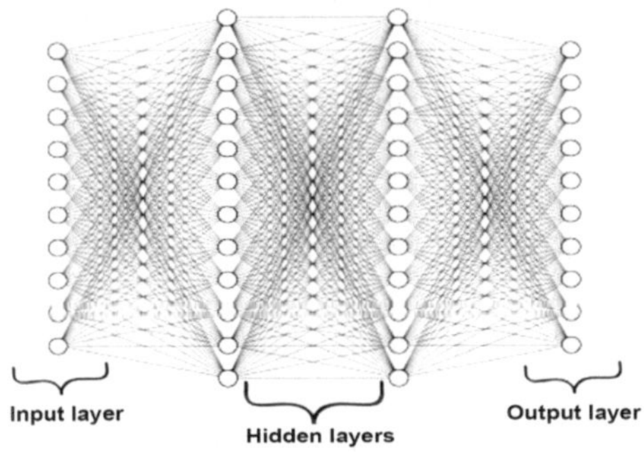

Figure 4.3. *Multilayer perceptron (MLP) structure.*

Source: https://blogger.googleusercontent.com/img/b/R29vZ2xl/AVvXsEhKeKx-tLbxWMTxLOp-VdWuMh5UNd--5JV9I_H-YvbCTlRbc3xafp8gNKqH610s9ETLm-t5U7dWWaS_K0USMlAzMgOaYRAe9MPrUJQiHkzNuvuhklnoOYk29kBY-A28MCDqVAcF71eZnYfT1X5_bkMQIGBq0BYO7ObHhD6-2R_bub5jZuMi8exvo-epazgXpw/w594-h334-rw/Neural%20network%20structure.png.

4.1.1. Input Layer and Its Function

The input layer is really the primary source of a Multilayer Perceptron (MLP), really receiving and processing external data before it continues on to the remaining layers of the network. This layer is made up of artificial neurons, where each neuron is associated with a specific feature of the input data set. For example, for a classification problem with images, each pixel value might be utilized as a neuron, all of them collectively to account for the entire image. Interestingly, the input layer does not process in a complicated way; rather, it preserves the innocence of the input and normalizes as well as transforms data, preparing it for manipulation within the hidden layers. This initial processing is significant, as it directly contributes to the network's ability to learn and generalize from training data, demonstrating the significance of a well-designed input layer in MLP architectures. As the data flows from the input layer to the hidden layers of an MLP through the process of transformation wherein the weights and the biases are used, the resulting system guarantees that the input layer not only provides raw information but also processed information that picks up on inherent patterns. The significance of such structured information is apparent in the application of handwriting character recognition, where the relationship between numerous features—like angles and curves—is able to affect the overall accuracy of predictions generated by a model. A good input layer maximizes the learning trajectory of the MLP so that it can bracket complex mappings between input and output. More recent works, as seen in studies utilizing tools such as the Bidirectional whitened neural networks, have shown the extent to which the employment of advanced input processing is capable of greatly improving performance, particularly in recognition tasks involving databases such as MNIST (Park et al., 2017). Functionality of the input layer also extends beyond representation of data; it is also important in managing information flow in the network. By setting up the foundation upon which information is dispersed throughout the MLP, the input layer dictates what comes next, e.g., error calculation during training sessions. This is particularly evident within complex applications where the input layer must effectively extract multidimensional information, e.g., the models analyzing wind energy harvests (Addison et al., 2000). Therefore, understanding the working nuances of the input layer not only explains its individual importance but also illustrates its interdependence with the efficiency and performance of the whole network. Therefore, careful attention to input layer design and functioning becomes core in the development of stable MLPs that can handle a range of computation tasks.

4.1.2. Hidden Layers and Their Significance

The role played by the hidden layers of Multilayer Perceptrons (MLPs) is crucial to the networks ability to capture sophisticated, non-linear data relationships. Hidden layers provide an intermediary position between the input and output layers in such a way that it enables the network to discover intricate patterns, which are not possible for a single-layer perceptron to do. The depth and width of the hidden layers decide the representational power of an MLP. Every hidden layer neuron is doing some transformation using activation functions, which introduce non-linearity to the system. This ability to generate complex mappings makes MLPs excel on many tasks from image recognition to natural language processing, where linear models have been known to not perform so well. Hidden layers also allow for hierarchical learning of features, which becomes the defining characteristic of MLPs. Lower levels are likely to extract simple features, such as edges or gradients on images, and upper levels compose these simple representations into more abstract representations. This hierarchical layout reflects cognitive processes that occur in human perception and allows MLPs to process high-dimensional data in a manner that is efficient. Consequently, hidden layers not only render learning more effective but also make the results easier to interpret by allowing for a structured representation of complicated data. It should be stressed that proper configuration of these layers—including the number of neurons and what kinds of activation functions they employ—plays a significant role in the performance of the neural network as a whole, which underscores their crucial role in MLP structure. Moreover, hidden layers exert leverage beyond mere representation, influencing the optimizability and generalizability of MLPs. By control over the depth and complexity of a neural network through its hidden layers, professionals can avert issues such as overfitting or underfitting. For instance, a well-tuned network can enhance prediction accuracy, for instance, in predicting survival from trauma, where sensitivity analysis can offer important information on clinical decision-making (Hunter et al., 2000). Because different data sets may require different architectures, it is critical to understand the function served by hidden layers to guide modifications in training and performance assessment. In the end, these layers are the foundation of MLPs, making the networks successful in wide applications and placing them at the cutting edge of neural network technology.

4.1.3. Output Layer and Interpretation of Results

The output layer of an Multilayer Perceptron (MLP) plays a critical role in the performance of the model, where the final processing step in which the learned representations of the networks are transformed into predictions. Unlike hidden layers that abstract and encode challenging data patterns, the output layer actively maps those patterns to generate the output in the required form, from classification labels to regression values. The choice of activation function in the output layer is critical in shaping the behavior of prediction, for example, softmax can be applied for multi-class classification scenarios so that output values are probabilities. The design of this layer is intricate as it requires in-depth understanding of the problem domain to enable the MLP to effectively transform its internal calculation into valuable information, thereby resulting in sound decisions based on the networks output. The interpretation of results obtained from using the output layer is also crucial for evaluating the performance of the MLP and the accuracy of the predictions. The assessment may include a set of metrics depending on output type: confusion and accuracy matrices are prevalent in classification issues, while mean squared error is common in regression issues. These measures not only assist in validating the predictive potential of the model but also identify areas of need for improvement. Interpretability takes on an even greater significance in disciplines such as medicine, where accurate predictions have material real-world consequences. For instance, the explanation of the output layers in using MLPs in trauma survival analysis identifies the effectiveness of the model to enhance patient outcomes and therefore the imperative to utilize thoughtful evaluation techniques to comprehend and accept the decision of the model (Hunter et al., 2000). Moreover, certain new approaches can enhance the outcome results interpretation of the output generated by MLPs. Methods such as feature importance estimation and decision boundary visualization are able to determine how input features influence the outputs. Methods in functional data analysis are employed in processing difficult data sets cost-efficiently by considering their functional structure, which can improve performance in practical applications. Precisely, employing projection-based MLPs can result in greater understanding of the mapping function between functional inputs and outputs, whereby the model is always generalizable without prediction errors. With such methods evolving further, output layer result explanation becomes increasingly sophisticated, allowing MLPs to increasingly offer solutions to an expanding array of problems with better explanatory power and prediction accuracy (Barron et al., 2006).

4.2. ACTIVATION FUNCTIONS

Activation functions are inherent components of multilayer perceptrons (MLPs) within neural networks as they regulate the output of each neuron by introducing non-linearity to the model. In a typical MLP architecture, these functions determine whether a neuron is activated or remains dormant depending on the sum of weighted inputs. Linear activation functions, though basic, fail to represent the complex interdependencies between the data and hence are limiting factors in the ability of the neural networks to generalize efficiently across various tasks. More complex functions like the sigmoid, hyperbolic tangent (tanh), and rectified linear unit (ReLU) have hence been more popular.

All of these functions possess individual strengths and weaknesses, with ReLU in particular gaining widespread use because it has the ability to alleviate vanishing gradient problem, a common problem in deep networks, thus making training easier. Secondly, an understanding of how different activation functions perform relative to one another in multilayer perceptrons is essential to the optimization of network effectiveness.

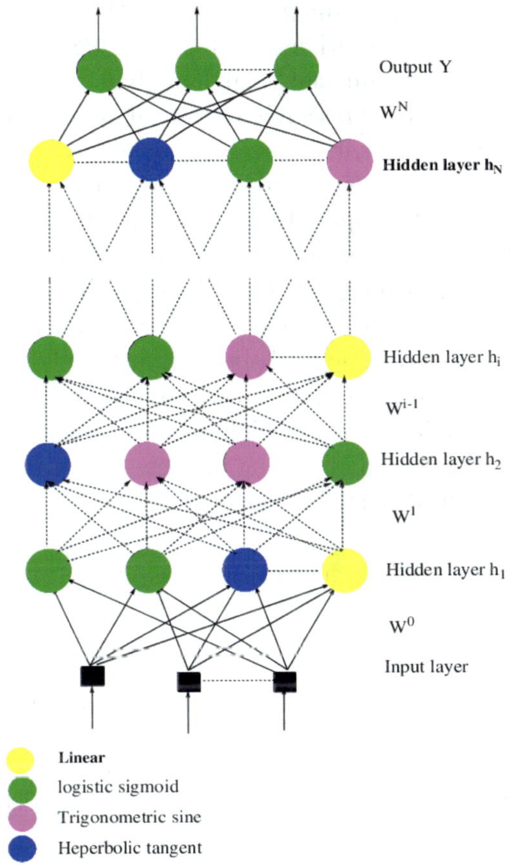

Figure 4.4. *Activation function structure in multilayer perceptron (MLP).*

Source: https://www.researchgate.net/profile/Youssef-Ghanou/publication/318239264/figure/fig1/AS:637028077142024@1528890737985/Activation-function-structure-in-Multilayer-perceptron.png.

The choice of activation function has the potential to make a very significant difference in regards to model convergence speed and accuracy. For instance, while the sigmoid function has the capability to scale inputs to a 0–1 range, it suffers from issues of saturation and thus is not as preferable for deep networks. In contrast, ReLU function, which allows linear growth of the output for positive inputs, has shown a superior ability to propagate gradients in backpropagation and thus ensure faster convergence rates. In addition, more recent variants such as Leaky ReLU and parametric ReLU have also emerged to address inherent flaws of the basic ReLU, namely the dying ReLU problem where neurons are deactivated and cease learning altogether. The addition of high-level activation functions can even drive MLPs' expressive capability all the way up to functional inputs, a significant breakthrough in neural network research. As also underscored in current research, functional multilayer perceptrons, too, have similar capability as their numerical equivalents, generating universal approximation outcomes that attest to their potency in describing intricate data. Such flexibility is especially required when applying MLPs to real-world issues, where disparate data modalities necessitate adaptive activation mechanisms to guarantee optimal performance. The breakthroughs in the activation function theory not only enrich our understanding of MLP architectures but also render them useful for practice to be applied across various fields, enabling multiple robots with the ability to interact cooperatively to accomplish tasks and decision-making in complex environments as highlighted in earlier work (Mansour et al., 2011) and once again demonstrating the need for well-defined parameter estimates for functional MLPs (Abraham et al., 2003) (Figure 4.4).

4.2.1. Role of Activation Functions in Multilayer Perceptrons (MLPs)

Activation functions are tasked with being the backbone in MLP architecture, having a major role in impacting the learning capacity and the overall performance of the network. Their primary role is to introduce non-linearity into the model so that the MLP can learn complex patterns and relationships in the data. Without such operations, an MLP with greater than a single layer would contract to an equivalent single-layer model and thus would not be capable of efficiently completing such tasks as classification and regression. Various activation functions, e.g., sigmoid, hyperbolic tangent (tanh), and rectified linear unit (ReLU), possess various characteristics that can be beneficial in different situations. Choice of an activation function is primarily accountable for convergence and stability in the process of training, which is paramount for establishing robust neural networks that are applicable in real-world scenarios. Choice of the activation function also affects gradients that are estimated with backpropagation, which underpins learning in MLPs. For instance, the sigmoid function will induce the vanishing gradient problem in the deep networks where gradients become too small for meaningful weight updates. Activation functions like ReLU mitigate this effect by maintaining a constant gradient for positive inputs, thereby more effective learning in deeper models. Such attributes have led ReLU and its variants to be the preference of choice in modern applications of MLPs. In addition, incorporating these with advanced techniques such as batch normalization maximizes the training by balancing the input distributions through each layer. Subsequently, understanding how activation functions affect the training behavior and accuracy of MLPs serves as the foundation of building effective neural network models. The analysis of activation functions is not just relevant to standard architectures; they transfer their importance to deeper forms of complexity, like functional MLPs. Recent studies have debated the viability of employing activation functions in functional MLPs, which handle functional inputs rather than scalar inputs typical in typical neural networks. In such contexts, activation functions must retain their fundamental properties while having the ability to support the complexity of functional data. Experimental findings confirm that the expressive capacity of functional MLPs is as great as classical numerical MLPs, further substantiating the grand significance of activation functions across various neural network designs. By working on universal approximation results, the literature highlights good activation function design as important in optimizing MLPs, either processing typical data sets or more advanced functional inputs, thus boosting their statistical efficiency and practical applicability (Abraham et al., 2003) (Figure 4.5).

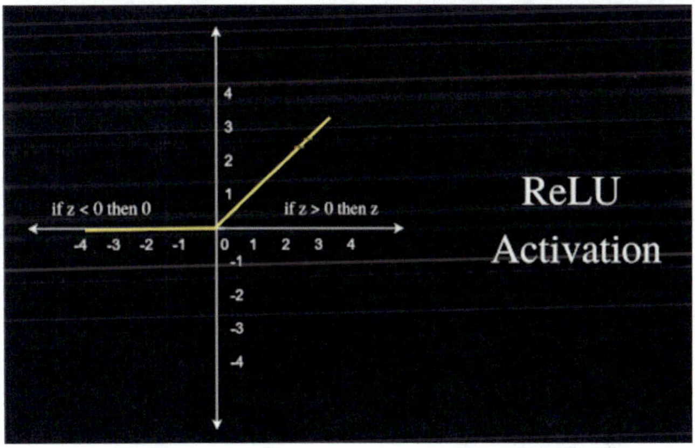

Figure 4.5. *Rectified linear unit (ReLU) activation function graph.*

Source: https://blogger.googleusercontent.com/img/b/R29vZ2xl/AVvXsEguG-JOpElvyN_70wXuAD7aLK02UOC-8oxO70sUGSEjWS2mdehVVCsiDZe3u-T0qTxKqHSrt6UmwEU0fCOeoO1lZQil_9UuklxjxEBJC0Bku9-UCUtfEXd-khHtrDDPlV1F79vtLnXaO9wEi9lZZ-jWHvB7b8BiAmedUjsjf0V9lqP6s2V2yw-cAHwxmrCqg/w552-h311-rw/ReLU%20graph%20(1).png.

4.2.2. Common Types of Activation Functions

During Multilayer Perceptron (MLP) design, the activation functions play a major role in what the network does with the data. Among the most common ones are Sigmoid, Hyperbolic Tangent (tanh), and Rectified Linear Unit (ReLU) functions. Sigmoid function with its S-shaped curve is particularly valuable in models that need to estimate probability as the output is bounded within the range 0–1. It suffers from the shortcoming of vanishing gradients, which occurs more often in deeper networks, and can act as a barrier in successful training. The tanh function, on the other hand, scales the output to the range -1–1, thus alleviating some of the problems the Sigmoid function faces by normalizing the data, leading to faster convergence when training. The various functions, based on their properties, dictate the neural networks' capacity to learn and act. Another well-known activation function is the Rectified Linear Unit (ReLU).

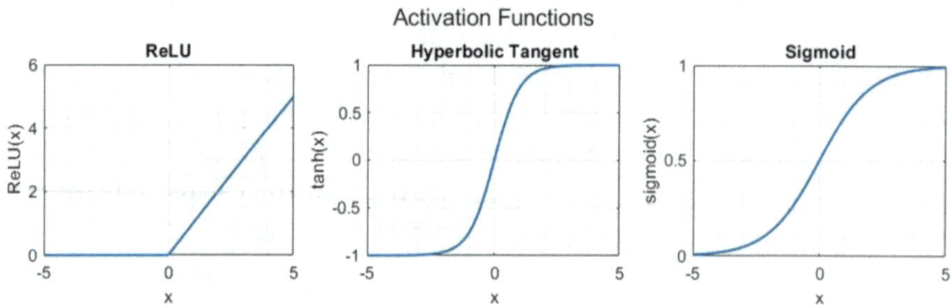

Figure 4.6. *Activation functions: Rectified linear unit (ReLU), tanh, sigmoid.*

Source: https://www.researchgate.net/publication/376193024/figure/fig3/AS:1143 1281209315146@1701720609015/Activation-Functions-ReLU-tanh-sigmoid.jpg.

This function simplifies computation by taking zero for negative inputs and the input itself for positive inputs. ReLU has gained popularity since it can silence vanishing gradient problems, which typically plague traditional activation functions like Sigmoid and tanh, especially in deeper layers of an MLP. By allowing models to train faster and be more performant on a variety of tasks, ReLU has become the go-to standard in modern uses of neural networks. But it's not perfect; it suffers from the dying ReLU problem, where neurons become "killed" in training. Consequently, other flavors, like Leaky ReLU and Parametric ReLU, have emerged to address these issues while still keeping the benefit of the ReLU function. Understanding various activation functions is important not only in constructing effective MLPs but also in enhancing predictive ability in real-world practice. Scientists, for instance, have explored applying neural networks with various activation functions to increase sensitivity analysis and survival prediction of trauma, illustrating the practical significance of these choices in critical areas like medicine (Hunter et al., 2000). Further, the selection of a proper activation function has the potential to go deep into a model's interpretability and its ability to generalize from training data to new instances. Therefore, the choice of activation functions is the final responsibility for the success of neural networks, and the necessity of ongoing research and experimentation in this ever-changing area of artificial intelligence (Figure 4.6).

4.2.3. Impact of Activation Functions on Learning

Choosing an activation function is perhaps the single most significant influence on the learning characteristics of multilayer perceptrons (MLPs) in neural networks. The sigmoid, tanh, and ReLU (Rectified Linear Unit) activation functions introduce varying degrees of non-linearity into the model, with significant impacts on how well the network is able to learn complex patterns within the data. Sigmoid and tanh, although widely applied in the past, have issues like vanishing gradients when backpropagation; this would realistically slow down learning, especially in deeper networks. But using ReLU avoids this from happening as gradients can now pass through more easily and therefore enhance faster convergence and more accurate representations of the input space. The activation function merely decides the direction of information flow in the network and impacts not just the effectiveness of learning but also the predictive performance of the models in tasks across various domains. Besides this, the design of a multilayer perceptron is also made better using an appropriate selection of activation functions based on the specific characteristics of the dataset and target task. For instance, in classification problems, employing softmax as the activation function in the output layer provides a probability distribution of the class labels. It diverges from the case of regression problems, where linear activation functions for the output are to be utilized. Leaky ReLU and Parametric ReLU have emerged as new variants to counter some of the disadvantages of typical activation functions. These modifications attempt to preserve the advantages of ReLU but provide non-zero gradients for every input so that the learning experience of the neural network is smoother and it is more capable of generalizing from training data. Activation functions also affect the stability of learning procedures. Neural networks, as they grow more sophisticated, are prone to such issues as instability and oscillation during training. This is also partly due to how the global updates of the weights affect learning dynamics and can cause unstable behaviors from the neural network. It has been discovered that changing the structure of the network, such as choosing the activation function, can significantly enhance learning efficiency and stability (Mansour et al., 2011). Therefore, careful consideration needs to be taken in the selection of activation functions, together with architectural design, to enhance training outcomes and have the multilayer perceptron model perform optimally in real-world applications, such as challenging tasks that involve the coordination of several robots to work together intelligently, for example, in line tracking or load balancing (Mansour et al., 2011).

4.3. TRAINING PROCESS

Training in Multilayer Perceptrons (MLPs) is a critical phase in their development and, basically, decides their ability to learn and generalize data. Backpropagation algorithm is the underlining method behind training, which adjusts the network weights by way of calculating gradients. Through minimization of the loss function, typically through application of the gradient descent, MLPs iteratively refine their parameters to better predict outputs. The success of this process depends upon a properly balanced dataset, learning rate, and appropriate activation functions that manage node conduct. This recurrent process, being strongly linked to the overall architecture and intricacy of the MLP, plays an immense role in the latter's performance and precision within functions as disparate as image recognition to natural language processing. Among the recent developments of new techniques are the Natural Gradient Descent, which enhances MLP training dynamics through the incorporation of a geometric framework. In contrast to regular gradient descent, which can be slow to converge, Natural Gradient Descent updates on Riemannian manifolds to minimize, thereby adapting the update process to the local geometry of the loss landscape. This approach utilizes the Fisher information matrix effectively to direct weight updates, offering improved search through the weight space of multiple dimensions. These innovative methods significantly raise convergence rates and training overall performance, as indicated in applications like handwritten character recognition on the Bidirectional whitened neural networks model that takes whitening operations in both forward and back-propagation phases (Park et al., 2017). Furthermore, the synchronization process in neural networks introduces a further intriguing element in training. By mutual adaptation, through co-connected networks evolving in an incremental manner toward each other's outputs, particular weight alignment patterns develop over time. The process demonstrates the potential of collaborative training methods for increasing the learning performance of MLPs, particularly in secrecy-rich tasks and safe data transmission. Using statistical physics, scientists have found dynamics in which networks are able to synchronize their weights and enhance performance and robustness in learning complex relationships among data. Such findings point to the importance of examining different training techniques in

MLPs and creating new prospects in their ability for engineering applications (Kanter et al., 2002) (Figure 4.7).

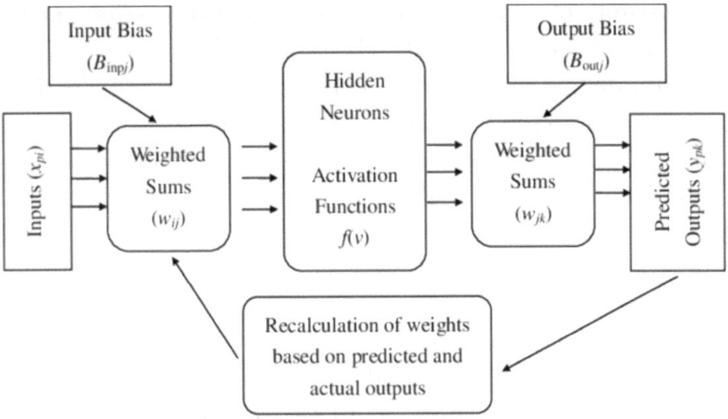

Figure 4.7. *A flow diagram of the training process in a multi-layer perceptron neural network.*

Source: https://www.researchgate.net/profile/Jeremy-Coid/publication/227212563/figure/fig1/AS:669029316456464@1536520427930/A-flow-diagram-of-the-training-process-in-a-multi-layer-perceptron-neural-network.png.

4.3.1. Overview of the Training Algorithm

Multilayer Perceptrons (MLPs) training algorithm is a critical component of designing neural networks and a primary factor influencing their potential to learn and make predictions. Essentially, this algorithm utilizes a method known as backpropagation to effectively adjust the weights of connection links between neurons with regards to the gradients of the loss function. This makes it possible for the network to minimize the difference between predicted output and target values by propagating the error backward through network layers. By making these weights incrementally smaller in size across multiple epochs with training data subsets, MLPs learn complex patterns and representations in the input data efficiently, and thus are most appropriate to handle tasks such as classification and regression. Further, the training algorithm efficiency is considerably enhanced by falling back on optimization techniques such as stochastic gradient descent (SGD) and its variants. These methods incorporate randomness into the weight update procedure, which is beneficial in preventing local minima and allowing quicker convergence to global minima. Regularization methods such as dropout and weight decay are often incorporated to prevent overfitting, especially in deep networks with lots of parameters. As is evident from studies, the delicate dance of minimizing training error and generalization is the key to algorithm success, observing the fine-grained nature of training MLPs and the ever-changing nature of techniques used in practice to maximize performance and robustness (Addison et al., 2000). The ramifications of a well-implemented training algorithm extend far beyond mere performance values; they directly aid in the application of MLPs in a broad range of activities. For instance, in the arena of robot applications, a complex MLP can facilitate communication and task completion between multiple robots, increasing overall operational efficiency. The ability of such networks to decipher complex sensor information and make decisions in real-time is crucial in developing autonomous systems that are capable of multitasking and communicating with one another. With further developments in the area, the integration of MLP training algorithms and sophisticated hardware capabilities will redefine opportunity across industries, further underscoring the need for ongoing research and innovation in the area (Mansour et al., 2011).

4.3.2. Backpropagation and Its Importance

Backpropagation serves as a foundation within the scenario of Multilayer Perceptrons (MLPs) of neural networks to facilitate the proper adjustment of weights through the calculated error from the predictions. Backpropagation operates through a twofold mechanism: the forward pass, during which input information is transmitted through the network to generate an output, and the backward pass, through which the error is back propagated to adjust the weights. Applying the chain rule of calculus, backpropagation calculates the gradient of loss with regard to each weight systematically in an efficient manner for optimizing learning across numerous layers. This is a critical process because it highlights the ability of MLPs in mapping intricate relationships between inputs and outputs, particularly in use cases such as financial time series analysis where data patterns can be complex and non-linear, as highlighted in previous research (Versace et al., 2009). There is also another level of importance in the capability of backpropagation to improve the efficiency of neural networks by allowing more extensive and more complicated structures without a proportional increase in computational resources. The algorithm enables MLPs to manage and optimize the numerous weights in such networks efficiently. In situations where there are many features, such as those found in financial datasets, determining the relevance and contribution of each feature may be essential. Backpropagation, not only helps facilitate such determination but also opens up the door for adapted models that consider feature importance, promoting precision in prediction. The integration of relevance in learning processes has been implemented in such techniques as Correlation aided Neural

Networks (CANN) that improve learning performance and speed depending on prior knowledge of the significance of features (Iqbal et al., 2011). The application of backpropagation lies not only in performance optimization but in the specification of flexibility and robustness of MLPs in evolving environments. Neural networks, particularly when applied to complex problems such as financial prediction, require learning to adapt to evolving patterns characterizing real-world data. Backpropagation enables the networks to re-tune based on new data so that learning is adaptive and not redundant. This adaptability is essential in a bid to guarantee predictive power and prevent the overfitting associated with rigid models of learning. In view of the changing nature of data, the application of dynamic algorithms like backpropagation will only become stronger, placing it as a cornerstone in the ongoing evolution of artificial intelligence techniques (Figure 4.8).

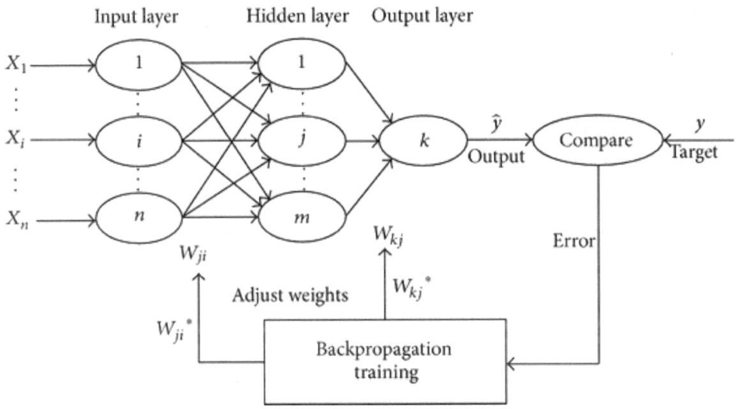

Figure 4.8. *Multilayer perceptron (MLP) based on backpropagation technique.*

Source: https://www.researchgate.net/profile/Saeed-Ghorbani-2/publication/326355575/figure/fig1/AS:649212618362889@1531795758778/MLP-Multi-layer-perceptron-based-on-backpropagation-technique.png.

4.3.3. Role of Learning Rate and Optimization Techniques

For the case of Multilayer Perceptrons (MLP), the learning rate is a determining factor when it comes to the training time and the quality of the process. It exists to be a scaling factor for weight updates in the process of optimization of the networks parameters. An overly high learning rate may lead to divergence, where the loss function oscillates or increases, while an excessively low learning rate can lead to immense training time and can lead to bad convergence to local minima. Hence, finding an optimal learning rate is important in an attempt to strike a balance between the speed of convergence and the stability of learning. A number of empirical methods suggest the use of strategies such as learning rate schedules or adaptive learning rates to dynamically adjust the rate during training, thereby enhancing the models capacity to generalize well on new data and overall performance in real-world applications. Optimization algorithms have a significant contribution to MLP training as they outline how well the network learns to optimize the error landscape in the process. Standard techniques for optimization such as Stochastic Gradient Descent (SGD), Adam, and RMSprop apply varying strategies to update weights based on calculated gradients. For instance, Adam is a combination of the strengths of both AdaGrad and RMSprop, learning parameter-specific adaptation with the inclusion of a momentum-like component. This is extremely useful in dealing with sparse data or if the data includes noise, allowing MLPs to learn trends effectively. Upon examining case studies, the integration of advanced optimization algorithms has been evidenced to make remarkable breakthroughs in model accuracy and training speed, validating their worth in practical applications, such as in MLP applications for electromagnetic duct height prediction (Earls et al., 2019). Moreover, how learning rate and optimization techniques interact can be evidenced by their collective contribution toward the efficiency of MLPs in practical applications. For instance, in multi-robot systems where different robots are synchronized to achieve a common goal, such as line-following robots, learning rate optimization and optimization techniques optimization are the priority. Through the optimization of such parameters, the robots will be able to coordinate their motion appropriately so that the task execution is more efficient than an individual robot could achieve due to limitations in load handling and capacity (Mansour et al., 2011). This synergy demonstrates how well-trained MLPs can be applied from theoretical models to actual applications and how learning rate and optimization techniques play significant roles as building blocks in designing intricate neural network architectures.

4.4. APPLICATIONS OF MULTILAYER PERCEPTRONS (MLPS)

The applications of MLPs cut across a wide range of fields, illustrating their versatility and applicability to the solution of complex problems. One such interesting application is in robotic systems, particularly where many robots are economically required to cooperate to achieve one operation. For instance, in projects focused on building line-following robots, MLPs can assist in follower-leader robot coordination and communication. By the processing of sensory information, the respective neural networks enable the robots to navigate and manage load sharing, thereby curing the frailties of single-robot systems. The ability of MLPs to learn by experience and react to dynamic environments not only improves task execution but also enhances the robustness and reliability of robot teams (Mansour et al., 2011). In the energy sector, MLPs exhibit great potential in prediction and optimization of energy yield from renewable sources. A good example is in estimation of wind energy, where MLP employs a measure-correlate-predict strategy. Based on analysis of historical wind trends and correlating it with system parameters, MLPs are able to estimate energy production with high accuracy, which proves useful in optimal usage of resources. This capability to predict is beneficial to utility firms as it aids in operations and planning, thus increasing the incorporation of renewable energy into grids. The capability of MLPs to cope with nonlinear associations in the data once again emphasizes their usefulness in predicting intricate phenomena that have been witnessed in the renewable energy sector (Addison et al., 2000). Furthermore, MLPs have been extensively applied in fields such as finance, medicine, and image processing. In finance, they are applied in the detection of fraud and credit scoring, where their ability to recognize patterns in large data helps institutions make informed decisions. In medicine, MLPs help identify diseases in their early stages by analyzing medical images, enabling doctors to diagnose conditions such as tumors more precisely. Also, their application in image processing involves areas such as object detection and facial recognition, further illustrating how diversified they are. The widespread use of MLPs across different sectors illustrates how they assist in advancing technology while addressing complex problems in society, making them a valuable resource in modern computing practices.

4.4.1. Use in Image Recognition

The application of multilayer perceptrons (MLPs) in image recognition is a foundation upon which most advances in computer vision have taken place. MLPs, defined in the context of their ability to learn complicated nonlinear relationships through densely interconnected layers of neurons, are able to process pixel data within images successfully. Through initiating training with large labeled sets, MLPs can identify automatically patterns and features, which are key to proper image classification. This ability to recognize complicated patterns—objects or specific environments—tells the worth of MLPs in work automation prior to that had relied on human percept. Moreover, with expanded cosmopolitanism of MLPs through more sophisticated image datasets, enhanced recognition accuracy is possible, making them invaluable assets for image inspection today. High-quality labeled dataset worth has become prominent in recent studies when training MLPs for image recognition purposes. For instance, the COCO dataset shows how dense and heterogeneous annotations enable better visual scene understanding by connecting diverse image-related tasks such as segmentation and VQA. Connecting diverse forms of annotations can enhance MLP performance because they can leverage knowledge from various domains. The incorporation of such data aims to facilitate the advancement of advanced recognition algorithms that not only improve classification but also improve the resilience of MLPs in real applications. As image recognition technology advances, application of multilayer perceptrons in such architectures will certainly result in epoch-making approaches that defy existing challenges and stretch the boundaries of innovation. The continued development of MLPs for visual recognition is a dramatic illustration of the interplay between machine capacity and human creativity. Techniques such as supervised attention for VQA have managed to demonstrate the capacity of MLPs to utilize segmentation-QA pairs as explicit supervisory signals and achieve state-of-the-art performance. This is one method that illustrates how segmentation and recognition operations can converge to enhance the effectiveness of MLPs. By empirical observations, it becomes evident that intricate interconnection between multilayer networks can re-design crude image data into useful recognition outcomes. With progressive studies, the focus will also be on fine-tuning MLP architecture to achieve maximum accuracy and computational costs so that they remain one step ahead of image recognition algorithms (Ho et al., 2010; Gan et al., 2017) (Figure 4.9).

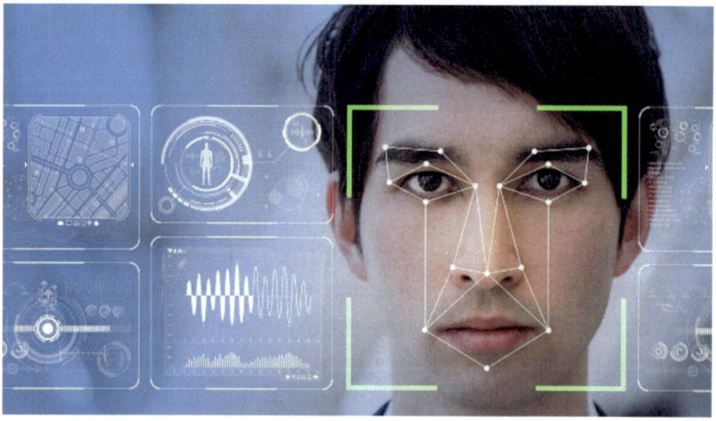

Figure 4.9. *Understanding image recognition.*

Source: https://kajabi-storefronts-production.kajabi-cdn.com/kajabi-storefronts-production/file-uploads/blogs/22606/images/ffb36af-fda-57fd-546-8e1e25788ca1_image-recognition.jpeg.

4.4.2. Applications in Natural Language Processing (NLP)

Multilayer perceptron (MLP) application to NLP is one of the avenues through which machines are capable of achieving better comprehension of human language complexities. MLPs, due to their capacity to learn nonlinear relationships between information, have become basic in many NLP applications, including sentiment analysis, language translation, and text summarization. Using deep learning techniques, MLPs can handle large datasets efficiently by taking advantage of copious amounts of annotated data for performance enhancement. Such a capability is particularly important in areas like VQA, where visual and text data fusion can lead to improved context and intention understanding. For instance, Gan et al. (2017) highlights the importance of layer-wise learning processes such that increasingly exhaustive human-labeled sets reinforce MLP performance in extracting correspondence among various language tasks and visual forms. The robustness of MLPs to NLP is also applicable to the investigation of complex communication patterns in datasets, as exemplified through recent advancements in machine translation and information retrieval. The neural topology fares best and structures input data, efficiently maintaining linguistic sequential dependencies. Notably, MLPs use attention mechanisms, whereby the model may assign particular attention to certain portions of text while it carries out information processing. This feature has been crucial in achieving advances in tasks like semantic segmentation and textual entailment, thereby enabling models to draw important conclusions from extensive text. Besides that, the incorporation of feature learning processes makes MLPs more generalizable to different tasks and domains. These advances further reflect the intrinsic contribution of MLPs to improving language models and applying them in NLP. Further, MLPs have been effective in countermeasure development for addressing problems of emerging security and privacy issues in natural language data applications, particularly in mobile settings. For example, the paradigm of integrating the usage of MLPs and static analysis enhances identification of communication connections among applications and gives a more accurate output compared to isolated usage of classical techniques. Type-directed encoders research indicates how the incorporation of MLP architectures enhances interpretability of models learned and accuracy of predictive outputs. Through the inclusion of statistical analysis into the design of the neural network, the probability of communication links in user data becomes readily quantifiable and understandable. Using multilayer perceptrons here is a testament to their flexibility in not only processing language but also making information exchange possible, thus proving more beneficial in the evolving context of natural language processing, as quoted in Martín et al. (2018).

4.4.3. Role in Financial Forecasting

The use of Multilayer Perceptrons (MLPs) in financial forecasting has altered the manner in which the financial analyst reads data and makes choices. Economic models have conventionally employed linear relationships that cannot cope with the complex, non-linear relationships found in the data used in finance. MLPs, however, exploit a layered architecture that enables them to discover multi-dimensional representations of inputs and thus identify sophisticated patterns that may slip the conventional model. This versatility towards multiple input properties enables MLPs to provide robust predictions, and that is why they are particularly valuable for situations of uncertainty and volatility. As financial markets are influenced by nonlinear, non-stationary, and oscillatory phenomena, the capability of MLPs to better represent such dynamics is a key asset in creating better predictive models of market trends and asset prices, as highlighted in current research on financial time series analysis (Versace et al., 2009). Furthermore, the ability of MLPs to predict finances is pointed out by their application in assessing whether economic indicators are sustainable, for example, a nation's current account deficit.

Figure 4.10. *Financial forecasting.*

Source: https://www.charcap.com/wp-content/smush-webp/2023/09/financial-forecasting-why-important-business.jpg.webp.

In neural network researches, it has been established that MLPs can efficiently examine the sustainability of seemingly unfavorable economic indicators, thereby offering a new aspect of financial fitness. For instance, although there are sizeable reported current account deficits in the Greek case, MLPs have shown that such deficits can be sustainable, reflective of the dynamics of structure at work below rather than simply the deficit size per se (Andreou et al., 2025). This not only shows the applicability of MLPs in real-world contexts to break down complex economic signals but also hints at their capacity for bridging discrepancies amongst current methods. In addition, MLPs amplify financial prediction by making it possible to include varied types of variables, thereby allowing for a thorough examination of a wide range of influencing variables. This feature makes it possible to incorporate macroeconomic signs, market sentiment, and past performance data into the predictive model, building a complete picture of probable future trends. Financial analysts using MLPs are therefore able to customize their strategies according to finer insights based on complex datasets. As these neural networks expand, their ability to process vast quantities of previous and current data will only improve ever more precise forecasting, thereby equipping decision-makers with the means to better navigate the complexities of the financial arena. Further research into the capabilities of MLPs in this arena is necessary for fostering financial predictive power and expanding market understanding (Figure 4.10).

4.5.ADVANTAGESOFMULTILAYERPERCEPTRONS (MLPS)

Multilayer perceptrons are very popular in the field of neural networks due to their robust ability to model complicated, non-linear interactions. The design of MLPs, with numerous layers of connected nodes, allows the network to identify complicated patterns that other models might overlook. Each layer operates hierarchically, transforming input data into abstract features that progressively extract high-level features. This stack processing is particularly helpful in applications such as speech and image recognition, whereby data encompasses high-dimensional characteristics. The capability of MLPs to map input to output through activation functions utilized within layers enables them to work better in scenarios requiring high-level understanding and interpretation of data. Multilayer perceptrons' other true strength lies in that they have flexibility for usage across applications within fields. MLPs can be effectively applied to regression problems, classification, as well as to time series forecasting, demonstrating their suitability. In financial forecasting, for example, MLPs have been very effective in detecting complex market processes. Immune-based neural networks, which include MLPs, have been shown to enhance profit gain and attain rapid convergence in prediction tasks with stationary and non-stationary signals, according to research (Al-Jumeily et al., 2025). This versatility not only contributes to MLPs robustness in academic research but also shows its practical applicability in commercial fields such as finance, health, and robotics, where diverse data patterns are prevalent. Moreover, the learning and optimization mechanism of MLPs further reveals its capabilities, particularly in creating accurate predictive models. Backpropagation, one of the most common algorithms for MLP training, allows efficient network weight updates in error rate terms. By this iterative scheme, learning power of models is enhanced and overfitting decreased by techniques such as regularization. MLPs also possess the generalization capability, which assists them in classification on unseen data, an important component in guaranteeing any predicting performance (Biehl et al., 1997). As machine learning and artificial intelligence continue to transform numerous industries, the benefits of multilayer perceptrons render them a fundamental tool for researchers and practitioners looking to maximize data-driven insights effectively.

4.5.1. Ability to Model Complex Relationships

The capacity of multilayer perceptrons (MLPs) to model complicated relationships lies in the structure of MLPs, which is characterized by several layers of neurons that are inter-connected. Every neuron calculates the weighted sum of its inputs and then executes a non-linear activation function. This renders MLPs able to model arbitrary data patterns. This design enables the networks to model complex mappings from inputs to outputs and accommodates a large spectrum of tasks, including classification and regression. Further, when the datasets grow larger and more complicated, the adaptability of MLPs becomes increasingly crucial. They can scale with inherent relationships in disparate data types such as image recognition or natural language, thereby increasing their predictive ability. This capability is also aided by advances in training procedures such as backpropagation and regularization mechanisms that together enhance the MLPs performance over a broad spectrum of applications. Under vision-language comprehension, MLPs demonstrate their potential in modeling high-level relations through engaging in innovative approaches that integrate various sources of information. For example, the evolution of visual question answering (VQA) opens up the question of how MLPs can learn from deep human-labeled data, and therefore enable the network to understand and respond to high-level questions related to visual information. The COCO dataset showcases this harmony by relating different annotations representing different perceptions of a single scene. MLPs with attention features and visual question and segmentation answer link training offer state-of-the-art VQA performance by using these relations in an efficient manner. This interaction not only enhances the performance of particular tasks but also offers new avenues for research, underscoring the MLPs capacity to identify complicated, multi-dimensional relationships in dense datasets, as evident from recent studies (Gan et al., 2017). Further, analysis of financial time series using MLPs showcases their capacity to recognize dynamic and complex relationships found in economic data. Regressive and traditional econometric models are often insufficient to account for the turbulent and non-linear nature of financial markets. MLPs, inspired by biological neural networks, however, offer a robust alternative as they effectively go through the complexity of variables with time dependence. Oscillatory structures as well as interactions among variables making up market dynamics can be modeled by them, thus yielding better forecasts. The ability to access financial data non-stationarity and noise positions MLPs as effective tools for researchers and analysts. By comparing MLP to traditional regression methods, one appreciates the flexibility and added modeling power of neural networks, establishing them as effective tools to model complex relationships (Versace et al., 2009).

4.5.2. Flexibility in Architecture Design

The flexibility in design is the ability to accommodate changing needs and technological advancements. Likewise, since neural networks, especially multilayer perceptrons (MLPs), have the dynamic power to learn from a very diverse range of inputs, architecture must evolve to suit changing society and environmental conditions. MLPs, in their nested and sophisticated computable model, are a metaphor for flexible architectural designs that can be readily extended with new functions. Flexibility is necessary because modern buildings are being asked to be multifunctional at the same time and respond in a timely manner to user demands, fostering in them an analogy with the way MLPs update weights and biases during training to optimize performance. Finally, flexibility in building design promotes innovation, allowing designers to create spaces that not only meet today's demands but also remain resilient against future demographic and use changes. Flexible design promotes sustainability too. A flexible building can be repurposed or redesigned, reducing the need for new buildings and mitigating environmental footprint. This idea embodies the way in which MLPs can redirect learning processes to concentrate on certain patterns of data and demote others, promoting effectiveness and engagement in neural network learning. As cities get populated and the necessity of resource conservation grows, architects must draw on the same level of creativity seen in the methods of neural networks. By being flexible, architects can create solutions that do not just comply with current building styles and codes but also compensate for challenges in the future, similar to how neural networks constantly update to achieve maximum predicting capabilities. This holistic design serves to preserve nature and society in the long term. Furthermore, the interplay between technology and architecture also offers deeper understanding of why flexibility is essential. The implementation of complicated models in

MLPs, as in literature, reflects the stunning advances in computational design that promote adaptive systems in both fields. Through the implementation of architectures that deploy complicated algorithms, such as those developed in neural networks, architects are able to create buildings that respond in real-time to environmental factors and users' needs, similar to how MLPs learn and process information. The application of flexibility in design does not only provide added functionality but also provides a smoother connection between humans and their environment. This union of artificial intelligence and architectural progress is exemplary of the manner in which the embracement of flexibility can have revolutionary effects, illustrating the relevance of flexible structures to sustained long-term sustainability and usability within the built environment, such as instances of neighboring discussion on flexible architectures that couple fuzzy expert systems with neural networks (Hunter et al., 2000; Ramamoorthy et al., 2025).

4.5.3. Robustness to Noise in Data

Multilayer perceptrons (MLPs) robustness to data noise is an important characteristic rendering them useful for application across a broad spectrum of disciplines. Noise can manifest itself in various forms like measurement errors, outliers, and inherent data variability, which can potentially jeopardize the performance of machine learning algorithms. MLPs, structured in several layers of interconnected neurons, possess an inherent capacity to minimize the effect of such noise through the use of their non-linear activation functions and hierarchical learning properties. This property allows MLPs to generalize from training examples to new situations well, provided their structure is well established and regularized. As can be seen in empirical research, MLPs can produce correct predictions even when training on datasets with heavy noise, demonstrating the strength of MLPs under real-world scenarios such as estimation of electromagnetic duct height in the marine atmospheric boundary layer, where observations might be sparsely sampled and noisy (Earls et al., 2019). Moreover, the architecture of a multilayer perceptron plays an important role in determining how resilient it is too noisy data. With the tuning of hyperparameters such as the number of hidden layers and the number of neurons in each layer, practitioners can optimize an MLP to increase its performance given various noise levels. The universal approximation theorem points toward the expressiveness of MLPs by proposing that they can successfully approximate a wide range of functions even in noisy input environments. This expressive ability is further supported by results showing that functional MLPs yield performance comparable to that of their numerical counterparts, emphasizing that the framework can efficiently handle complex patterns in noisy data (Abraham et al., 2003). The ability to filter relevant patterns while neglecting noise goes a significant distance in operational efficiency of MLPs in their different applications. In practice, the ability of MLPs to work well even amidst data noise is proof of their usability in scenarios involving real-time processing and decision-making. For instance, in environmental monitoring or disease diagnosis, noise contaminates input signals to a severe degree. MLP flexibility through various means of training such as dropout and early stopping makes it remain accurate amidst data anomalies. It has been proved through research that with appropriate training, even noisy and sparse data can make good predictions, thereby expanding the uses of MLPs in dynamic environments. This feature makes them more desirable not only in research but also in industrial use where precision and reliability are crucial. In general, the robustness of MLPs to noisy data is an indication of their effectiveness as a versatile machine learning tool (Earls et al., 2019).

4.6. LIMITATIONSOFMULTILAYERPERCEPTRONS (MLPS)

The shortcomings of MLP in neural networks are numerous, impacting their efficiency in various uses. That they are prone to overfitting is one of the largest shortcomings, particularly when the model complexity is more than the inherent patterns within the data. Overfitting occurs when an MLP is learned to learn the noise in the training data instead of relevant features, leading to poor generalization when seen with new data. This situation is especially aggravated when there is high-dimensional space where the quantity of data necessary to train the model well is unrealistically large. Consequently, practitioners would find it difficult to balance model performance with complexity, and MLPs would be less appropriate for datasets having limited size or representational diversity. The other disadvantage is based on training time and computational resources required by MLPs. Backpropagation is an algorithm used for weight updates in the network, and it could be very slow, especially for deeper models. Converging to a proper solution generally requires numerous iterations, adding to the complexity of training. Such increased computational requirement can make MLPs less practical for real-time processing when efficiency and speed are critical. Apart from that, MLP performance can also be influenced by hyperparameter tuning, which requires more time and experience. Addressing these training and resource constraints is paramount to optimization of MLP utility, particularly within high-speed technology environments where speed of deployment is imperative. Furthermore, MLPs have been faulted as non-interpretable, a drawback that makes it difficult in applications such as medicine and finance where model decision understanding is paramount. Unlike simpler models, MLPs are "black boxes," rendering their reasoning behind outcomes untransparent. This transparency can hinder trust among stakeholders and complicate regulatory compliance, especially for domains in which decision transparency is necessary. The interpretability problem is compounded by the interaction of non-linear activation functions, which are able to produce surprising outputs. Even sophisticated algorithms struggle with stability and variability issues in studies evaluating gene regulatory networks, which emphasizes the necessity for robustness in interpretation. As such, further developing the interpretability of MLPs continues to be a prime objective for researchers and practitioners working to enhance their usability in various industries (Barabasi et al., 2010; Turing et al., 2012).

4.6.1. Overfitting and Underfitting Issues

Multilayer perceptron (MLP) performance is frequently impaired by the twin problems of overfitting and underfitting, both of which are caused by the complexity of the model compared to training data. Overfitting is a condition where a model learns to recognize noise as well as the true patterns within the training set and, in the process, results in high training accuracy but low generalizability on new information. It is extremely common in MLPs since they contain numerous layers and parameters by which they are able to fit intricate functions and end up with a highly specialized model. Techniques such as regularization, dropout, or cross-validation are generally employed to avoid this risk by simplifying the model enough yet maintaining it balanced in terms of bias and variance so that it functions accurately on fresh data. Underfitting is when a model is so basic that it cannot learn the underlying pattern of the data and does not do well during training as well as testing phases. In the case of MLPs, it can happen if the network structure is not deep enough or when training time is insufficient. When an MLP underfits, its predictions are poor, and learning as a whole is not able to take advantage of the rich relationships that might exist in the data. Therefore, the models complexity adjustment is crucial; the form must be selected carefully to balance to learn as much as one can without falling victim to either issue, since a model that constantly underfits cannot generate useful results for practitioners in domains that utilize neural networks extensively. Overfitting and underfitting must be addressed on several fronts, particularly when handling complicated real-world problems with MLPs. Careful design of network architecture with layers and neurons based on data complexity is essential. For instance, although the representation of nonlinear relationships is well facilitated by multilayer perceptrons, hyperparameter adjustment of learning rate and batch size becomes an essential issue in solving these problems. Moreover, using techniques like early stopping, it is possible to observe the training process so that practitioners can prevent overfitting by stopping the training before the model has become too complex. In practice, as in applications such as algorithms comparing MLP and CNN classifiers for environmental monitoring use, understanding and application of these principles can lead to incredible model reliability and accuracy boosts (Castañeda et al., 2017; López et al., 2019) (Figure 4.11).

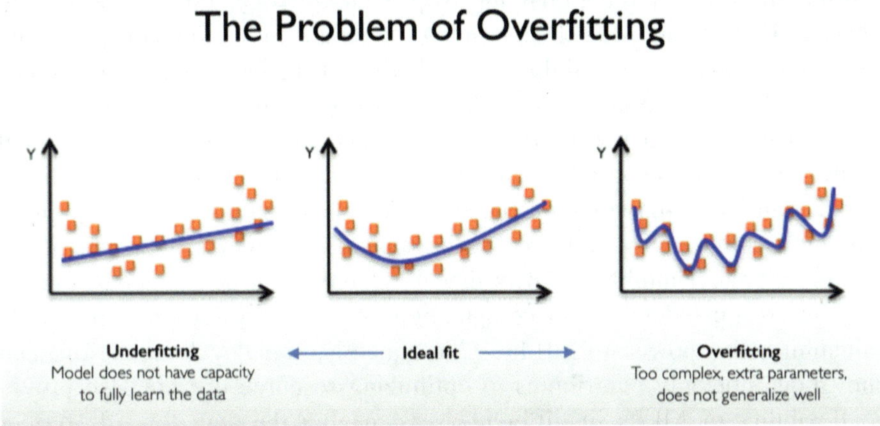

Figure 4.11. *Depicting underfitting, ideal fit, and overfitting in neural network training.*

Source: https://aiml.com/wp-content/uploads/2023/10/problem-of-overfitting_nn_mit.png.

4.6.2. Computational Cost and Resource Requirements

Computational costs of Multilayer Perceptrons (MLPs) are heavy burdens that define both their feasibility and performance in various applications. MLPs rely upon a series of mathematical operations, mainly matrix multiplications and activations, that grow to be time- and energy-consuming as the complexity of the network increases. For instance, with the number of layers and neurons on the rise, the operational demands are multiplied exponentially, resulting in increased computational burden. This excessive burden on computation often necessitates the use of specialized hardware in order to make real-time processing possible or reduce latency, particularly in applications such as image recognition or natural language processing where models have to live off large datasets. As such, learning and optimizing the computational cost of MLPs is crucial to effective deployment in low-resource settings. Resource requirements of MLPs extend beyond raw computation costs to memory utilization and energy usage as well. Overall, storage requirements for training data, parameters of the model, and calculations in between may prove to be a strain on available resources, especially in using MLPs on embedded systems or FPGA boards. Such systems as outlined in Sharma et al. (2007) demonstrate how to optimize hardware implementations of MLPs in optimizing precision vs. resource usage. Efficient usage of resources decreases operation costs while ensuring the models functional integrity. Consequently, ongoing efforts to enhance MLP structures, such as pruning the redundant neurons or quantizing the weights, enhance the viability of employing MLPs in practical applications at negligible resource costs. In addition, emerging advances, such as those presented in Mart'in et al. (2020), place focus on methods to trim computational overhead through innovative architectures like ThumbNet. This approach has a direct solution to the voracious needs of deep learning models by exploiting techniques compressing and accelerating neural networks using input image transformations. ThumbNet shows that the deployment of thumbnail images suggests drastic reductions in computation and memory requirements while maintaining the power of MLPs. Consequently, the development of such innovations not only contributes to optimizing resource use but also proves the flexibility of MLPs in different areas, paving the way towards further applications in more resource-constrained applications. Basically, integrating such innovations in today's MLP progress could greatly enhance their practicality and effectiveness for real-world applications.

4.6.3. Challenges with Large Datasets

Large sets of data pose significant issues for training and applying Multilayer Perceptrons (MLP) in neural networks. One significant concern is the computational expense entailed in dealing with large datasets. With increasing sets of data, training times for MLPs to achieve the optimal weights increase exponentially. These extended training periods pose the potential risk of inefficiencies during resource usage and model construction stages. Additionally, as data dimensionality increases, there is a higher likelihood of overfitting, resulting in models that will perform well on the training data but fail to generalize to new instances. Therefore, data quality and quantity management strategies must then be ironed out by the researchers to validate the integrity of the training process, which remains a central problem with the use of MLPs (Burger et al., 2012). The other significant issue associated with big datasets is the need for effective data preprocessing techniques, which are crucial to enhance the performance and effectiveness of MLPs. Data preprocessing typically entails reducing dimensions to lower the computational burden so that the model can handle big datasets more effectively. Poor handling of data, such as the insertion of missing values at this point, has an adverse impact on model performance.

PWLA work is an excellent illustration of a new remedy for such challenges through the integration of normalization, dimension reduction, and pre-training. By way of preprocessing in the form of producing standardized input values before applying them to the MLP, PWLA enhances the effectiveness of the learning process overall. Preprocessing measures of this nature are important in augmenting the ability of MLPs while mitigating the character of the challenges posed by big data (Asadi et al., 2009). Moreover, the inherent noisy complexity of noise within big data adds to the problem of training MLPs. Noisy data has the ability to mask the underlying patterns that the MLP is intended to learn from, leading to suboptimal performance and increased training time. Recent advancements in image denoising using the employment of MLPs demonstrate the potential of such networks to be greater than the traditional methods if trained from vast image databases. Techniques such as the combination of block-matching algorithms with MLP have shown promising performance in the image denoising task of improving the signal-to-noise ratio of photographic data. The performance of such techniques is, nevertheless, greatly reliant on the adequate modeling of noise models and related variations. Therefore, employing MLPs for learning mappings between noisy input and cleaner output encompasses both the advantage and the limitation in employing the networks to their full potential when they are dealing with large datasets (Burger et al., 2012).

SUMMARY

In conclusion of this research on MLPs, there is proof that it has great potential in transforming various disciplines through its capacity to model intricate functions. MLPs, as a basis for the majority of neural network models, utilize their layered structure to learn exceptionally well from large quantities of input data. Their ability to discern complex patterns within data sets has enormous implications for application in everything from visual recognition to financial prediction. However, good usage of MLPs depends on good training methodologies as well as tunability of the parameters of MLPs, who in turn have control over the predictive strength and generalizability of the networks. Therefore, the scenario of MLPs is not just optimized to be used but also acts as a pointer towards further development in the field of neural networks. Also, a systematic investigation of the dynamics in MLPs acts to bring forth the fine balance needed for training such models. Evidence indicates that the identification of invariant sets of weights, as noted by Ho et al. (2010), is essential in improving the learning process. Through the description of the weights, it is possible to evaluate the dynamic range of the perceptrons performance and thus ensure that the training algorithms yield stable and reliable results.

In addition, comprehension of conditions for the injective property of weight dynamics can have profound effects on the overall performance of MLPs. In the absence of these analytical schemes, the potential for overfitting or underfitting problems arises, which can compromise the prediction power of models. Finally, the relevance of MLPs goes beyond abstract concepts, demonstrating their potential applications in real-world contexts. The synthesis of sensitivity analysis and neural networks offers opportunities for greater predictability in fields such as the prediction of surviving trauma, as discussed in Hunter et al. (2000). This link demonstrates the ability of MLPs not only to be useful in academic research but also to introduce tangible improvements in essential areas such as health and emergency systems. As the knowledge of MLPs is further understood, it is crucial to keep investigating their uses and limitations to open the door for developments that take full advantage of neural network technologies in solving intricate problems across many fields.

The investigation of MLPs points to a number of important issues that indicate its importance in the field of artificial intelligence and machine learning. Behind the MLP architecture is the layer principle of neurons, typically an input layer, one or more hidden layers, and a layer of outputs. This layered design allows for complex data transformation, so MLPs are well adapted to pattern classification and recognition tasks. Moreover, activation functions such as sigmoid or ReLU introduce non-linearity within the network so that MLPs can model intricate relationships between sets of data. Thereafter, MLPs have been used in a wide range of applications including image and speech recognition, which demonstrates their ability to handle various sources of information as well as learning computations in an efficient manner. Another core characteristic of MLPs is their process of learning, which is predominantly managed by the backpropagation algorithm. The feedback mechanism facilitates the weight adjustment within the network in terms of error in prediction. As the error is reduced by gradient descent, MLPs gain precision with time. Further, the ability to train MLPs on large sets of data has been facilitated by advancements in computing and the availability of hardware such as Graphics Processing Units (GPUs). Thus, currently, MLPs can be applied to more advanced tasks, which lead to improved machine learning models that not only perform well on training data but also generalize efficiently to new data. These developments emphasize the evolving function of MLPs in the landscape of AI technology. Finally, the collaboration potential of MLPs in robot systems is an intriguing research and application frontier. Based on a number of studies, integrating MLPs into robot control systems can facilitate coordinated behavior by many robots working towards a common goal. This approach enables robot units to collaborate in a process of following each other and share workload and thereby overcome limitations that come with one-robot operation, such as load capacity restrictions. The MLPs' unique capability of responding effectively to complicated decision-making processes enables them to be a useful asset in robotics, where systems guided by MLP can optimize the carrying out of tasks and facilitate the collaboration of robots to enhance effectiveness and functionality in varying working environments (Mansour et al., 2011). The meeting of MLPs with robotics is illustrative of the wider implications of neural networks on shifting operational paradigms in various fields.

REFERENCES

1. Abadi, M., Allamanis, M., Elish, K. O., Kim, Y., Kremenek, T., et al. (2018). Neural-augmented static analysis of Android communication. http://arxiv.org/abs/1809.04059 (accessed on 25th September 2025).
2. Abadi, M., Han, S., He, Y., Hinton, G. E., Ioffe, S., Li, Y., Luo, J. H., et al. (2020). ThumbNet: One thumbnail image contains all you need for recognition. http://arxiv.org/abs/1904.05034 (accessed on 25th September 2025).
3. Abraham, A., Besse, P., Breiman, L., et al. (2003). Functional multi-layer perceptron: A nonlinear tool for functional data analysis. https://core.ac.uk/download/50360245.pdf (accessed on 25th September 2025).
4. Addison, J. F. D., Bass, J., Hunter, A., et al. (2000). A neural network version of the measure correlate predict algorithm for estimating wind energy yield. https://core.ac.uk/download/53912.pdf (accessed on 25th September 2025).
5. Al-Jumeily, D., & Hussain, A. (2025). The performance of immune based neural network with financial time series prediction. https://core.ac.uk/download/42477499.pdf (accessed on 25th September 2025).
6. Andreou, A. S., Stylianou, C., & Zombanakis, G. A. (2025). The Greek current account deficit: Is it sustainable after all? https://core.ac.uk/download/pdf/6505283.pdf (accessed on 25th September 2025).
7. Asadi, R., Mustapha, N., & Sulaiman, N. (2009). Training process reduction based on potential weights linear analysis to accelerate back propagation network. https://core.ac.uk/download/153801401.pdf (accessed on 25th September 2025).
8. Bader, S., Hitzler, P., & Hoelldobler, S. (2004). The integration of connectionism and first-order knowledge representation and reasoning as a challenge for artificial intelligence. https://core.ac.uk/download/36748820.pdf (accessed on 25th September 2025).
9. Barabasi, A., Baralla, A., Braunstein, A., Krishnan, A., Margolin, A., Di Camillo, B., et al. (2010). Reverse engineering gene networks with ANN: Variability in network inference algorithms. https://core.ac.uk/download/pdf/8662758.pdf (accessed on 25th September 2025).
10. Barron, A. R., Brumback, B. A., Conan-Guez, B., Abraham, C., Hoover, D. R., Ferraty, F., Rossi, F., et al. (2006). Theoretical properties of projection based multilayer perceptron's with functional inputs. https://core.ac.uk/download/50459392.pdf (accessed on 25th September 2025).
11. Biehl, M., Opper, M., Kinzel, W., & Yeomans, J. (1997). Phase transitions of neural networks. http://arxiv.org/abs/cond-mat/9704098 (accessed on 25th September 2025).

12. Burger, H. C., Harmeling, S., & Schuler, C. J. (2012). Image denoising with multi-layer perceptrons, part 1: Comparison with existing algorithms and with bounds. http://arxiv.org/abs/1211.1544 (accessed on 25th September 2025).

13. Chicaiza, J., García, J., López, J., et al. (2008). Study of the application of neural networks in Internet traffic engineering. https://core.ac.uk/download/62659012.pdf (accessed on 25th September 2025).

14. Earls, C. J., & Sit, H. (2019). Characterizing evaporation ducts within the marine atmospheric boundary layer using artificial neural networks. http://arxiv.org/abs/1903.03010 (accessed on 25th September 2025).

15. Gan, C., Gong, B., Li, H., et al. (2017). VQS: Linking segmentations to questions and answers for supervised attention in VQA and question-focused semantic segmentation. http://arxiv.org/abs/1708.04686 (accessed on 25th September 2025).

16. Grzes, M., & Shannon, J. (2018). Reinforcement learning using augmented neural networks. http://arxiv.org/abs/1806.07692 (accessed on 25th September 2025).

17. Ho, C. Y. F., IU, H. H. C., & Ling, B. W. K. (2010). Invariant set of weight of perceptron trained by perceptron training algorithm. https://core.ac.uk/download/54225.pdf (accessed on 25th September 2025).

18. Hunter, A., Champion, G., Gedeon, T., Hannan, M., Ferguson, I., Jain, R., Henry, J., et al. (2000). Application of neural networks and sensitivity analysis to improved prediction of trauma survival. https://core.ac.uk/download/1644813.pdf (accessed on 25th September 2025).

19. Iqbal, R. A. (2011). Using feature weights to improve performance of neural networks. https://core.ac.uk/download/pdf/14876.pdf (accessed on 25th September 2025).

20. Kanter, I., & Kinzel, W. (2002). Interacting neural networks and cryptography. http://arxiv.org/abs/cond-mat/0203011 (accessed on 25th September 2025).

21. López, R. (2019). Flood: An open-source neural networks C++ library. https://core.ac.uk/download/pdf/296535037.pdf (accessed on 25th September 2025).

22. Mansour, S. F. (2011). Corporation robots. https://core.ac.uk/download/12007787.pdf (accessed on 25th September 2025).

23. Medina Castañeda, E. E. (2017). Deep CNN and MLP-based vision systems for algae detection in automatic inspection of underwater pipelines. https://core.ac.uk/download/295394937.pdf (accessed on 25th September 2025).

24. Park, H., Cardoso, J. F., & Amari, S. I. (2017). A neural network model with bidirectional whitening. http://arxiv.org/abs/1704.07147 (accessed on 25th September 2025).
25. Ramamoorthy, P. A. (2025). A neural network architecture for implementation of expert systems for real time monitoring. https://core.ac.uk/download/pdf/42814708.pdf (accessed on 25th September 2025).
26. Sharma, P. (2007). FPGA implementation of artificial neural networks. https://core.ac.uk/download/53188814.pdf (accessed on 25th September 2025).
27. Turing, A. M., Bhattacharjee, D., Zadeh, L. A., Sugeno, M., Kohonen, T., Balas, V. E., & McCullock, W. (2012). Examples of artificial perceptions in optical character recognition and iris recognition. http://arxiv.org/abs/1209.6195 (accessed on 25th September 2025).
28. Versace, M., & Wong, C. (2009). Modeling financial time series with artificial neural networks. https://open.bu.edu/bitstream/2144/1976/1/TR-09-012.pdf (accessed on 25th September 2025).

CHAPTER 5

TRAINING AND OPTIMIZATION

Contents

INTRODUCTION

The area of neural networks has witnessed explosive growth, driven by advances in machine learning and artificial intelligence. With deeper computational resources, scientists and practitioners have been able to develop increasingly powerful models with the ability to conduct complex tasks across various fields. Training and optimization are central elements in applying these neural networks and influence their efficiency, performance, and accuracy. With so many model training methodologies, from supervised to unsupervised paradigms of learning, the intricacies of optimization lie at the heart of achieving intended outcomes. Thus, understanding the paradigms of optimization and training may provide insight into state-of-the-art neural network models utilized. Problems inherent in neural network training present very challenging obstacles for effective performance. For example, issues such as overfitting, underfitting, and convergence stability always confront researchers and developers.

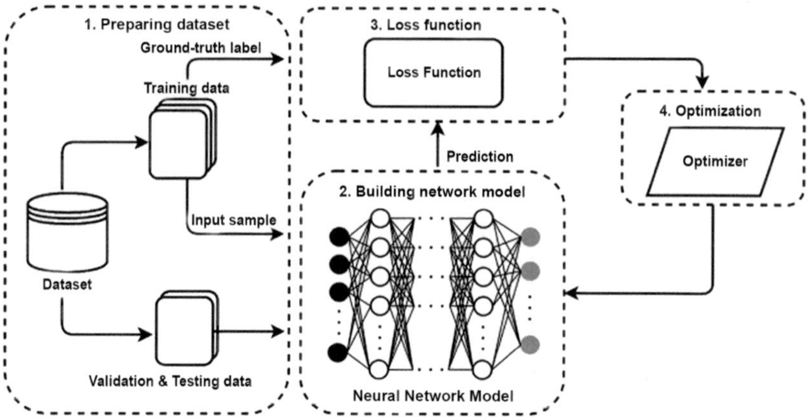

Figure 5.1. *Schematic diagram of the neural network training procedure.*

Source: https://ars.els-cdn.com/content/image/3-s2.0-B9780323901987000069-f02-04-9780323901987.jpg.

These need to be explored using many techniques, for example, architectural modifications and coming up with novel optimization algorithms. Techniques for overcoming these difficulties normally involve adjusting network structure or changing the way in which gradients are computed during training. In particular, successful implementations of neural networks in certain applications, e.g., particle accelerator control systems, point to the necessity for design optimization. A solution designed specifically to manage RF electron gun resonance controls at Fermilab is characteristic of how specially designed neural network applications can streamline control procedures with favorable results demonstrating the correlation between fidelity of training and operation efficiency (Biedron et al., 2016). In addition to structural minimization, the advent of advanced generative models like Generative Adversarial Networks (GANs) has transformed data generation in neural networks and distribution modeling in high dimensions. Training GANs is plagued by issues of mode collapse and convergence instability. Overcoming these necessitates innovative approaches to network design, objective function definition, and algorithm selection. The existing research puts stress on a broad spectrum of solutions that aim to improve GAN training protocols towards more stable outcomes across different applications such as image and audio synthesis (Cao et al., 2020). By categorizing innovation into these paradigms, researchers can explain significant issues while proposing a novel taxonomy of solutions that create doors for future breakthroughs and success in neural network optimization (Figure 5.1).

Definition of Neural Networks

The concept of neural networks is rooted in the biological process of the human brain, where neurons are interconnected and they communicate to process information. For artificial intelligence, the neural network is a computational structure that aims to simulate this biological setup. In effect, the networks consist of stacks of nodes, or artificial neurons, which have been coded to identify patterns and make decisions on the basis of input information. Through a mechanism known as training, the weights given to the connections between the nodes are adjusted to minimize errors in forecasting or classification. This paradigmatic approach allows neural networks to find complex patterns in massive datasets, and they are consequently priceless in many applications ranging from image perception to natural language processing. Multiple algorithms, including backpropagation, have to be used for training neural networks, such as modifying the weights in accordance with errors. One of the primary aspects of this learning process involves minimizing the loss function, which measures the difference between the prediction output and the actual target value. Additionally, neural network optimization may involve techniques like dropout or regularization in order to prevent overfitting, thereby enhancing the network's generalization performance on novel data. As is evident in the description of adversarial input generation, the robustness of the neural networks is of the utmost importance; slight perturbations in the input can lead to severe errors in the output, displaying the necessity for rigorous training and optimization procedures (Dreossi et al., 2019). Recent advances in neural networks broaden their scope of use across scientific fields, showcasing their versatility as well as robustness. For instance, in control systems of particle accelerators, researchers have explored the utilization of neural networks to enhance efficiency in operation and optimize system performance. By utilizing methods of neural networks, as shown using the example of RF electron gun at Fermilab, control systems may adapt to evolving operational conditions more effectively (Biedron et al., 2016). This latest trend not just emphasizes the concept of neural networks as robust tools for pattern recognition but also depicts their capability in practical real-life intricate scenarios. Ultimately, the ongoing improvement in training and optimization techniques is crucial for realizing the utmost potential of neural networks in every discipline (Figure 5.2).

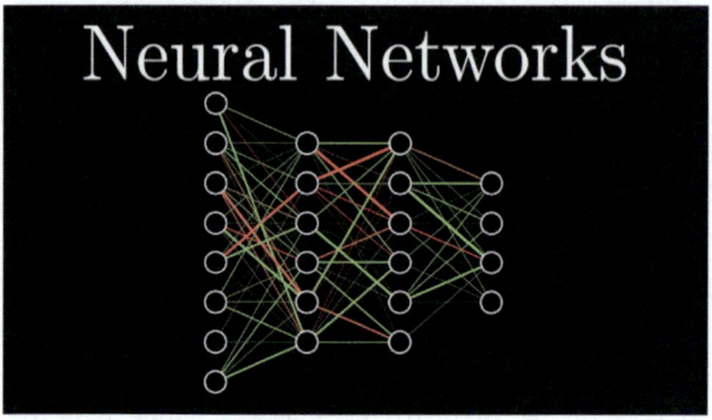

Figure 5.2. *Understanding neural networks.*

Source: https://i9.ytimg.com/s_p/PLZHQObOWTQDNU6R1_67000Dx_ZCJB-3pi/landscape_sddefault.jpg?sqp=CJznlcUGir7X7AMICNGyiNsFEAE=&rs=AOn4CLAtAbGbPYfillabY9-bj_mK8dPLMQ&v=1533155665.

Importance of Training and Optimization

The robustness of neural networks primarily relies on the efficacy of train and optimize processes. Neural network training is a procedure that entails connection weight adjustments from data input, thereby influencing the performance of models. Bat algorithm is one of the techniques that are gaining popularity as it enhances the conventional back-propagation method. This meta-heuristic also helps in resolving the local minima issue as well as improving the convergence rate of the training algorithm. It has been established by recent studies that integrating the Bat algorithm with the back-propagation neural network (BPNN) greatly improves models learning efficiency significantly, with improved time performance as well as solution quality compared to traditional methods. These advances remind us once again of the need to use new optimization techniques in order to improve the overall performance of the neural networks and enable their effective deployment into complex tasks (Hafifi et al., 2016). Optimization in neural networks is not just about improvement in performance metrics; it also requires important theoretical supports. Recent research on loss regularizations, like local entropy and heat regularization, indicates new optimization strategies that provide both efficiency and interpretability. Such approaches leverage a two-step process that reduces reliance on standards on gradients and instead uses sampling algorithms. Such paradigm shift allows for a non-gradient-required training procedure and is additionally parallelizable, supporting more stable learning under conditions that change. By optimizing optimization, practitioners are able to gain a deeper sense of network functioning while also optimizing computational effectiveness. This theoretical advancement is important as it paves the way for innovation in future training methodologies of neural networks (Kaplan et al., 2019). In addition to improving theoretical models, neural network optimization is behind major advancements in application in real-world settings. Healthcare, finance, and autonomous vehicles rely on the reliability of neural networks to handle enormous databases and deliver actionable data. As datasets grow more complex, training requirements that not only enhance algorithmic performance but also ensure robustness towards outliers and adversarial samples have never been more of an issue. Hence, it is crucial to spend on sophisticated optimization techniques for building stable models with the potential to generalize well in real-world applications. Completely understanding and applying hard training and optimization methods is required to push the boundaries of what neural networks are capable of, thus proving their relevance in contemporary technology (Hafifi et al., 2016; Kaplan et al., 2019).

5.1. THE TRAINING PROCESS

The process of training neural networks is a fundamental step that determines the effectiveness and performance of these models in learning from data. It takes a series of crucial steps, beginning with the generation of training datasets that should be large and representative of the underlying patterns. The process has a direct contribution to the generalizability of a neural network to new instances. During training, the network is tweaked where the weights are adjusted using algorithms such as backpropagation so that the model minimizes the gap between predictions and actuality. This feedback loop process tends to involve delicate tuning of hyperparameters, including learning rates and batch sizes, whose adjustment has a great impact on convergence rates and the overall performance of the model. Additionally, the integration of neural networks in complicated systems, such as controls for particle accelerators, illustrates the need to optimize the training process. Emerging discoveries have unveiled the potentials for the successful integration of neural networks into such sophisticated applications, according to recent research (Biedron et al., 2016). The success of a neural network control system implementation at the Fermilab Accelerator Science and Technology center indicates the adaptability of such models in expert environments. These tasks not only demonstrate the ability of neural networks to manage real-time feedback but also emphasize the significance of rigorous training protocols designed to instill dependability and accuracy in high-risk operating situations, ultimately resulting in better system performance. In addition, some networks like Generative Adversarial Networks (GANs) have special difficulties while training, which emphasize the significance of tailored optimization regimes. Issues such as mode collapse and instability can arise because of badly designed architectures or inappropriate objective functions, making the training process problematic (Cao et al., 2020). Issues like these can be mitigated by embracing deep knowledge of optimum design principles and new training methods. In recent surveys, future research directions have been envisioned to promote GAN training for improved stability and convergence (Cao et al., 2020). Through step-by-step resolution of these challenges, the research community can maximize training protocols so that enhancements will extend the scope of applicability and the efficacy of GANs in a broad range of areas (Figure 5.3).

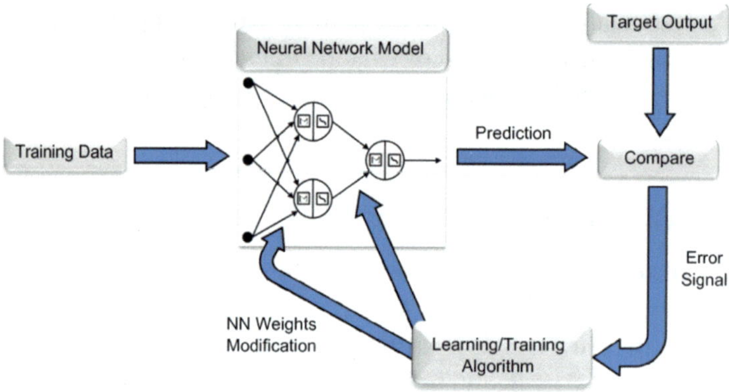

Figure 5.3. *The representation of neural network training process.*

Source: https://www.researchgate.net/profile/Syariful-Shamsudin/publication/299390844/figure/fig5/AS:650029635235894@1531990550259/The-representation-of-neural-network-training-process.png.

5.1.1. Data Preparation and Preprocessing

The efficiency of neural networks relies heavily upon data preparation and preprocessing as fundamental procedures that have direct influences on training outcomes. Inefficient handling of data can lead to learning inefficiencies in the model, which in turn influence performance and accuracy. Some forms of preprocessing, such as normalization and dimensionality reduction, are employed to enhance data quality and make training easier. For instance, normalization maps input features into a scaled format, enabling the model to learn effectively without biased representation for larger values. Additionally, dimensionality reduction algorithms, while helping to minimize computational expense and training time, can also alleviate issues with the curse of dimensionality. All this, as a result of their realization and execution, is crucial for data scientists looking to enhance the performance of neural networks as well as achieve precise observations from high-dimensional data. Advanced preprocessing techniques also emerge in contrast to the challenges posed by traditional methods. One of the novel approaches being debated in the literature is Potential Weight Linear Analysis (PWLA), which incorporates normalization, dimensionality reduction, and pre-training. This method attempts to generate normalized input values in anticipation of efficient training by initializing potential weights before reducing the dimensions of the input matrix. This integrated approach promises to accelerate Back Propagation Networks (BPN) and greatly enhance their accuracy within a single training epoch. Experiments have shown that the application of PWLA could reduce BPNs to Supervised Multi-Layer Feed Forward Neural Networks (SMFFNN), highlighting the significance of newer data preprocessing techniques in overcoming the intricacies of neural network structure and enhancing overall model performance (Asadi et al., 2009). Additionally, implementation of deep learning structures, specifically deep convolutional neural networks (DCNNs), indicates the ongoing advancement in data preprocessing techniques. These networks are capable of handling high-dimensional data and can automatically calculate effective features, far superior to traditional preprocessing techniques. For example, in computational imaging tasks, DCNNs have demonstrated spectacular success in reconstructing high-resolution images from fewer input data than traditional methods, thus signifying the significance of sophisticated preprocessing techniques. As neural networks require humongous amounts of training data, techniques that manage this data economically and preserve its quality come into focus. Successful integration of advanced preprocessing techniques can thus enrich the performance of neural networks in various applications, from imaging to real-time analysis of data up to finally enhancing their predictability and effectiveness (Nehmetallah et al., 2019).

5.1.2. Forward Propagation

Forward propagation is a fundamental process in neural network optimization and training that transforms input data into an output prediction. Within this process, the network processes data sequentially layer by layer and applies learned weights and biases to produce a prediction from features present in the input. The received inputs are given to the input nodes as raw input, which again pass through hidden layers in which different activation functions explore the complexity of the data. The activations help guide the models in learning non-linear patterns, thus allowing the network to approximate complex functions. Hence, proper forward propagation is necessary as it directly affects the accuracy of the predictions created by the neural network and thus ranks as a crucial step in the broader model training process. Besides, forward propagation is not merely a matter of generating outputs but also setting the stage for learning stages that follow, most importantly back-propagation. When the predictions are made, they are normally compared to actual target values by a loss function to quantify the models prediction error. This measurement is very vital as it determines the weights and biases update during the back-propagation phase in a way that minimizes error in later outputs. A well-optimized forward propagation step provides informative gradients to guide the optimization algorithms towards refining the model. As emphasized by recent research, accuracy of forward propagation can be decided by various elements including neural network architecture and type of activation function, highlighting necessity for careful model design consideration (Das et al., 2012). Moreover, studies necessitate enhancing the efficiency of forward propagation using integration strategies such as hybridization with nature-inspired algorithms. For example, artificial bee colony algorithm has been found beneficial in optimizing forward propagation processes through derivative-free solutions that address complex training problems faced by traditional methods. Such advancements not only accelerate the rates of convergence but also set the stage for improved predictive outcomes. Implementing these new techniques in forward propagation models can lead to dramatic improvement in the overall optimization and training of neural networks. Hence, the strategic R&D of forward propagation methods can yield great benefits in a variety of applications, particularly when neural networks are applied to sophisticated tasks (Obaid et al., 2021) (Figure 5.4).

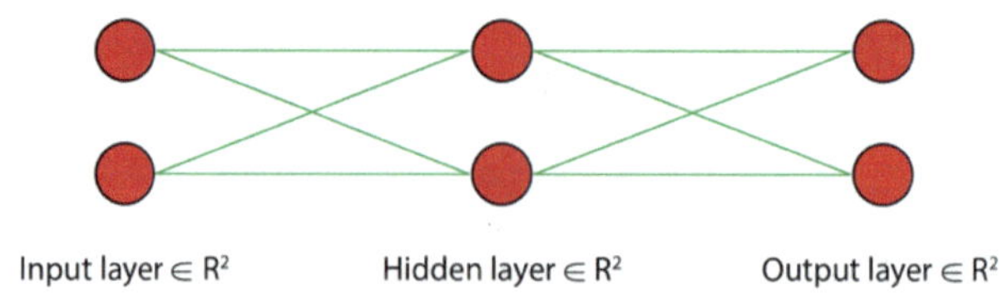

Figure 5.4. *Components of forward propagation.*

Source: https://d1rwhvwstyk9gu.cloudfront.net/2024/06/Components-of-forward-propagation.png.

5.1.3. Backpropagation and Error Calculation

The sophisticated backpropagation mechanism is a cornerstone for the training and optimization of neural networks, allowing for efficient error calculation. This algorithm computes the gradient of the loss function with respect to each weight by the chain rule of calculus. A forward pass through the network first computes the output that's been predicted, then it's compared against the actual output and it generates an error signal. This error is backwards propagated through the network, adjusting the weights such that they're computed to reduce the overall error in future predictions. The backpropagation architecture of the past, while reliable, is limited in application to more complex neural network architectures, such as those that include recurrent interconnections. Recent developments have made error gradient calculation in networks with temporal dynamics possible, enhancing its application in systems identification and control (Pineda et al., 1989). In addition to traditional backpropagation methods, the emergence of automatic differentiation (AD) has revolutionized the error computation paradigm in machine learning. Since backpropagation is sometimes regarded as a special-purpose technique for neural networks, AD provides a more general mechanism for computing derivatives in a more universal programming context. With efficient computation of gradients of numerical functions, AD enables dynamic computation graph construction that describes computation flows adjustively. This flexibility allows machine learning experts to make use of eminent programming for advanced optimization problems, making it unnecessary to code gradient calculations manually. Hence, the integration of AD and backpropagation not only streamlines the computation of errors but also extends the regions of application in areas of computational fluid dynamics and engineering design, and fills gaps that were not previously attended to in machine learning and numerical computing domains (Baydin et al., 2018). As backpropagation and error approximation become better, their integration with current computational algorithms holds potential for future application in neural network training. The positive direction towards adapting dynamic computational graphs mirrors the increasing relevance of automatic differentiation in machine learning applications. As these methods converge, the ability to solve increasingly difficult higher-dimensional and abstract optimization problems comes into view. This integration provides gates to sophisticated models that are able to learn and improve from changing environments, further enhancing the proficiency of artificial intelligence systems. Future research can focus on sharpening these combined methods, examine their impact on computational efficiency, and ultimately give rise to yet more superior neural networks that function optimally across a broad spectrum of applications. Thus, the training of neural networks in the future will be transformed through the relentless enhancement of backpropagation and the merging of automatic differentiation techniques (Baydin et al., 2018; Pineda et al., 1989) (Figure 5.5).

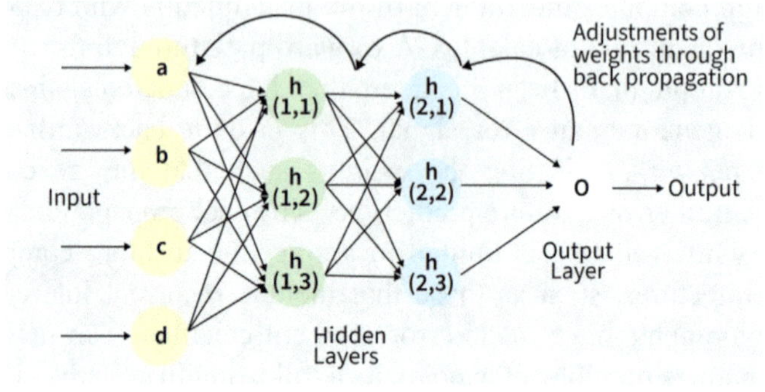

Figure 5.5. *A simple illustration of how the backpropagation works by adjustments of weights.*

Source: https://media.geeksforgeeks.org/wp-content/uploads/2025070 1163824 448467/Backpropagation-in-Neural-Network-1.webp.

5.2. OPTIMIZATION TECHNIQUES

In neural networks, optimization techniques are important for maximizing performance and yielding good results. These techniques significantly adjust the parameters of a neural network to minimize the loss function, the quantity that represents the difference between predicted outputs and true labels. One optimization method commonly employed is stochastic gradient descent (SGD), which adjusts weights in small increments from small batches of data, achieving a good balance between computation speed and rate of convergence. Adding versions of SGD, such as Adam or RMSprop, can also accelerate training by varying learning rates based on past gradients. The exploration-exploitation tradeoff in such methods is critical; it guards against overfitting but also ensures the model converges appropriately toward a global optimum, hence improving the performance of the neural network to generalize unseen data. Apart from traditional methods, advanced optimization techniques are increasingly being used for the optimization of training for neural networks. For instance, practices like dropout, batch normalization, and weight decay include practices that enhance robustness and performance. Dropout randomly disables neurons during training, forcing the network to learn more general patterns and avoid overfitting. Batch normalization also normalizes inputs to each layer, regularizing optimization and accelerating convergence. Regularization methods like weight decay also penalize large weights, promoting better generalization. Each of these techniques contributes large amounts of model performance to stability and flexibility in varied training conditions. Hence, wise use of such advanced techniques illustrates a general approach towards optimal neural network training to yield better predictive capability. Moreover, innovative optimization techniques are being conceived more and more by virtue of the complexity of neural network design and application needs. Techniques such as bootstrap aggregation, where multiple neural network models' predictions are aggregated, have been proven to improve predictive accuracy. This method utilizes resampled training set subsets, creating diverse models whose overall results are improved (Li et al., 2015). Similarly, convolution beamforming techniques have entered the optimization discussion, providing computationally efficient speech enhancement methods best tailored for denoising, dereverberation, and source separation simultaneously (Boeddeker et al., 2020). The creation and deployment of these novel optimization techniques not only show the versatility of neural networks to various domains but also show the ongoing creation of techniques aimed at overcoming traditional limitations in model performance and efficacy (Figure 5.6).

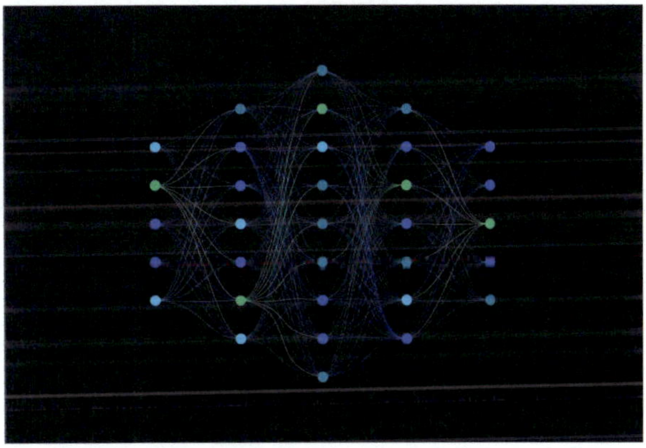

Figure 5.6. *Neural network optimization techniques.*

Source: https://images.prismic.io/codiste-website/a15c8936-b7ce-46b9-9cf3-71829f7aaf85_A+Comprehensive+Guide+on+Neural+Network+Optimization++.webp?auto=compress,format.

5.2.1. Gradient Descent Variants

Gradient descent, a fundamental optimization algorithm, is the backbone for training neural networks. Its basic structure relies on calculating the gradient of the loss function over the model parameters and thereafter iteratively adjusting the parameters in order to minimize the loss. The simple-to-implement gradient descent approach often struggles, however, with high-dimensional spaces and the non-convex functions typical of deep learning. As a counter to these difficulties, numerous extensions of gradient descent have been developed, each designed to further accelerate convergence rates or modify the performance of the fundamental algorithm in reaction to particular limitations. Most relevant are methods like Stochastic Gradient Descent (SGD) and its generalization to incorporate momentum that introduce stochasticity and have the ability to avoid local minima while accelerating convergence with large data sets, thereby improving the efficacy of the training process for high-complexity neural architectures. Except for vanilla gradient descent, advanced versions apply techniques that adjust adaptively the learning rates during training, addressing the instabilities and inefficiencies of standard methods. Of these most known is the Adaptive Normalized Risk-Averting Training (ANRAT), which introduces a novel framework in order to improve the deep neural network training.

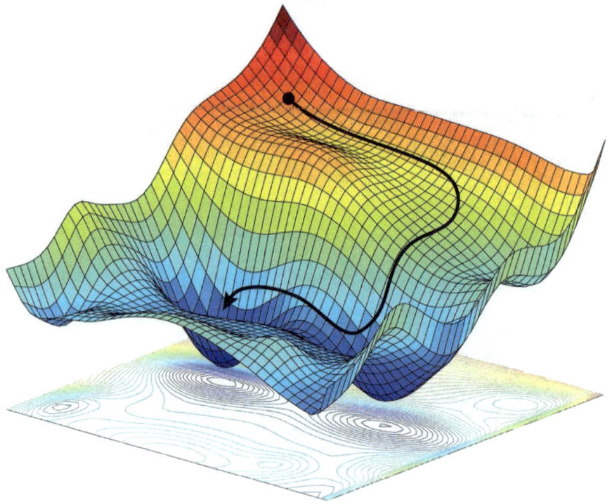

Figure 5.7. *Gradient descent.*

*Source: https://miro.medium.com/v2/resize:fit:4800/format:webp/1 *KTyZVGHy XXMrum-pY8OchQ.jpeg.*

This method specifically solves the non-convex optimization problem that besets most conventional approaches through locally and globally adapting the learning criteria based on convexity indices. ANRAT demonstrates high performance gains on typical datasets like MNIST and CIFAR-10, producing consistently competitive state-of-the-art results without pretraining or advanced auxiliary methods. These advancements are the ongoing progress of gradient descent algorithms toward enhancing the quality and effectiveness of neural network training (Lo et al., 2016). In addition, the inclusion of meta-learning principles in gradient descent variants also presents interesting avenues for future research. Recent advances exist in the guise of algorithms that are based on past gradient behaviors to leverage learning rate landscapes, which allow models to provide correct predictions of optimal scaling of observed gradients. This new approach enhances the capability of gradient-based optimizers to dynamically learn new tasks, significantly speeding up the learning process in batch and online modes. Such techniques are applied particularly in real-time systems such as robotics and adaptive control systems since they exploit previously learned data to direct and improve existing optimization methods. Overall, the development of variants of gradient descent exhibits a direction towards more stable and efficient training mechanisms for neural networks that ensure a boost in speed and performance in vast applications (Kappler et al., 2018) (Figure 5.7).

5.2.2. Learning Rate Adjustments

The concept of learning rate adjustments is a pivotal aspect in training and optimizing neural networks, providing a critical balance between convergence rate and model accuracy. Learning rate, a hyperparameter that controls the magnitude of the weight updates during training, has a significant influence on the path of models in the loss landscape. Set too high, it induces divergence during learning, leading to instability and lack of convergence. A learning rate that is too low, on the other hand, leads to sluggish training times and risk of getting stuck in local minima. The pattern of behavior for this parameter can be regulated through various methods such as learning rate decay, whereby the learning rate is slowly reduced as training progresses, thus enabling more accurate updating in the later phases of learning. This technique helps achieve stronger convergence throughout the process as well as overall performance of the neural network. It can also be implemented through adaptive optimization algorithms like the Adam optimizer, which are able to adjust the learning rate on a parameter basis. This ability is required in handling the varying convergence rates of different features learned by the neural network. By having a subtle sense of the landscape of loss, methods such as Adam leverage the first and second moments of the gradients to guide learning rate updates so that training dynamics stay efficient even in complicated settings. Such updates have been shown to be able to evade the shortcomings of conventional methods for learning rate scheduling by being able to let the model learn progressively about the form of the loss surface during training time. Thus, by combining them with deeper learning architectures such as Convolutional Neural Networks (CNNs), these approaches lead to effective enhancements in classification issues and other applications of neural networks, as noted in the research articles on numerical recognition issues and computer vision applications (Agarwal et al., 2024). Further, the interaction between the learning rate and the network architecture as well as the optimization problem landscape is an intricate problem. Experimental results demonstrate that sharpness of the loss landscape plays a critical role in determining the efficacy of learning rate updates. Analyzing the eigenvalues of the Hessian matrix sheds light on the training dynamics—discerning four distinct phases from the transient early behavior to late stability regimes. This learning rate sensitivity is particularly significant across varying neural network depths and widths and produces an advanced interaction that should be well-tuned (Kalra et al., 2023). Emphasizing the importance of learning rate adjustment, practitioners may employ practices such as cyclical learning rates or warm restarts. By doing so, they can recursively explore different learning rate regimes, finally achieving better training performance and optimal model accuracy in several deep learning applications.

5.2.3. Regularization Methods

Under training and neural network optimization, regularization techniques are essential methods employed to combat overfitting and enhance the model's generalization. As neural networks become more complex, overfitting—the situation in which a model will excel on the training data but will do badly on previously unseen data—is rapidly increased. Regularization methods, including L1 and L2 regularization, add constraints to penalize too complex of models, bringing effectively a balance to the fit vs. generalization trade-off. By adding these penalties, researchers have found that performance is better on a wide range of tasks, bringing to light the importance of regularization in real-world neural network applications. With an evolution of models, the innovative application of such outdated methods is still fundamental towards developing stable machine learning solutions to lead to future empirical enhancements. Additional checks of regularization verify that more advanced techniques such as Adaptive Normalized Risk-Averting Training (ANRAT) are efficient, providing a novel method of addressing non-convex optimization issues prevalent in deep learning. ANRAT achieves this by adaptively modifying the training process based on the gradient of a convexity index to deliver efficiency improvements in training deep neural networks from challenging datasets like MNIST and CIFAR-10. Not only does this method equalize performance with best practices, but it also delivers a theory that confirms its adaptive practice. By validating the experimental significance of ANRAT towards visual recognition issues, researchers underscore the importance of using new regularization methods for ensuring optimal model training. These advancements put more focus on how the use of the latest methods should be brought into the broader context of neural network optimization (Lo et al., 2016). Regularization also needs to address unconventional practices, such as the use of reproducing kernel Hilbert space (RKHS) norms. This perspective nicely brings together a variety of regularization principles available in a single framework for traditional penalties as well as new methods like spectral norm and gradient penalties. In addition to merely offering a new outlook, it also leads to practical application strategies that benefit model training, particularly when working with small datasets or requiring adversarial robustness. Using upper and lower bounds of RKHS norms, researchers can study novel hybrid regularization techniques to make model stability and performance enhancement possible. These techniques prove the adaptability and effectiveness of regularization techniques in shifting conditions of deep learning, pointing out their vital role in optimizing neural networks for real-world applications (Bietti et al., 2019) (Figure 5.8).

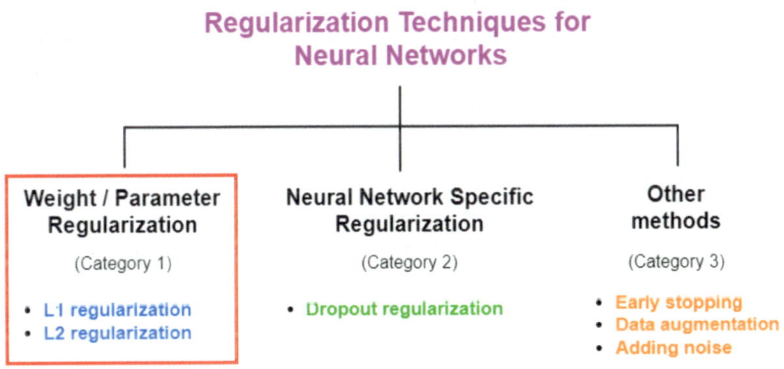

Figure 5.8. *Overview of regularization techniques for neural networks.*

Source: https://miro.medium.com/v2/resize:fit:4800/format:webp/1 DmK-wOZ5F1kDoReXj0-7xUA.png.*

5.3. HYPERPARAMETER TUNING

Hyperparameter tuning plays a crucial role when one is training and optimizing the neural networks, and it plays the role of being an interface between performance output and architecture design. Hyperparameters are also known as configuration parameters that dictate the training process but do not get trained from the data. Learning rates, batch sizes, and the number of hidden layers are some of the parameters that fall under the category. Careful selection of hyperparameters is important, as hyperparameters influence greatly not just the convergence speed of the training algorithm, but also the ultimate accuracy of the model. A well-calibrated model can achieve higher performance than similar models with the same architectures, so hyperparameter selection needs to be conducted systematically. There are many hyperparameter tuning methodologies, each with advantages and limitations. Random search, while basic, is not effective, unable to take advantage of improved configurations discovered in the process. Instead, advanced techniques such as Bayesian optimization or the Successive Halving and Classification (SHAC) algorithm yield a more accurate solution by iteratively improving the search space based on prior estimations. SHAC, for example, operates at various stages where it trains classifiers to remove suboptimal parameter regions efficiently (Dahl et al., 2018). Not only does this conserve computational resources but also ensures the greatest possible likelihood of finding hyperparameter settings that lead to improved model performance. More importantly, hyperparameter tuning is of huge significance in adversarial training, where sensitivity to a few hyperparameters can break or create a model's adversarial robustness. The richness of the adversarial robustness surface highlights the demand for careful parameter tuning, as changing settings can yield dramatically different outcomes. The research indicates that employing hyperparameter optimization methods is capable of navigating the accuracy-versus-robustness trade-off in models, offering a structured method for enhancing adversarial training procedures (Duesterwald et al., 2019). Thus, effective hyperparameter tuning is a critical component of the end-to-end training and optimization cycle for neural networks, allowing for the creation of better and stronger models (Figure 5.9).

Figure 5.9. *Hyperparameter tuning.*

Source: https://images.shiksha.com/mediadata/ugcDocuments/images/wordpressImages/2022_03_feature2-1.jpg.

5.3.1. Definition and Importance of Hyperparameters

Hyperparameters are the most important factor in defining the performance and output of the models in the scenario of neural networks. Hyperparameters are parameters set before training and are not learned from the data directly. Hyperparameters include variables such as learning rate, batch size, layer numbers, and regularization types. These parameters fundamentally set the manner in which the model will learn from the training data, the rate of convergence, and the ultimate accuracy of the predictions. Hyperparameter tuning is a topic of utmost significance as they decide how the learning algorithm games with the data and are therefore vital for neural network optimization during training. In their absence or improper tuning, even the most sophisticated neural architectures can only perform at suboptimal levels, thereby showcasing their significance in machine learning.

Their importance is most evident when model optimization is involved. Tuning the hyperparameters to be too poorly can lead to overfitting and underfitting, both of which compromise the generalizability of the model. For instance, too high a learning rate may make the optimization process converge in an unstable manner, and too low a learning rate can lead to convergence at unacceptably slow speeds, making the training inefficient. Recent advances, such as new stochastic gradient descent mechanisms that eliminate the need for setting learning rates in advance, illustrate a growing recognition of the sophistication of selecting hyperparameters. These advances not only aim to improve models but also express the vital role played by hyperparameters in advancing deep learning techniques across various uses, as addressed in successful uses across various domains (Orabona et al., 2017). Additionally, the use of heterogeneous features through hyperparameter tuning can produce notably enhanced predictive accuracy, demonstrating their usage across domains.

For example, evidence exists that prediction accuracy can be enhanced in specific situations, such as the prediction of electricity prices, by the effective exclusion of relevant and irrelevant data inputs using a feature selection algorithm in conjunction with hyperparameter tuning (Ridder et al., 2017). This interplay of hyperparameters and feature engineering highlights the mutual relationship between them in determining model effectiveness. With the development of neural network architectures, the importance of hyperparameter tuning remains keen, with continued research to improve methods for ensuring optimal model training and strong performance. Hence, profound knowledge of hyperparameters is essential for everyone working on optimization and training of neural networks as they are the building blocks of effective model construction.

5.3.2. Techniques for Hyperparameter Optimization

Simplifying, hyperparameter optimization, or HPO, is a critical component of neural network training because the functionality of neural networks is highly influenced by the choice of the hyperparameters. Various approaches have been devised to manage the intricacies of HPO, some being grid search, random search, and even more advanced techniques such as Bayesian optimization and genetic algorithms. Grid search, although straightforward, is computationally costly as it is exhaustive. Random search, however, is a cost-effective alternative as it samples configurations randomly, which is likely to provide better results with fewer evaluations. Nevertheless, in order to further boost optimization, more recent studies put more focus on applying meta-heuristic approaches like genetic algorithms that explore the hyperparameter space adaptively. Such approaches not only enhance performance but also reduce training time, which fits well the needs of fast development of optimal models in artificial intelligence and machine learning (Narmontas et al., 2024). The combination of early stopping techniques with hyperparameter optimization gives another new approach towards increasing training efficiency.

Early stopping works by stopping training the moment model performance no longer improves, thereby preventing overfitting and conserving computational resources. This technique is particularly useful when used with other types of optimization, as it allows for more dynamic evaluation of model performance. In addition, techniques like successive halving and learning curve extrapolation pruning selectively reduce time spent on underperforming models. Researchers can thereby compare candidate models based on training performance at various checkpoints instead of waiting for full convergence. The compromise between drastic elimination of underperforming models and maintenance of predictive accuracy is an important equilibrium as it has considerable implications on overall performance results and resource expenditure (Egele et al., 2024). New approaches that apply mixes of the aforementioned methods further streamline the hyperparameter tuning process.

For instance, auto machine learning (AutoML) platforms integrate various optimization strategies, including ensemble strategies and meta-learning, to apply automation to the HPO pipeline. With the capability to leverage past experiences and patterns, the systems can explore hyperparameter spaces adaptively to minimize the training process in terms of efficiency and efficacy. Apart from this, the adaptive nature of these frameworks makes them optimize across different data and architectures with minimal human intervention, representing a key milestone in training neural networks. As advancements continue in the field, the combination of manual and automatic approaches is set to dominate hyperparameter optimization methods for high performance under limited resources in practical applications (Egele et al., 2024; Narmontas et al., 2024) (Figure 5.10).

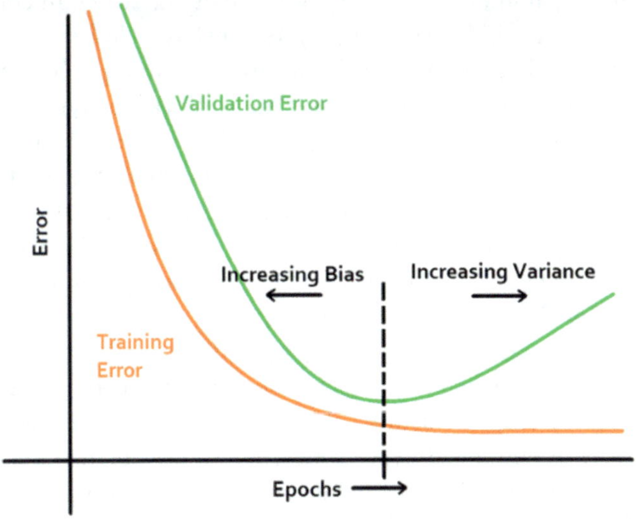

Figure 5.10. *Early stopping.*

Source: https://miro.medium.com/v2/resize:fit:720/format:webp/0 FMS-8L7Agx8XO7D7D.png.*

5.3.3. Impact of Hyperparameters on Model Performance

Hyperparameters play an essential role in regulating the performance and efficiency of neural network models. Unlike model parameters, which are learned during training, hyperparameters are selected prior to training commencing and can potentially significantly influence how well a model is able to learn from data. Their selection usually means striking a compromise between preserving model complexity and preventing overfitting. For instance, the choice of learning rate may control how rapidly a model converges to a loss minimum, and therefore how well it generalizes to unseen data. In turn, the proper tuning of hyperparameters may differentiate an optimal model from an average model, and therefore carefulness must be exercised when optimizing many times over hyperparameters to prevent unnecessary over-tuning. The estimation of the significance of hyperparameters has been empirically demonstrated in experimental studies, where evidence indicates that some hyperparameters, e.g., the choice of optimization procedures and learning rate schedules, can impact a model's performance substantially. Evidence has been demonstrated in research studies that specific settings, e.g., pre-trained word vectors, attain substantial improvement in tasks such as linguistic sequence tagging, indicating the value of informed hyperparameter choices (Gurevych et al., 2017). In contrast, other factors like the count of hidden units or layers may have a lesser impact on model output. This means that while it is relevant to learn multiple hyperparameters, it is more crucial to set priority to the high-relevance hyperparameters in order to have more efficient training protocols. Hence, adopting a focused approach towards hyperparameter tuning can enhance the performance as well as explainability of neural networks. The presence of state-of-the-art hyperparameter optimization methods is also important for the purpose of attaining best model performance, particularly in heavily complex applications such as electricity price forecasting. Models with market integration as well as proper interconnected features, for example, experience considerably improved forecasting performance when advised by meticulous hyperparameter selection (Ridder et al., 2017). Using feature selection methods that are more advanced and combined with optimized hyperparameter values can also improve model predictions so that the most influential data points impact outputs. With the rise of machine learning, the sophistication of methodologies for hyperparameter tuning, including methods such as Bayesian optimization, is quickly becoming more prestigious. Through systematic management of the intricate effects of hyperparameters, researchers are able to significantly improve the performance and trustworthiness of neural network models in diverse application domains.

5.4. CHALLENGES IN TRAINING NEURAL NETWORKS

Training neural networks comes with many challenges that have significant impacts on their performance and feasibility in a wide range of applications. Non-stationarity of data, particularly in dynamical environments, poses one of the greatest challenges, resulting in enormous prediction errors. For instance, in solar forecasting applications, traditional point forecasting methods cannot be able to reflect the variability involved in solar power generation. These issues not only lead to greater uncertainties when operating a system but also raise the expense of operating, thereby affecting the reliability of grid management. Eliminating these issues demands innovative architectural approaches, such as the integrated architecture being utilized for multi-time-horizon prediction based on RNN, which demonstrates greater accuracy compared to existing models. This is indicative of the necessity to devise robust strategies that enhance performance and minimize errors in reality. Another primary challenge in training neural networks is their optimization. Not only is optimization in this context setting the weights, but it is also keeping away from complicated error landscapes with saddle points and local minima that will strongly hinder convergence. The very large decision space, particularly for deep learning models, further contributes to the complication of the optimization process. Each architecture of the neural network can also have its own set of requirements, so the training process becomes more complex. For example, in video games, different genres put different demands on the learning process, and hence there are specialized optimization strategies required. As witnessed in recent studies, employing deep learning methods across various environments, such as general game playing, reveals inherent issues with sparse rewards and enormous decision spaces that must be addressed by researchers for effective model training. In total, the path towards effective training of neural networks is fraught with issues beyond sheer computational complexity. Difficulties such as data variability, optimization complexity, and context-aware tuning emphasize the ongoing research to fill the voids. Furthermore, as the area keeps evolving, the implementation of effective methodologies such as deep architectures and optimized ones will be required to enhance neural networks' adaptability and reliability to different applications. The engagement with such challenges is not simply academic but also heavily critical to the practical application of neural network systems, particularly in high-risk contexts like energy management and automated decision-making systems. Further research into these challenges is therefore still significant to advance the science of neural networks.

5.4.1. Overfitting and Underfitting

The overfitting and underfitting are the core in training and optimizing the neural networks and are behind the models performance as well as the models ability to generalize. Overfitting occurs when a model is learning the noise along with the underlying patterns in the training data and therefore creates a model that performs extremely well on the training data but fails to generalize to new data. This occurs typically with complex models in which the number of coefficients is large relative to the training data size. To avoid overfitting, techniques which include adding a penalty on large coefficients to the model and cross-validation are employed. Pruning mechanisms can also be employed in removing complexity without any loss of performance. Therefore, one should be cautious not to overfit while still managing to pick up on basic trends in the data. Underfitting is the opposite problem, which indicates that the model is too simple to accommodate the underlying pattern in the data. This occurs when a model is not complex enough for the task at hand and hence doesn't perform optimally on training as well as validation sets. Underfitting is generally due to insufficient model capacity, leading to high bias and failure in modeling the data's' complexity. Underfitting typically results by not being able to learn from the given data and creates high error rates when both training and testing. To avoid underfitting, the model complexity of the architecture of the neural network may be enhanced by introducing neurons or layers or more complex algorithms that can identify more intricate relationships between the data. The right balance between model complexity and capacity has to be determined for effective training and optimization. Lastly, learning the trade-off between overfitting and underfitting is significant in developing efficient models of neural networks. With the unprecedented degree of data and computational capacity, machine learning techniques have become more and more in demand, requiring an efficient model development and testing framework (Simeone et al., 2018). With increasing applications of neural networks in different fields, including in optical communication networks, requiring insights are necessitated through fine-grained analysis of data as well as decision-making (Macaluso et al., 2018). An age-old cycle of model tuning, validation, and improvement is necessary to peak performance. With the use of techniques such as dropout, early stopping, and ensembling methods, researchers are able to increase the generalizability of neural networks. Lastly, proper management of overfitting and underfitting not only enhances the performance of the model but also guarantees the reliability and effectiveness of AI-driven solutions (Figure 5.11).

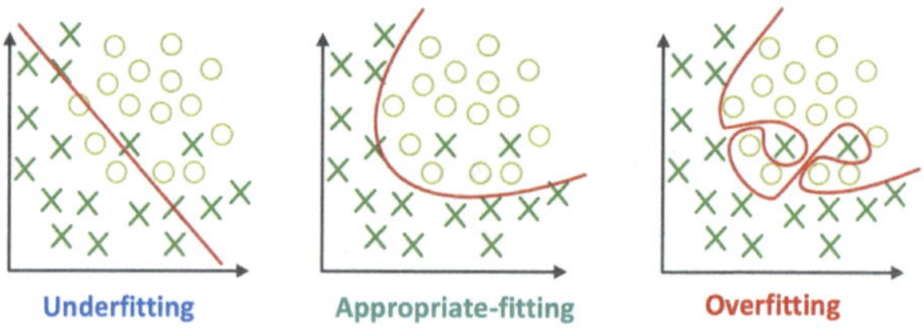

Figure 5.11. *Overfitting and underfitting.*

*Source: https://miro.medium.com/v2/resize:fit:4800/format:webp/1*vc6qBD_l3RF89dNtRqj-Ig.png.*

5.4.2. Vanishing and Exploding Gradients

The vanishing and exploding gradients phenomenon is very problematic when training deep neural networks, particularly when dealing with deep networks such as recurrent neural networks (RNNs) and their deeper versions such as long short-term memory networks (LSTMs). These issues are primarily caused by the manner in which gradients propagate between layers when backpropagating, essential for updating the network weights. In the exploding gradient problem, the gradients grow exponentially and thus cause very large weight updates and result in numerical instability that effectively stops the training process altogether. In the vanishing gradient problem, the gradients become smaller and smaller as they travel through many layers. This makes the weight updates inefficient for the early layers and results in slow learning or even complete stagnation of the learning process. These problems have to be addressed in order to ensure stable and robust neural network training. Several solutions and architectural updates have been proposed in response to the effects of exploding and vanishing gradients. For instance, application of activation functions such as ReLU (Rectified Linear Unit) and its variants is argued to be a key advancement as these functions provide positive gradients in every layer and are less prone to saturation compared to traditional sigmoid or tanh activations. Furthermore, recurrent neural networks have become more robust architectures, particularly by developing LSTMs. With the use of memory cells and gates, LSTMs are designed such that they preserve gradients over long sequences by enhancing the network's ability to learn from data in a very substantial manner.

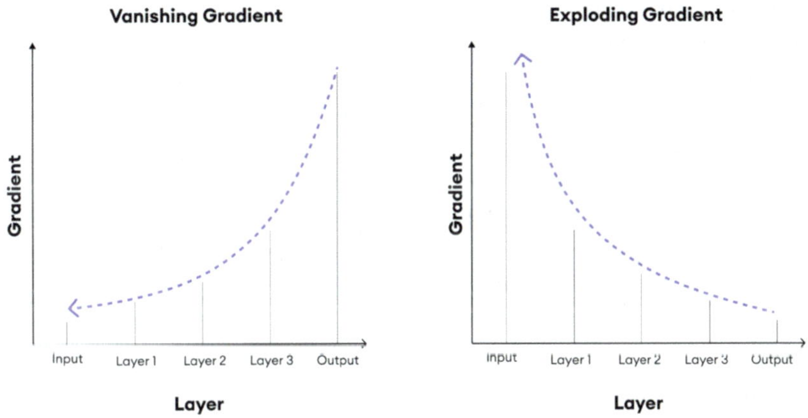

Figure 5.12. *Vanishing and exploding gradient.*

Source: https://aiml.com/wp-content/uploads/2023/11/vanishing-and-exploding-gradient-1.png.

These architectural improvements are central to counterbalancing training degradation due to ordinary gradient difficulties, thus facilitating improved optimization through learning. Literature indicates that supplementing the fundamental architecture of neural networks with complex-valued representations may offer promising solutions to rendering networks robust against such gradient-related challenges. Employing complex numbers over simple real-valued computations, neural architectures may exhibit superior representational ability and improved performance over a broad spectrum of tasks. Complex-valued neural networks, as used in recent research, can be expected to outperform real-valued neural networks in certain applications, specifically in audio processing and computer vision. For instance, architectures such as complex convolutional LSTMs use the natural property of complex numbers to improve memory recall and minimize instances of vanishing gradients. This strategy proposes that innovation in theory and implementation is necessary to move our knowledge forward on training dynamics in neural networks while at the same time minimizing performance on a wide range of machine learning tasks (Bengio et al., 2018; Sherstinsky et al., 2020) (Figure 5.12).

5.4.3. Computational Resource Limitations

In the field of neural networks, computational resource constraints severely impede training and optimization procedures of such models. With increasing model depth and larger datasets, as neural networks deepen, the required computational power increases. Deep learning models often include enormous calculations that, lacking adequate hardware, result in prolonged training and inefficiency. Academics and practitioners frequently find themselves in a situation where their computational resources are a limitation, hampering progress and innovation. The necessity of giving efficient results forces them to search for solutions like model pruning and architectural simplification to transcend these limits, a task that demands the delicate balancing of model performance preservation with computational efficiency. The equipment employed for the training of neural networks plays a significant role in deciding the efficiency with which resources are consumed. CPUs are sufficient for small models but, as network size increases and dataset complexity also increases, GPUs and specialized processors play vital advantages. The application of Field Programmable Gate Arrays (FPGAs) illustrates a promising direction toward deep learning system optimalization, according to findings demonstrating shocking gains in processing speed and energy efficiency (Ding et al., 2018). The adoption of new strategies like algorithm-hardware co-optimization enables deep learning practitioners to achieve exponential levels of computational efficiency gains. Therefore, awareness and exploitation of the hardware platform are essential to outsmarting computational resource limitations in training and optimizing neural networks. The implications of outsmarting computational resource limitations extend beyond the efficiency of training; they extend to broader deployment of neural networks into practical applications. As new smart machine learning technologies, including those targeted at 6G wireless communication systems, continue to evolve, computational resource collaboration and efficiency in the models also become increasingly essential

(Abbas et al., 2020). As high-performing neural networks remain in high demand, it is crucial that not only are smart algorithms designed but also in the manner through which they exploit current computational resources. Emphasizing energy-efficient designs and research into novel optimization techniques can unlock pathways to environmentally sound applications of neural networks in many fields, so that technological advancement goes hand in hand with wise use of resources.

5.5. ADVANCED TRAINING STRATEGIES

Advanced training techniques are at the core of enhancing the functioning of neural networks. Among these, semi-supervised learning has been of particular interest as it can solve the problems that arise due to a lack of adequate labeled data. In the majority of actual applications, it is time-consuming and expensive to acquire labeled datasets, thus generally excluding the use of supervised learning approaches. By leveraging both labeled and unlabeled data, semi-supervised learning enlarges the training dataset size, allowing enriched learning experience. This method employs sparse signal representations alongside unsupervised and supervised methods, allowing for effective detection and retrieval of novel signals, particularly in complication-dense situations, such as identification of radio emitters. As detailed in Chapelle et al. (2017), such advanced methods not only improve learning but also performance in general by providing generalization from existing data to future tasks. Reinforcement learning (RL) is another advanced training method which promises to revolutionize neural networks, particularly recommendation systems. Traditional RL methods have a propensity to center around individual optimization strategies, and as they are faced with complex, sequential user behaviors, can lead to sub-optimal outcomes. DeepChain system, for instance, outlines a multi-agent RL approach that takes advantage of interdependencies between sequential contexts to enhance the effectiveness of the recommendations. By making it possible for recommender agents to possess a collective memory of user behavior, this technique makes it easier for information-based decisions, maximizing total reward in a session. In solving the problem of data sparsity and reward skewness, model-based RL techniques have been able to reduce the requirement for training data as well as produce more accurate updates, showing how important such methods are to optimization in neural networks as is noted in Liu et al. (2020). Combining state-of-the-art training techniques not only improves constituent aspects of neural networks, but system performance in general as well. Techniques such as transfer learning and meta-learning have been trendy for their capacity to adapt pre-trained models to new tasks with limited data. Transfer learning moves knowledge learned from one domain to enhance learning on a related yet different task, basically reducing the time to train and resources needed. Similarly, meta-learning, or learning to learn, enables models to develop more efficient learning algorithms that can learn quickly to cope with numerous various situations and sets of data. As these approaches increasingly remain popular, they hold the promise of simplifying neural network training and making it more efficient, ultimately resulting in more stable programs across a wide range of studies. Finally, the use of cutting-edge training methods paves the way for generations of advancements in neural network training and optimization.

5.5.1. Transfer Learning

Transfer learning has emerged as a key method of training and optimizing neural networks, particularly in cases where there exists sparse labeled data for a specific task. With the help of experience gained by models that have been trained on large data sets previously, transfer learning allows the fast adjustment of neural networks to new but related issues. The technique reduces the time and energy required for model training enormously, as it utilizes pre-made features and representations. For instance, a model that has been trained using a general image data set can be adapted for an application that is specific, such as detection of specific agricultural pests. As highlighted in the latest studies, transfer learning makes it easier to optimize the model and is thus a first choice for researchers who want to enhance performance at lower computational cost (Abbas et al., 2020). As the technology improves, applications of transfer learning continue to expand across various fields, including natural language processing and autonomous systems. Transfer learning plays a central role in wireless communications in developing models that can adapt in real-time to the dynamics of network conditions. This capability is central in that it allows systems to optimize performance even where there is not a significant amount of training data. Techniques such as zero-touch optimization take advantage of the principles of transfer learning to dynamically adjust parameters to optimize the network to make it more efficient and reliable (Abbas et al., 2020). Furthermore, this aspect enables the integration of machine learning solutions into future 6G networks, which will have a vital role to offer end-to-end seamless connectivity and rich features on heterogeneous devices and applications. In addition, the combination of progress in model architecture and transfer learning has helped significantly enhance the robustness and accuracy of neural networks. The addition of new algorithms in precision agriculture, for example, demonstrates how transfer learning can be utilized to allow autonomous systems to be created that could operate in varying environments. Due to the initial training of deep learning models with full datasets, the models can then be tuned for specific agriculture tasks in ongoing learning from fresh, contextually relevant data.

The repeated cycle of developing and tuning the model not only enhances working efficiency but also shows the elastic nature of transfer learning to span industries. Consequently, ongoing research into transfer learning methods remains the overriding focus within the broader framework of neural network training and optimization as researchers strive to unlock fresh machine learning capability.

5.5.2. Data Augmentation

Data augmentation is an increasingly significant technique within the training and optimization of neural networks, particularly in terms of enhanced performance and robustness within models dealing with small datasets. By artificially expanding the range of available training data through various transformations, such as rotation, scaling, flipping, and noise addition, data augmentation allows models to learn more general features rather than memorizing training samples. This is particularly crucial in fields like medical imaging, where it can be extremely time-consuming and costly to acquire large, annotated datasets. For instance, in stroke detection from CT scans, a convolutional neural network (CNN) employs data augmentation during training to increase the accuracy of classification and prevent overfitting with an accuracy of 97.2% for validation in stroke detection (Abdi et al., 2025). Thus, data augmentation not only facilitates the learning process but also improves the reliability of model predictions in real situations. Moreover, data augmentation plays its part to ensure that the machine learning model retains its ability to function well under different situations. The inclusion of augmented data can help the model be less input-sensitive to variations, particularly when handling medical image data that can be different due to different scanning machines or the health of the patients. Enhanced model robustness, achieved through well-designed augmentation procedures, can further contribute toward improved generalization on unseen data. While training models employing optimization techniques, such as linear or quadratic programs, augmentation can introduce variations that help identify and preserve optimal solutions (Qian et al., 2025). By applying such innovative techniques, researchers are able to enhance training of models with an encouragement towards adaptability in the face of an array of challenges within a variety of domains. As machine learning becomes increasingly prominent by the day, the development of more sophisticated data augmentation techniques becomes an increasing imperative. Recent research extends beyond traditional image manipulations and includes the application of advanced algorithms like generative adversarial networks (GANs) to produce synthetic data that resembles reality. Such a move expands the augmentation horizon to enable the synthesis of entirely new samples that inherit the underlying characteristics of real data. The use of data augmentation methods in self-supervised learning techniques is also increasingly common, enabling models to learn representations without the need for large labeled datasets. These developments place emphasis on the vital importance that data augmentation plays in training and fine-tuning neural networks, raising the boundaries on model efficiency and accuracy and paving the way for future technological advancements in machine learning applications (Figure 5.13).

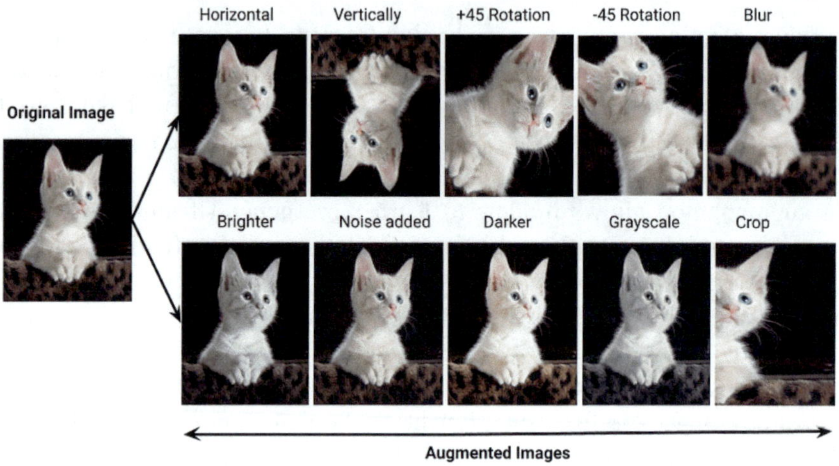

Figure 5.13. *Data augmentation.*

*Source: https://miro.medium.com/v2/resize:fit:4800/format:webp/0*PI-A460EY-7Crj49M.*

5.5.3. Ensemble Methods

Usage of ensemble methods is crucial in boosting the performance of neural networks, particularly in complex prediction tasks. By combining multiple models, ensemble methods can tap the best of each individual component, thereby reducing the likelihood of overfitting and improving overall accuracy. This is especially necessary in instances where models may vary significantly in the learning patterns. For instance, when it comes to gene expression profiling, extreme gradient boosting with deep neural networks (DNNs) has been demonstrated to yield improved predictive performance, such as in studies with the L1000 assay. The pre-training and ensemble methodology introduced in the chapter presumes that initial training of DNNs by techniques like autoencoders not only positions them favorably in the optimization space but also produces a heterogeneous set of outputs, which is essential for the success of ensembles

(Lee et al., 2025). Moreover, ensemble techniques are particularly valuable in environments involving dynamic and unpredictable data, such as found in mobile edge computing environments. The method called density clustering and ensemble learning training-based deep reinforcement learning (DCEDRL) is a good instance of this application. In utilizing multiple deep neural networks, DCEDRL effectively manages the task of calculating task distribution over edge servers. Adaptive characteristics of such ensembles allow real-time adjustment based on the computed priority of tasks, a determinant for latency reduction and improving resource allocation. This sheds light on how ensemble techniques not only solidify individual model predictions but also provide a sustainable system for decision-making in evolving computational demands (Qin et al., 2025).

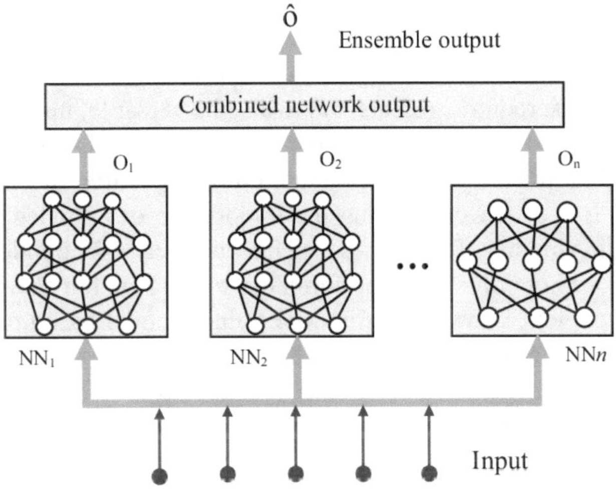

Figure 5.14. *A neural networks ensemble.*

Source: https://www.researchgate.net/publication/334747885/figure/fig1/AS:786056853082112@1564421966028/A-neural-networks-ensemble.png.

In terms of neural network training, using ensemble techniques ensures a context more amenable to optimization by sustaining diversity among models. This diversity is important because it avoids the systematic flaws that would result from too much reliance on one model. With neural networks pretrained over many configurations or datasets, they will settle on a variety of solutions, and with this rich wealth of knowledge from which an ensemble can benefit, it is possible to get a more global perspective on the data presented. While research continues to make advancements in this field, the new applications of ensemble techniques, particularly in the instance of gene expression analysis and mobile computing, bring to the fore their potential in accelerating the precision and effectiveness of the training of neural networks as well as optimization methods (Lee et al., 2025; Qin et al., 2025) (Figure 5.14).

SUMMARY

The complications involved in training and conforming neural networks demand extensive understanding of the same processes and issues of the models. The final part of this chapter emphasizes the need for continued research and development, particularly the solution to noticeable issues such as mode collapse and non-convergence, which significantly hinder the efficiency of models such as Generative Adversarial Networks (GANs) (Cao et al., 2020). As these issues evolve and progress, new architectures, optimization methods, and training protocols must be created and experimented with. This constantly evolving landscape requires researchers to also be versatile, implementing new techniques in their efforts to optimize the performance and resilience of neural networks in all domains of use. Reflecting on the evolution of neural network optimization, it is also worth noting the importance of knowledge extraction from challenging models. Techniques which reduce network complexity through pruned iterations not only enable performance to run lean but also facilitate the extraction of explicit knowledge from the trained model based on pioneering methodologies (Gorban et al., 2002). This groundbreaking technique enables researchers and practitioners to derive operational knowledge from neural network behavior without losing interpretability. The integration of efficient training methods with rule extraction methods having explicit rules promises future potential to make the neural networks more usable and accessible on real-world problems, thereby extending their applications in different fields. Lastly, the journey of training and optimizing the neural networks is one of problems and innovations that continue to revolutionize the field of artificial intelligence. Since the region is making progress, it will be important to future development to have a foundation of best practice and to build on what has been learned in prior studies. The call for systematic taxonomies and surveys of optimization methods, particularly of GANs Cao et al. (2020), indicates the need for an international overview of developments. Through cooperation and information sharing, the scientific community is able to utilize the potential of neural networks while keeping them at the forefront of solving complex problems and advancing technology in the years to come.

In the area of neural networks, the importance of understanding the nuances of optimization and training must be understood in order to have them unlock their potential. Key methodologies have been established that address the fundamental issues in optimally training the models. Amongst these techniques are various forms of regularization, which prevent overfitting by adding generalization-favoring constraints. Furthermore, the optimization landscape has been revolutionized with the development of adaptive learning rate techniques, such as Adam and RMSprop, to significantly enhance convergence rates in training. By modifying the learning rate based on parameters gradients, these algorithms have become considerable improvements on traditional methods, enabling faster and more stable training procedures. These advancements are a standard component of modern neural network training techniques, enabling models to not only be highly capable but also robust in changing environments. Its use across various fields, such as fluid mechanics, attests to the efficacy and versatility of neural networks in numerous applications. As argued in recent publications, machine learning is full of methodologies with which to model and analyze complex systems. For instance, within fluid mechanics, data quantities from experiments and simulation are the foundation for the application of methods based on neural networks for optimizing flow control. Through the utilization of historical information and live data, these methods can improve the precision of forecasts on fluid behaviors considerably. The continued application of neural networks in this and other fields brings with it opportunities for optimization and control advances, hinting at the revolutionary potential of these technologies for scientific research and practical applications, as acknowledged within the discussion on emerging potential within machine learning for fluid mechanics (Brunton et al., 2020). Generative Adversarial Networks (GANs) are an innovation in optimization of neural networks, but they are defined by specialized difficulties to be addressed for effective utilization. Mode collapse and convergence obstacles are just some of the matters that highlight the critical necessity of new solutions for training GANs. Recent studies have uncovered approaches that enhance GAN structure and optimization techniques to achieve more stable and high-performance results. Through exploring new objective functions and reimagined architectures, researchers have gone a step further in tackling the innate difficulties associated with GANs. The methodical exposition points to the necessity of determining a complete understanding of various GAN models as well as optimization methods. The more light that is cast on the subject, a taxonomy of solutions by large research challenges will increasingly influence future work, propelling the creation of this promising area of neural network application (Cao et al., 2020).

REFERENCES

1. Abbas, R., Ahmad, I., Ali, S., et al. (2020). 6G white paper on machine learning in wireless communication networks. http://arxiv.org/abs/2004.13875 (accessed on 25th September 2025).
2. Abdi, H., Hasan, M. S. R., Dattana, V., & Mahmood, S. (2025). Stroke detection in brain CT images using convolutional neural networks: Model development, optimization and interpretability. Information. https://www.semanticscholar.org/paper/a25ce4634c3e1c3bed63cd85a4fb531fdbf2f6f6 (accessed on 25th September 2025).
3. Agarwal, M., Gill, K. S., Malhotra, S., & Devliyali, S. (2024). Exploring numerical analysis with sequential convolutional neural networks leveraging Adam optimization technique. 2024 International Conference on Innovations and Challenges in Emerging Technologies (ICICET). https://www.semanticscholar.org/paper/f7b5fce8cd3c99ee3689a7951cf8b265d623285f (accessed on 25th September 2025).
4. Aghi, D., Chiaberge, M., & Mazzia, V. (2020). Local motion planner for autonomous navigation in vineyards with a RGB-D camera-based algorithm and deep learning synergy. https://core.ac.uk/download/pdf/327177639.pdf (accessed on 25th September 2025).
5. Asadi, R., Mustapha, N., & Sulaiman, N. (2009). Training process reduction based on potential weights linear analysis to accelerate back propagation network. https://core.ac.uk/download/153801401.pdf (accessed on 25th September 2025).
6. Audrius Narmontas, Jankevičiūtė, R., Bliujus, T., Vaičekauskas, E., & Abromavičius, V. (2024). Exploration of genetic algorithm-driven hyperparameter optimization for convolutional neural networks. 2024 IEEE Open Conference of Electrical, Electronic and Information Sciences (eStream). https://www.semanticscholar.org/paper/bfb2ceb8f6707fc4be965c939c50c8e2e7e7e743 (accessed on 25th September 2025).
7. Baydin, A. G., Pearlmutter, B. A., Radul, A. A., et al. (2018). Automatic differentiation in machine learning: A survey. https://core.ac.uk/download/297029995.pdf (accessed on 25th September 2025).
8. Bengio, Y., Bilaniuk, O., Mehri, S., et al. (2018). Deep complex networks. http://arxiv.org/abs/1705.09792 (accessed on 25th September 2025).
9. Biedron, S. G., Chase, B. E., Edelen, A. L., et al. (2016). Neural networks for modeling and control of particle accelerators. http://arxiv.org/

abs/1610.06151 (accessed on 25th September 2025).

10. Bietti, A., Chen, D., Mairal, J., et al. (2019). A kernel perspective for regularizing deep neural networks. https://core.ac.uk/download/200162956.pdf (accessed on 25th September 2025).
11. Boeddeker, C., Delcroix, M., Haeb-Umbach, R., et al. (2020). Jointly optimal denoising, dereverberation, and source separation. http://arxiv.org/abs/2005.09843 (accessed on 25th September 2025).
12. Bontrager, P., Justesen, N., Risi, S., et al. (2019). Deep learning for video game playing. https://core.ac.uk/download/289098923.pdf (accessed on 25th September 2025).
13. Brunton, S., Koumoutsakos, P., & Noack, B. (2020). Machine learning for fluid mechanics. http://arxiv.org/abs/1905.11075 (accessed on 25th September 2025).
14. Cao, J., & Saxena, D. (2020). Generative adversarial networks (GANs): Challenges, solutions, and future directions. http://arxiv.org/abs/2005.00065 (accessed on 25th September 2025).
15. Chapelle, C., Ester, M., Kingma, D., LeCun, Y., Maaten, L., et al. (2017). Semi-supervised radio signal identification. http://arxiv.org/abs/1611.00303 (accessed on 25th September 2025).
16. Dahl, G. E., Kumar, M., Norouzi, M., et al. (2018). Parallel architecture and hyperparameter search via successive halving and classification. http://arxiv.org/abs/1805.10255 (accessed on 25th September 2025).
17. Das, A., Nandy, S., & Sarkar, P. P. (2012). Training a feed-forward neural network with artificial bee colony-based backpropagation method. http://arxiv.org/abs/1209.2548 (accessed on 25th September 2025).
18. Dayal Singh Kalra, & Barkeshli, M. (2023). Phase diagram of early training dynamics in deep neural networks: Effect of the learning rate, depth, and width. https://www.semanticscholar.org/paper/f739de44605f35481066fdff0f9be89d8a5728d6 (accessed on 25th September 2025).
19. De Ridder, F., De Schutter, B., Lago, J., et al. (2017). Forecasting day-ahead electricity prices in Europe: The importance of considering market integration. http://arxiv.org/abs/1708.07061 (accessed on 25th September 2025).
20. Ding, C., Li, Z., Liao, S., et al. (2018). Towards ultra-high performance and energy efficiency of deep learning systems: An algorithm-hardware co-optimization framework. http://arxiv.org/abs/1802.06402 (accessed on 25th September 2025).

21. Dreossi, T., Ghosh, S., Sangiovanni-Vincentelli, A., et al. (2019). A formalization of robustness for deep neural networks. http://arxiv.org/abs/1903.10033 (accessed on 25th September 2025).
22. Duesterwald, E., Murthi, A., Sinn, M., et al. (2019). Exploring the hyperparameter landscape of adversarial robustness. http://arxiv.org/abs/1905.03837 (accessed on 25th September 2025).
23. Egele, R., Mohr, F., Viering, T., & Balaprakash, P. (2024). The unreasonable effectiveness of early discarding after one epoch in neural network hyperparameter optimization. https://www.semanticscholar.org/paper/661de816d5c7e3b556c3bcb5c02f60d586922b91 (accessed on 25th September 2025).
24. Gorban, A. N., Mirkes, E. M., & Tsaregorodtsev, V. G. (2002). Generation of explicit knowledge from empirical data through pruning of trainable neural networks. http://arxiv.org/abs/cond-mat/0307083 (accessed on 25th September 2025).
25. Gurevych, I., & Reimers, N. (2017). Optimal hyperparameters for deep LSTM-networks for sequence labeling tasks. http://arxiv.org/abs/1707.06799 (accessed on 25th September 2025).
26. Hafifi, N., Khan, A. M. Z., Rehman, M. N., et al. (2016). BAT-BP: A new BAT based back-propagation algorithm for efficient data classification. https://core.ac.uk/download/42954000.pdf (accessed on 25th September 2025).
27. Kaplan, Z., Sanz-Alonso, D., & Trillos, N. G. (2019). Variational characterizations of local entropy and heat regularization in deep learning. http://arxiv.org/abs/1901.10082 (accessed on 25th September 2025).
28. Kappler, D., Meier, F., & Schaal, S. (2018). Online learning of a memory for learning rates. http://arxiv.org/abs/1709.06709 (accessed on 25th September 2025).
29. Lee, D. B., & Hwang, K. B. (2025). Pre-training and ensembling of deep neural networks for target gene expression prediction from landmark genes. IEEE Transactions on Computational Biology and Bioinformatics, 22, 1574–1586. https://www.semanticscholar.org/paper/a257b62f600d3aa95612c689d1f492398f26e539 (accessed on 25th September 2025).
30. Li, F., Oko, E., Wang, M., et al. (2015). Modelling of a post-combustion CO_2 capture process using neural networks. https://core.ac.uk/download/151159410.pdf (accessed on 25th September 2025).
31. Liu, H., Tang, J., Xia, L., et al. (2020). Whole-chain recommendations. http://arxiv.org/abs/1902.03987 (accessed on 25th September 2025).

32. Lo, J., Oates, T., & Wang, Z. (2016). Adaptive normalized risk-averting training for deep neural networks. http://arxiv.org/abs/1506.02690 (accessed on 25th September 2025).

33. Macaluso, I., Musumeci, F., Nag, A., et al. (2018). An overview on application of machine learning techniques in optical networks. https://core.ac.uk/download/224788320.pdf (accessed on 25th September 2025).

34. Mishra, S., & Palanisamy, P. (2018). Multi-time-horizon solar forecasting using recurrent neural network. http://arxiv.org/abs/1807.05459 (accessed on 25th September 2025).

35. Nehmetallah, G., Nguyen, T., & Tian, L. (2019). Deep learning in computational microscopy. https://open.bu.edu/bitstream/2144/40200/1/1099007.pdf (accessed on 25th September 2025).

36. Obaid, M. K. (2021). Causative factors of construction and demolition waste generation in Iraq construction industry. https://core.ac.uk/download/12008479.pdf (accessed on 25th September 2025).

37. Orabona, F., & Tommasi, T. (2017). Training deep networks without learning rates through coin betting. https://core.ac.uk/download/154948072.pdf (accessed on 25th September 2025).

38. Pineda, F. J. (1989). Recurrent backpropagation and the dynamical approach to adaptive neural computation. https://core.ac.uk/download/4881017.pdf (accessed on 25th September 2025).

39. Qian, C., & Morris, C. (2025). Principled data augmentation for learning to solve quadratic programming problems. ArXiv, abs/2506.01728. https://www.semanticscholar.org/paper/6dccfdcac3d9fa0545e8f36a69d6fe6752a01e8c (accessed on 25th September 2025).

40. Qin, Y., Chen, J., Jin, L., Yao, R., & Gong, Z. (2025). Task offloading optimization in mobile edge computing based on a deep reinforcement learning algorithm using density clustering and ensemble learning. Scientific Reports, 15. https://www.semanticscholar.org/paper/9eb0f823781ec4a408e155e82de30c875e0aba07 (accessed on 25th September 2025).

41. Sherstinsky, A. (2020). Fundamentals of recurrent neural network (RNN) and long short-term memory (LSTM) network. http://arxiv.org/abs/1808.03314 (accessed on 25th September 2025).

42. Simeone, O. (2018). A very brief introduction to machine learning with applications to communication systems. https://core.ac.uk/download/195274082.pdf (accessed on 25th September 2025).

CHAPTER 6

CONVOLUTIONAL NEURAL NETWORKS (CNNS)

Contents

INTRODUCTION

Convolutional Neural Networks (CNNs) have triggered an unprecedented revolution in the field of artificial intelligence, particularly for image processing. Inspired by the human vision system's anatomy and working mechanism, CNNs are designed to learn automatically and adaptively spatial hierarchies of features from images. Their use is more than just basic classification; CNNs provide intricate uses such as object detection, semantic segmentation, and even video analysis. With scientists learning more about how they function, the ability of CNNs to extract salient features has made them a corner-stone in sectors such as healthcare, autonomous vehicle driving, and entertainment. The excellent performance of CNNs for image recognition tasks highlights their potential to revolutionize most areas that are vision-dependent. Despite high capabilities, the application of CNNs poses some challenges. The overfitting issue, enormous demands on computational resources, and lack of interpretability can curtail their use under certain conditions. Although the deep learning community continually develops new architectures and techniques to balance these issues, it is essential to familiarize oneself with the fundamentals of CNNs.

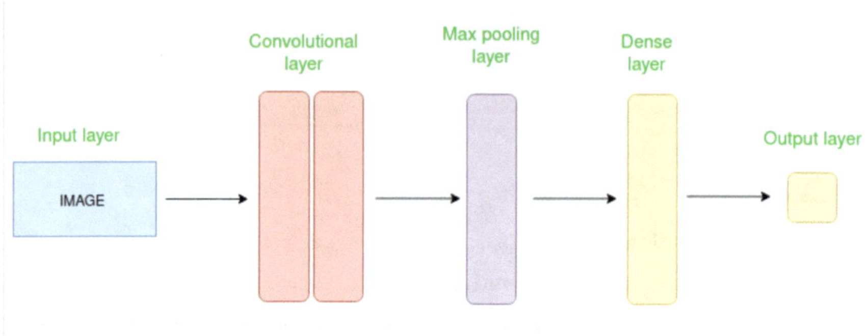

Figure 6.1. *Simple convolutional neural network (CNN) architecture.*

Source: https://media.geeksforgeeks.org/wp-content/uploads/20231218174301/max.png.

For instance, researchers have begun exploring dynamic network configurations to address the constantly shifting input data scenario, as in real-world applications. The use of dynamic graph neural networks offers promising breakthroughs in supplementing CNNs' typical functionality, thus broadening their use for dealing with complex, temporal data structures in a vast array of disciplines, such as social network analysis and real-time object recognition (Gabrys et al., 2021). In addition, ongoing advancements in CNN architectures and loss functions serve to indicate the requirement for a fine-line approach towards improving their performance. Improvements such as WordFence's architecture illustrate how integrating semantic segmentation methods can make word recognition in natural images more effective, with fewer needs for complex post-processing steps (Polzounov et al., 2017). This change is part of an even broader trend across the field in which multi-task learning and end-to-end processes not only provide consistency but also allow for more accurate and effective outcomes in a number of applications. As CNNs evolve, understanding the interaction between architecture design, training mechanisms, and application spaces will be critical to best harness their potential. Throughout the rest of this chapter, this chapter will critically analyze the mechanics of CNNs, explore their fundamental building blocks, and analyze their impact on artificial intelligence research and applications in practice (Figure 6.1).

Definition of Convolutional Neural Networks (CNNs)

The definition of CNNs is key to understanding their applications and application in numerous fields, particularly image processing and computer vision. CNNs are a category of deep learning algorithms that are specifically designed to process structured grid data, such as images, in a series of convolutional layers. CNNs differ from traditional neural networks, which rely on fully connected layers, since CNNs utilize convolutional layers that perform a filter or kernel operation on input data. This is a process that allows CNNs to detect spatial features and patterns automatically, reducing feature extraction manually. The hierarchical structure of CNNs not only enhances their ability to encode local spatial structures in data, but also gives them translation invariance, which makes them qualified to handle variation in input. The CNN structure consists of convolutional layers, pooling layers, and fully connected layers, each with a distinct purpose. Feature extraction is performed by convolutional layers via sliding filters convolving across the input to produce feature maps. Pooling layers, typically max or average pooling-based, then follow convolutional layers to down-sample feature maps, effectively reducing dimension but preserving important information. Fully connected layers then combine the extracted features to a final output, enabling classification or regression task presented to the network. This hierarchical method of processing ensures that CNNs are capable of learning and processing complex patterns from the data, thereby making them especially useful for high-dimensional inputs like images and videos. Furthermore, the flexibility of CNNs is not just limited to classical computer vision tasks but can be extended to complex realms like time series classification and non-Euclidean data structures. Transfer learning, which is a leading technique in the deployment of CNN, is to first pre-train a network on a large dataset and then fine-tune it on a target dataset to acquire a higher accuracy. The method strengthens the models ability to generalize across tasks and has played a key role in expanding the application domain of CNNs from conventional image recognition to more complex tasks such as time series analysis. Therefore, CNNs are an essential component of the machine learning arsenal, displaying awe-inspiring flexibility in solving a vast assortment of problems in numerous scientific and engineering fields, highlighting their importance in contemporary research and applications (Bronstein et al., 2016; Fawaz et al., 2018) (Figure 6.2).

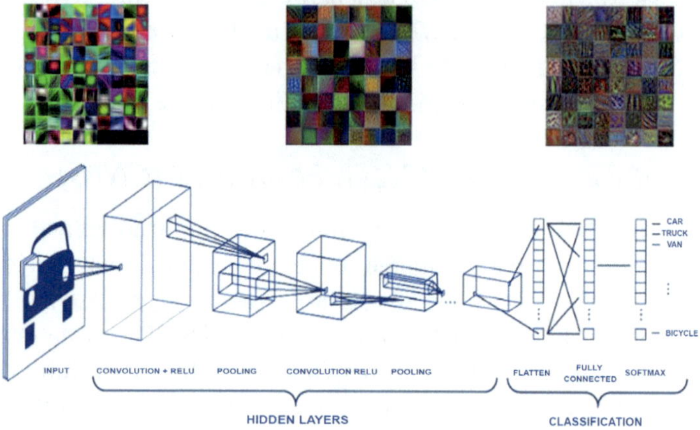

Figure 6.2. *Convolutional neural network (CNN).*

*Source: https://miro.medium.com/max/984/0*YVT_vA0cgiwkKkPX.png.*

Importance in the Field of Artificial Intelligence

The relevance of CNNs in artificial intelligence extends beyond efficiency in image processing. As leading players in computer vision applications, CNNs have demonstrated an unprecedented ability to learn hierarchical features without human intervention from raw images, thereby eliminating the necessity for time-consuming manual feature extraction. Such a feature has revolutionized applications such as facial recognition, autonomous vehicles, and medical imaging. Interestingly, research indicates that CNNs are capable of enhancing their learning process from adaptive connections focusing only on informative inputs, enhancing the accuracy of classification in numerous various applications (Tek et al., 2020). Not only do the enhancements optimize performance, but they also facilitate the development of more sophisticated AI systems for nuanced tasks impossible using previous neural network designs. Moreover, the versatility of CNNs contributes to their relevance in a broad array of sectors, including medicine and diagnostics. For instance, a recent publication illustrated the effective application of a 2D U-Net CNN to automate liver segmentation with multiple imaging modalities, showing the capability of CNNs to perform complex segmentation tasks with high accuracy (Bahrami et al., 2019). The training process involved employing different imaging techniques to develop a generalized model, demonstrating the inbuilt flexibility which is typical of CNNs. This capacity to deal with variability inherent across different applications enables the possibility of CNNs being relevant across different applications, including tissue characterization and volumetry development. Therefore, CNNs are not just facilitators of improved data analysis but also blocks to develop dynamic AI systems to carry out complicated clinical and medical tasks. In summary, the value of CNNs in artificial intelligence is compounded by their ability to learn deeply, versatility, and flexibility across fields. Their ability to facilitate informative input prioritization at minimal computational expenses makes them imperative components towards developing intelligent systems that can autonomously process and comprehend sophisticated data sets. As demand for effective and accurate AI technology continues to rise, research on developing CNN architectures will keep yielding more innovations. In addition to widening computational capacity, they will also enhance the capability of artificial intelligence technology application in all industries, further solidifying the core role of CNNs in shaping the future of this burgeoning scientific field.

Overview of Applications in Various Domains

CNNs have also significantly changed numerous areas, particularly in computer vision when it comes to image recognition. CNNs find application in computer vision for object detection, image classification, and segmentation. The CNN architecture inherently learns spatial hierarchies using convolutional layers, such that sophisticated patterns in visual information can be recognized. This capability has spurred innovation in applications such as autonomous driving, where high-definition real-time image processing is critical to safe navigation and operation. Recent research ensures that the use of deep learning techniques like CNNs has resulted in better performance measures across these applications, asserting their significance in enabling systems that require high visual acuity in dynamic situations (Gashler et al., 2017). Apart from visual understanding, CNNs are also improving in the medical arena, particularly when it comes to analyzing medical images. CNNs are extremely capable of detecting pathology in images taken from MRI, CT scans, and X-rays, facilitating early detection of diseases such as tumors and fractures. Healthcare providers can avoid significant diagnostic errors and improve the quality of care by training CNNs on enormous databases of medical images. The use of CNNs has the potential to transcend personalized medicine and enhance the value of patient care through predictive models recommending customized treatment plans from patient data analysis. The advantages brought by healthcare use of CNNs show the possibility of effective resource allocation and enhanced access to health services, aiming for better quality of patient care (Bronstein et al., 2016). In addition to their application in vision-critical tasks and medicine, CNNs are additionally being put to new applications in the field of robotics, proving themselves to be flexible across domains. With robotics systems advancing, deep learning approaches, particularly CNNs, have an important role to play in sensor interpretation and improving robotic interactions with the world. The networks enable robots to learn through vision and engage in tasks ranging from navigation to object manipulation. The application of CNNs is not only limited to vision processing; they are also used to enhance the interaction of human operators with robotic systems. Through the application of CNNs, researchers are realizing new capabilities in robotics that lead to the development of smart systems that have the capability to make complex decisions as well as adaptive actions (Gashler et al., 2017).

6.1. HISTORICAL BACKGROUND

The history of the development of Convolutional Neural Networks (CNNs) is a pathbreaking journey in the fields of machine learning and artificial intelligence. Initially created in the 1980s by pathbreaking research by Kunihiko Fukushima, CNNs were initially aimed at replicating how vision is processed in the human brain. Early models, such as the Neocognitron, were the precursors to the multilevel hierarchy that is common in CNNs today but were limited by computing capabilities of the time. The subsequent resurgence of interest in the 1990s, spearheaded by Yann LeCuns influential LeNet-5 architecture, validated CNNs as valuable aids for digit recognition in special cases. This was the breakthrough, as it demonstrated that feature learning significantly enhanced image tasks, paving the way for future work and innovation in neural networks. The rapid advancements in computing power, particularly with the advent of Graphics Processing Units (GPUs), boosted the development of CNNs during the 2010s. Researchers began to research deeper and complex structures, which led to significant improvements across various branches of computer vision. Particularly compelling was the 2012 introduction of AlexNet, the winner of the ImageNet Large Scale Visual Recognition Challenge, and showing the dramatic performance increase with CNNs over conventional methods. This shift highlighted not just the potential of deep learning but also spurred the creation of other neural network structures as well as transfer learning breakthroughs—an approach that is integral to enabling CNNs to transfer learning across numerous datasets without requiring a lot of retraining. The shift into these more complex models paved the way for them to be adopted in numerous applications, including medical imaging and self-driving cars. In further espousing CNNs' flexibility, recent research has begun implementing them in new applications beyond traditional image processing into manuscript baseline detection and time series classification. For instance, advances in baseline extraction with deep learning validate CNNs more widespread application in addressing complex data challenges, which traditional algorithms could not accomplish. The use of CNNs for similar specialized tasks proves their adaptability and effectiveness in extracting meaningful information from varied sources of data, confirming their place as a powerful tool across the board. Moreover, the usage of techniques like transfer learning enables researchers to leverage existing models and adapt them to a specific function, elevating accuracy and effectiveness in areas like document analysis and classification. This adaptability further solidifies CNNs as a foundational technology in modern machine learning, further cementing their long-term evolution and ongoing dominance of the field (Fawaz et al., 2018; Fink et al., 2018) (Figure 6.3).

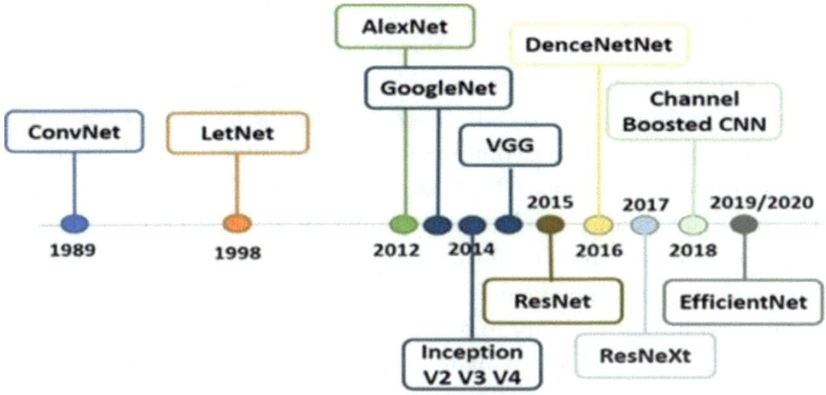

Figure 6.3. *A brief history of convolutional neural network.*

Source: https://www.researchgate.net/publication/372925804/figure/fig4/AS:11431281179546515@1691247477667/A-brief-history-of-convolutional-neural-network.jpg.

6.1.1. Early Developments in Neural Networks

The origins of neural networks are traceable to the mid-20th century when researchers initially began testing computational models that mimic how human brains process information. The initial tests involved relatively primitive architectures, such as the perceptron, developed by Frank Rosenblatt in 1958. This model furnished the foundation upon which to grasp how interconnected nodes would process binary data. But the perceptron's limitations were soon apparent, particularly when faced with linearly inseparable data, which the model couldn't process effectively. Despite these failings, the early experiments spurred a tidal wave of interest that spurred further research into the discipline. The popularity of neural networks ebbed and flowed from time to time, but ideas established at the time, such as the idea of a multi-layered structure, were the building blocks of later developments and ultimately led to more powerful models, including Convolutional Neural Networks (CNNs). The renewed interest in neural networks during the 1980s stemmed primarily from the availability of backpropagation. This technique, developed by the work of various researchers, enabled efficient training of multi-layered neural networks, and the weight adjustment procedure based on errors became available to all. As research and commercial entities saw the potential of these breakthroughs, applications rose exponentially. The growth of larger datasets and greater computing power during this time made exploration of deeper architectures more feasible, setting the stage for the innovations like Convolutional Neural Networks. This evolutionary process shows how crude neural network models, as poor as they were, provided valuable insight into non-linear processing and adaptive learning, thereby allowing researchers to better their artificial intelligence strategies. The evolution from rudimentary neural networks to advanced structures such as CNNs is a remarkable innovation in artificial intelligence. The architectural improvements of CNNs, derived from past advancements, enhance their performance in spatial data processing, particularly effective in image classification applications. By implementing stacked architecture with the capability to hierarchically abstract features, CNNs have outstanding performance in recognizing patterns that earlier models were unable to differentiate. This process of transformational abstraction, as described in current critiques, indicates that neural architectures can become proficient in coping with complexity by systematic refinement of inputs and thereby tolerating nuisance variations. The implications of these early neural network advancements extend beyond technical advances; they have actually changed the character of machine learning, as evidenced by ongoing advancement that further closes the gap between mind theories in psychology and the computer programs we employ today (Brunton et al., 2020; Buckner et al., 2018).

6.1.2. Introduction of Convolutional Layers

The introduction of convolutional layers is a milestone in neural network development, significantly enhancing their capacity for dealing with image data. Convolutional layers are distinct from the fully connected layers of traditional neural networks because they take advantage of an expertly designed structure that makes use of local structure in the data. By applying convolution operations over small regions of the input data, those layers can effectively identify features such as edges, textures, and shapes, which are critical to image recognition issues. This feature detection mechanism allows CNNs to reduce the input dimensionality without destroying the spatial hierarchies, hence making the model more efficient as well as capable of handling complex image data. Therefore, convolutional layers are transformed into vital building blocks in CNN architectures such that they can provide exceptional performance capabilities in various tasks from image classification to object detection. In CNNs, the arrangement of convolutional layers is very much planned to enhance model performance even further. Each convolutional layer is typically followed by an activation function, such as the ReLU (Rectified Linear Unit), which adds non-linearity to the model and allows it to discover complex patterns. Furthermore, pooling layers are also added between convolutional layers to reduce computational expenses and prevent overfitting. These pooling operations downsample the feature maps generated by the convolutional layers so that they preserve the most significant features while reducing the dimension size. By this hierarchical layering and merging of activation and pooling functions, CNNs can attain high accuracy in challenging tasks such as face recognition and medical image analysis. The architectural design strategy of convolutional layers enhances the overall learning efficiency of CNN models and facilitates advancements in deep learning technologies. Use cases of convolutional layers extend beyond simple image processing and have significant impacts in fields such as autonomous driving and medical imaging diagnosis.

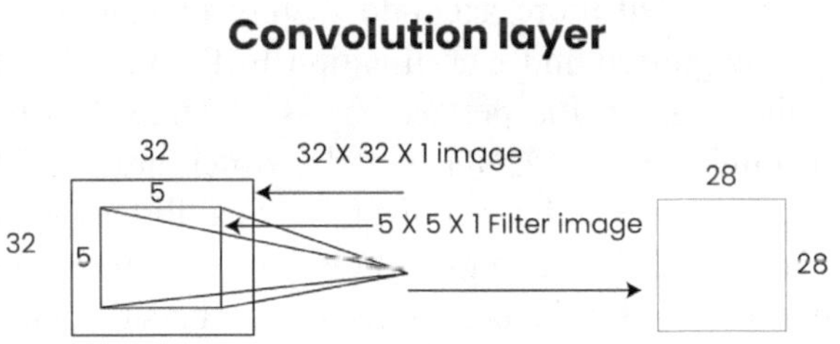

Figure 6.4. *Convolution layer.*

Source: https://media.geeksforgeeks.org/wp-content/uploads/20240605123653/Convolution-layer.webp.

In pedestrian detection systems, for example, convolutional layers enhance the realization of multiple features critical to ensuring safety and enabling decision-making in advance to prevent accidents. As demonstrated in recent advances, pedestrian detectors based on CNN apply convolutional layers to achieve near-state-of-the-art accuracy with low computational expenses, which is a prerequisite for their integration in embedded systems (Baroffio et al., 2016). Besides, the ability of convolutional layers to extract intricate patterns from diverse data streams, like wireless signal modulation identification, demonstrates their versatility across disciplines (Gamal et al., 2018). As the importance of convolutional layers grows, their role in driving innovation and enhancing accuracy in machine learning solutions remains a central focus area of research and development in artificial intelligence (Figure 6.4).

6.1.3. Milestones in Convolutional Neural Network (CNN) Research and Development

he past of CNNs has been marked by a series of milestone events that have significantly contributed to their application in various fields, particularly computer vision. One of the most influential breakthroughs was in 2012, when AlexNet was created and won the ImageNet Large Scale Visual Recognition Challenge (ILSVRC). By using more profound architectures and the incorporation of techniques such as dropout for regularization and ReLU activations for non-linearity, AlexNet did justice to the immense potential of CNNs for image classification. The innovation achieved by this model gave a tremendous push to deep learning methods, and researchers started exploring more advanced architectures. Follow-up advancements such as VGG19 further refined the principles established by AlexNet using uniform architecture and deeper models that enabled more accurate feature extraction, advancing the science of image recognition and classification to the next level. In addition to architecture enhancement, the pervasiveness of large datasets has played a critical role in training robust CNN models, which are capable of directly influencing the performance and generalization capability of these models. As projects such as the RISE dataset gained popularity, capturing environmental phenomena such as factory smoke emissions, researchers recognized a demand for comprehensive and quality datasets. The RISE dataset, grown under citizen science, consists of over 12,000 labeled video segments for smoke detection, indicating the paramount importance of data quality to CNN performance. The inclusion of community participation in the process of data gathering creates a new era of opportunity for CNN use, particularly in environmental monitoring social justice causes. This partnership showcases the manner in which CNN studies not just benefit technology but also provide solutions to urgent societal problems that are enhanced by greater observation and evidence-based advocacy. As new breakthroughs in CNN research are developing, the endless stream of more and more sophisticated architecture and data sets has profound implications across much of the field. The combination of strong models and large data sets has produced performance milestones that constantly expand the limits of what CNNs can do, with implications in areas ranging from facial recognition and medical imaging to autonomous vehicles. Comparative analyses between multiple architectures, such as those using both AlexNet and VGG19, have accentuated the potential area under the receiver operating characteristic curve scores reaching near 99.6% in detecting complex patterns from images. As this research goes on, CNN architectures and their implementation into beneficial applications still remain crucial, a sign of how an adaptive learning system still evolves with technological advancements as well as societal needs, molding the future of artificial intelligence across various sectors (Figure 6.5).

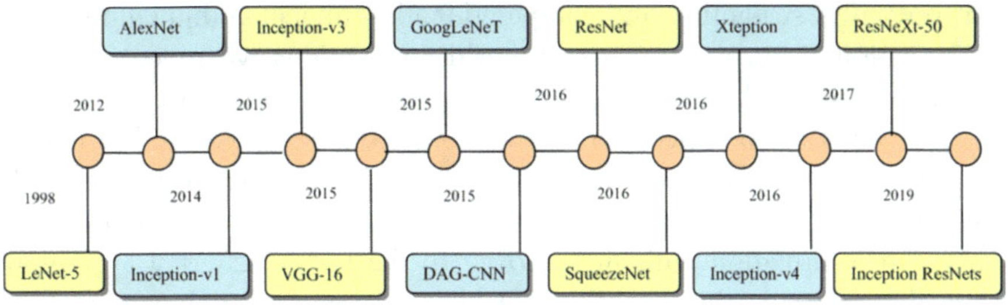

Figure 6.5. *A timeline showing development of convolutional neural network (CNN) models.*

Source: https://www.researchgate.net/publication/369379085/figure/fig15/AS:11431281360346001@1744090321814/A-timeline-showing-development-of-CNN-models.png.

6.2. ARCHITECTURE OF CONVOLUTIONAL NEURAL NETWORKS (CNNS)

The CNN architecture is naturally suited to handle intricate data structures, especially images, using a hierarchical processing approach. The convolutional layer is the key element of this architecture, and it employs a collection of filters on input data in order to enable the extraction of spatial hierarchies of features. This stacked approach enables the learning of increasingly abstract attributes at every subsequent deeper layer, ranging from simple edges in earlier layers to complex object representations in the bottom layers. The general structure may include more components such as pooling layers, which are reduction-in-dimensional aspect, and fully connected layers for enabling classification of the learned features.

The systematic method of designing CNNs renders them very efficient in image recognition and segmentation, performing better than traditional methods. The effective CNN architecture design also nullifies the issue of high computational power consumption and memory requirement characteristic of deep models. A standard CNN is likely to have millions of parameters to calculate that demand huge computational powers, and therefore, it's an issue in terms of deploying them in real-time scenarios or on low-processing devices. As a response, there has been significant work on compressing and optimizing such networks. For instance, some implementations utilize multilinear projections so that the number of parameters is greatly reduced while retaining performance on par with the standard CNN. This new approach not only reduces the architecture but also enables scalability and computationally efficient computation, which can be exploited even more in real-world applications where resources are scarce (Gabbouj et al., 2017). In expanding the capabilities of CNNs, recent innovations have also focused on introducing motion analysis ability into the architectural framework. By decoupling network structures from principles of signal processing, certain models can natively represent dense optical flow from video information without resorting to the use of external algorithms. This further advances the capability of CNNs to comprehend dynamic scenes, providing a strong framework for action and interaction perception in video streams. Such designs emphasize special significance on contrast and rotation variation invariance, hence lowering the complexity of learning required. The resulting networks have significantly fewer parameters and can deliver comparable performance to traditional methods with end-to-end training on small data sets. The adaptability predicts a future full of promise for CNNs, in which their architectural structure may be scaled from static image analysis to complex temporal data (Horn et al., 2016) (Figure 6.6).

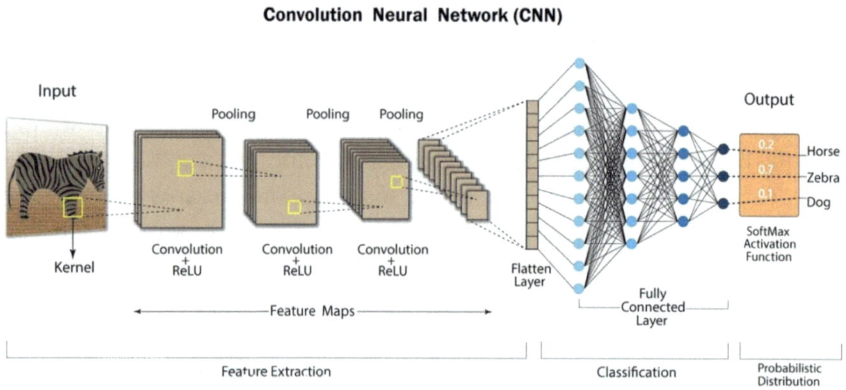

Figure 6.6. *Convolutional neural network (CNN) architecture.*

Source: https://media.licdn.com/dms/image/v2/D5612AQGOui8XZUZJSA/article-cover_image-shrink_720_1280/article-cover_image-shrink_720_1280/0/1680532048475?e=2147483647&v=beta&t=5gZVHYNL2Vc2mK3iKrpK-FcpURIFdyaP-4Vi38eeeZyM.

6.2.1. Layers in a Convolutional Neural Network (CNN): Convolutional, Pooling, and Fully Connected

The CNN architecture is essentially composed of three principal layers: the convolutional, pooling, and fully connected layers. They each have a distinctive function and play their respective role in the networks' capacity to learn from complex data structures. The convolutional layer forms the core of CNNs, which is trained to automatically detect features from the input data with learnable filters. The filters convolve over the input data, changing it through the convolution operation, allowing the model to capture spatial hierarchies in an efficient manner. As a result, CNNs demonstrate better performance in tasks such as image and speech recognition and display the capability to process variations of input data and provide higher overall accuracy in tasks of various classifications. Pooling layers follow convolutional layers and are a critical part to reduce the dimensionality of the feature maps created by the convolutions. By retaining the most significant data and discarding less crucial features, pooling layers decrease computational complexity and prevent overfitting within the network.

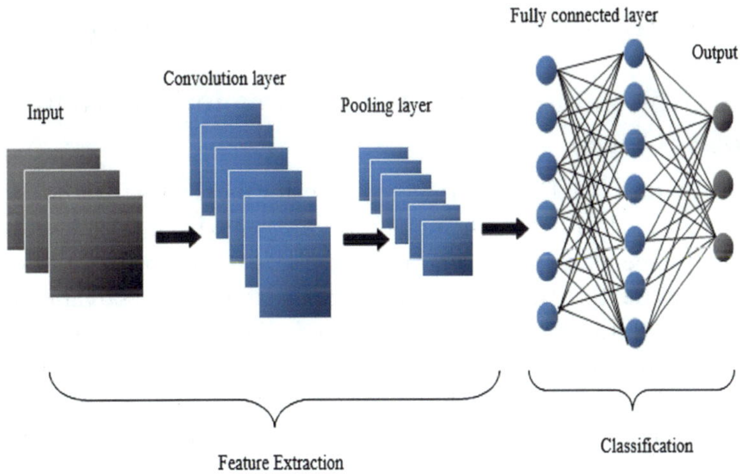

Figure 6.7. *Architecture of convolutional neural network (CNN) with convolutional, pooling, fully connected layer and output.*

Source: https://www.researchgate.net/publication/374143931/figure/fig4/AS:11431281190918268@1695521918070/Architecture-of-CNN-with-convolutional-pooling-fully-connected-layer-and-output.png.

Techniques like max pooling, in which the highest value from sub-regions of feature maps is employed, maintain the essential features needed for effective classification. Furthermore, pooling serves to guarantee the translational invariance of CNNs, allowing the model to discover patterns regardless of their position within the input. As depicted in most research, wise utilization of pooling techniques has realized improved performance in computer vision tasks up to speech recognition, confirming the role of this layer in model performance (Aravkin et al., 2013). The final CNN architecture phase consists of fully connected layers, where the model learns to mix the features learned by past layers in an attempt to make final predictions. In the fully connected layers, all neurons are connected to all neurons in the preceding layer, which facilitates a full integration of the learned features. This connectivity enables the model to learn subtle interactions among the features extracted by the convolution and pooling operations, ultimately transforming these into target outputs. Recent studies have demonstrated the effectiveness of adding techniques such as dropout within fully connected layers for enhancing generalization and overcoming overfitting (Bassett et al., 2017). Through architecture and hyperparameter optimization by techniques like the Evolutionary DEep Networks (EDEN), researchers keep pushing the depth of CNN performance to yield exceptional results across a variety of applications and demonstrating the revolutionary nature of such layering within deep learning processes (Figure 6.7).

6.2.2. Activation Functions Used in Convolutional Neural Networks (CNNs)

The architecture of CNN heavily relies on choosing the right activation functions, and they are tasked with introducing non-linearity into the model. Non-linearity is important since it allows for learning complex patterns in data beyond linear relationships. The Rectified Linear Unit (ReLU) is a popular activation function used in CNNs. ReLU functions by returning the input itself when it is positive and zero otherwise. This move effectively prevents gradient saturation, therefore allowing for faster learning and allowing models to converge more quickly. Further, its computational ease makes it a good pick for deep learning models. However, it is not without restrictions, e.g., the dying ReLU issue where neurons become inactive and fail to learn when training (Cai, 2024). Besides ReLU, additional activation functions have been developed to counter its limitations. The Leaky ReLU is an answer to the dying ReLU problem by introducing a small, non-zero gradient when the unit isn't active. The amendment ensures that there is still some degree of learning in neurons that otherwise wouldn't be. Additionally, the Parametric ReLU (PReLU) and Exponential Linear Unit (ELU) are a couple of other variations that have gained popularity for their improved performance in certain cases. These functions work particularly well in object recognition and image segmentation problems, where finding subtle patterns is crucial. With more complex and deeper neural networks, the activation function remains a key to maintaining learning and the overall performance of the model (Awasthi et al., 2024). Swish is a newer activation function that has become increasingly popular as a highly desirable substitute with superior performance on deep learning tasks compared to standard ReLU use. Swish can mathematically be expressed as f(x) = x * sigmoid(x), creating a non-monotonic, smooth function in which higher-level representations can be learned by the model. This property has made Swish particularly convenient in scenarios where it is needed to model rich relationships in data. Furthermore, empirical analysis has shown that models incorporating Swish perform better than those with ReLU or its modification when accuracy on benchmark datasets is used for comparison. As the research of convolutional neural networks progresses, it continues to uncover a deeper understanding of activation functions and how they are at the forefront of maximizing CNN potential and changing applications in computer vision and beyond (Cai, 2024).

6.2.3. Importance of Architecture Design in Performance

Convolutional Neural Network (CNN) architecture design plays a vital role in determining how proficient they become at performing an array of visual and analytical tasks. By using good layering and parameters, the models capacity to detect fine-grained patterns in data, as needed by image recognition and sentiment analysis, can be enhanced. A good CNN employs hierarchical representation learning, and hierarchical features are learned at multiple levels of abstraction. This is particularly true for use cases involving sentiment harvested from visual content since it needs a model that can catch subtle emotional cues. Work on fine-tuning such architectures suggests that judicious tuning can lead to significant gains in performance, pointing to the linear correspondence between architectural choice and the efficacy of CNNs in practical applications (Jiang et al., 2015). Furthermore, the addition of specialized modules to CNN architectures can also make them more effective in dynamic contexts such as video action recognition. Baseline CNNs might be difficult to manage long-term dependencies since their architecture is designed with spatial features and there is no consideration for temporal dynamics. However, the incorporation of mechanisms from Recurrent Neural Networks (RNNs) that possess a strong ability to deal with temporal data can also further equip the architectures motion understanding ability over time. This composite approach allows CNNs to learn both spatial appearance and motion dynamics, which break the limitations imposed by models strictly convolutional. With the employment of memory-augmented mechanisms, as in recent advancements, the architecture can selectively retain useful information, thus augmenting recognition precision in complex video streams. Advances such as these show the central role architectural design plays in obtaining optimum performance in all areas (Wang et al., 2019). Finally, experimental validation in architecting design cannot be overstressed. Quantifying CNNs against benchmark datasets makes it possible to quantify the impact of design choices on performance. This serious testing makes possible more insight into how layer placement, activation functions, and pooling strategies all contribute to the overall performance of models. For instance, in the case of action recognition datasets, the insights gained from architecture-specific experiments reveal the fine-grained patterns through which structural variations can introduce performance differences. This supports the argument that thoughtful architectural design is no longer a matter of abstract theory but a concrete reality determining the success or failure of CNN deployments. As advancements in the field continue to unravel, the necessity of continuing to innovate architectural designs will remain essential to ensuring improvements are made in CNN performance and dependability.

6.3. TRAINING CONVOLUTIONAL NEURAL NETWORKS (CNNS)

Training CNNs is a difficult task involving close monitoring of numerous factors, including architecture, dataset size, and computational power. Increased complexity in CNN models has unleashed spectacular advances in their application towards image recognition issues. But how much subtle feature capture relies on the balance between network depth and training data volume is increasingly open to evidence suggesting that methods such as Efficient Network Training can radically increase training effectiveness by allowing small datasets to be used without needing to compromise on accuracy. This method, particularly with pre-trained models such as ResNet, exploits pre-existing features which can alleviate the training process, hence enhancing overall model performance and efficiency in most domains (Frohn et al., 2018). Training optimization for CNNs can also include pretraining approaches that simulate traditional feature extraction methods traditionally employed in computer vision. By combining decades of learned from image feature design, CNNs can mimic processes such as histogram of oriented gradients. The pretraining provides a solid foundation for fine-tuning on specific tasks afterward, ultimately allowing the network to learn richer, task-specific representations (Chen et al., 2016). The employment of these advanced techniques enables the CNNs to learn better for new datasets and thereby improve their classification capacity and be used in real-world situations. Meanwhile, these techniques minimize overfitting hazards, which is a common problem when there are limited training samples. The presence of high-performance computing resources such as cloud GPUs has transformed the scene of CNN training entirely, allowing researchers and practitioners to experiment with various training protocols on scales that were not possible before. Efficient Network Training practices are particularly useful in such a situation because they maximize accuracy while maintaining computational cost at an absolute minimum by performing wise resizing of images during training. This method not only helps enhance the performance of the networks but also help optimize the inference times, especially where there are tight runtime constraints (Frohn et al., 2018). With the ongoing development in the field, the fundamental dynamics of these training techniques will be crucial to know. Future research into standard dataset's domains and comparisons with other paradigms in machine learning has the potential to reveal valuable information regarding the efficiencies of training methods in CNNs (Figure 6.8).

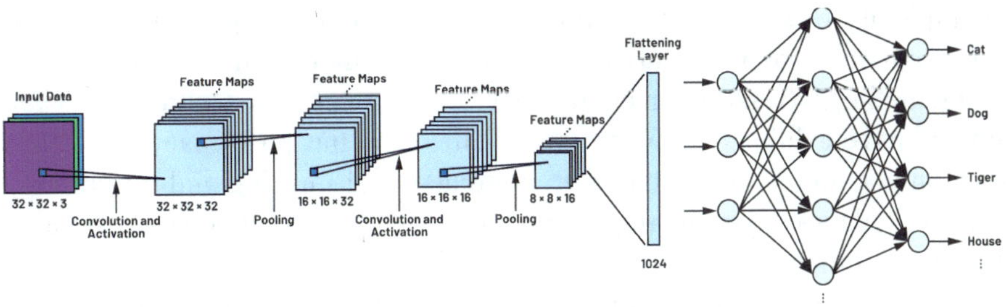

Figure 6.8. *CIFAR convolutional neural network (CNN) architecture.*

Source: https://www.analog.com/en/_/media/images/analog-dialogue/en/volume-57/number-1/articles/training-convolutional-neural-networks-what-is-machine-learning-part-2/491280-fig-01.svg?w=900&rev=5638128a3e8548faa89644 05084c875a.

6.3.1. Dataset Preparation and Augmentation Techniques

Preparation of the dataset is a critical foundation for the successful training of Convolutional Neural Networks (CNNs). It encompasses a number of processes, including data collection, cleaning, and preparation. Proper data collection guarantees that the dataset is a true representation of the problem space, an essential requirement for the model to learn valuable patterns. Data cleaning also involves the removal of noise and inconsistencies in the data that can potentially perplex the training process. This is especially crucial in applications like image classification and object detection, where mislabeled images can have drastic consequences for the performance of the models. Partitioning of the data into train, validation, and test sets makes the correct evaluation and prevents overfitting. These processes are all crucial in deciding whether the models can generalize well to out-of-sample cases. Data augmentation techniques are employed in order to boost the diversity of training sets through artificial boosting of their size by creating transformed copies of existing samples. It is particularly beneficial for use in scenarios where obtaining huge data sets is not possible or expensive. Rotation, scaling, flipping, and color variation are some of the techniques that can provide better examples on which models can be trained, thus overfitting is less likely to occur. In applications such as medical imaging, where there is limited annotated data, data augmentation can be an effective tool. Furthermore, sophisticated augmentation approaches, like Smart Augmentation, enable networks to learn to automatically create optimal augmentations from the training dynamics of themselves. This technique not only boosts accuracy but can also reduce the complexity of the whole network, achieving improved performance with fewer parameters, thereby surpassing current limitations in resource-hungry training methods (Bazrafkan et al., 2017). Augmentation techniques when combined have exhibited amazing improvements in the performance of CNNs in most applications. For instance, in computational imaging and microscopy applications, data availability improvements can be converted into more reliable and accurate outcomes. With deep convolutional neural networks (DCNNs), researchers have overcome complex problems such as 3D inverse scattering and microscopy phase recovery by leveraging the higher variability made available through augmentation methods (Nehmetallah et al., 2019). This technique not only assists in better feature learning from complex datasets but also enhances model resistance to noise and variability present in real-world scenarios. As the demand for advanced AI systems increases, focus on effective dataset preparation and augmentation will remain vital in ensuring advancements and efficiency of CNNs.

6.3.2. Backpropagation and Optimization Algorithms

Backpropagation algorithm is a basis for training Convolutional Neural Networks (CNNs) and provides efficient weight tuning via gradient descent techniques. Backpropagation enables systematic computation of loss function gradients with respect to network parameters, which enables backpropagation to assist the network in learning from mistakes. Backpropagation begins at the output node, where the difference between the output and true values is calculated. This error is thus propagated backward within the network, allowing each layer to modify its weights based on the error propagated from the next layer. Such efficient weight modification is crucial within deep networks, where many layers can accumulate errors should not be ruled out. Such knowledge of backpropagation is therefore crucial in designing stable CNN architectures that can improve performance through iterative learning (Aizenberg et al., 2024). The application of optimization algorithms also enhances the performance of backpropagation in CNNs. Stochastic Gradient Descent (SGD) is one of the most widely used optimization algorithms and modifies the weights from training data subsets, optimizing between performance and cost of computations. Variations such as Momentum and Adam include adaptive mechanisms that help adjust learning rates, hence overcoming issues such as slow convergence and oscillation at local minima.

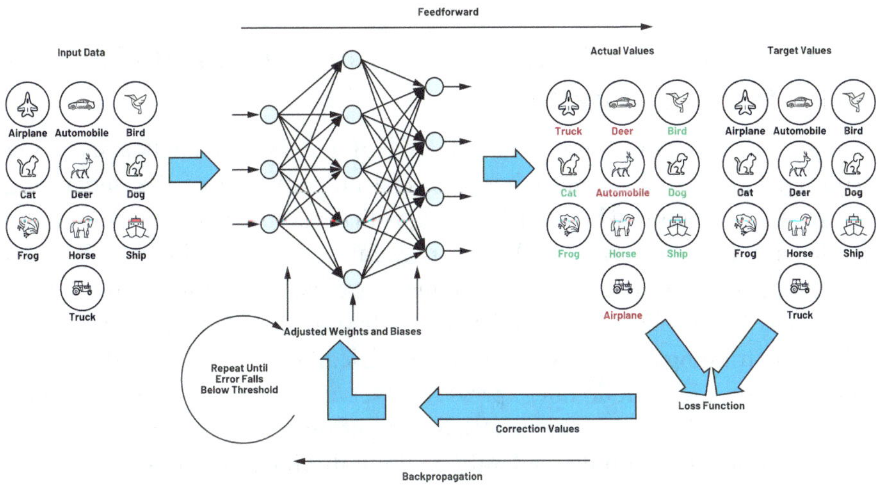

Figure 6.9. *A training loop consisting of feedforward and backpropagation.*

Source: https://www.analog.com/en/_/media/images/analog-dialogue/en/volume-57/number-1/articles/training-convolutional-neural-networks-what-is-machine-learning-part-2/491280-fig-02.svg?w=900&rev=34ea0a41d829451fb5c68c2a635008c5.

These optimization techniques are particularly significant while processing deep structures and intricate datasets as they stabilize the learning procedure and improve convergence rate. Through selecting proper optimization algorithms, researchers and practitioners can essentially improve CNN performance and deploy it to address challenges like image recognition and classification more effectively (Xu et al., 2024). In CNNs, optimization algorithms and backpropagation both work synergistically rather than additively. Backpropagation formulates the fundamental framework of error correction, while optimization algorithms refine the process to make it faster and more efficient with respect to the quality of outcomes. For instance, the adaptive learning rate innovation based on methods like Adam facilitates CNNs to navigate the optimization topography more intelligently, effectively bypassing plateaus where learning becomes stalled. This symbiotic phenomenon is observed in different applications, including driver behavior recognition systems, whose accurate predictions are predicated upon the networks' capacity to leverage abstract patterns in training datasets. A close understanding of both aspects emboldens researchers and developers to create more sophisticated neural designs that stretch the boundaries of what CNNs are capable of Aizenberg et al. (2024) and Xu et al. (2024) (Figure 6.9).

6.3.3. Challenges in Training Convolutional Neural Networks (CNNs), Including Overfitting

Training CNNs is not straightforward, one of the largest challenges being overfitting. Overfitting occurs when a model not only learns the underlying structure in the training set but also the noise, with the consequence that the model generalizes poorly to new data. This is particularly frequent in environments where the quantity of training data is limited or biased, resulting in the failure of models to learn robust features that generalize. If the model memorizes the training set, training set accuracy may be misleading, as evidenced by high performance metrics that do not express themselves in actual usage. Therefore, measures have to be taken so that CNNs are not only able to attain very high accuracy but also perform equivalently well on all kinds of, different datasets. One of the best strategies to resist overfitting is by using data augmentation. This method entails artificially enriching the training dataset by subjecting the present images to different types of transformations like rotation, scaling, or translation. By introducing variability in the training set, CNNs can learn more universalized features that improve the performance of test and validation sets. For instance, in the reported work by Li et al. (2025), the application of data augmentation techniques significantly enhanced the accuracy of classification in detecting complex patterns such as Dongba pictographs. But while data augmentation is a very powerful tool, it can introduce new issues such as increasing the training time and computational costs, which may be beyond the means of all laboratory facilities. Another issue with training CNNs is the architectural complexity and the related hyperparameter tuning that must be achieved for maximum performance. DenseNet-201, as illustrated in Chouat et al. (2025), achieves deep architectures that optimize feature propagation and avoid the vanishing gradient problem but with strict parameter tuning, e.g., learning rate, batch size, and training epochs. This intricate process of tuning is not exactly simple because an optimal parameter setting for a particular dataset may not yield similar results for another dataset. Thus, it is necessary to attempt numerous different setups in experiments, which is time-consuming and computationally expensive. Also, the need for a balanced approach in model selection and hyperparameter tuning emphasizes the multi-aspect challenges in training CNNs, necessitating an interdisciplinary blend of theoretical knowledge and practical know-how to create effective solutions.

6.4. APPLICATIONS OF CONVOLUTIONAL NEURAL NETWORKS (CNNS)

Among CNN's many uses, medical image analysis has been one of the most revolutionary. The capacity to automatically classify and analyze medical images such as X-rays, MRIs, and CT scans has revolutionized diagnostic procedures. CNN's cascaded structure is utilized to learn advanced features from images to apply to tasks of image classification, segmentation, and object detection. Current surveys have indicated that over 300 contributions have explored the intricacy of deep learning methods pertinent to medical image analysis, demonstrating the profound interest and new directions in this subject (Bejnordi et al., 2017). Despite the promising promise of CNNs, the need for large labeled datasets and the characteristics of medical images remain considerable challenges. Solving these issues will be critical in maximizing the performance and utility of CNNs in clinical settings. Besides clinical applications, CNNs have been applied in environmental and climate data analysis, where they are the strong drivers in the detection of patterns and classification. The ability of CNNs to handle spatio-temporal data is particularly relevant in this field, which involves large and unstructured datasets. But proper utilization of CNNs in environmental science requires proper attention to the datas inherent complexities, necessitating specialized architectures for specialized datasets and tasks. Research has proposed innovative solutions, such as auto-labeling techniques via unsupervised clustering algorithms, as a means to compensate for the challenges imposed by sparse labeled examples. For instance, a CNN trained on thousands of labels for weather patterns revealed impressive accuracy rates well over 90%, which underscores the strength of such techniques in solving real-world climate problems (Chattopadhyay et al., 2018). Such flexibility makes CNNs valuable assets in the fight against climate change and environmental loss. Furthermore, their application extends into autonomous systems, where they enable sophisticated abilities in robotics and autonomous driving. The ability of CNNs to process visual information from cameras makes such systems capable of viewing and comprehending the world around them, a necessity for safety in navigation and interaction in dynamic space. This application needs real-time processing to enable instant decision-making as delay or error will result in catastrophic outcomes. Application of CNNs in autonomous systems not only improves their performance but also user experience in the form of enhanced predictive analysis and situational awareness. With researchers developing CNN's training procedures and architectures more finely, their ability to advance autonomous technologies grows, further solidifying their role in building the future of intelligent systems (Figure 6.10).

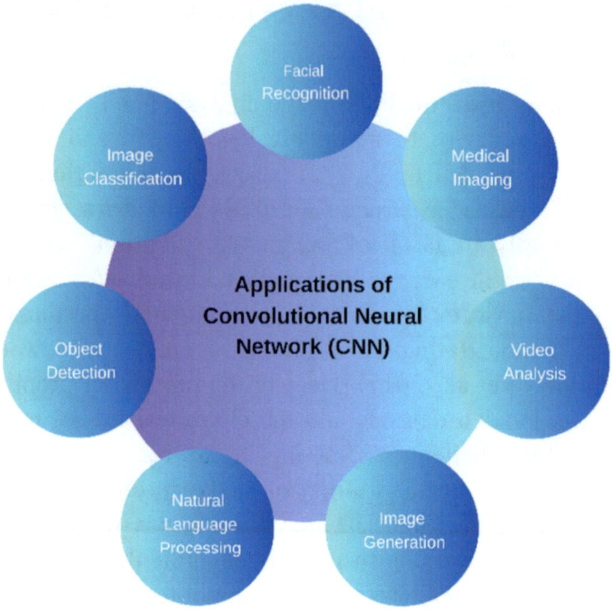

Figure 6.10. *Applications of convolutional neural network (CNN).*

Source: https://www.researchgate.net/profile/Amrish-Kumar-4/publication/374167758/figure/fig1/AS:11431281256820511@1719573685259/Applications-of-Convolutional-Neural-Network-CNN.png.

6.4.1. Image Recognition and Classification

Image recognition and classification have greatly evolved due to advancements in deep learning technology, namely Convolutional Neural Networks (CNNs). These neural networks draw on hierarchical features present in images and can learn features at multiple levels of abstraction. For instance, lower levels can identify edges or textures, but more advanced layers can identify more sophisticated ideas, such as shapes and objects. This enables CNNs to process images more efficiently compared to traditional image processing techniques in applications such as medical imaging, self-driving cars, and face recognition systems. Through their capacity to handle large-sized datasets, CNNs have emerged as the de facto method for image classification tasks with impressive gains in recognition algorithms' accuracy and resilience. Success by CNNs in image classification is typically a function of the architecture design and the specific training methods used. The recent advancements have introduced new methodologies such as the Latent CNN model, which selectively emphasizes those portions of an image that are more informative and overlooks the uninformative background to the largest possible extent. This model is significant in reducing the issues of data sets being skewed in which certain classes might be underrepresented. Also, techniques like Multiple Instance Learning Convolutional Neural Networks are more flexible when it comes to labeling by allowing the strict requirements to be minimized, thereby accommodating even more complex situations that arise in real-world applications. Such strategic advancements focus not only on the CNN architectures but also the techniques employed to propel them towards classifying tasks more effectively (Sun et al., 2025). Even recent research has also proposed new building blocks that enhance CNN architectures, further maximizing image recognition capabilities. Among them is the incorporation of epitomic convolutions, which replace normal layers with a superior feature extraction mechanism. The epitomic convolutional layers raise the accuracy of recognition by allowing for small translations and spatial hierarchies in images. Experiments have also indicated that models employing epitomic convolutions exhibit improved performances on benchmark datasets such as Imagenet, outperforming traditional CNN designs. By plugging the loopholes in existing designs, such advancements have the potential to put image classification to new heights, registering significant improvements in precision and performance (Papandreou et al., 2014) (Figure 6.11).

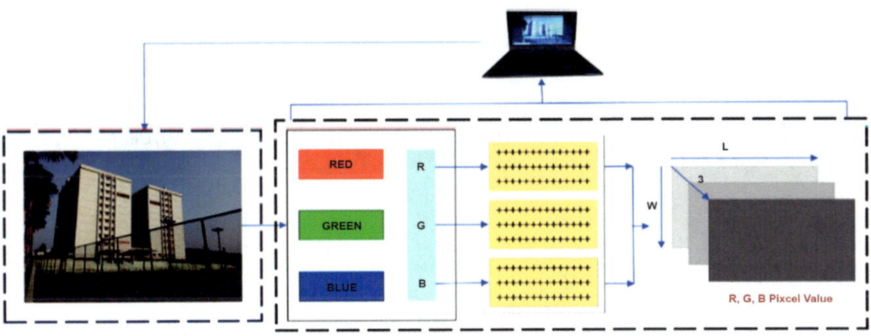

Figure 6.11. *Process of image recognition in a computer.*

Source: https://media.springernature.com/full/springer-static/image/art%3A10.1038%2Fs41598-023-49739-1/MediaObjects/41598_2023_49739_Fig1_HTML.png?as=webp.

6.4.2. Object Detection and Segmentation

The advancements in object detection and segmentation from convolutional neural networks (CNNs) have been most impactful across various fields like computer vision and medical imaging. Detection of objects refers to the identification and classification of objects in an image, while segmentation partitions an image into meaningful regions. These operations are crucial to technologies like autonomous vehicles and surveillance systems, where identification and boundary specification of objects are very crucial. The effectiveness of CNNs in performing these tasks lies in their ability to learn automatically hierarchical feature representations. It is observed in recent research that employing novel architectures especially designed for semantic segmentation enhances the performance of CNNs, providing a robust mechanism for object and boundary separation.

Figure 6.12. *In image segmentation, our goal is to classify the different objects in the image, and identify their boundaries.*

Source: https://miro.medium.com/v2/resize:fit:720/format: webp/1 Ndwf-HMrW3rpj5SW_VQtWVw.png.*

Another contribution of the paper is that it introduces specialized frameworks to support word recognition in natural images with semantic segmentation techniques. The WordFence structure, for instance, greatly identifies word boundary positions to more effectively detect text from scene images. By the pixelwise weighted softmax loss function design, the design favors smaller text regions against background noise reduction and hence addresses common issues faced by recognition performance. The end-to-end system outperformed traditional approaches with a 92% recall rate against benchmark data, showing the capability of CNNs not only for object detection but also domain-specific tasks such as text recognition across diverse environments (Polzounov et al., 2017). In medical image analysis, CNNs have proven to be a go-to method of object detection and segmentation, which enhances diagnostic processes of their own accord. Deep learning techniques enable precise anatomical structure classification and localization in medical images, an imperative aspect of radiology and pathology. As evident from recent surveys, CNNs have shown promising results in solving image registration and analysis problems, praising their adaptability across various fields. Regardless of these developments, a number of obstacles lie ahead, such as the requirement of big annotated datasets and the difficulty of transferring models from one imaging modality to another. It will be essential to overcome these obstacles in order to progress, extending the frontiers of CNNs in complicated image examination tasks (Bejnordi et al., 2017) (Figure 6.12).

6.4.3. Use in Medical Imaging and Diagnostics

Application of Convolutional Neural Networks (CNNs) in medical imaging and diagnosis has rapidly transformed the healthcare landscape, making possible more accurate and less time-consuming analyses than traditional methods. These deep learning models have been particularly beneficial for image classification, object detection, and segmentation tasks, with many studies published that validate their efficacy. According to Böhle et al. (2019), more than 300 recent advances in medical image analysis have been reported, emphasizing the growing reliance on CNNs to bridge challenges in clinical environments. The potential of CNNs to learn independently from raw image data minimizes the need for manual feature extraction, and thus, diagnosis is faster and replicable. As physicians and clinicians discover ever greater utility for such technologies, it is important to measure their performance as well as effects on patient outcomes. In specific applications, CNNs have done well in detecting Alzheimer's disease (AD) from structural magnetic resonance imaging (MRI) data analysis. One of the most noted applications of layer-wise relevance propagation (LRP) highlighted CNN decision interpretability in AD diagnosis, producing heatmaps that labeled the most important locations in the brain images for classification outputs (Bejnordi et al., 2017). Not only is this type of visualization useful for the interpretation of network decisions, but also for clinicians in that it pinpoints why a given patient would exhibit signs of AD. The ability to correlate such results with existing medical literature underscores the potential of CNNs in returning accuracy and transparency during diagnosis. Through enhanced interpretability of CNN outcomes, clinicians are able to make better-informed clinical decisions that ultimately feed through to better patient care. Although significant progress has been made, some issues remain that must be addressed in order for sustained implementation of CNNs into medicine to occur. Issues such as the sensitivity of LRP and other methods to parameters of computation and the models used may affect the reliability of the results. In addition, while CNNs can identify significant locations such as the temporal lobe and hippocampus in AD patients, inconsistency of individual case studies necessitates approaching implementation with caution in clinical practice (Böhle et al., 2019). Future research should focus on developing robust algorithms that ensure consistency in their execution in solving these problems. Moreover, exploring other available challenges in deep learning applications can unlock more sophisticated methodologies that will consolidate the role of CNNs in diagnostics and lead to improved healthcare results and patient experiences (Bejnordi et al., 2017) (Figure 6.13).

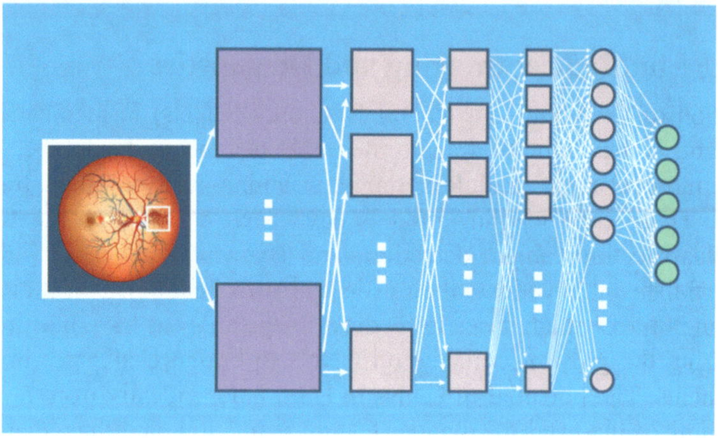

Figure 6.13. *Using convolutional neural networks (CNNs) in medical image analysis for automated diagnostics.*

Source: https://www.scnsoft.com/healthcare/trick-or-treat-using-cnns-in-medical-image-analysis-for-automated-diagnostics/training-testing.png.

6.5. ADVANTAGES OF CONVOLUTIONAL NEURAL NETWORKS (CNNS)

The applicability of CNNs is indicated by their ability to work effectively in the tasks of image recognition and classification, and this has serious implications in various sectors. Through the proper utilization of spatial hierarchies in images, CNNs apply convolutional layers that allow them to learn intricate patterns and features with little preprocessing. This aspect greatly enhances the accuracy and reliability of the models when compared to traditional machine learning models. Specifically, CNNs are designed to learn local features, so they are extremely capable at object recognition in an image. This has been responsible for their widespread application from facial recognition systems to computer vision-based quality inspection in manufacturing lines, where accuracy is vital. One of the great advantages of CNNs is the network structure that keeps the usage of parameters to a large extent compared to fully connected networks. The saving is achieved by sharing weights in convolutional layers, and thus CNNs can make optimal use of computational resources while achieving high performance. Ou et al. (2017) provides a striking illustration wherein TRFs of the neural variety, that are based on deep CNNs, are miles ahead of regular recurrent models in terms of speed and accuracy. This renders CNNs not just more and more deployable in real-time scenarios but also scalable in larger data sets. This efficiency is critical in applications such as medical image analysis, where accurate and timely diagnosis can make a huge difference in patient recovery. CNNs also bring the benefit of multi-channel representation for images. This capability extends the model's ability to perform classification tasks from various data sources. For instance, in dental health assessment through quantitative imaging, CNNs can classify multi-channel images taking into account various color channels to improve classification accuracy for plaque and other ailments. Crielaard et al. (2017) depicts the way in which a CNN image classification model significantly outperformed shallow classification methods, thus validating the appropriateness of deep learning models for processing complex data types. This multi-aspect approach not only enhances performance but also provides a robust mechanism to deal with difficulties across various applications, thus CNNs are valuable in the data-driven age today.

6.5.1. Ability to Automatically Extract Features

The ability to automatically extract features is the characteristic that defines Convolutional Neural Networks (CNNs) and enables them to distinguish minute patterns in dense data sets. Standard machine learning approaches are prone to requiring hand-engineered feature extraction, which is as time-consuming as it is biased on the operator's skill level. However, CNNs access hierarchical layers that learn progressively more abstract features of the raw input. These range from convolutions that react to textures and edges to deeper layers that react to more abstract features, such as shapes and object parts. This capability of automatic feature extraction significantly enhances the models flexibility and performance, allowing CNNs to perform very well across a broad spectrum of applications, such as image and speech recognition, demonstrating their strength and robustness in handling various inputs and tasks. Unveiling the hidden efficiency of CNN architectures is made possible through a deep exploration of the dynamics of automatic feature extraction. It has been proven from studies that CNNs are capable of achieving high levels of performance with smaller models as seen from the utilization of StochasticNets. The design encompasses sparsely connected deep neural networks, which enhance speed and efficiency in feature extraction without losing classification accuracy. It has been proven experimentally that relative error rates are reduced, which displays the practical benefits associated with this new approach. For instance, StochasticNets was able to effectively achieve a relative test error improvement of ~4.5% on classification problems in the STL-10 dataset. Such performance highlights how CNNs are able to evolve to improve their learning capacity as well as their functional performance in practical applications, making them priceless assets in modern machine learning. In practical usage, the potential of CNNs to automatically extract features has revolutionary applications, especially in fields like healthcare, where proper analysis of data can influence critical interventions. An example of such applicability of CNNs is the identification of Stereotypical Motor Movements (SMMs) in Autism Spectrum Disorder (ASD) patients. Through the use of deep learning techniques that enable automatic feature extraction of relevant features from multi-sensor accelerometer signals, researchers are able to design strong SMM detection systems that can overcome inter-subject and intra-subject variability issues. This not only facilitates more accurate SMM detection but also enables real-time monitoring, making personal therapeutic interventions a possibility. In line with the ongoing advancement of the discipline, the use of CNNs in feature extraction methods is a perfect representation of the harmony between real-world application and machine learning, with reference to the likelihood of transforming diagnostic and treatment strategies in many different environments (Bizzego et al., 2015; Fieguth et al., 2015).

6.5.2. Robustness to Variations in Input Data

The stability of Convolutional Neural Networks (CNNs) against input data variations is a vital characteristic that makes them more useful across various domains. Robustness can be understood as the ability of a model to perform irrespective of changes in input conditions, particularly under practical scenarios where environmental factors may change data behavior significantly. This robustness is critical in tasks such as visual place recognition, where CNNs must correctly identify locations despite variations in lighting, view, and context. Based on studies, tailoring CNN architectures to specific tasks and employing multi-scale feature encoding contributes to the development of invariant representations and thereby improving robustness against such variations. By leveraging patterns that span a wide range of experimental conditions, CNNs achieve a remarkable performance increase, as indicated by significant gains over baseline recognition methods and pre-trained models on challenging datasets (Chen et al., 2017). Outside of visual domains, CNN robustness extends to bioacoustic applications, where they are applied to recognize and classify animal vocalizations in noisy environments. The inherent randomness of background noise presents a significant difficulty for unsupervised sound event detection (SED) systems. A research article highlights the adoption of noise adaptation techniques that enhance the CNN models' generalizability upon being deployed in multi-scene acoustic conditions. Employing methodologies like per-channel energy normalization and context-adaptive neural network layers, the authors observe a dramatic boost in detection accuracy. These advances indicate that CNNs can handle diverse input data in a good manner and be consistent in performance in the presence of noise interference. Thus, CNNs' capability to handle variability of inputs not only reflects their adaptability but also their potential in practical applications where variability is inevitable (Bello et al., 2019). Moreover, advances in training processes hold key in building CNN's robustness to variability. The advent of large-scale datasets aimed at covering a large number of scenarios, such as the Specific PlacEs Dataset used for place recognition, represents this novel trend. Systematically covering multiple instances of appearance variations of places, CNNs are able to learn from a richer feature set, producing more robust models. Their evaluation on benchmark data sets has presented evidence of improved performance, validating the implication that strict training regimens can directly influence the reliability of CNNs in real-world use. As the field progresses, such evolution of these training techniques will be essential, particularly as CNNs attempt to address ever-more dynamic data universes in which variations are not merely a fact but also an inherent element of the operational environment they have to grapple with (Chen et al., 2017).

6.5.3. Efficiency in Processing Large Datasets

Efficiency in processing large datasets is one of the critical issues in applying Convolutional Neural Networks (CNNs), particularly where computer vision and deep learning are in question. As these models are computationally intensive, their efficiency to process the data and segment it is what determines the overall systems performance. For instance, recent advances in CNN architectures leverage the capabilities of cloud-based solutions and on-premises infrastructure in order to maximize training process utilization of available hardware like GPUs. This double approach enhances improved efficiency by lessening training durations while enhancing the correctness of resulting classifiers, and hence it is crucial to employ proper data processing techniques and infrastructures particular to specific applications like automotive recognition and visual inspections (Ashcraft et al., 2017). The inherent limitations that come with conventional backpropagation algorithms also highlight inefficiencies in processing big datasets. Weight transfer problem, which is a result of uninhibited data movement demands, can limit DNN scalability, particularly in the case of deeper networks. Recent advancements bring bio-plausible solutions, such as sparse feedback alignment methods that reduce the computational load. With only a fraction of the information utilized in the past, such methods significantly lower the time and energy spent on training CNN. Consequently, such innovations not only mitigate memory bandwidth challenges but also enhance end-to-end processing efficiency when handling large volumes of data, which is a sign of progression towards more environmentally friendly deep learning conduct (Crafton et al., 2019). In addition, practical applications derived from CNNs all stress the importance of efficient ways of handling processing. As data volumes grow, coupled with growing complexity, and there is more reliance on pre-curated, labeled data, there is an evolving necessity for creative steps towards optimizing training outcomes. The automobile manufacturing sector, for example, illustrates this by creating specialized datasets which support automatic detection of car features. Utilizing CNNs along with optimized cloud platforms provides improved management of the data, leading to high-performing classification models. As such networks continue to develop and transform, benefiting from expanded computing and storage capabilities while addressing existing inefficiencies is key to unlocking the full value of CNNs for processing massive data sets (Ashcraft et al., 2017).

6.6. LIMITATIONS OF CONVOLUTIONAL NEURAL NETWORKS (CNNS)

Despite all their advancements, CNNs possess significant disadvantages that can restrict their applicability in various domains. One of the core issues is that they are prone to adversarial attacks, where slight, and in others, even unnoticeable modifications of input lead to extreme output classification discrepancies. This sensitivity poses quintessential difficulties in safety-critical uses, such as facial recognition and self-driving cars, where errors can have catastrophic effects. In addition, CNNs rely on vast amounts of labeled training data and, therefore, are resource-intensive and difficult to utilize in applications where data gathering is prohibitively expensive or challenging. Such reliance on large datasets reflects the difficulties researchers face in trying to employ CNNs in a variety of real-world tasks. More critically, interpreting results produced by CNNs is another intrinsic limitation. While such networks can achieve remarkable performance results in problems of classification, the black-box decision process of their results is objectionable in regards to accountability and transparency. Their non-interpretable nature makes their decision processes more difficult to comprehend, especially in industries like healthcare or finance where stakeholder trust has to be unequivocal. For example, when constructing convolutional neural networks for the detection of seizures early from EEG, reliability and accuracy are more immediate requirements. As noted, many neural networks can perform in certain conditions but are lacking where optimizing them to work for low-power microcontrollers involved in long-term monitoring is concerned, thus emphasizing a discrepancy between model performance and practical application (Blum et al., 2018). Besides, CNNs suffer the disadvantage of failing to generalize to new or unseen information with ease, thereby leading to overfitting. This is further pronounced in specialized applications such as gravitational wave detection, where CNNs have yet to reach the level of performance achieved using traditional methods (Gebhard et al., 2019). Overfitting occurs when a model learns noise and random fluctuations in the training data rather than the actual patterns. It is a phenomenon that can drastically reduce a network's performance on new data, and thus make the network weaker for practical applications. The computational expense of training deep CNN models also discourages smaller groups of researchers and organizations from accessing it. Thus, while CNNs are promising across various fields, these issues raise a need for more research aiming to enhance their robustness, interpretability, and generalizability for practical applications.

6.6.1. Requirement for Large Amounts of Labeled Data

Substantial amounts of annotated data are the biggest obstacle in the successful use of Convolutional Neural Networks (CNNs). These networks function best with comprehensive datasets that allow them to learn deep structures and features to improve the accuracy of their predictions. However, getting comprehensive annotated datasets is typically faced by practical constraints like the time-consuming task of annotating data and the requirement for expertise to correctly label. In areas like medical imaging, where there is a need for sensitivity, the non-availability of labeled data turns out to be a limitation in exploiting the full potential of CNNs. Consequently, the inefficiencies inherent in traditional supervised learning approaches highlight the pressing necessity for alternative methods that are capable of bridging the gap caused by non-availability of adequate amounts of labeled data. In response to the limitations due to excessive demand for labeled data, new approaches such as semi-supervised learning have emerged. Semi-supervised approaches can leverage the presence of limited amounts of labeled data and a more extensive collection of unlabeled data. Semi-supervised approaches enable CNNs to enhance their learning capabilities without requiring intensive labeling operations, hence enabling a more practical path towards cost-effective model training. Utilizing a combination of supervised and unsupervised learning techniques, these techniques allow for significant performance enhancements while reducing the requirements for large volumes of human-labeled datasets. This adaptability is particularly prevalent within most applications, including radio emitter detection, where access to enormous, but untagged, data can be used to customize learning performance to achieve best results (Chapelle et al., 2017). Furthermore, there are particular applications of CNNs that enhance additionally the necessity to handle solutions to the need for labeled data. For example, in medical imaging, a Convolutional Neural Network-based Unsupervised Body part Regression (UBR) has demonstrated that unlabeled CT volumes can be employed efficiently, sidestepping challenges with big labeled datasets. The UBR approach is one instance of intrinsic relationships in unlabeled data directing training and outlines one self-organizing method for building a continuous score for each axial slice based solely on inter-slice relationships (Lu et al., 2018). This hints at a significant paradigm shift in how efficiently CNNs can be trained, suggesting that machine learning's future may be linked to new learning paradigms that are capable of tapping into unlabeled data.

6.6.2. Computational Resource Demands

The computational resource demands of Convolutional Neural Networks (CNNs) have become a focal point of debate within the field of artificial intelligence, particularly when said networks are used to power more advanced applications. When researchers are trying to make CNNs more accurate, they will primarily look towards increasing or expanding network architecture. However, this will only fuel computational costs, doubling both resources required for training and time taken by these models to generate predictions exponentially. The challenge lies in balancing the requirement for high accuracy against the constraint of computational limits, which are keenly experienced in cases that involve computationally limited edge devices. Bao et al. (2019) makes the observation that enhancing performance through the restriction of model size—rather than growing it—is able to deliver significant gain in accuracy while simultaneously reducing the computational burden. Besides, hardware technologies such as resistive random-access memory (ReRAM) have been proposed as solutions to help address the memory bottleneck of CNNs. This kind of technology allows for a processing-in-memory paradigm that can effectively bridge the gap between computational capabilities and memory capacity. Its unique architecture design allows for tremendous improvement in efficiency and density, both being highly valued in coping with the growing demands of CNNs. However, as pointed out in Hu et al. (2019), the full potential of these innovations remains unrealized due to the communication overhead among the processing elements and peripheral circuit complexity management. The focus on developing a more efficient and smaller system structure is thus crucial in addressing these issues and maintaining high-performance computing capabilities. In addition to hardware developments, ongoing optimization of software systems is also essential to manage computational resource demands. The idea of reconfigurable architectures, i.e., Field Programmable Synapse Arrays (FPSA), and a software stack integrated all together can improve the utilization of pre-trained deep learning models. Those frameworks can customize routing and placement algorithms to find a compromise between storage and computation needs, enhancing overall performance and inference speed. As evidenced by the advances brought by FPSA in comparison to state-of-the-art structures, hardware and software optimization are critical to preserving the boost in CNN usage. Lastly, the marriage of new hardware and adaptive software strategies will address increasing resource demands, allowing more and effective use of CNNs across many areas.

6.6.3. Vulnerability to Adversarial Attacks

The increasing applications of Convolutional Neural Networks (CNNs) in critical applications, such as medical image processing, testify to the necessity of addressing their vulnerability to adversarial attacks as a priority. Adversarial examples are inputs that have been slightly perturbed to cause a misclassification by the neural network, and in most instances without noticeable changes to human observers. The phenomenon poses a particular threat in instances such as COVID-19 diagnosis, where DNNs such as CNNs have been employed to diagnose chest X-ray images. It has been found in research that such networks are vulnerable to universal adversarial perturbations (UAPs) leading to classification failure, posing a major threat to their reliability and robustness. As detecting accuracy remains a matter of utmost importance in medical settings, discovery of such vulnerabilities and remedying them will be of paramount importance to ensure patient safety and trust in automated decision-making systems (Hirano et al., 2020). The implications of adversarial vulnerability extend far beyond mere misclassification errors; they pose serious questions regarding the ethical deployment of CNN-based systems. Those concerns are amplified in autonomous systems, where the consequences of misclassification can have dangerous implications. For instance, the reality that CNN output can be manipulated using adversarial examples poses threats throughout a variety of applications, from autonomous vehicles to security. Adversarial manipulation exploits the natural processes of CNNs, typically insufficiently robust to counter such attacks, as evidenced through various empirical works. By illustrating that standard learning algorithms can violate smoothness assumptions, researchers show the potential of vast safety breaches inherent in deep-learning designs (Biggio et al., 2017). Hence, making sure a photo of these vulnerabilities exists is crucial to the development of secure, reliable AI systems. Mitigation methods against adversarial attacks focus on enhancing the robustness of CNN models, but it is challenging. Techniques such as adversarial training involve exposing the CNN to adversarial examples while training, which causes some form of resistance against such manipulation. Nevertheless, such techniques are typically resource time-consuming and do not necessarily eliminate the vulnerability altogether against optimally crafted attacks. In addition, solutions like input rejection hold promise, but the need to detect abnormal inputs complicates things. As the terrain of AI develops, then, research must keep up with developing new solutions, such as improved model forms and noise-injection methods, to aid in defense against adversarial attack. Implementing effective countermeasures is imperative to ensure the secure deployment of CNNs to high-risk environments, ultimately safeguarding the integrity and performance of AI applications across multiple domains (Hirano et al., 2020).

SUMMARY

Overall, the evolution of CNNs is a paradigm shift in computer vision and pattern recognition. Understanding the history of neural networks helps us grasp the significance of CNNs. As seen in this chapter, CNNs perform optimally in deriving hierarchical feature representations from data to carry out high-level tasks such as image classification, detection of objects, and segmentation with great accuracy. The evolution of architectures combining low- and high-level features has proven the importance of utilizing contextual information in improving the model's performance. For instance, it has been shown through experimentation that the incorporation of context closer to top-level layers can result in a 1%–2% error reduction in classification without having an appreciable increase in computational costs (Afzal et al., 2017). Such developments not only enhance performance but also open up avenues for investigation in further developing CNN architecture, thus opening up a lever for theoretical advancement as well as practical deployment. Moreover, CNN applications extend beyond visual image processing tasks to permeate areas such as medical diagnosis and autonomous systems. For example, in pulmonary nodule detection, the integration of Maximum Intensity Projection (MIP) images for nodule detection represents the effectiveness of CNNs in real clinical application. By integrating two-dimensional (2-D) CT scans and MIP images, researchers achieved an astounding sensitivity of 92.67% with extremely minimal false positives, successfully demonstrating the potential of CNNs in aiding healthcare professionals with decision-making that has life-altering consequences (Cui et al., 2019). The above example demonstrates the ways in which CNNs can enhance diagnostic accuracy, thereby enhancing patient outcomes. The findings confirm an increased possibility for further integration of CNNs into the healthcare technology field, thus affirming the networks' flexibility. In general, the history of Convolutional Neural Networks demonstrates a remarkable overlap of innovation and utilization across many disciplines. With scientists continually developing and innovating the networks, the prospects of CNNs addressing more sophisticated problems become increasingly evident. The potential to advance object recognition, augment medical diagnosis, and augment user interaction in interactives is great. These achievements testify to the importance of ongoing research and development within the domain of CNNs, such that future iterations will propel maximum performance while limiting constraints to the bare minimum. Therefore, the demand for a combined effort by academia, industry experts, and healthcare practitioners is most important to leverage the full potential of CNNs and provide breakthrough development across various fields.

When considering the advancement and applications of CNNs, there are a number of points that come into focus and underscore their importance in contemporary machine learning. One key point that stands out is that CNNs can learn high-level features from complicated data inputs, and in particular, images. This feature extraction capability allows CNNs to efficiently process visual data and recognize patterns, making them useful in computer vision applications such as image classification, object detection, and medical imaging. They have been constructed in various architectures over the years to enhance their performance, and researchers continue to seek optimization methods for CNNs to eliminate redundancy and optimize efficiency and accuracy. The recent findings of the research point towards the adaptability of CNNs in diverse settings and emphasize their application in bringing in revolutionary advancements in diverse fields. The second important feature is the relation of CNNs with new modules for enhancing performance. For instance, the development of architectures involving specialized modules like the Differentiable Spatial Normalization Technique (DSNT) has proved to have favorable impacts on specific applications. A study evaluated three CNN architectures for detection of important points on the Chinese mitten crab carapace and determined that the DSNT module significantly enhanced detection accuracy and used fewer resources (Wu et al., 2025). This addition of new modules shows how typical CNN structures could be expanded to meet specific needs in specialized domains, leading to improved outcomes in areas like aquaculture monitoring, where accuracy and dependability are paramount. In conclusion, the future of CNNs is being driven by the need to incorporate temporal data in the form of information beyond spatial data. Although CNNs are effective in capturing spatial features, researchers have attempted recurrent architectures due to their limited performance in temporal processing. For example, recent developments in spiking neural networks (SNNs) focus on modeling spatio-temporal features and efficiently extracting data from dynamic environments. The proposed recurrent spiking neural network model, with a state-of-the-art spiking convolutional block attention module (SCBAM), integrates the spatial and temporal information, reflecting an exciting step towards the solution of the present shortcomings of CNNs (Xu et al., 2024). This convergence of techniques not only enhances model performance but also increases the flexibility of CNNs to a wider range of datasets and real-world problems, further embedding them in their continued relevance in the evolving landscape of machine learning.

REFERENCES

1. Afzal, M. Z., Kölsch, A., & Liwicki, M. (2017). Multilevel context representation for improving object recognition. http://arxiv.org/abs/1703.06408 (accessed on 25th September 2025).
2. Aizenberg, I. N., & Vasko, A. (2024). Frequency-domain and spatial-domain MLMVN-based convolutional neural networks. Algorithms, 17, 361. https://www.semanticscholar.org/paper/986b5bc1811138024fd348c4f63aad42dc67990b (accessed on 25th September 2025).
3. Aravkin, A. Y., Beran, T., Dahl, G. E., et al. (2013). Improvements to deep convolutional neural networks for LVCSR. http://arxiv.org/abs/1309.1501 (accessed on 25th September 2025).
4. Ashcraft, N., Cook, M., Djerekarov, E., et al. (2017). Deep learning in the automotive industry: Applications and tools. http://arxiv.org/abs/1705.00346 (accessed on 25th September 2025).
5. Awasthi, A., Rao, S. B., & Acharjya, K. (2024). Efficient image feature extraction using convolutional neural networks. 2024 3rd International Conference for Advancement in Technology (ICONAT). https://www.semanticscholar.org/paper/40497c1b01cf4c5b5304e44a759542b8ab9893e5 (accessed on 25th September 2025).
6. Bahrami, N., Bass, E., Blansit, K., et al. (2019). Automated CT and MRI liver segmentation and biometry using a generalized convolutional neural network. https://core.ac.uk/download/286729450.pdf (accessed on 25th September 2025).
7. Bao, C., Chen, J., Gao, A., et al. (2019). Be your own teacher: Improve the performance of convolutional neural networks via self-distillation. http://arxiv.org/abs/1905.08094 (accessed on 25th September 2025).
8. Baroffio, L., Bondi, L., Pau, D., et al. (2016). Reduced memory region based deep convolutional neural network detection. https://core.ac.uk/download/477685912.pdf (accessed on 25th September 2025).
9. Bassett, B. A., & Dufourq, E. (2017). EDEN: Evolutionary deep networks for efficient machine learning. http://arxiv.org/abs/1709.09161 (accessed on 25th September 2025).
10. Bazrafkan, S., Corcoran, P., & Lemley, J. (2017). Smart augmentation–Learning an optimal data augmentation strategy. https://core.ac.uk/download/227529778.pdf (accessed on 25th September 2025).
11. Bejnordi, B. E., Ciompi, F., Ghafoorian, M., et al. (2017). A survey on deep learning in medical image analysis. http://arxiv.org/abs/1702.05747 (accessed on 25th September 2025).

12. Bello, J. P., Farnsworth, A., Kelling, S., et al. (2019). Robust sound event detection in bioacoustics sensor networks. http://arxiv.org/abs/1905.08352 (accessed on 25th September 2025).
13. Biggio, B., Brown, G., Demontis, A., et al. (2017). Is deep learning safe for robot vision? Adversarial examples against the iCub humanoid. http://arxiv.org/abs/1708.06939 (accessed on 25th September 2025).
14. Bizzego, A., Furlanello, C., Jurman, G., et al. (2015). Convolutional neural network for stereotypical motor movement detection in autism. https://core.ac.uk/download/593039281.pdf (accessed on 25th September 2025).
15. Blum, M., Boedecker, J., Dümpelmann, M., et al. (2018). Early seizure detection with an energy-efficient convolutional neural network on an implantable microcontroller. http://arxiv.org/abs/1806.04549 (accessed on 25th September 2025).
16. Böhle, M., Eitel, F., Ritter, K., et al. (2019). Layer-wise relevance propagation for explaining deep neural network decisions in MRI-based Alzheimer's disease classification. https://core.ac.uk/download/227044275.pdf (accessed on 25th September 2025).
17. Bronstein, M. M., Bruna, J., LeCun, Y., et al. (2016). Geometric deep learning: Going beyond Euclidean data. https://core.ac.uk/download/148026047.pdf (accessed on 25th September 2025).
18. Brunton, S., Koumoutsakos, P., & Noack, B. (2020). Machine learning for fluid mechanics. http://arxiv.org/abs/1905.11075 (accessed on 25th September 2025).
19. Buckner, C. (2018). Empiricism without magic: Transformational abstraction in deep convolutional neural networks. https://core.ac.uk/download/186330867.pdf (accessed on 25th September 2025).
20. Cai, G. (2024). Advanced image classification using convolutional neural networks. Science and Technology of Engineering, Chemistry and Environmental Protection. https://www.semanticscholar.org/paper/4122da01403873b8ba25126161ed3c0210089aaf (accessed on 25th September 2025).
21. Chapelle, C., Ester, M., Kingma, D., LeCun, Y., Maaten, L., et al. (2017). Semi-supervised radio signal identification. http://arxiv.org/abs/1611.00303 (accessed on 25th September 2025).
22. Chattopadhyay, A., Hassanzadeh, P., & Pasha, S. (2018). A test case for application of convolutional neural networks to spatio-temporal climate data: Re-identifying clustered weather patterns. http://arxiv.org/abs/1811.04817 (accessed on 25th September 2025).

23. Chen, X., Liu, M. Y., Mallya, A., Tuzel, O., et al. (2016). Unsupervised network pretraining via encoding human design. http://arxiv.org/abs/1502.05689 (accessed on 25th September 2025).

24. Chen, Z., Jacobson, A., Liu, L., Milford, M., et al. (2017). Deep learning features at scale for visual place recognition. http://arxiv.org/abs/1701.05105 (accessed on 25th September 2025).

25. Chouat, I., Echtioui, A., & Ghorbel, M. (2025). Lung disease classification in X-ray images using a modified deep convolutional neural network. In 2025 IEEE 22nd International Multi-Conference on Systems, Signals & Devices (SSD). https://www.semanticscholar.org/paper/89412fb81b6686b0897746f86183bfa2d332c524 (accessed on 25th September 2025).

26. Crafton, B., Gebhardt, E., Parihar, A., Raychowdhury, A., et al. (2019). Direct feedback alignment with sparse connections for local learning. https://core.ac.uk/download/200898225.pdf (accessed on 25th September 2025).

27. Crielaard, W., Imangaliyev, S., Keijser, B. J. F., Levin, E., et al. (2017). Classification of quantitative light-induced fluorescence images using convolutional neural network. http://arxiv.org/abs/1705.09193 (accessed on 25th September 2025).

28. Cui, X., Guo, J., Oudkerk, M., van Ooijen, P., et al. (2019). Automatic pulmonary nodule detection in CT scans using convolutional neural networks based on maximum intensity projection. https://core.ac.uk/download/322977421.pdf (accessed on 25th September 2025).

29. Dille, P., Hoffman, R., Hsu, Y. C., Hu, X., et al. (2020). Project RISE: Recognizing industrial smoke emissions. http://arxiv.org/abs/2005.06111 (accessed on 25th September 2025).

30. El Gamal, A., Liu, X., & Yang, D. (2018). Deep neural network architectures for modulation classification. http://arxiv.org/abs/1712.00443 (accessed on 25th September 2025).

31. Fawaz, H. I., Forestier, G., Idoumghar, L., Muller, P., et al. (2018). Transfer learning for time series classification. http://arxiv.org/abs/1811.01533 (accessed on 25th September 2025).

32. Fieguth, P., Shafiee, M. J., Siva, P., Wong, A., et al. (2015). Efficient deep feature learning and extraction via StochasticNets. http://arxiv.org/abs/1512.03844 (accessed on 25th September 2025).

33. Fink, M., Layer, T., Mackenbrock, G., Sprinzl, M., et al. (2018). Baseline detection in historical documents using convolutional U-Nets. http://arxiv.org/abs/1810.09343 (accessed on 25th September 2025).

34. Frohn, P., & Wanger, T. C. (2018). Testing the efficient network training (ENTR) hypothesis: Initially reducing training image size makes convolutional neural network training for image recognition tasks more efficient. http://arxiv.org/abs/1807.11583 (accessed on 25th September 2025).

35. Gabbouj, M., Iosifidis, A., & Tran, D. T. (2017). Improving efficiency in convolutional neural network with multilinear filters. http://arxiv.org/abs/1709.09902 (accessed on 25th September 2025).

36. Gabrys, B., Musial, K., & Skarding, J. (2021). Foundations and modelling of dynamic networks using dynamic graph neural networks: A survey. http://arxiv.org/abs/2005.07496 (accessed on 25th September 2025).

37. Gashler, M. S., & Pierson, H. A. (2017). Deep learning in robotics: A review of recent research. http://arxiv.org/abs/1707.07217 (accessed on 25th September 2025).

38. Gebhard, T. D., Harry, I., Kilbertus, N., Schölkopf, B., et al. (2019). Convolutional neural networks: A magic bullet for gravitational-wave detection? https://core.ac.uk/download/227487708.pdf (accessed on 25th September 2025).

39. Hirano, H., Koga, K., & Takemoto, K. (2020). Vulnerability of deep neural networks for detecting COVID-19 cases from chest X-ray images to universal adversarial attacks. https://core.ac.uk/download/390099118.pdf (accessed on 25th September 2025).

40. Horn, B. K. P., Fleet, D., Fortun, D., Butler, D. J., Heeger, D. J., Adelson, E. H., Solari, F., et al. (2016). Learning to extract motion from videos in convolutional neural networks. http://arxiv.org/abs/1601.07532 (accessed on 25th September 2025).

41. Hu, X., Ji, Y., Li, S., Wang, Y., et al. (2019). FPSA: A full system stack solution for reconfigurable ReRAM-based NN accelerator architecture. http://arxiv.org/abs/1901.09904 (accessed on 25th September 2025).

42. Jiang, Y. G., Krizhevsky, A., Lang, P., LeCun, Y., Plutchik, R., Szegedy, C., & Tang, Y. (2015). Diving deep into sentiment: Understanding fine-tuned CNNs for visual sentiment prediction. https://core.ac.uk/download/41824045.pdf (accessed on 25th September 2025).

43. Li, S., Nguyen, L. T., Chansanam, W., Iam-on, N., & Boongoen, T. (2025). Enhancing Dongba pictograph recognition using convolutional neural networks and data augmentation techniques. Information. https://www.semanticscholar.org/paper/460bbc3d7bf3bf221bea3b1d00b02c2a8fbd6208 (accessed on 25th September 2025).

44. Lu, L., Summers, R. M., & Yan, K. (2018). Unsupervised body part regression via spatially self-ordering convolutional neural networks. http://arxiv.org/abs/1707.03891 (accessed on 25th September 2025).

45. Nehmetallah, G., Nguyen, T., & Tian, L. (2019). Deep learning in computational microscopy. https://open.bu.edu/bitstream/2144/40200/1/1099007.pdf (accessed on 25th September 2025).

46. Ou, Z., & Wang, B. (2017). Language modeling with neural trans-dimensional random fields. http://arxiv.org/abs/1707.07240 (accessed on 25th September 2025).

47. Papandreou, G. (2014). Deep epitomic convolutional neural networks. http://arxiv.org/abs/1406.2732 (accessed on 25th September 2025).

48. Polzounov, A. (2017). WordFences: Text localization and recognition. https://core.ac.uk/download/81581052.pdf (accessed on 25th September 2025).

49. Roig Marí, C. (2016). Deep learning architectures for computer vision. https://core.ac.uk/download/81572231.pdf (accessed on 25th September 2025).

50. Sun, M. (Engineer). (2025). Large scale image classification and object detection. https://core.ac.uk/download/98352271.pdf (accessed on 25th September 2025).

51. Tek, F. B. (2020). An adaptive locally connected neuron model: Focusing neuron. http://arxiv.org/abs/1809.09533 (accessed on 25th September 2025).

52. Wang, D., Wang, Q., & Yuan, Y. (2019). Memory-augmented temporal dynamic learning for action recognition. http://arxiv.org/abs/1904.13080 (accessed on 25th September 2025).

53. Wu, C., Wang, S., Zhang, S., Zheng, H., Wang, W., & Yang, S. (2025). Enhancing landmark point detection in Eriocheir sinensis carapace with differentiable end-to-end networks. Animals: An Open Access Journal from MDPI, 15. https://www.semanticscholar.org/paper/457b6cd74613ee79c987c60cb96a37dddcc30c79 (accessed on 25th September 2025).

54. Xu, Q., Gao, Y., Shen, J., Li, Y., Ran, X., Tang, H., & Pan, G. (2024). Enhancing adaptive history reserving by spiking convolutional block attention module in recurrent neural networks. https://www.semanticscholar.org/paper/bd429686b9b3bc1d060ee1fe8ef8f1d0f017112c (accessed on 25th September 2025).

CHAPTER 7

RECURRENT NEURAL NETWORKS (RNNS)

Contents

INTRODUCTION

The past few years have witnessed tremendous growth in artificial intelligence at a rapid pace, leading to unprecedented development in machine learning in the field of temporal sequence processing. Of all the architectures that have been invented to address this intricate field, Recurrent Neural Networks (RNNs) are particularly distinct due to their exclusive capacity to look back and retain contextual information through time. This ability thus positions RNNs to be employed in time series analysis, speech recognition, and natural language processing. As the world continues to demand new ways to process and analyze large volumes of sequential data, the work of RNNs in facilitating this demand becomes increasingly obvious, particularly since traditional approaches are likely to fall behind the exponential growth in the volume and complexity of the data. There is a greater need for effective sequence learning algorithms in the environment of next-generation hardware platforms, such as the neuromorphic platforms on which they require specially designed algorithms to take advantage of the hardware capabilities. While RNNs have been useful in numerous sequence-based tasks, their application on neuromorphic hardware is an area of ongoing research interest. For example, new research has innovated techniques such as the train-and-constrain technique, which allows for the transfer of machine-learned RNNs to spiking neuron substrates. This technique breaks through several impediments by matching the dynamical nature of RNNs with the operations of neuromorphic systems, allowing for novel applications in fields demanding quick, power-efficient computation.

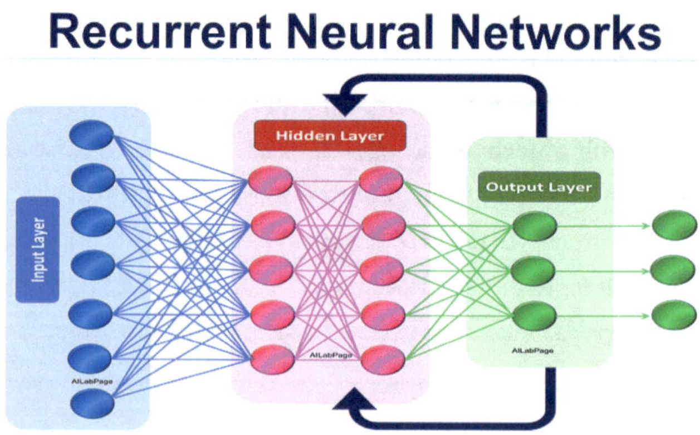

Figure 7.1. *Recurrent neural network (RNN).*

*Source: https://miro.medium.com/v2/resize:fit:4800/format:webp/1*5bjD7kmtaJI-n3qztBC2Ig.png.*

The promise of this work not only retains the benefits of RNN architectures but gets them nearer to the stringent demands of future neural computational models (Cassidy et al., 2016). As document classification emerges as a crucial application of RNNs, there emerges a necessity for more complex and hierarchical approaches, especially with the data explosion taking place in available data to be processed. Traditional classifiers tend to struggle with growing document numbers and category nuance, making it necessary to investigate avenues that improve the fidelity of the classification. Hierarchical Deep Learning for Text classification (HDLTex) is representative of this trend, leveraging stacked deep learning architectures in order to gain more sophisticated understanding at different levels of document hierarchy. By combining cutting-edge RNN methodologies with hierarchical models, researchers seek to build systems that can meaningfully decompose large and diverse datasets. These breakthroughs are a breakthrough in the ability to classify and organize information in a systematic way, further solidifying the relevance and usability of RNNs as computational demands evolve (Barnes et al., 2017) (Figure 7.1).

Definition of Recurrent Neural Networks (RNNs)

RNNs are a class of artificial neural networks specifically constructed to process sequential information. Unlike regular feedforward neural networks, RNNs possess the unique capability of retaining previous input information in their internal state or memory. This characteristic becomes priceless in numerous applications where context in prior data points is useful in prediction and interpretation. For instance, on such natural language processing tasks as machine translation or sentiment analysis, the meaning of words typically depends on context, which RNNs can well capture. An RNN's structure contains loops within the network, where information can pass from one timestep to another, providing a temporal dependency at the heart of their mechanisms. The adaptability of RNNs is also reflected in how they can manage and learn from time-series data and therefore are invaluable to speech recognition and medicine. In the medical field, for example, RNNs find application in heart rhythm classification, processing enormous amounts of electrocardiogram (ECG) data to identify vital heart rhythms such as atrial fibrillation (Delai et al., 2017). The time-varying nature of ECG signals lends itself well to the capabilities of RNNs, which are capable of observing changes in rhythm over time and accurately predicting abnormalities through learned patterns. These types of uses further illustrate the value of RNNs in allowing medical practitioners to more effectively monitor patients with high-risk conditions, offering real-time analysis that captures the significance of understanding sequences of events in high-stakes environments. Moreover complementing their ability, advancements in RNN architecture, such as Bidirectional RNN, have emerged to overcome the limitations of standard RNNs. Bidirectional RNN processes input in forward and reverse directions, tapping into all information within the sequence to generate richer context outputs. This addition is especially beneficial in sequence labeling tasks, where an element's understanding relies on both the elements preceding and following it. For example, research has shown the effectiveness of Bidirectional RNNs in a wide range of situations to yield stable learning with satisfactory computational complexity (Anandkumar et al., 2016). As applications of RNN continue to grow, the superior capability of such high-quality architectures reflects an expanded set of opportunities for researchers and practitioners who wish to tackle complex problems involved with sequential data (Figure 7.2).

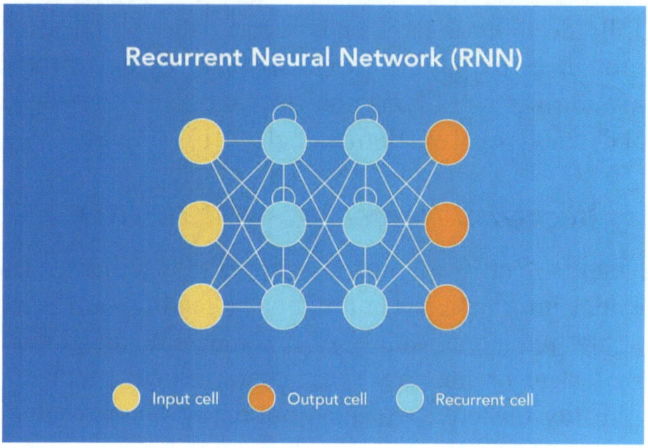

Figure 7.2. *Understanding recurrent neural network (RNN).*

Source: https://www.mygreatlearning.com/blog/wp-content/uploads/2020/05/Blog-images_21_5_2020-03-1536x1024.jpg.webp.

Importance in the Field of Machine Learning

Over the recent past, RNNs have transformed the field of machine learning, particularly in time-series forecasting and natural language processing. RNNs are able to handle sequences of data much better compared to normal models, which allows them to learn temporal patterns and dependencies that regular models cannot address very effectively. This capacity plays a crucial role in applications such as speech recognition, in which understanding context over time is a matter of greatest concern. Through the use of the internal organization of sequential data, RNNs facilitate improved predictive performance and enable machines to process human languages more effectively, demonstrating the main contributions they make to the construction of AI technologies. Also, the creation of architectures like Long Short-Term Memory (LSTM) also addressed the limitations of the conventional RNNs, minimizing the difficulty of vanishing gradients and enhancing their applications in the majority of fields, including finance, medicine, and weather forecasting. Moreover, RNNs' adaptability extends from simple sequence handling to more abstract domains such as ionic liquids (ILs) simulation, where their predictive abilities enable scientists to design chemical properties to meet industrial applications. ILs' unique attributes, dependent on their cation and anion structure, call for advanced machine learning methods to accommodate exact modeling and prediction. The conventional models might not have a chance to accurately model the behavior within this broad range of variations. RNNs, as well as other ANN networks, exhibit remarkable virtues in that aspect, as highlighted by recent literature. The networks can efficiently probe the complex relationships between inputs and outputs and hence facilitate better prediction of thermodynamic and physical IL properties. The importance of using RNNs resonates with their ability to promote innovation and efficiency in various scientific and industrial uses, paving the way for better research methods and outcomes (Racki et al., 2025). Furthermore, the interaction of RNNs with other complex structures, such as transformers, underscores their pivotal position in machine learning. Recent research has found that such factors as recurrence and gating mechanisms are crucial in improving model performance in many forecasting tasks, from text proccssing to dynamic systems analysis. The combination of RNNs with sophisticated methods not only improves prediction capability but also engenders necessary discussions concerning model interpretability and transparency. The necessity for ablation studies to evaluate and comment on the performance of different architectural components is of critical significance, but very often overlooked. Through the incorporation of RNNs into mixed frameworks, scientists are able to construct powerful models that combine the optimal from various strategies, ultimately advancing the machine learning paradigm and making it more useful in solving complex real-world problems (Heidenreich et al., 2024). This ongoing discovery emphasizes the foundational importance of RNNs, as they continue to shape the emerging direction of artificial intelligence and machine learning advancements.

7.1. HISTORICAL BACKGROUND

The history of Recurrent Neural Networks (RNNs) is rooted in pioneering studies of artificial intelligence and neural computing during the 1980s. The initial architecture of RNNs was created when scientists tried to build models that would learn from sequences of data. This was a significant shift from the classical feedforward neural networks, which had primarily addressed fixed-size inputs. RNNs introduced the concept of recurrence links so that information could persist from one time step to the next, thus allowing them to learn temporal patterns behind sequential data. This advance led to several breakthroughs in areas involving time-series analysis, e.g., natural language processing and speech recognition. Theoretical basis of RNNs was further developed by the use of backpropagation through time (BPTT), a critical algorithm for learning RNNs, with emphasis on the significance of RNNs in challenging, time-variant applications. With the development of technology into the 1990s and early 2000s, RNNs were experiencing problems, particularly pertaining to their ability to learn long-range dependencies due to the vanishing gradient problem. Consequently, researchers began exploring special forms of RNN architecture to tackle these limitations. The introduction of Long Short-Term Memory (LSTM) networks and Gated Recurrent Units (GRUs) were breakthroughs in the development of RNNs. These models incorporated gate mechanisms that helped manage the information flow, significantly enhancing their capacity to learn from longer sequences without the problem of vanishing gradients. The advancements came to assume a key part in revolutionizing applications like machine translation, wherein contextual understanding born out of past inputs became imperative. The advances made by LSTMs and GRUs reinstated the strategic significance of RNNs in modern machine learning to perform with hitherto unprecedented accuracy and effectiveness in time-series data-based operations. In contemporary settings, RNNs have been discovered to demonstrate robustness in numerous scenarios well beyond simple sequence prediction use cases. For instance, the development of systems like Tiresias demonstrates their use in computer security, where upcoming malicious actions can be predicted to prevent potential attacks. With RNNs, Tiresias analyzes enormous amounts of security event data to forecast future occurrences with excellent accuracy, up to 0.93. This capability of predicting as well as anticipating event patterns raises the flexibility and capability of RNNs in real-world use. Furthermore, as computation capabilities have advanced, techniques like optimized training methods such as optimal batch bucketing have improved faster learning processes. The sustained advances continue to highlight the chronic significance of RNNs, validating their ground-breaking role in advancing artificial intelligence as well as real-world implementations across diverse fields (Bokhan et al., 2017; Le et al., 2018).

7.1.1. Development of Neural Networks

Neural network architectures have played a crucial role in developing Recurrent Neural Networks (RNNs). Evolving from perceptron designs, neural networks have undergone multiple stages, each of which was characterized by increasing computational sophistication and more sophisticated models. Models at their initial stages were limited by linear activations that made them unable to capture complicated patterns in sequential data. With greater research, advances in non-linear activation functions and multi-layered architectures facilitated deeper representations. This fundamental transformation paved the way for RNNs, which are specifically built to handle time-variant data. RNNs leverage the memory concept via the use of recursive linkages so that they can remember information when iterating through an input sequence and are well suited to sequence-holding tasks such as language modeling or predicting time series. More complex tasks were accompanied with greater neural network capabilities. RNNs came up with more advanced architectures such as Long Short-Term Memory (LSTM) and Gated Recurrent Unit (GRU), which addressed the vanishing gradient problem that has plagued earlier RNN implementations. These architectures contain memory cells and gates that allow them to forget or recall selectively, thereby enhancing their ability to learn long sequences. The advent of LSTMs in particular was a paradigm shift, both extending the capabilities of RNNs and also improving performance on standard benchmark tasks for speech recognition and natural language processing. Improvements in training algorithms such as backpropagation through time (BPTT) also continued to fuel the field by allowing more efficient learning from huge temporal data. Furthermore, RNN applications in real-life demonstrate how their impact can be far-reaching across a broad range of domains from image classification to natural language processing. For instance, Speech Activity Detection (SAD) systems have been revolutionized by the use of RNN architecture combined with convolutional layers. In a particular experiment, Convolutional Recurrent Neural Network (CRNN) was employed to solve SAD problems by transforming audio classification into a two-dimensional multilabel image classification problem and gaining significant performance improvement over traditional methods (Chen et al., 2019). Similarly, RNNs have been extremely useful in word segmentation, wherein they use language models to add or delete word boundaries in sequences of characters for unstructured text data processing (Doval et al., 2018). Such breakthroughs not only confirm the usability of RNNs but also their ability to learn different challenges in diverse applications, transforming the machine learning front entirely.

7.1.2. Emergence of Recurrent Neural Networks (RNNs) in the 1980s

The emergence of RNNs in the 1980s was a milestone in the history of neural computing and artificial intelligence. This was a period characterized by overwhelming advances in understanding temporal dependencies in data. Compared to other neural network architectures previously, RNNs introduced the concept of networks that can retain and utilize hidden states such that they can efficiently model sequences of data. This aspect contributed significantly to RNNs outperforming traditional feedforward networks in a number of applications, particularly language processing and time series analysis. The initial ideas formed during this decade serve as the basis for future advancements in deep learning architectures (Gashler et al., 2017). David Rumelhart and Geoffrey Hinton were two of the most significant contributors to the theoretical framework of RNNs by then. They not only researched the backpropagation algorithm but also demonstrated how RNNs can be trained to learn over time. The union of these new approaches revealed the potential for RNNs to tackle more complex challenges, like linguistic issues and sequential decision-making. Further, the arrival of LSTMs (Long Short-Term Memory networks) late in the decade brought with it methods to defend against the vanishing gradient problem that typically plagued regular RNNs. These advancements revealed the potential of the way architectural modifications would significantly enhance the capacity of neural networks to learn temporal dynamics (de Castro et al., 2019). While the promise of RNNs existed as early as the 1980s, their practical usage was held back by computer constraints and unavailability of large training sets at first. However, the groundwork established here provided a stepping stone for subsequent researchers to explore and simplify these models considerably. By the 1990s and 2000s, with increasing computational power and availability of big datasets, RNNs began performing much better on a wide range of applications. With movement gathering pace in the region, the early thoughts of the 1980s were wedded into new paradigms, setting off new curiosity about RNNs that would prove to be a significant influence on the success of deep learning technologies in the next decades (Gashler et al., 2017).

7.1.3. Key Milestones in Recurrent Neural Network (RNN) Research

The evolution of RNNs is marked by a series of key milestones that have significantly enhanced their capabilities and applications across various domains. One of the most important advancements was when the Long Short-Term Memory (LSTM) architecture arrived in the 1990s. The breakthrough resolved the vanishing gradient problem that was characteristic of the conventional RNNs by way of a variety of applications towards capturing long-term dependencies in sequential data. LSTMs have since then formed the basis of various applications, ranging from natural language processing to time series prediction, testifying to their relevance in different fields. Moreover, the architectures novel gating mechanism allows for more controllable information flow, which renders it proficient at finding latent patterns in long sequences, a trait that has been highly valuable in many real-world systems, particularly in Automatic Speech Recognition (ASR) systems (Bengio et al., 2018). Another core innovation in RNN work is the discovery of Gated Recurrent Units (GRUs) that came in 2014 as a simpler alternative to LSTMs. GRU modeling merges the update operations of the forget gate and the input gate into a single update gate, making the architecture simpler without losing a lot of the LSTMs' efficiency. Experiments have shown that GRUs can match LSTMs in various tasks, but use less computational power since they are less complex. GRUs have also made the utilization of RNNs more democratized, such that practitioners with no large computational capabilities can now utilize the ability of recurrent models in sentiment analysis and toxicity detection in text, among other tasks (Martin et al., 2018). This simplification is one of the most important reasons why RNNs have become commonly used in typical deep learning architectures. Additionally, the use of advanced techniques such as batch normalization and activation functions employed in RNN architectures has also significantly affected recurrent neural networks. Improvements in training algorithms and regularization methods have also immensely improved the stability and performance of RNNs to sustain more complex tasks. The replacement of the older activation functions by newer ones, such as ReLU, has been successful in accelerating training and enhancing the ability of the network to learn long-term dependencies without falling into numerical instability. These advances indicate the continued progress in RNN research, which reflects an active body of research that continues to shape itself to meet the demands of advancing technology and application demands (Bengio et al., 2018).

7.2. ARCHITECTURE OF RECURRENT NEURAL NETWORKS (RNNS)

RNN structure is one of the main features that distinguish RNNs from the typical feedforward neural networks. RNNs can process sequential data and contain loops in their structure which allow information to be held over time steps. This memory capacity allows RNNs the potential to build dependencies in the data, which is particularly valuable in handling sequences such as time series or natural language. RNNs can view temporal patterns and learn context relations with hidden states serving as their memory. RNNs are therefore particularly suited to speech recognition, language modeling, and anything else where sequence and order must be taken into account. A key characteristic of RNN design is the use of activation functions that determine the way the data flows through the network. The most commonly utilized activation functions are the hyperbolic tangent (tanh) and the rectified linear unit (ReLU), both of which provide room for non-linear transformation to effectively learn. However, standard RNNs may fall short with issues such as vanishing and exploding gradients, reducing their ability to learn long-term dependencies. To overcome these constraints, more recent architectures like Long Short-Term Memory (LSTM) and Gated Recurrent Units (GRUs) have been developed. These additions include gate mechanisms to manage the flow of data that further enhances the networks capability to retain important information for long sequences, opening up more real-world applications of RNNs in complex environments. Furthermore, applications of RNNs have been highly beneficial in an extensive range of applications extending far beyond traditional areas. For example, they have been recognized in dynamic network analysis for their versatility in monitoring changes in network structures through time. Though they are well-established in most fields, the combination of RNNs with newer methods like Graph Neural Networks (GNNs) has been an area of increased interest in recent times. This union aims to combine both temporal depth of RNNs and structural insight provided by GNNs, thus allowing for improved performance in network-related tasks. With research development still ongoing, understanding the architecture of RNNs remains vital in tapping their utility in new areas across different fields, particularly with increasingly growing interconnectivity and data complexity (Gabrys et al., 2021; Gashler et al., 2017) (Figure 7.3).

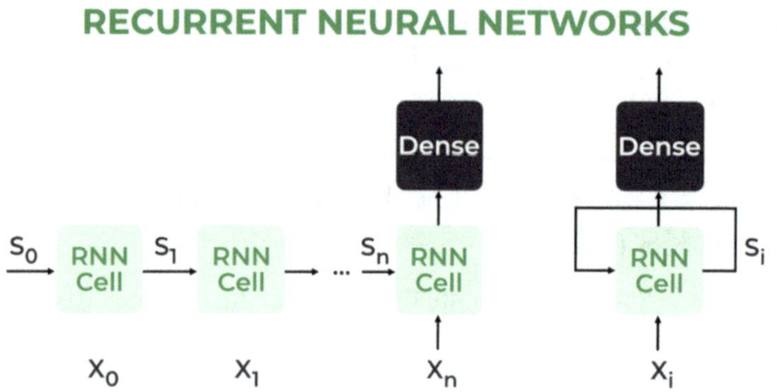

Figure 7.3. *Architecture of recurrent neural networks (RNNs).*

Source: https://media.geeksforgeeks.org/wp-content/uploads/20231204131544/recurrent_neural_networks-768.png.

7.2.1. Basic Structure of Recurrent Neural Networks (RNNs)

The fundamental structure of RNNs establishes a structure other than traditional feedforward neural networks, primarily due to the inherent feedback loops within the system. This feedback allows RNNs to enjoy a form of memory, in that they are able to retain information from previous inputs while sequencing. Central to the design of an RNN are a sequence of input layers that exchange information with one another over time via feedback loops throughout the network. Each neuron's output during the last time step is fed back into the network as input to the following step and thus results in a dynamic representation capable of handling inputs of varying lengths. This single property is most critical when dealing with time-series data and sequence-dependent calculations, embodying the central concept that "present states" are informed by "previous states," thereby enhancing their worth for applications like natural language processing. RNNs are not without limitations, though, and notable issues arise when dealing with longer sequences or being tasked with learning long-term dependencies. The vanilla RNN structure has issues such as the vanishing and exploding gradients problem, which manifests during training. These issues can hamper learning significantly because gradients become very small or excessively large, limiting effective weight updates and, consequently, capacity for learning.

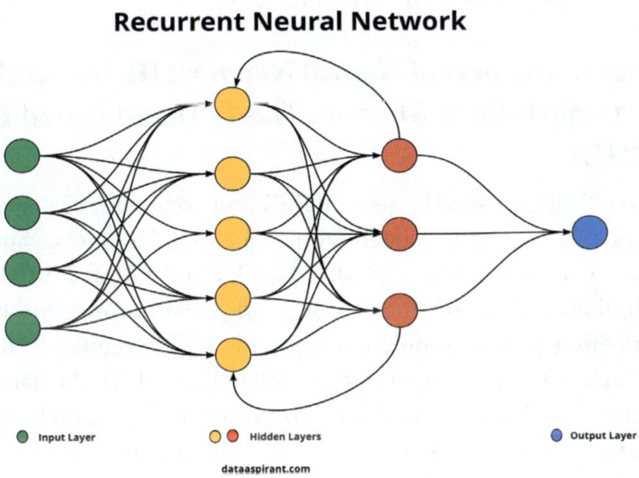

Figure 7.4. *Basic structure of recurrent neural networks (RNNs).*

Source: https://dataaspirant.com/wp-content/uploads/2020/11/3-Recurrent-Neural-Network-1536x1138.png.

To overcome these constraints, more advanced forms of RNNs have emerged, the most prominent of which are Long Short-Term Memory (LSTM) networks and Gated Recurrent Units (GRUs). LSTM networks also have gating systems that efficiently manage the information flow, permitting critical content to be preserved for long periods of time and removing less critical content. This versatility makes LSTMs and GRUs superior to simple RNNs in several applications, showing how they represent an evolutionary step in deep learning (Arnau et al., 2017). Furthermore, ongoing research into the use of RNNs matches the evolution of energy-efficient hardware technology aimed at optimizing their performance. The growing interest in neuromorphic computing reflects this trend, with these systems like IBMs TrueNorth attempting to take advantage of the capabilities of RNNs by employing spiking neuron models. These architectures aim at power efficiency and latency-tolerant temporal sequence processing and emphasize the variability of RNN applications beyond ordinary computational paradigms. For example, an important methodology involves backpropagation through time for training Elman RNNs and then converting them to spiking RNNs, which aligns with the constraints of neuromorphic platforms. The train-and-constrain approach offers valuable mapping and transferability to other platforms, demonstrating how progress on the hardware side can render RNN architectures deployable and more efficient for real-world applications (Cassidy et al., 2016) (Figure 7.4).

7.2.2. Types of Recurrent Neural Network (RNN) Architectures (e.g., Long Short-Term Memory (LSTM) and Gated Recurrent Units (GRU))

The domain of RNNs is ruled by several different architectures that are designed to address specific issues associated with sequential data processing. The most popular among them include LSTM networks and GRU. LSTMs introduce memory cells that are able to memorize long-range relationships without suffering from the vanishing gradient problem that usually afflicts regular RNNs. Through the use of a series of gates—input, forget, and output—LSTMs manage the flow of information such that networks can learn from past inputs on long sequences. Meanwhile, GRUs simplify such architecture with the combination of the forget and input gates into an update gate in an effort to increase computation efficiency without loss of the essence of LSTMs. Such advancements make the LSTM and GRU frameworks particularly useful in applications that require highly sensitive appreciations of temporal dynamics, e.g., natural language processing and time series prediction. Recent developments in RNN architectures have immensely expanded their areas of application, and their ability to incorporate contextual information has become ever more intriguing. For example, research on venue recommendation systems utilizes various forms of RNN architectures for recommending venues ordered by users, based on previous check-in data to personalize suggestions. These architectures were successful in capturing the dynamic nature of user behaviors in taking contextual hints such as time of day and location of the venue into account. However, traditional methods have a tendency to disregard varying impacts of contexts on user preferences. To address such problems, innovative architectures like the Contextual Attention Recurrent Architecture (CARA) have been developed, involving multiple gate mechanisms to classify normal and transition contexts, improving flexibility and prediction precision in actual application (Diederik et al., 2018). For use in health monitoring, RNN architectures like Fast LSTMs and GRUs have played a crucial role in developing fall detection systems using accelerometer data. The complexity of human movement calls for robust algorithms able to discriminate serious patterns characteristic of imminent falls. Studies have shown that deep learning algorithms, especially those using LSTM and GRU architecture, are capable of significantly enhancing the accuracy of fall detection while reducing the computational cost. In studies of various setups of the recurrent frames on sufficiently labeled datasets, researchers have noted the enhancement of detection effectiveness with average F1-scores greater than 0.73, thus outdoing existing state-of-the-art systems. This success reiterates the versatility of RNN designs in addressing immediate real-world challenges, such as the safety of older people and sending timely warnings in event of falls (Rodríguez et al., 2019) (Figure 7.5).

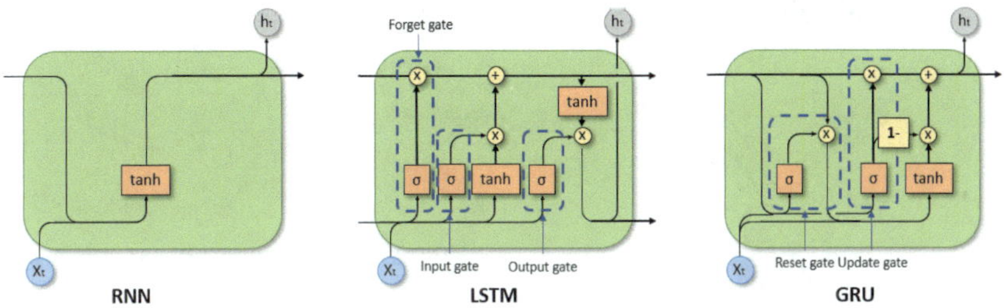

Figure 7.5. *Recurrent neural network (RNN), long short-term memory (LSTM) and gated recurrent units (GRU) cells.*

Source: https://towardsdatascience.com/wp-content/uploads/2022/12/1B0q2ZLsUUw31eEImeVf3PQ.png.

7.2.3. Comparison with Traditional Feedforward Neural Networks

The evolution of the neural network architecture has yielded the basic distinction between traditional feedforward neural networks and recurrent neural networks (RNNs). Feedforward networks process inputs unidirectionally, in that data travels from the input layer through the hidden layers to the output layer without loops. The linear flow typically limits their capacity to learn temporal relationships in sequential data, such as time series and natural language. In comparison, RNNs possess an intrinsic architectural advantage in the form of the inclusion of the feedback loops that allow them to hold information about previous inputs and hence are highly capable of processing time-dependent data. The capacity to remember past occurrences is vital for the purpose of analysis of sequences and hence characterizes RNNs as a highly versatile tool compared to their feedforward counterparts. RNNs ability to learn long-term dependencies is also exemplified by their advanced variants, including Long Short-Term Memory (LSTM) networks. Feedforward neural networks fail to have the capacity to memorize for long sequences of data and therefore cannot learn tasks involving context from past data points. For instance, in time series forecasting, conventional methods such as ARIMA models and feedforward networks fail in capturing complex non-linear correlations between data points. While LSTMs, in contrast, have been shown to work better in the same environment by effectively picking up and processing temporal data with less feature engineering, closely resembling the nature of real-world data. Evidence has been shown that LSTMs beat the traditional methods by far in mean absolute error and root mean squared error and thus is a sought-after tool for time-series analysis (Uppalaiah et al., 2025).

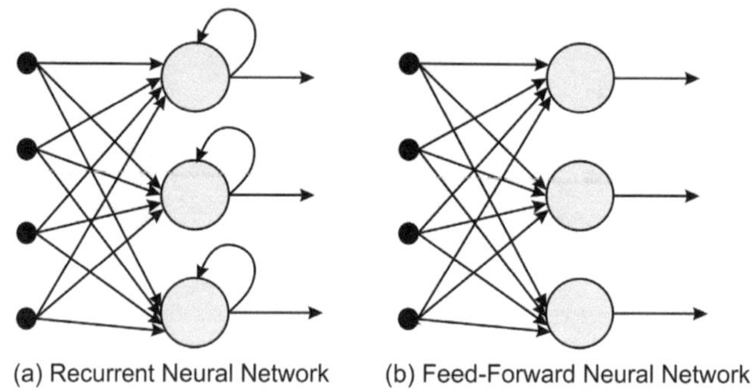

Figure 7.6. *The comparison between recurrent neural network (RNN) and feed-forward neural network (FFNN). It demonstrates in FFNN there is only one direction for the data to move, whereas in RNN there is a loop.*

Source: https://www.researchgate.net/publication/338672883/figure/fig1/AS:864764884422656@1583187423806/The-comparison-between-Recurrent-Neural-Network-RNN-and-Feed-Forward-Neural-Network.jpg.

Besides, relative strengths of RNNs, especially LSTMs, have been highlighted to a great extent in fault detection tasks. In industrial applications, standard diagnostic methods are lacking in robustness, resulting in weak identification of faults, especially in complex systems where data are bound to be noisy or imbalanced. RNNs, especially when applied in the processing of acoustic signal analysis, have been able to improve diagnostic accuracy by good learning from temporal patterns in data obtained from running machines. The novel application of RNNs in combination with Bayesian Neural Networks in this context has achieved higher fault detection performance compared to traditional approaches, highlighting their potential in safety-critical situations where precise and explainable predictions are vital (Bauer et al., 2025). By demonstrating these developments, it is apparent that RNNs not only improve current techniques but also open the door for more advanced methodologies in many fields (Figure 7.6).

7.3. WORKING MECHANISM

The working mechanism of Recurrent Neural Networks (RNNs) lies essentially in its ability to handle sequential data employing a hidden state that varies over time. This property is essential for tasks that require to capture context or interdependence between inputs, such as language modeling or time series prediction. Compared to feedforward networks, RNNs utilize the hidden state to maintain a memory of past inputs, in a manner that allows them to "remember" previous observations. This recurrent characteristic enables them to be more expressive in capturing dynamic temporal patterns in the data, and RNNs become most suitable for tasks involving sequences of varying length. By repeated utilization of the same weights across time steps, RNNs can learn complex relationships within sequences, which is a necessity for tasks like natural language processing and speech recognition. To avail themselves of the cost-effectiveness of RNNs, recent developments have led to novel approaches like the train-and-constrain method, which enables the use of RNNs in neuromorphic hardware. This approach begins with the training of typical RNN architectures using backpropagation through time, followed by discretization of the weights in order to meet the specific connectivity needs of neuromorphic hardware. The strategy is demonstrated in question classification using IBMs TrueNorth architecture. Here, the limitation on connectivity and synaptic parameters of the architecture necessitates careful adaptation so that the model's performance is not compromised while power consumption is significantly reduced. The successful mapping also demonstrates the possibility of utilizing RNNs in low-power spiking neural networks, thus facilitating more efficient computation for sequence learning tasks (Cassidy et al., 2016). Although effective in learning complex temporal information, traditional RNNs have been accompanied by the drawbacks of interpretability, especially when employed in models like deep learning-based knowledge tracing (DLKT) models. The reliance on sophisticated architectures can mask understanding of decision making, instilling barriers to application to real life such as educational technology. Scholars have therefore begun examining the methods of interpretability, of which one is the layer-wise relevance propagation (LRP) method, allowing to track the relevance scores from output to input layers. With the application of LRP to RNN-based DLKT models, predictions for every component can be interpreted, showing a greater insight into the operation of such models. This also enhances not only the transparency but also the application of RNNs in life-critical domains such as personalized learning and intelligent tutoring systems (Arbabzadah et al., 2020).

7.3.1. How Recurrent Neural Networks (RNNs) Process Sequential Data

RNNs are particularly designed to handle sequential data, as opposed to the standard feedforward neural networks. This is due to their internal architecture, summarized by the existence of loops in the network that allow information to persist from one time step to the next. When RNNs are presented with a sequence, they possess an internal state or memory that keeps useful information from previous inputs. This memory is engaged when carrying out tasks like language modeling or time-series prediction, where context created from prior inputs is crucial in determining the meaning of the current input. This feedback architecture enables RNNs to capture temporal dependencies in sequences of times and hence are incredibly robust in tasks that must comprehend context. The various RNN architecture, such as Long Short-Term Memory (LSTM) and Gated Recurrent Unit (GRU), enhance their sequential data handling by preventing the vanishing gradient problem that standard RNNs typically face. The gated design offers the capacity to control the information flow and permit or reject utilization of past details depending on relevance. These mechanisms allow RNNs to handle long-range dependencies effectively, which comes in handy for those applications that deal with complex sequence patterns, such as natural language processing. In more recent studies, the application of bidirectional RNNs, where two layers have read the sequence from opposite directions, has further solidified models' understanding of context by aggregating conclusions of both previous and following data points that demonstrate its flexibility in handling sequential data (Heidemann et al., 2018). In addition, RNNs bring vast improvements in other uses due to the sequential processing capability. As an example, in speech recognition, RNNs are capable of processing a sequence of phonetics and translating into text with great accuracy. This capability is applied in other areas such as music generation and human movement detection, where sequential data pattern detection is crucial. The present work on enhancing RNN architectures, for example, exploring novel combinations with frameworks like Markov Random Fields, is proof of the drive toward enhancing RNNs expressive power. Hybrid frameworks are able to tap the strengths of RNNs while outreaching intrinsic weaknesses in traditional formulations and, hence, advancing the boundary of sequential data processing (Dempster et al., 2016). This constant evolution reflects the importance of RNNs in not just understanding but creating many fields that are based on sequential information.

7.3.2. Role of Hidden States in Recurrent Neural Networks (RNNs)

The role of hidden states in RNNs is important in enabling the models to process sequential information effectively. Hidden states are dynamic memory cells, remembering information from previous time steps and hence enabling the network to learn temporal dependencies. This capability is responsible for the critical functionality of most applications, natural language processing, where the history of surrounding words is a major contributor to subsequent meaning. The ability to store and refresh latent states enables RNNs to detect long-term patterns, which is crucial for tasks like speech recognition and machine translation. This memory-like property ultimately improves the models performance, as it is able to leverage prior data in order to affect current predictions, illustrating how RNNs exploit hidden states in order to develop a richer sense of sequential data. To address the challenges in learning long-term dependencies, some alterations to standard RNN architectures have been proposed. Techniques to improve the strength of hidden states include training auxiliary models to predict future states based on current context. One example is training a backward recurrent network trained on reversed sequences that can reinforce the forward model's hidden states. The technique not only enhances the ability to hold onto informative information but also acts as a solution to the vanishing gradient problem usually faced with normal RNNs. Through the incorporation of forward and backward processing methods, researchers recognized quantifiable improvements in performance measures for a number of applications, such as speech recognition, through the facilitation of a more robust representation of temporally long-range dependencies (Bengio et al., 2018). The developments reinforce the critical role of hidden states in achieving performance improvements in sequence data tasks. Further, advancements like the Recurrent Memory Network (RMN) have provided insight into how RNNs operate internally, particularly the hidden states. The RMN architecture refines the initial RNN model while allowing researchers to identify patterns in the hidden layers more effectively. This model transforms the hidden state representation such that it incorporates both past and present information, and this leads to improved task efficiency and language modeling in situations requiring higher-level understanding, such as sentence completion. The ability of RMNs to surpass LSTM networks in some tasks underscores the significance of understanding hidden states so that the complexities involved in sequential data processing are better separated. This advancement allows the study of linguistic properties and determines the manner in which the alteration of back-end state structure can bring immense performance leaps along natural language tasks (Bisazza et al., 2016) (Figure 7.7).

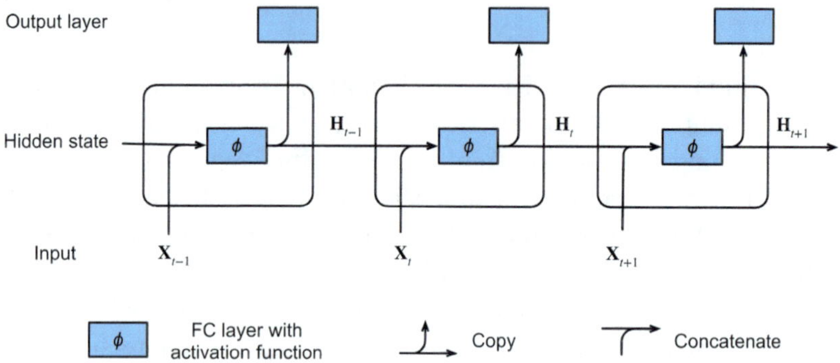

Figure 7.7. *An recurrent neural network (RNN) with a hidden state.*

Source: https://d2l.ai/_images/rnn.svg.

7.3.3. Backpropagation Through Time (BPTT)

BPTT is a central algorithm applied to training recurrent neural networks (RNNs) that is specifically designed to address problems of relevance to temporal sequences of information. By unrolling the RNN along the time dimension, BPTT facilitates computing gradients at each and every time step, which then allows for learning from sequential dependency in an efficient way. This unrolling process provides an explicit structure for evaluating how the output of each unit contributes to the overall loss, which is critical for weight optimization over all time steps. The choice of training procedures, as reported in research work, is generally overlooked, though BPTT is a simple method in efficient training of RNNs on several tasks, including sequence prediction and language modeling (Boom et al., 2018). An awareness of the nuances of BPTT can significantly enhance the performance and ability of RNNs in many applications. Useful though it is, BPTT presents some difficulties for researchers to overcome, such as computational cost and vanishing gradients, which can impede learning over long sequences. The intrinsic complicacy of BPTT can lead to issues such as unstable training dynamics, especially when the hidden states are propagated during model startup on subsequences. Instability is dataset-dependent, meaning learning techniques must be adjusted for optimal performance. Additionally, the usage of BPTT may rely heavily on the choice of hyperparameters and network architecture, with a focus on experimentation and tweaking in practice (Boom et al., 2018). As the growing field of RNN applications unfolds, comprehension and solution to such issues remain a central factor for successful model deployment. Finally, advances in computing techniques and technology have enabled better implementations of BPTT with enhanced performance and tolerable complexity. Reducing the word-length of signals and weights in RNN architectures, researchers have managed to lower the hardware demands without compromising the performance of the model. For instance, quantization methods such as retraining the network are very important in this optimization process, enhancing the fixed-point behavior of RNNs. These advances not only simplify the training process but also enable real-time usage of RNNs, like language modeling and phoneme recognition tasks. The development of BPTT and its applications thus represent a wider trend in machine learning in which performance and efficiency must converge, and therefore, there is always a call for innovation in algorithmic development (Figure 7.8).

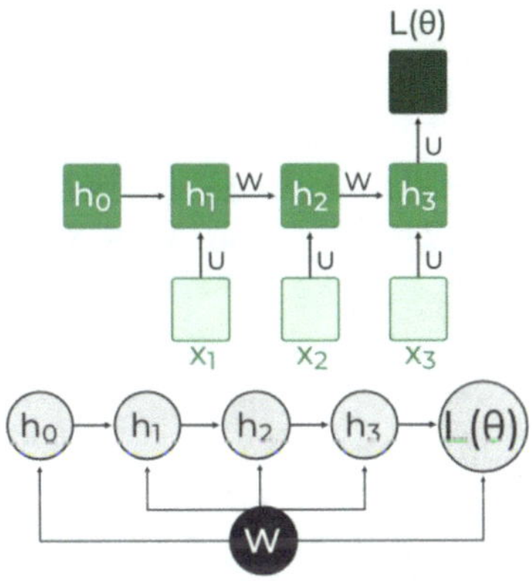

Figure 7.8. *Backpropagation through time (BPTT) in recurrent neural network (RNN).*

Source: https://media.geeksforgeeks.org/wp-content/uploads/20231204132128/Backpropagation-Through-Time-(BPTT).webp.

7.4. APPLICATIONS OF RECURRENT NEURAL NETWORKS (RNNS)

RNNs are now at the forefront of sequential data processing across various domains, especially natural language processing (NLP). Its memory of past time steps makes it a good fit for applications such as language modeling and sentiment analysis. Contextual understanding of text, as per conventional methods, used to involve extensive feature engineering. However, RNNs, especially the ones enhanced with Long Short-Term Memory (LSTM) units, have revolutionized text comprehension to a large degree, enabling better context perception. RNNs' capability to recognize patterns in longer sequences has enabled vast advancements in tasks such as machine translation and text creation. These skills show their role as a pillar of many modern-day NLP applications as an essential tool for developers and researchers trying to increase user interaction with technology through superior language understanding. Another notable application of RNNs is speech recognition, where their temporal signal processing skill proves very useful. With the application of RNNs, programmers were able to achieve tremendous gains in recognizing spoken words and converting them into text.

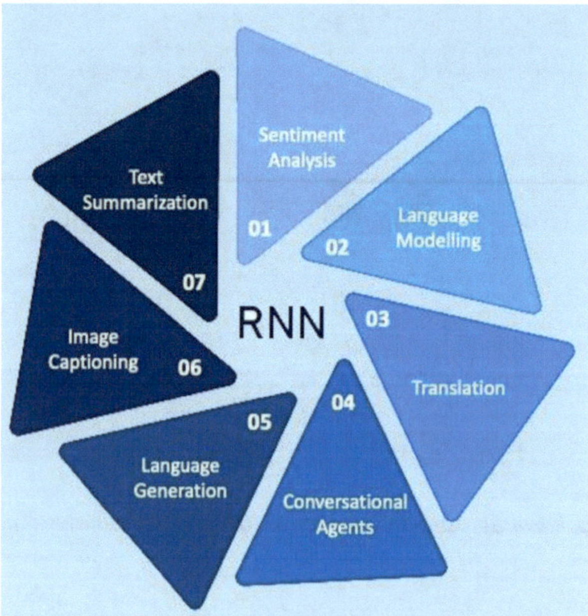

Figure 7.9. *Applications of recurrent neural networks (RNNs).*

Source: https://almablog-media.s3.ap-south-1.amazonaws.com/image3_1_ba01a376b5.jpg.

Human speech, as it is dynamic in nature and varying in terms of pace, tone, and accent, is a gigantic issue for conventional models. RNNs address such issues by efficiently managing context knowledge retention and sequential audio signal learning. That adaptability enables speech recognition systems to enhance their accuracy over time as they learn from different data sets, including numerous speakers and scenarios. RNN designs, especially with Gated Recurrent Units (GRUs), are said to have improved performance metrics, hence solidifying their position in transforming how machines understand human language, ultimately creating enhanced user experiences across various systems. Furthermore, RNNs expand their use to robotics, proving their mettle beyond traditional data processing tasks. RNN application in robotic systems has fueled new approaches to motion detection and control. For instance, skeleton-based human motion recognition has been improved by bidirectional RNN architectures, which analyze movement from multiple perspectives to enhance precision and reliability in robotics. As recorded in recent reviews, the application of RNN with conventional machine learning techniques has displayed significant advancements in interpreting complex movements, which enables robots to interact more normally within common spaces with humans. This convergence aligns with the common direction of embedding deep learning theory into robotic technologies, which consequently sparks more innovations in automation and intelligent behavior, thereby driving future R&D efforts in the field (Gashler et al., 2017; Heidemann et al., 2018) (Figure 7.9).

7.4.1. Natural Language Processing (NLP)

NLP has fundamentally changed how computers interact with human language, enabling a multitude of applications from sentiment analysis to translation. RNNs lie at the heart of this transformation, having been responsible for processing sequential data such as text. RNNs particularly thrive in capturing relationships in context within language and facilitating deeper understanding and text generation. This capability is priceless especially in applications like Automatic Speech Recognition (ASR) where the output tends to be unstructured and devoid of basic formatting and punctuation. As mentioned in existing research, how bidirectional RNNs can work together on functions like punctuation and capitalization can significantly enhance the performance, thereby improving the overall quality of NLP applications, which are largely dependent on well-structured input to enable efficient processing, to be better (Kotlerman et al., 2017). In addition to advancements in structure, RNNs have also made it possible to advance more sophisticated forms of combining disparate fields of AI, such as computer vision and NLP. The creation of text descriptions of pictures from pictures is one such merging, wherein RNNs can be trained to interpret visual information and then translate that information into meaningful language. Current approaches in this area are likely to take a top-down or bottom-up approach, but recent advances have prompted a novel combination of these approaches based on RNNs. With the application of a semantic attention model, which selectively fuses semantic concept proposals, there is the capability to produce more precise and contextually informative descriptions.

This cross-methodology not only advances the frontiers of image captioning but also increases the capabilities of NLP systems since they will now be able to understand and describe complex visual information (Fang et al., 2016). The advancements of these innovations in NLP and RNN technology extend beyond the capability of present applications; they signal the advent of a new wave of interactive and responsive machine learning systems. As RNNs continue to improve at analyzing and understanding natural language, the technology will make it possible for even more dynamic interactions between man and machine. Opportunities for future evolution include enhancing RNN design to handle more advanced linguistic frameworks and integrating them with other machine learning platforms in order to handle multidimensional tasks. The continuous growth of NLP, driven by the advances in RNNs, offers promising directions for research and development, holding a rosy future for the scientific community as well as for other industrial areas. With the growing significance of NLP, understanding what is behind these improvements remains essential in order to take full advantage of their potential (Figure 7.10).

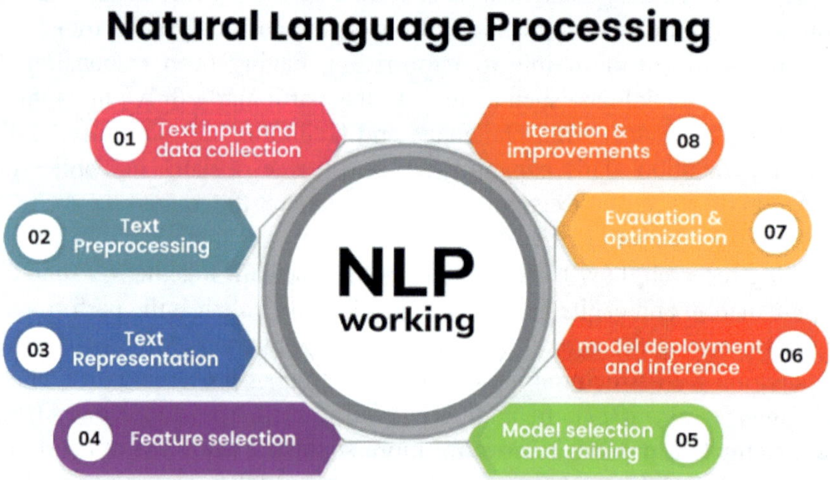

Figure 7.10. *Natural language processing (NLP) working.*

Source: https://cdn.botpenguin.com/assets/website/image_663eaffbc2.png.

7.4.2. Time Series Prediction

The accuracy of time series prediction is crucial in many applications, including finance, weather forecasting, and healthcare, where the prediction informs critical decision-making. Recurrent Neural Networks (RNNs) have been found to be a successful solution in this context since they can process sequential data and learn temporal relationships. Compared to traditional statistical methods, RNNs can identify patterns in complex datasets and learn from past values in an adaptive manner, raising forecasting accuracy. The employment of advanced architectures, such as the application of Long Short-Term Memory (LSTM) networks, enhances RNNs ability to retain information for extended periods and suppresses the vanishing gradient phenomenon that typically weakens simple RNN architectures. Hence, the application of RNNs in predicting time series has made enormous strides, which have seen their performance in predicting future values based on past trends excel. The adaptability of RNNs in forecasting in a time series is also evidenced by their deployment on many well-known benchmark problems successfully. As an example, studies contrasting different architectures bring forth the fact that although straightforward recurrent models such as the Elman and Jordan networks deliver acceptable results, hybrid models uniting the strength of both have proved superior in predictive accuracy. Precisely, it has been noted that the Jordan neural network outperforms its alternatives in many contexts, demonstrating the strength and effectiveness of the network in managing temporal dependencies. This flexibility of architecture allows practitioners to tailor models to the specific character of their datasets in a bid to achieve optimal performance even for complicated time series. The inclusion of methods like Resilient Propagation in addition to RNNs has significantly improved training stage convergence speed, hence improving model efficiency (Abdulkarim et al., 2016). The prospects for time series forecasting with RNNs look promising with scientists exploring new concepts in order to further improve model performance. Some of these developments include Higher Order Neural Networks (HONNs) and Pi-Sigma Neural Networks (PSNN), both aimed at boosting input representation and learning ability. HONNs, for instance, introduce more advanced interactions in the input space, which can detect subtle relationships undetected by typical RNNs. Moreover, the unique features of PSNN, which combine advantages of higher-order networks and recurrent architectures with error feedback, constitute a compelling alternative for time series analysis. As the field moves forward, ongoing research into these methods, alongside the elaboration of better current RNN architectures, has the ability to push the current boundaries of what is achievable in exact time series prediction, ultimately equating to advantage a broad array of applications and industries (Akram et al., 2017) (Figure 7.11).

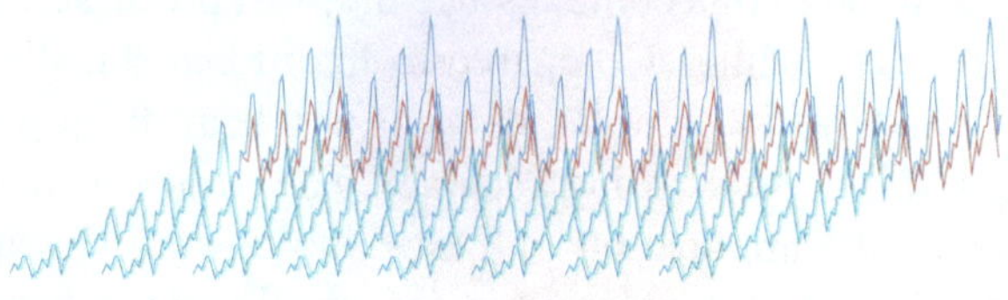

Figure 7.11. *Time series predictions with recurrent neural networks (RNNs).*

Source: https://images.prismic.io/encord/93d426cc-ec5e-4c66-88b3-54ef05c098d7_Time+series+w+RNN.png?auto=compress%2Cformat&fit=max&w=1812&h=1276&fm=webp.

7.4.3. Speech Recognition

The advent of speech recognition technology has transformed various industries, from personal digital assistants to automated customer care solutions. These innovations are spurred by sophisticated algorithms powered by recurrent neural networks (RNNs) that excel at handling sequential information by encoding temporal relationships. RNNs are particularly geared to model the dynamic nature of human speech to facilitate real-time transcription and understanding of verbal communication. However, unformatted raw output of Automatic Speech Recognition (ASR) systems is typically one that lacks punctuation and capitalization, thereby being in an unusable form for purposes of later natural language processing tasks. Filling this gap, new approaches are proposed in recent research that utilize the application of bidirectional recurrent neural networks for modelling punctuation and capitalization together, thereby enhancing the general speech recognition system performance. This shared approach not only improves the quality of transcriptions but also allows for more rational and contextually suitable communication (Kotlerman et al., 2017). Beyond the accuracy of transcription, the architecture of RNNs also makes them less prone to adapt in different acoustic environments. The time-variant characteristic of speech may vary immensely between different contexts, and therefore, it is also important for subtle audio signals to be identified. Research has revealed that the application of convolutional neural networks (CNNs) coupled with gated recurrent units (GRUs) enhances the ability of the RNNs to learn and handle such long temporal patterns in audio signals. This configuration has been of enormous utility in tackling audio tagging problems, an important aspect of speech recognition systems that involve the annotation of certain sounds or events in a given input audio stream. By capitalizing on robust features mined from mel-filter banks or spectrograms, the combination of CNNs and GRUs has achieved gigantic reductions in error rates, demonstrating the potential of new neural architectures to improve speech recognition (Huang et al., 2017). As time goes by, the continued growth of RNNs has the potential to further transform speech recognition. Because the technology involves machine learning approaches and data from various linguistic origins, it is rendered even more effective in understanding accents, dialects, and other speech patterns. This capability is extremely significant in offering more personalized and efficient user experiences across applications ranging from virtual assistants to language translation services. In addition, as RNNs are upgraded using advanced research techniques, the field will probably witness the introduction of systems that can predict user intention and circumstance and facilitate smoother interaction. Thus, the integration of RNNs and speech recognition technologies forms a critical foundation for more advanced, easier-to-use devices for communication and drives the further integration of natural language processing in various applications (Figure 7.12).

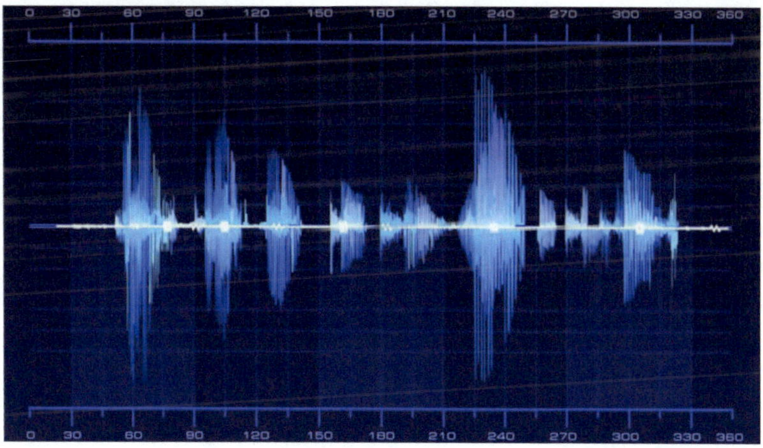

Figure 7.12. *Automatic speech recognition (ASR).*

Source: https://usabilitygeek.com/wp-content/uploads/2018/05/automatic-speech-recognition-lead.jpg.

7.5. ADVANTAGES OF RECURRENT NEURAL NETWORKS (RNNS)

The development of RNNs has made a tremendous difference in the field of deep learning, particularly in sequence-related operations. One of the key advantages of RNNs is that they are capable of maintaining memory across sequences, thereby facilitating the processing of varying-length inputs without information loss in context. This time aspect of RNNs makes them particularly well adapted to handling tasks such as time series prediction, natural language processing, and speech recognition. For instance, RNNs can read the history states in a sequence in order to make informed predictions about future states and thereby perform better than regular feedforward neural networks. This aspect not only enhances the predictive ability of the models but also enables the development of sophisticated applications, like real-time translation and chatbots, that require encoding fine-grained context information over time (Avacharmal et al., 2024). Another fascinating aspect of RNNs is the ability to share weights across multiple time steps, which maintains the model's complexity significantly lower and prevents overfitting.

This weight-sharing process allows RNNs to generalize more effectively over a broad range of categories of data without the need for many training parameters. Thus, RNNs can improve computational effectiveness and facilitate training, particularly when combined with processes such as Backpropagation Through Time (BPTT). In addition, if equipped with models like Long Short-Term Memory (LSTM) and Gated Recurrent Units (GRUs), RNNs are less susceptible to issues like the vanishing gradient problem. Such improvements render RNNs especially resilient to applications involving long-term dependencies, for instance, text generation and video analysis (Rai et al., 2024). The diversity of RNN architectures even further indicates the importance of strengths in a wide range of different applications. RNNs can be trained for a variety of tasks and converge quickly to the needs of varying domains, from finance to healthcare. For example, in speech-to-text conversion, RNNs employ their sequential processing capabilities to address voice recognition issues with great accuracy. Furthermore, the integration of convolutional layers with RNNs yields advanced hybrid models that are able to extract spatial features without losing temporal dynamics. This combination leads to innovation in fields like sign language interpretation, where sounds are initially converted by the model and then leads to respective movements through the application of RNNs (Avacharmal et al., 2024; Rai et al., 2024). The ease of use and efficiency of RNNs make them invaluable in solving actual-world problems in numerous applications.

7.5.1. Ability to Handle Sequential Data

Handling sequential data is a feature of Recurrent Neural Networks (RNNs), especially designed to handle information that is mutually dependent in time. Feedforward neural networks are not very effective with this kind of data because they process each input separately and do not capture temporal dynamics. On the other hand, RNNs contain a current hidden state with each successive input, where they can retain knowledge about previous data points. This is particularly beneficial in applications such as NLP and time-series prediction, where sequence and context play a significant role in impacting predictions. Through the capture of sequential dependencies, RNNs are able to learn to effectively scan trends, identify patterns, and interpret predictions based on previous sequences, positioning them as potent resources in tasks requiring memory and context sensitiveness. Contributing to the potency of RNNs in handling sequential data further is the incorporation of more evolved architectures such as Long Short-Term Memory (LSTM) networks. LSTMs address the vanishing gradient problem that usually plagues standard RNNs, making it possible for them to capture long-distance relationships more effectively. This stability is crucial when handling complex sequences in which significant connections may extend over many time steps. For instance, in healthcare applications, a RNN can analyze multimodal time series on weight, sleep, and exercise. Through the use of models such as the cross-modal LSTM (X-LSTM), researchers are able to achieve optimal parameter efficiency while facilitating well-informed cross-links between heterogeneous data, thereby boosting prediction performance. The combination yields valuable insights that enhance the appreciation of the interaction between various variables over time, a perfect illustration of RNN strength in practical applications (Bellahsen et al., 2017). Besides, RNNs can handle censored data issues that are prevalent in most fields such as clinical trials. By exploiting the sequential nature of data, RNNs can predict the probability of occurrences and the survival rate over a time interval without stringent assumption about the underlying probability distributions. Cases like Deep Recurrent Survival Analysis demonstrate that RNNs can be used extensively to tackle such complexities in an intelligent manner and give deeper insights into survival analysis. The model allows the occurrence of events to be predicted and challenges of censorship of data to be tackled, demonstrating how RNNs not just solve temporal dependency but are also more adaptable in addressing real-world complexities. As a result, RNNs are extremely valuable in numerous applications dealing with sequence data, with widespread advantages over traditional approaches (Qin et al., 2018).

7.5.2. Memory Retention Through Hidden States

In the context of recurrent neural networks (RNNs), memory retention is closely tied to the concept of hidden states. Hidden states are internal representations of knowledge, holding insight based on sequences of input data. In contrast to the typical feedforward neural networks that lack the ability to memorize over time, RNNs rely on hidden states to remember context information so that they can efficiently process and forecast time-series sequences. The architecture of RNNs allows for this retention through mechanisms directly embedded in their recurrent connections, enabling the network to maintain previous inputs and employ this memory in subsequent computation. This temporal ability is imperative to operations that entail understanding dependencies over time, such as natural language processing and voice recognition, further ensuring the importance of latent states in enhancing RNN efficiency. The capacity of storage in memory within RNNs is also best enhanced with advanced methods, such as long short-term memory (LSTM) networks. LSTMs are specifically designed to address the vanishing gradient problem that is typically found in RNNs, allowing them to store and manage memory in long sequences. This is achieved through the use of a gate mechanism used to regulate information flowing into and out of the memory cell, thus optimizing storage of useful information while discarding noisy irrelevant information. Past work also focused more on the superior predictive abilities of LSTMs compared to other models in dealing with challenging sequence prediction, with a 0.902 accuracy in predicting protein subcellular locates from their sequences alone. The capability of the architecture to process long sequences underscores the significance of good memory maintenance through hidden states in enhancing RNN performance (Graves et al., 2015). Furthermore, research demonstrates that incorporating attention mechanisms into RNN models such as LSTMs can enhance memory retention capabilities even further. Attention mechanisms allow networks to focus on specific regions of input data and thus prioritize the most relevant features needed for predictions while maintaining long-term context sensitivity. This concentrated attention enhances the ability of networks to make accurate predictions based on key elements from long sequences. By combining the strong recall of memory offered by hidden states with the discriminative aspect of attention, RNNs become more sophisticated models for extracting biologically significant information in a variety of applications. With such advancements evolving further, the workings of latent states, memory, and processes of attention have the capacity to significantly advance the performance of RNNs in tackling more difficult problems in computational as well as biological contexts (Abbott et al., 2019).

7.5.3. Flexibility in Various Applications

Flexibility of Recurrent Neural Networks (RNNs) is one of the key strengths in various applications, particularly sequence prediction and temporal data analysis. RNNs' intrinsic structure enables them to process variable-length input sequences and are therefore best suited to applications such as natural language processing and speech recognition. This versatility allows practitioners and researchers to apply RNNs to a broad spectrum of applications, ranging from text processing to music composition, where retention of context of previous inputs is crucial. The value of such versatility is also seen with the myriad of applications in robotics, where deep learning techniques are being continuously applied to boost operational efficiency and task precision. The adaptability of RNNs thus testifies to their essential role in spearheading technological frontiers across different disciplines (Gashler et al., 2017). In the financial sector, RNNs have proved beyond any doubt when it comes to predicting and modeling volatility, showing their ability to examine and understand complex time series information. Recent trends involve the integration of statistical models with RNNs to create advanced frameworks that can capture the temporal nature of volatility in a better way than in the past.

As an illustration, the new approach presented in recent studies depicts how complementary stochastic RNNs can significantly improve volatility estimation over the traditional approaches like GARCH models. With effective duplication of the joint distribution of stochastic processes, these RNNs make more precise predictions and uncertainty estimation. Advances such as these show how RNN's adaptability allows them to move beyond the general application, developing financial analysis and risk management into new areas (Luo et al., 2018). Flexibility offered by RNNs is carried to their real-time learning ability and adaptation, which is particularly beneficial in dynamic environments. This property is particularly valuable to utilize in autonomous systems and mobile learning environments, where the conditions change quickly and models need to update simultaneously. As RNNs can remember relevant information from previous time steps while dismissing insignificant details, they are well-suited to excel at fine-tuning predictions with current information. This ability not only allows them to perform exceptionally well in extremely variable environments but also reduces the need for extensive retraining processes. The feature of ongoing learning highlights RNNs' relevance to various sectors of industry, such as healthcare and telecommunications, where timely and context-dependent decision-making is essential. The flexibility inherent in RNN design hence positions them as a potent instrument in addressing contemporary challenges industry-wise.

7.6. CHALLENGES AND LIMITATIONS

The use of Recurrent Neural Networks (RNNs) is confronted by some challenging and constraining problems that hinder their expansion to numerous applications. Vanishing and exploding gradients are root RNN problems that arise when training deep neural networks. In propagating the values of gradients through several layers, they can decrease to values close to zero or, contrarily, become overwhelmingly large, leading to inefficient learning or model instability. This phenomenon particularly renders long sequence training challenging, as RNNs' capacity to maintain long-term relationships is greatly impaired. Thus, scientists are compelled to look for alternative architectures, such as Long Short-Term Memory (LSTM) networks or Gated Recurrent Units (GRUs), that try to mitigate these issues but introduce their own complications and computational expenses. Still, another important RNN weakness is in performance when handling non-stationary data, particularly in predicting sequences that are driven by variable external sources. For instance, the solar power industry has demonstrated that traditional forecasting methods fail due to large prediction errors that add to grid operation uncertainties and therefore affect reliability and operation costs. The research highlights that while RNNs can be adapted for multi-time-horizon forecasting, enabling greater robust forecasting with real-time inputs, they still do not exhibit high accuracy in different time scales. The intrinsic nature of limitations in forecasting with RNNs necessitates investigations into integrated architectures that leverage their potential while mitigating their weaknesses, as discussed in various works toward enhancing prediction efficiency in dynamic scenarios (Mishra et al., 2018). Last but not least, RNN interpretability is an issue that holds back RNNs from being widely adopted in high-risk sectors, such as healthcare and finance, where model choices have to be comprehensible. Even with advancements in training RNNs for most applications, their internal functioning tends to be complex, turning them into black boxes. This opacity creates accountability and trust issues when RNNs produce predictions that significantly impact human life. BlackboxNLP workshop focused on various approaches to providing transparency, such as systematic input manipulation to quantify performance impact and analysis of intermediate representations for transparent knowledge extraction. As long as more is not done towards explaining RNNs, their use in high-risk domains remains controversial, compelling practitioners to balance effectiveness with clarity (Alishahi et al., 2019).

7.6.1. Vanishing and Exploding Gradient Problems

Vanishing and exploding gradients are fundamental issues in the training of recurrent neural networks (RNNs), quite literally arising from the nature of gradient descent optimization. As gradients approach very close to zero, they vanish, and in the process, they help weights vary very minimally in training and thus lead to learning stalling, particularly in long sequences. When gradients explode, they induce extreme updates in weights, and more commonly, this leads to learning diverging. These issues can significantly impede the functioning of RNNs, inhibiting long-term dependencies required for tasks such as language modeling and sequence prediction from being established. Traditional RNN designs, in their original form, are particularly susceptible to these problems, hence the need to explore innovative means of enhancing their training stability as well as performance in advanced sequence processing tasks. In order to solve vanishing and exploding gradient issues, scientists introduced several architectures and methods. One of the significant methods is using orthogonal or unitary recurrent weight matrices to keep the magnitude of gradients during backpropagation through time. For instance, the scaled Cayley orthogonal recurrent neural network (scoRNN) incorporates an orthogonal recurrent weight matrix that is parameterized via a scaled Cayley transform, which can mitigate these gradient issues without strongly impacting the learning process. This paradigm shows how accurate mathematical structures can be instrumental in enhancing RNN stability and performance. By refining recurrent weight dynamics, scoRNN can effectively manage gradients, yet it requires hyperparameter adjustment to achieve optimal performance. These advancements reflect the ongoing pursuit within the discipline for robust solutions in order to enhance the learning capacity of RNNs in relation to these pervasive gradient issues. Other innovations, like batch normalized recurrent highway networks, indicate another means of managing gradient flow extremely effectively. Through normalizing inputs at each recurrence loop, the model minimizes the chances of gradients exploding or vanishing and promotes faster convergence during training. This approach is particularly remarkable in that it maintains eigenvalues of the temporal Jacobian at unity across time steps, thus stabilizing the learning trajectory. Empirical findings offer evidence for the efficacy of such models, with improved performance on image captioning compared to state-of-the-art Long Short-Term Memory (LSTM) networks and recurrent highway networks (RHNs). As exemplified in the works, creating metrics for gradient control techniques is of the highest priority to ease the intrinsic complexity brought about by the exploding and vanishing gradient problems of RNNs and paving the way for more reliable metrics in sequence learning tasks (Helfrich et al., 2019; Loui et al., 2017).

7.6.2. Computational Complexity

Computational complexity is the essence of understanding the strength and weaknesses of Recurrent Neural Networks (RNNs). These networks are designed to process sequential data in such a way that temporal dependencies that are inherent to applications like language modeling and time series prediction can be supported. Precisely, RNNs' sophistication can be explained in terms of their attractor dynamics. With the identification of a more refined attractor-based measure of complexity for Boolean RNNs, researchers have begun to unravel the intricate interplay between the dynamics of these networks and their computational capability. This approach provides a hierarchical network categorization based on attractor dynamics that elucidates how varying dynamics can suggest varying computational capability and efficiency. Such discoveries ultimately enhance our understanding of how to tailor RNNs for specific applications, thus making complexity measurement a fundamental area of research in the study of neural networks (Cabessa et al., 2014). Moreover, the comprehension of temporal gates within recurrent architectures, such as Long Short-Term Memory (LSTM) networks, is one of the biggest advances in addressing computational complexity. These gates play a critical role in controlling the flow of information such that the network is able to selectively remember or forget information between sequences. This selective memory is crucial in alleviating the vanishing gradient problem that plagues most RNNs in learning long-range dependencies. The inclusion of learned temporal gates provides an avenue for RNNs not just to process sophisticated patterns but to do so at a more efficient rate. As empirically shown, the new paradigm has attained state-of-the-art performance on various question-answering benchmark test sets, which means the adaptive mechanisms can control computational complexity and thereby enhance the performance of RNN architectures (Hui et al., 2017). The marriage of subtle complexity measures with mechanisms like temporal gates points to a future when RNNs can be engineered better for specific tasks. With the evolution of the discipline, understanding how computational complexity influences the structural dynamics of RNNs will be key to their future development. Such an understanding could facilitate the creation of more advanced models that not only process intricate temporal patterns but also optimize computation. These developments are particularly important in real-time computation and flexible applications such as natural language processing and robotics. Hence, research into the computational complexities behind RNNs keeps improving the theoretical foundation and practical applications of neural network technology, with the proliferation of continued breakthroughs in this constantly developing field (Cabessa et al., 2014; Hui et al., 2017).

7.6.3. Difficulty in Training on Long Sequences

RNN training on long sequence is a particularly demanding task, most critically due to the frailties in backpropagation through time (BPTT) algorithm. BPTT, which is capable of handling sequential data, has severe problems when inputs are long. The network having been unrolled through time, the gradient signals could get watered down—a phenomenon known as vanishing gradients. This is a problem that makes RNNs perform poorly in learning dependencies over very long time scales and leads to poor performance in applications involving understanding context or relationships over extended sequences. The performance of RNNs is thus compromised, especially when they are applied to catch up on intricate patterns or temporal dynamics needed in sophisticated applications. In more recent efforts to alleviate these training issues, researchers have sought alternatives beyond the conventional gradient-based approaches. Perturbation-based learning approaches, for instance, offer a fresh relief through the use of global feedback signals instead of depending solely on exact gradient data. This allows training to move forward without the extensive backtracking found in BPTT, at significantly lower computational expenses and essentially eliminating the vanishing gradient issue. Integration of this method into training RNNs holds potential since it maintains levels of performance while scaling up. Moreover, strategies like the activity-based node perturbation (ANP) method have also shown efficacy when applied towards time-domain processing, highlighting the capability of emerging methods to revolutionize the way RNNs are trained on long sequences (Jesús García Fernández et al., 2024). The challenge of RNN training on long sequences is largely evident in practical applications such as genomic sequence analysis, in which models have to rapidly and accurately process and classify long data. Recent work illustrates the limitations experienced with standard RNN architectures in effectively understanding long genomic sequences, which may contain valuable information over long durations. These limitations are countered by deep learning architectures like the long-short term memory (LSTM) networks. Nevertheless, even these highly evolved architectures portray challenges in preserving relative positions of input data over large intervals, introducing a performance shortfall compared to shorter sequences (Rani et al., 2025). Consequently, ongoing attempts to find efficient training techniques continue to concentrate on the need to continue innovating in order to enable the performance of RNNs to more effectively handle difficult and high-dimensional data tasks.

SUMMARY

RNNs have developed machine learning significantly overall, particularly in processing temporal and sequential data. By virtue of their ability to maintain an input memory of earlier inputs, they can model complex dependencies between data sequences. This capability is especially useful in applications such as speech recognition and natural language processing, where context and temporal order of the inputs need to be understood. Even if RNNs have been successful in these applications, problems intrinsic to training such networks—such as the vanishing gradient problem—emphasize the need for ongoing work and research. Resolving these issues is required to enhance the stability and interpretability of RNNs in such a way that their application remains effective and reliable in achieving desired outcomes under practical circumstances. Furthermore, the evolving landscape of machine learning indicates that RNNs are hardly the sole player in town when it comes to sequence data processing. Advanced techniques, including hybrid models and reinforcement learning frameworks incorporation, are paving the way for innovation leveraging RNN advantages while alleviating their disadvantages. For instance, incorporating probabilistic graphical models and switching systems can be a robust approach to factorizing advanced dynamics, as described in related recent research (Abdulsamad et al., 2020). This integration of technologies not only increases the arsenal of researchers but also opens up new fronts for the development of intelligent systems that have the capacity to perform sophisticated decision-making processes under dynamic data environments. Ultimately, the future of RNNs is all about balance between complexity and interpretability. As deep learning research draws widespread interest to a variety of applications, for instance, robotics and autonomous systems, the real-world implications of these technologies grow more critical to understand (Gashler et al., 2017). Additional study of RNN structures and integration into other models of learning can give systems both proficiency and clarity. Hence, while RNNs form a landmark in the machine learning paradigm, the future holds ongoing research and inter-disciplinary work with collaboration that can usher innovations that can redefine theoretical frameworks and practical implementations in the field.

In encapsulating the essence of the most important features of RNNs, an utmost amount of emphasis must be placed on their inherent capacity for treating sequential data comprehensively. RNNs are specifically designed to process sequences of variable lengths as inputs, keeping a hidden state that summarizes information from previous time steps. This property is particularly important in applications dealing with time series, natural language, and even in sophisticated cases such as 3D scene understanding, where the temporal dynamics are to be captured exactly. Relevant innovation in this domain is the creation of Data Associated Recurrent Neural Networks (DA-RNNs), which combines semantic labeling and 3D scene mapping. This format permits increased robot-environment interaction, as semantic data is integrated into the reconstructed scenes, thus showcasing an innovative application of RNN technology outside of common uses (Fox et al., 2017). Besides, the advancements in RNN models have also given rise to specialized variants such as Long Short-Term Memory (LSTM) networks. Unlike standard RNNs, LSTMs can model long-range dependencies due to their new gating mechanisms that enable them to learn from sequences that span greater than very large temporal separations. This capability is of special significance in use cases such as Network Traffic Matrix (TM) prediction, where long-term trends and short-term fluctuations must be comprehended. The LSTM architecture has been found to perform particularly well in temporal sequence modeling, thus greatly altering data scientists' approach to solving network planning and resource allocation. Empirical evidence indicates that LSTM-based models have the ability to converge quickly and outperform traditional methods, a highly important development in predictive analysis for large networks (Azzouni et al., 2017). Lastly, RNNs' flexibility and the various architectures they enable highlight their impact on a wide range of applications. From enhancing machines' ability to comprehend and generate human language to enabling robots to navigate around and understand complex spatial configurations, the scope of RNN application is vast. As neural network work continues to improve, further development of RNN technologies can be anticipated that might lead to even more sophisticated models. These developments not only will push the functional boundaries of RNNs farther but also improve the accuracy and efficiency with which they perform. This ongoing innovation is a watershed in machine learning and artificial intelligence, recording the revolutionary capabilities of recurrent neural networks in handling sequential data and making precise predictions in multiple disciplines.

REFERENCES

1. Abbott, B., Bartolozzi, B., Benjamin, B., Bi, G., Bohte, S., Detorakis, G., et al. (2019). Spiking neural networks for inference and learning: A memristor-based design perspective. https://core.ac.uk/download/323310558.pdf (accessed on 25th September 2025).
2. Abdulkarim, S. A. (2016). Time series prediction with simple recurrent neural networks. https://core.ac.uk/download/478433971.pdf (accessed on 25th September 2025).
3. Abdulsamad, H., & Peters, J. (2020). Hierarchical decomposition of nonlinear dynamics and control for system identification and policy distillation. http://arxiv.org/abs/2005.01432 (accessed on 25th September 2025).
4. Akram, U., Ghazali, R., & Mushtaq, M. F. (2017). A comprehensive survey on pi-sigma neural network for time series prediction. https://core.ac.uk/download/18264205.pdf (accessed on 25th September 2025).
5. Alishahi, A., Chrupała, G., & Linzen, T. (2019). Analyzing and interpreting neural networks for NLP: A report on the first BlackboxNLP workshop. http://arxiv.org/abs/1904.04063 (accessed on 25th September 2025).
6. Amaya Rodríguez, I., Civit Balcells, A., Civit Masot, J., Domínguez Morales, M., et al. (2019). An automated fall detection system using recurrent neural networks. https://core.ac.uk/download/286564597.pdf (accessed on 25th September 2025).
7. Anandkumar, A., & Sedghi, H. (2016). Training input-output recurrent neural networks through spectral methods. https://core.ac.uk/download/216302370.pdf (accessed on 25th September 2025).
8. Arbabzadah, F., Yang, H., Arras, L., Feng, M., Grégoire, M., Schuster, M., Baker, R. S. J., et al. (2020). Towards interpretable deep learning models for knowledge tracing. http://arxiv.org/abs/2005.06139 (accessed on 25th September 2025).
9. Arnau, J. M., Dot, G., Gonzalez, A., Silfa, R., et al. (2017). E-PUR: An energy-efficient processing unit for recurrent neural networks. http://arxiv.org/abs/1711.07480 (accessed on 25th September 2025).
10. Avacharmal, R., Pamulaparthyvenkata, S., Pandiya, D. K., Prakash, R. K., Ranjan, P., Balakrishnan, A., & Maheswaran, S. (2024). Comprehensive investigation on deep learning models: Applications, advantages, and challenges. In 2024 15th International Conference on Computing Communication and Networking Technologies (ICCCNT). https://www.semanticscholar.org/paper/

b06bac1cd22d235305b46e7ea83a415fb8410a9f (accessed on 25th September 2025).

11. Azzouni, A., & Pujolle, G. (2017). A long short-term memory recurrent neural network framework for network traffic matrix prediction. http://arxiv.org/abs/1705.05690 (accessed on 25th September 2025).
12. Barnes, L. E., Brown, D. E., Gerber, M. S., Heidarysafa, M., et al. (2017). HDLTex: Hierarchical deep learning for text classification. http://arxiv.org/abs/1709.08267 (accessed on 25th September 2025).
13. Bauer, W., & Baranowski, J. (2025). Comparison of deep recurrent neural networks and Bayesian neural networks for detecting electric motor damage through sound signal analysis. https://www.semanticscholar.org/paper/56230353ad0b5e5856983dc390a3d5fd57d8359c (accessed on 25th September 2025).
14. Bellahsen, O., Bhattacharya, S., Chieh, A., Karazija, R., et al. (2017). Cross-modal recurrent models for weight objective prediction from multimodal time-series data. http://arxiv.org/abs/1709.08073 (accessed on 25th September 2025).
15. Bengio, Y., Brakel, P., Omologo, M., Ravanelli, M., et al. (2018). Light gated recurrent units for speech recognition. http://arxiv.org/abs/1803.10225 (accessed on 25th September 2025).
16. Bengio, Y., Ke, N. R., Pal, C., Serdyuk, D., et al. (2018). Twin networks: Matching the future for sequence generation. http://arxiv.org/abs/1708.06742 (accessed on 25th September 2025).
17. Bisazza, A., Monz, C., & Tran, K. (2016). Recurrent memory networks for language modeling. https://core.ac.uk/download/376875358.pdf (accessed on 25th September 2025).
18. Blanes Martin, V. (2018). Toxic comment classification using convolutional and recurrent neural networks. https://core.ac.uk/download/187264887.pdf (accessed on 25th September 2025).
19. Bokhan, K., Khomenko, V., Radyvonenko, O., Shyshkov, O., et al. (2017). Accelerating recurrent neural network training using sequence bucketing and multi-GPU data parallelization. http://arxiv.org/abs/1708.05604 (accessed on 25th September 2025).
20. Cabessa, J., & Villa, A. E. P. (2014). An attractor-based complexity measurement for Boolean recurrent neural networks. https://core.ac.uk/download/132562993.pdf (accessed on 25th September 2025).
21. Cassidy, A., Diehl, P. U., Neftci, E., et al. (2016). Conversion of artificial recurrent neural networks to spiking neural networks for low-power

neuromorphic hardware. http://arxiv.org/abs/1601.04187 (accessed on 25th September 2025).

22. Chen, L., Fanioudakis, E., Giakoumis, D., Hamzaoui, R., et al. (2019). Two-dimensional convolutional recurrent neural networks for speech activity detection. https://core.ac.uk/download/228189775.pdf (accessed on 25th September 2025).
23. De Boom, C., Demeester, T., & Dhoedt, B. (2018). Character-level recurrent neural networks in practice: Comparing training and sampling schemes. https://core.ac.uk/download/159321980.pdf (accessed on 25th September 2025).
24. de Castro, F. Z., & Valle, M. E. (2019). A broad class of discrete-time hypercomplex-valued Hopfield neural networks. http://arxiv.org/abs/1902.05478 (accessed on 25th September 2025).
25. Delai, M., Karlen, W., Scebba, G., Schwab, A., et al. (2017). Beat by beat: Classifying cardiac arrhythmias with recurrent neural networks. http://arxiv.org/abs/1710.06319 (accessed on 25th September 2025).
26. Dempster, A., Graves, A., Dong, C., Ising, E., Hinton, G. E., Cross, G. R., Rue, H., et al. (2016). Deep Markov random field for image modeling. http://arxiv.org/abs/1609.02036 (accessed on 25th September 2025).
27. Doval, Y., & Gómez-Rodríguez, C. (2018). Comparing neural- and n-gram-based language models for word segmentation. https://core.ac.uk/download/614587948.pdf (accessed on 25th September 2025).
28. Fang, C., Jin, H., Luo, J., Wang, L., et al. (2016). Image captioning with semantic attention. http://arxiv.org/abs/1603.03925 (accessed on 25th September 2025).
29. Fox, D., & Xiang, Y. (2017). DA-RNN: Semantic mapping with data associated recurrent neural networks. http://arxiv.org/abs/1703.03098 (accessed on 25th September 2025).
30. Gabrys, B., Musial, K., & Skarding, J. (2021). Foundations and modelling of dynamic networks using dynamic graph neural networks: A survey. http://arxiv.org/abs/2005.07496 (accessed on 25th September 2025).
31. García Fernández, J., Keemink, S. W., & Gerven, M. (2024). Gradient-free training of recurrent neural networks using random perturbations. Frontiers in Neuroscience, 18. https://www.semanticscholar.org/paper/a9d0f92621b6915a42ea1da2cc5e53b52effd152 (accessed on 25th September 2025).
32. Gashler, M. S., & Pierson, H. A. (2017). Deep learning in robotics: A review of recent research. http://arxiv.org/abs/1707.07217 (accessed on 25th September 2025).

33. Graves, A., Höglund, A., Prlić, A., Magnan, C., Dahl, G., Xiong, H. Y., Maaten Van Der, L. J. P., et al. (2015). Convolutional LSTM networks for subcellular localization of proteins. https://core.ac.uk/download/43255023.pdf (accessed on 25th September 2025).
34. Heidemann, G., & Tanisaro, P. (2018). An empirical study on bidirectional recurrent neural networks for human motion recognition. https://core.ac.uk/download/161589401.pdf (accessed on 25th September 2025).
35. Heidenreich, H., Vlachas, P. R., & Koumoutsakos, P. (2024). Deconstructing recurrence, attention, and gating: Investigating the transferability of Transformers and gated recurrent neural networks in forecasting of dynamical systems. https://www.semanticscholar.org/paper/0d9171e8fd811e1fe57c4e36ad0ce1af556497f7 (accessed on 25th September 2025).
36. Helfrich, K. E., Maduranga, K. D. G., & Ye, Q. (2019). Complex unitary recurrent neural networks using scaled Cayley transform. http://arxiv.org/abs/1811.04142 (accessed on 25th September 2025).
37. Huang, Q., Kong, Q., Plumbley, M. D., Wang, Y., et al. (2017). Convolutional gated recurrent neural network incorporating spatial features for audio tagging. https://core.ac.uk/download/77612902.pdf (accessed on 25th September 2025).
38. Hui, S. C., Tay, Y., & Luu, A. T. (2017). Cross temporal recurrent networks for ranking question answer pairs. http://arxiv.org/abs/1711.07656 (accessed on 25th September 2025).
39. Hwang, K., Shin, S., & Sung, W. (2016). Fixed-point performance analysis of recurrent neural networks. http://arxiv.org/abs/1512.01322 (accessed on 25th September 2025).
40. Kingma, D., Liu, Q., Neil, D., Rendle, S., Yuan, F., Zhang, Y., & Zhao, S. (2018). Contextual attention recurrent architecture for context-aware venue recommendation. https://core.ac.uk/download/155789835.pdf (accessed on 25th September 2025).
41. Kotlerman, L., Laha, A., Lev, G., Mirkin, S., et al. (2017). Joint learning of correlated sequence labelling tasks using bidirectional recurrent neural networks. http://arxiv.org/abs/1703.04650 (accessed on 25th September 2025).
42. Le, B. S., Brown, P. F., Chua, Z. L., Gu, G., Ho, G., Liu, Y., Melicher, W., et al. (2018). Tiresias: Predicting security events through deep learning. http://arxiv.org/abs/1905.10328 (accessed on 25th September 2025).
43. Loui, A., Nguyen, T., Ptucha, R., Sah, M., et al. (2017). Batch-normalized recurrent highway networks. http://arxiv.org/abs/1809.10271 (accessed on 25th September 2025).

44. Luo, R., Wang, J., Xu, X., Zhang, Y., et al. (2018). A neural stochastic volatility model. http://arxiv.org/abs/1712.00504 (accessed on 25th September 2025).

45. Mishra, S., & Palanisamy, P. (2018). Multi-time-horizon solar forecasting using recurrent neural network. http://arxiv.org/abs/1807.05459 (accessed on 25th September 2025).

46. Qin, J., Qiu, L., Ren, K., Yang, Y., et al. (2018). Deep recurrent survival analysis. http://arxiv.org/abs/1809.02403 (accessed on 25th September 2025).

47. Racki, A., & Paduszyński, K. (2025). Recent advances in the modeling of ionic liquids using artificial neural networks. Journal of Chemical Information and Modeling, 65, 3161–3175. https://www.semanticscholar.org/paper/7a14762ef4ba44ef4408692f22cae2fbf2006a8c (accessed on 25th September 2025).

48. Rai, D., Rana, N., Kotak, N., & Sharma, M. (2024). Real-time speech to sign language translation using machine and deep learning. In 2024 11th International Conference on Reliability, Infocom Technologies and Optimization (Trends and Future Directions) (ICRITO). https://www.semanticscholar.org/paper/cad731ebfb219e62cbd6666a4c7a9fc224262991 (accessed on 25th September 2025).

49. Rani, G., Misra, A., Kundu, N., Dhaka, V., & Lather, P. (2025). Neural genome sequence encoding for downy mildew pathogen detection: A spatial pyramid and dual-attention approach. IEEE Access, 13, 65478–65489. https://www.semanticscholar.org/paper/935c99406894115c0e864df821899763a92db63e (accessed on 25th September 2025).

50. Uppalaiah, B., Ahmad, A. A., Lotus, A. A., Al-Shammari, A. H., Hassan, S. I., & Dhaaraani, R. (2025). Recurrent neural networks for efficient solutions to time-series forecasting in complex mathematical models. In 2025 3rd International Conference on Smart Systems for Applications in Electrical Sciences (ICSSES). https://www.semanticscholar.org/paper/0413bcfbaed48778e49682841d48c7210734c939 (accessed on 25th September 2025).

CHAPTER 8

ADVANCED ARCHITECTURES

Contents

INTRODUCTION

The development of neural network architectures has revolutionized a wide range of disciplines, providing the building blocks for sophisticated artificial intelligence systems. The advent of deep learning, a subfield of machine learning, has precipitated improvements in computer vision, natural language processing, and speech recognition, to mention a few. Sophisticated architectures, such as Convolutional Neural Networks (CNNs), have been extremely effective at executing complex tasks that were hitherto reserved for human cognitive functions. As revealed in Marí et al. (2016), these architectures are better than identifying patterns and features from big data sets, and this has significant implications for facial recognition and image categorization applications. Thus, the basic impact of these new neural network architectures not only has a beneficial influence on performance in most areas but also compels research today to work on enhancing their capabilities and broadening their range of application. One key area of research is comparative analysis of deep learning architectures compared to classical machine learning approaches. Classical methods use feature engineering and domain knowledge, while new architectures like Deep Neural Networks (DNNs) use raw inputs to learn important features in multiple abstraction levels automatically.

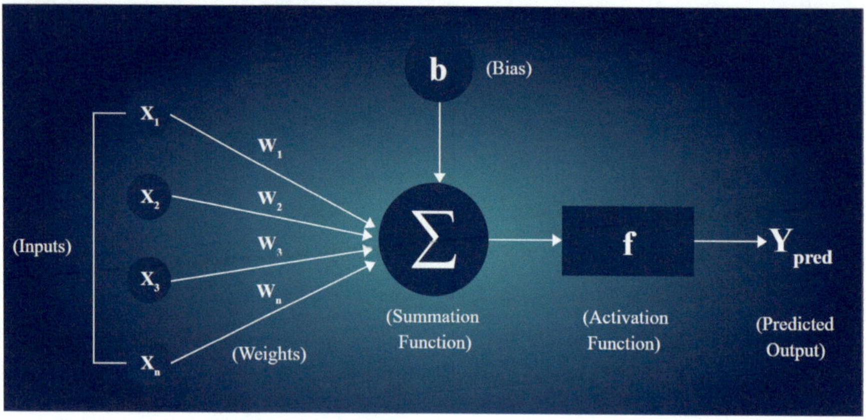

Figure 8.1. *Neural networks: architecture.*

Source: https://d3lkc3n5th01x7.cloudfront.net/wp-content/uploads/2023/05/30234805/ What-are-neural-networks-Banner.svg.

This trait is particularly seen in applications such as malware classification, where deep learning models can outperform traditional models in certain circumstances, as seen in Rathore et al. (2018). Such architectures' computational burden, however, may be demanding, as deeper networks tend to require more resources and longer training periods. So, it is crucial for practitioners to understand the trade-offs between latest architectures and classical strategies such that they would be able to optimize model performance while keeping practical considerations in check while constructing models in real-world applications. As the frontier is pushed further in this direction, hybrid models and ensembling strategies have become a thrilling area of research. These strategies try to aggregate the strengths of multiple architectures to yield better performance across a variety of tasks. For instance, blending CNNs with conventional classifiers has achieved great performance in most image recognition problems, as can be observed by research work and real-world applications. In addition, the need to attain state-of-the-art performance necessitates continuous upgrading of architecture design, hyperparameter tuning, and integration of new methods such as transfer learning. Ultimately, the ongoing evolution of advanced neural network structures is not merely a sign of progress in technology; it reveals the promise that these systems hold to address increasingly complex problems in many fields, while a clearer understanding is gained about the place of artificial intelligences in society (Figure 8.1).

Definition of Neural Networks

The concept of neural networks has evolved a lot since it was created, and it has been at the core of artificial intelligence practice. Essentially, a neural network is a computational model inspired by the biologically occurring neural networks in the human brain. A neural network consists of layers of linked nodes or neurons, and each connection contains a weight that differs the signal from one to another. This structure allows for the processing of intricate input data, enabling the network's ability to learn patterns through a mechanism known as training. Training involves the modification of the weights using the learning algorithm which repeatedly enhances the models accuracy. The capacity of neural networks to learn from vast amounts of data renders it an important instrument in modern computation, particularly in image and language processing. As neural networks developed, various architectures emerged to extend their capacities, addressing specific issues in various domains. Advanced architectures like convolutional neural networks (CNNs) and recurrent neural networks (RNNs) are case in point. CNNs are particularly suited to handle grid-structured data, such as images, through layers that apply convolutional filters in order to identify spatial hierarchies. Conversely, RNNs are designed for sequential data, hence they can be used for tasks that need time-series forecasting or natural language processing. Specialized architectures like such show the great strides the field has made because they enable more complex learning and enable networks to handle more complex datasets better. Specialization, in turn, not only improves performance but also expands the application of neural networks to so many various fields like medical imaging and autonomous systems. The significance of neural networks transcends mere computational superiority; it also encompasses their potential for creative problem-solving. New technologies have introduced concepts such as relational reasoning networks (RRN), which use deep learning to identify patterns of relationships between various points of data without needing forced segmentation, demonstrating an astronomical leap in capability. This design takes advantage of the inherent relations in the data for decision-making, something that can potentially revolutionize surgical planning in fields such as craniomaxillofacial surgery, as pointed out by recent studies (Bagci et al., 2019). In addition, the use of advanced machine learning techniques in network optimization is an example of interdisciplinary problem-solving. For instance, cognition-inspired networks utilize the principles of cognitive science for maximizing network control, demonstrating the power and flexibility of neural networks in addressing complex, multi-faceted issues (Grazia et al., 2015). All these advances depict the revolutionary impact of neural networks on modern computational challenges (Figure 8.2).

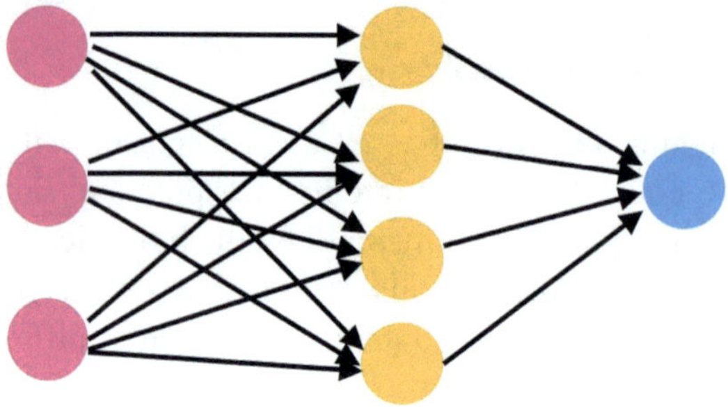

Figure 8.2. *Neural Networks.*

Source: https://www.specbee.com/sites/default/files/inline-images/neural-network-min.jpg.

Importance of Advanced Architectures

The importance of advanced architectures in neural networks cannot be overstated since they are the key to improving computational efficiency and performance in many applications. As a result of the advancing field of deep learning, tasks have grown more demanding, necessitating the existence of architectures that are capable of handling huge amounts of data efficiently and providing low latency. For instance, Multi-GPU systems with a high density are utilized as a solution for the increasing demands of high-performance computing environments. In particular, MPI+CUDA frameworks are utilized to enable the systems to perform massive computation effectively by streamlining inter-GPU communication processes. The development of specialized libraries like NVIDIA NCCL has also enhanced performance even more, enabling operations like data broadcasting to numerous GPUs to be enhanced significantly, thus demonstrating how better architectures are contributing to more efficient and optimized workflows in deep learning workloads (Banerjee et al., 2017). In addition, more recent designs enable the incorporation of machine learning techniques into standard areas such as fluid mechanics, whereby they introduce new possibilities for theoretical understanding as well as application. Recent advances have served to highlight the ability of machine learning algorithms to identify patterns in large data sets drawn from experiments and simulations, thereby offering a better understanding of fluid dynamics. Such architectures not only automate flow control and optimization functions but also enhance existing domain knowledge seamlessly to support the researcher's role better. Modeling and optimizing fluid flows using machine learning frameworks provide an example of how top architectures promote innovation by remapping data usage and taking advantage of novel analysis schemes. This capacity to integrate data-driven methods with traditional scientific research constitutes the revolutionizing power of new architectures across fields (Brunton et al., 2020). Secondly, application of new architectures is imperative to counter the challenge posed by rapidly rising volumes of data and computational needs in today's technology-dominated era. As neural networks continue to advance, scalability and flexibility are ever becoming a necessity in architecture. Elegant designs, such as those facilitating pipelined communication between several GPUs, are classic examples of how architectural innovation is key to maintaining system efficiency and performance. Additionally, competitive edge afforded by such innovations may be observed when parallel processing is carried out with multiple GPUs, emphasizing the value of efficient communication protocols. With the growing scope of artificial intelligence, the utilization of advanced architectures for performance and efficiency will rise even more, making them prominent in upcoming deep learning research on neural networks and applications.

8.1. CONVOLUTIONAL NEURAL NETWORKS (CNNS)

The invention of CNNs represents an important milestone in deep learning, particularly in computer vision. Initially inspired by the form of the visual cortex, CNNs are adept at recognizing patterns in information, something essential for tasks such as image classification, object recognition, and video analysis. Their design typically consists of convolutional layers, pooling layers, and fully connected layers, each serving a particular purpose. Convolution layers are optimal in extracting local features from input data by convolving through filters, while pooling layers carry out dimension and computation reduction through down-sampling of feature maps. This hierarchical structure allows CNNs to construct increasingly abstracted representations and hence enhance the ability to tackle advanced visual issues. The recent advancements in CNNs have expanded their applications in various domains other than traditional image processing. As an example, CNN application to video analysis has been promising, as evidenced by recent systems of state-of-the-art video classification. Such systems demultiplex video frames to disentangle basic texture and motion representations for enabling spatio-temporal analysis using CNNs. Video capture separation from CNN processing, however, introduces bandwidth and power consumption issues that are substantial in Internet-of-Things applications. Leveraging the limitations of such has led to innovative solutions, e.g., selective retention of motion vectors and textures at much lower bitrates without sacrificing performance in classification. These solutions not only improve efficiency but also leverage the adaptive and robust nature of CNNs to function with a variety of mixed and demanding tasks in real-time environments (Abbas et al., 2018). In medicine, CNNs have demonstrated immense potential for enhancing diagnostic accuracy and effectiveness, particularly in cancer detection. Under confocal laser microscopy application, CNNs have been used to classify images automatically to differentiate between malignant and benign tissues. The effectiveness of transfer learning approaches has been explored to improve performance when dealing with sparse datasets, proving that fine-tuning pre-trained models can provide remarkable gains in classification. For example, studies exhibit robust accuracy in the discrimination between colorectal cancer metastases through CNNs, showing even sparse datasets can be valuable within intraoperative decision-making. The different applications of CNNs illustrate their versatility and success across multiple domains, making them a cornerstone of strong neural network architectures (Bengs et al., 2019) (Figure 8.3).

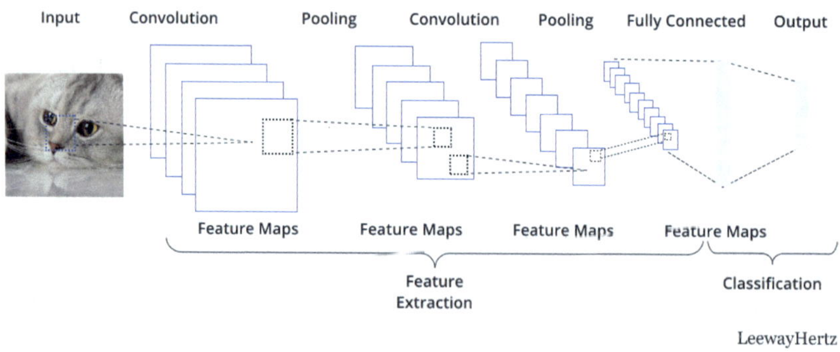

Figure 8.3. *Convolutional neural networks (CNNs).*

Source: https://d3lkc3n5th01x7.cloudfront.net/wp-content/uploads/2023/05/31063205/Convolutional-Neural-Networks-CNN.png.

8.1.1. Structure and Function of Convolutional Neural Networks (CNNs)

The design of CNNs is naturally built for emulating the hierarchy of pattern in data, particularly in image processing. Essentially, CNNs have a number of layers that transform input images to draw increasingly important features. The architecture typically consists of convolutional, pooling, and fully connected layers. Convolutional layers utilize a collection of learnable filters that recognize spatial hierarchies so the network can recognize patterns such as edges, textures, and shapes. Pooling layers then decrease the dimensionality of the feature maps, enhancing the computational efficiency without sacrificing essential features. Layered learning not only accelerates learning but also enhances the network's capacity to generalize from training data to novel data, allowing enhanced performance on novel data. CNNs perform better since they have a unique ability for spatial hierarchies with local connectivity and weight sharing, distinguishing them from traditional neural networks. The process of convolution guarantees local feature learning, which may be pooled to capture global features.

The intensive process enables CNNs to achieve incredible accuracy in image classification and object detection alongside other applications. For example, advances in the CNN architecture have brought about a significant surge in benchmark datasets, whereby existing models record greater accuracy rates. Besides, CNNs can be enhanced using various training mechanisms, such as residual connections and dropout, that preclude overfitting by encouraging learned representation robustness. Thus, CNNs have been conventional models used in computer vision tasks. Recent developments have also explored new methodology with the objective of enhancing the structural effectiveness of CNNs. Techniques such as evolutionary algorithms have gained prominence, embodied by the EXACT algorithm where CNN structure is evolved in distributed computing platforms (Krizhevsky et al., 2017). The technique facilitates automated optimization of network structure, resulting in new structures that are capable of superior performance compared to conventional networks in performance metrics. Pruning techniques, such as Sparse Structure Selection, are also designed to minimize computational complexity while preserving accuracy. These methods leverage sparsity regularization to eliminate secondary parameters or structures, flattening the networks' operation without affecting its performance (Beck et al., 2018). These advances are a step towards adaptive and low-resource CNNs that are even more suitable to the real-world applications in which computational resources are generally limited (Figure 8.4).

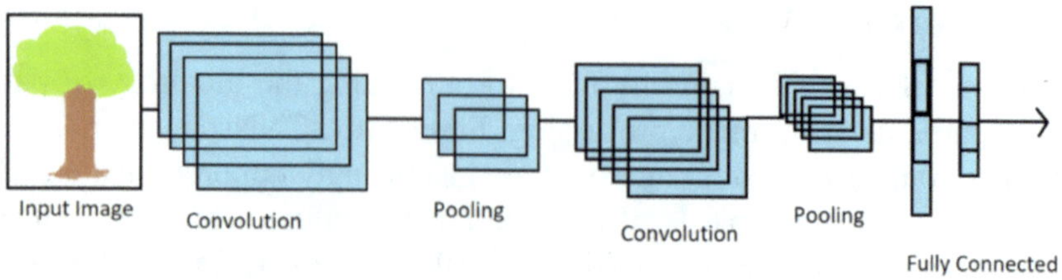

Figure 8.4. *Typical convolutional neural network (CNN) architecture.*

Source: https://debuggercafe.com/wp-content/uploads/2019/06/conv-1-e1561089320572.png.

8.1.2. Applications in Image Processing

The creation of new neural network architectures has, in significant ways, revolutionized image processing applications, particularly through the use of convolutional neural networks (CNNs). CNNs have performed extremely well in image classification, object detection, and segmentation. They possess a layer structure enabling hierarchical features to be extracted automatically, thereby simplifying the recognition of complex patterns from images. For instance, in industrial settings, CNNs are used in visual inspection processes to carry out swift quality control. Through the use of curated databases, CNNs are able to learn to recognize defects or classify products efficiently, showcasing their high performance in real-world applications. As cited, custom automotive dataset generation has shown the way deep learning ensures maximum vehicle property identification, emphasizing even more the important role structured data plays in the successful training of neural networks (Ashcraft et al., 2017). For actual applications of image processing, choosing computing infrastructure has a radically critical bearing on performance outcomes. Recent studies have established that using tensor processing units (TPUs) lowers the training time considerably in handling large data, and thus they are a better choice than traditional GPUs (Alienin et al., 2018). During experiments conducted with both MNIST and Fashion-MNIST datasets, TPUs showed a large speedup and had up to tenfold efficiency improvements during training times. This improved performance highlights the necessity of selecting proper batch sizes to ensure maximum utilization of the computing power of these architectures. Such efficiency gains aren't at the expense of prediction accuracy, being extremely close to the parity of GPU outputs, which is important for applications that require speedy, certain image processing solutions. Furthermore, the contribution of deep learning in image processing extends far beyond manufacturing to other sectors like healthcare, security, and autonomous vehicles. The ability of advanced neural network architectures to handle and interpret vast quantities of visual data has propelled diagnostics imaging and surveillance systems. In the medical field, for instance, medical imaging is processed through deep learning algorithms to detect abnormalities such as tumors, which result in timely diagnosis and improved patient outcomes. Similarly, in autonomous driving, real-time processing of images is crucial to safe driving and avoidance of obstacles. As neural networks continue to evolve to become more specialized across a range of applications, their roles in image processing will definitely grow, leading to revolutionary advancements across many sectors, similar to computational power and structured data (Ashcraft et al., 2017) (Figure 8.5).

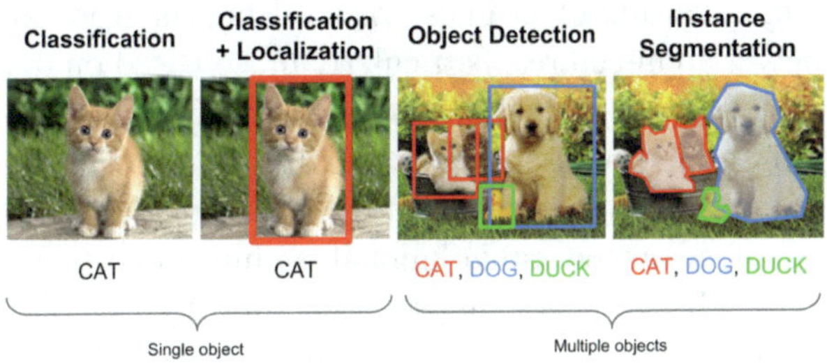

Figure 8.5. *The image shows the difference between different tasks in computer vision, both for single and multiple objects.*

Source: https://svitla.com/wp-content/uploads/2024/06/localizationVsDetection-1024x426.png.

8.1.3. Advantages Over Traditional Neural Networks

In recent years, there have been advanced neural network architectures that have challenged traditional neural networks seriously and proved themselves superior in performance in a broad array of applications. Their enhanced efficiency in data management, particularly in dynamic environments, is one significant advantage they enjoy. For instance, event cameras, which emulate biological vision, exhibit outstanding ability in motion and light change processing without too much redundancy. These sensors coupled with deep learning models result in significant breakthroughs in tasks such as motion estimation, providing more stable estimates under challenging conditions where regular cameras fail. These breakthroughs underscore one of the fundamental strengths of new structures: the capacity to alter data representation dynamically and so optimize predictive performance at the cost of computing burdens (Gallego et al., 2018). In addition, advanced architectures exhibit a highly dramatic reduction in the amount of human labor required for effective learning. Traditional neural networks generally have high demands on complex feature engineering and lots of domain expertise to yield decent results. In contrast, deep learning models, particularly those based on representation learning, remove much of this work. As an example, newer research shows that employing the coding criterion to analyze programs enables deep learning models to outperform logistic regression and support vector machines with less human effort. Not only does this development accelerate the building of neural network models, but it also democratizes advanced machine learning in terms of access so that more people from various fields can participate (Jin et al., 2014). Furthermore, the newer neural network architectures' scalability presents an evident advantage over the older ones. When data sets grow larger and more complicated, newer architectures, particularly those based on transfer learning approaches, can leverage pre-trained models to achieve high performance with comparatively low training data. This is especially discernible in situations where acquiring data is challenging, such as autonomous vehicle navigation systems. Implementation of advanced convolutional architectures that are tuned for event camera output has proven to improve steering angle predictions, showing the power and capability of such newer models in real-world applications. The ability to learn and tune for specific applications ensures higher-grade neural networks constantly update and improve, hence asserting their supremacy and usability in the ever-accelerating world of artificial intelligence (Gallego et al., 2018).

8.2. RECURRENT NEURAL NETWORKS (RNNS)

Within the context of complex neural network architectures, RNNs have proven to be a very powerful paradigm for dealing with sequences of data. Unlike conventional neural networks, RNNs are specifically constructed to identify patterns over time sequences in that they preserve some kind of memory by utilizing their hidden states. It enables them to process variable-length inputs, which is essential for functions such as time-series forecasting and natural language processing. RNN design inherently makes training the process challenging, especially when dealing with long sequences, due to things such as vanishing and exploding gradients. To deal with these constraints, a number of innovations like the Long Short-Term Memory (LSTM) networks have been suggested, allowing RNNs to effectively learn relationships over extended time horizons. Advances in RNN architectures in recent times have also expanded their modeling ability as well as efficiency. For instance, the creation of Recurrent Highway Networks (RHNs) extends the conventional LSTM framework by allowing greater depth for transition functions. This architectural innovation enables RHNs to utilize deeper layers for processing sequences, thus increasing their power of representation without any parameter increase. Consequently, when applied to tasks of language modeling, RHNs have achieved major improvements in terms of performance efficiency. For example, on the Penn Treebank data set, raising the depth of transitions significantly reduced word-level perplexity, showcasing the effectiveness of this new approach (Koutník et al., 2017). These developments are a significant step towards overcoming the inherent weaknesses of RNNs, particularly in their applications on multiple sequential processing tasks.

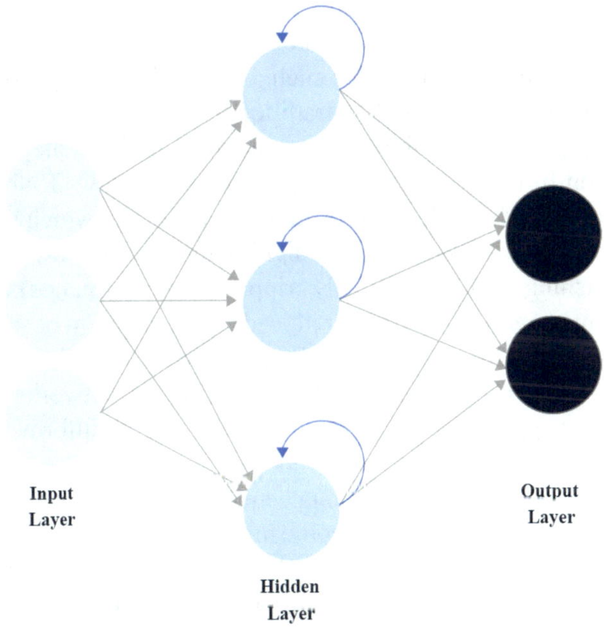

Figure 8.6. *Recurrent neural network (RNN).*

Source: https://d3lkc3n5th01x7.cloudfront.net/wp-content/uploads/2023/05/31063055/Recurrent-Neural-Networks-RNN.svg.

The integration of RNNs with other architectures also reflects a growing trend toward high performance across many various applications, particularly audio processing tasks. For instance, the integration of Convolutional Neural Networks (CNNs) and RNNs has led to a significant break-through in sound event detection. In this convolutional recurrent hybrid model, CNNs first learn local features in both frequency and time, whereas RNNs are able to retain the temporal context required to comprehend sound events over longer periods. This fusion of architectures, termed Convolutional Recurrent Neural Networks (CRNNs), has been found to outperform conventional classification algorithms on several datasets, providing very high performance gains in recognizing compound sound events (Heittola et al., 2017). These measures highlight the versatility of RNNs as they serve a crucial role in enhancing the accuracy and efficiency of neural network models as part of the broad artificial intelligence (Figure 8.6).

8.2.1. Mechanism of Recurrent Neural Networks (RNNs) and Sequence Processing

The RNN mechanism naturally tackles the issue of dealing with sequential data, which is critical in many applications such as natural language processing and time series prediction. Compared to traditional feedforward neural networks, RNNs naturally possess the ability to maintain a hidden state, and thus can keep information from previous time steps. This loop allows RNNs to process sequences of any length and learn time-step dependencies, which is particularly helpful for working with sequences of significant length. However, the usual problem of vanishing gradients typically cripples the performance of basic RNNs because gradients of earlier layers are reduced significantly in backpropagation, which makes it difficult to learn dependencies across long distances. As such, methods such as Long Short-Term Memory (LSTM) networks that include mechanisms to support better memory retention and information passing through long sequences have been proposed. Another enhancement of the capability of RNNs in dealing with long sequences is the concept of auxiliary mechanisms such as the SkipFlow in some modern architectures. This approach imitates interactions among snapshots of latent representations as the network operates across inputs, effectively bridging the gap left by the flaws of vanilla LSTM networks, particularly in processes operating on long text data. Through several snapshots, the SkipFlow mechanism facilitates an evasion of vanishing gradient issues, allowing the model to generate richer representational features across long sequences. In addition, these snapshots support the extraction of so-called neural coherence features that enhance the models ability to recognize and predict textual coherence effectively. This double benefit enhances the architectures performance, particularly for use in applications such as Automatic Text Scoring (ATS), where recognizing long-term dependencies and context relationships is of paramount importance (Hui et al., 2017). Outside of LSTM and its extensions, the general area of deep learning highlights RNNs as robust systems in a number of fields, though challenges continue. The use of RNN is not confined to text but also spreads across image processing and remote sensing, each having its own special ways of dealing with sequential data. Though there is an overwhelming power associated with them, there still exists a common argument that circulates in the scientific community over the black box nature of deep learning models. Critics suggest that the black-box nature of neural networks can conceal critical interpretability features required in strict scientific analysis (Fraundorfer et al., 2017). Therefore, in adopting deep learning techniques, it is vital that domain experts combine their professional expertise with these new technologies. Such collaboration can usher in revolutionary solutions to societal issues through the synergies between the profound capabilities of deep learning and the nuanced wisdom of seasoned experts across various fields.

8.2.2. Use Cases in Natural Language Processing (NLP)

NLP has evolved rapidly through the advent of new architectures for neural networks, giving us a variety of interesting applications that reflect the promise of the technology. One of the most prominent applications is sentiment analysis, where deep learning models scan text data to identify the emotional undercurrent of user-generated content. Such research is crucial for businesses that want to track customer happiness and create products around feedback. Businesses can survey big volumes of text-based data, draw conclusions, and make data-driven decisions with the assistance of recurrent neural networks and transformer models. As nuances of language constitute an obstacle, deep learnings capacity for understanding context and semantics allows corporations to forecast more accurately, thereby optimizing their action strategies in real time. Another essential application of NLP is machine translation, where new neural architectures, such as sequence-to-sequence models, have completely transformed the way differences between languages are overcome. The development of these models has progressed incredible translation of languages with high levels of accuracy. In contrast to classical statistical models, which sometimes used literal phrase translations, deep learning architectures facilitate the comprehension of whole sentences instead of individual words, with enhanced fluency and readability. Attention mechanisms are some of the techniques that increase translation quality by enabling the model to assign importance to different parts of the input sequence dynamically. This capability not only facilitates communication among speakers of different languages but has also opened up cross-cultural access to information, bringing huge strides towards global communication. Chatbots or conversational agents are another interesting use of NLP with the help of advanced neural network architectures. With architectures like generative adversarial networks and transformers, chatbots have developed leaps and bounds, providing users with coherent and contextually relevant conversations. These systems accept natural language as input and generate responses, simulate human conversation, and assist in a variety of applications, ranging from customer service to personal productivity tools. Furthermore, the integration of deep learning enables continuous learning and adaptation from interactions and hence enhances the accuracy and responsiveness of these AI assistants. When firms invest in such technologies, they introduce improved user experience and operational efficiency, the first-ever impact of deep neural networks on everyday interactions and decision-making processes.

8.2.3. Limitations and Challenges of Recurrent Neural Networks (RNNs)

RNNs, despite being powerful for sequence prediction tasks, suffer from humongous flaws that affect their performance and usability. Another crucial challenge is the vanishing gradient problem, whereby gradients of the loss function exponentially reduce in magnitude during backpropagation. It is this phenomenon that results in RNNs being unable to learn long-range dependencies effectively, rendering them powerless to extract essential contextual information in sequences. If the length of the input data is large, the models' performance decreases significantly, limiting the functionality of RNNs in tasks with long sequences, such as time-series prediction or language modeling. These problems necessitate the exploration of more advanced architectures that are able to overcome these issues, and this has led to the exploration of alternatives like Long Short-Term Memory (LSTM) networks and Gated Recurrent Units (GRUs), which provide mechanisms for carrying gradients over extremely long time frames, enhancing learning ability within sequential contexts. Another significant hindrance to the use of RNNs is its computational inefficiency, particularly within the context of large datasets or very long sequences. While RNNs are able to process sequential data sequentially, this is a time-consuming and computationally costly approach due to their recurrent nature. This therefore makes training time longer, consuming large amounts of time and computation resources that may not be financially viable for all applications. The inefficiency can be significantly exacerbated in real-time environments where predictability must occur in real time, such as online recommendation systems where immediacy is extremely important. With real-time demands for processing being on the rise in numerous applications, reliance on RNNs grows to become a concern, which inspires researchers to venture into other neural network structures that optimize performance and reduce resource utilization efficiency to be able to accelerate training and inference speed. Furthermore, RNNs have interpretability and hyperparameter optimization complexity problems. The typically opaque operations of deep learning models also make it difficult for researchers to know why a particular prediction is being made, generating roadblocks in those places where transparency is required, like healthcare or finance. Furthermore, tuning hyperparameters such as learning rates, layer sizes, and activation functions are required to maximize model performance, although RNNs can be particularly sensitive to these changes. For that reason, overfitting then becomes an increasingly likely threat as well, especially in small datasets. Removing these limitations is necessary to advance the development of RNNs and harness their advantages effectively. New methods bringing in explainable artificial intelligence (XAI) concepts and automated machine learning (AutoML) techniques are crucial in overcoming these limitations to enhance the real-world applications of RNNs and advance the development in the overall field of neural networks.

8.3. GENERATIVE ADVERSARIAL NETWORKS (GANS)

GANs are a revolutionary class of deep generative models that are primarily known for their ability to learn implicit complex and high-dimensional distributions. By employing a novel structure in the form of a generator and a discriminator, GANs are capable of producing high-quality data samples, including images and sound. This new architecture aids the learning process by placing the generator in competitive context with the discriminator, which tries to distinguish real data from generated data. While GANs have shown phenomenal results across various fields, they also undergo extreme challenges during training, including mode collapse, non-convergence, and instability. These issues commonly arise from a faulty design of the network structure, the choice of optimization algorithms or the objective function, and hence require careful study of their solution. In recent years, these limitations have been overcome through new methods with emphasis on evaluating the improvement in the design and optimization of GAN structures. Scientists have also been seeking ways to better design the network architecture, such as re-designing the discriminator and generator topology to yield enhanced performance. Novel objective functions have also been focal points of research, allowing for more effective learning processes that avoid limitations from standard GAN training. Optimization processes are also being transformed, with novel algorithms being suggested to reduce instability and provide convergence during training. The enhancement of these efforts has led to a systematic investigation of various proposed solutions, thereby forming a platform on which future progress can significantly enhance the performance of GANs. All of these enhancements together indicate the dynamism and evolving nature of GAN architectures within the overall neural network framework. Aside from the overall advancement in network structure, GANs are also advancing towards understanding complex data manifolds more dynamically. New methods facilitate a probe into the use of acquired distribution to specific target properties, for example, cluster shapes or style transitions, instead of the traditional holistic distribution imitation (Alvarez-Melis et al., 2019). The evolution of metrics such as the Gromov-Wasserstein distance makes this subtle strategy possible by considering distributions in relation, thus enhancing manifold and relational learning tasks. This adaptability not only extends the use of GANs to various domains but also enhances their application in cross-domain learning scenarios. By proving the diversity of GANs in handling multi-aspect tasks, continued research underscores the possibility of such advanced neural network architectures spearheading new paradigms and areas of application in generative modeling (Alvarez-Melis et al., 2019) (Figure 8.7).

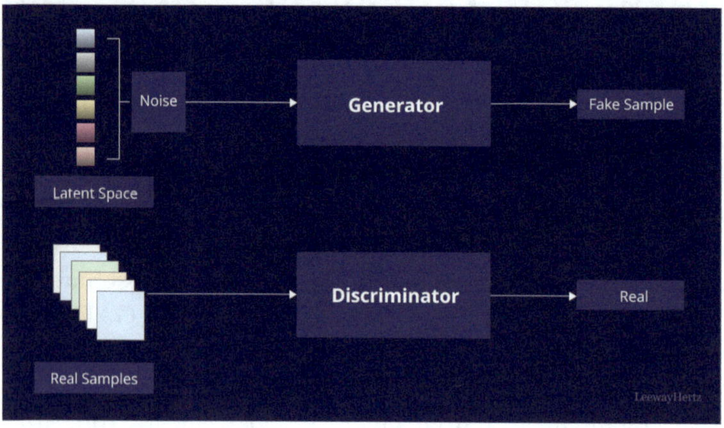

Figure 8.7. *Generative adversarial networks (GANs).*

Source: https://d3lkc3n5th01x7.cloudfront.net/wp-content/uploads/2023/03/28045210/Generative-Adversarial-Networks-5.png.

8.3.1. Architecture and Working Principle of Generative Adversarial Networks (GANs)

The GAN architecture is a great achievement of two neural networks: the discriminator and the generator. The generator tries to generate data that cannot be distinguished from real data, whereas the discriminator attempts to identify whether data generated by the generator is real. This competitive process fosters a competition environment where the generator constantly improves its capacity to produce realistic results as a function of the feedback it gets from the discriminator. Each architecture for the network is customizable to be employed within specific applications, and this flexibility makes it possible for GANs to find application in numerous sectors such as image generation, video generation, and even text generation. With researchers continuing to push the frontiers of neural network design, the foundation principles of GAN architecture remain at the forefront of research and development. The mechanism of GAN operation is indeed based in game theory, where the discriminator and the generator are in a position of a zero-sum game. As the generator is trying to produce quality outputs that can fool the discriminator, the discriminator is engaged in refining its ability to recognize real versus fake data.

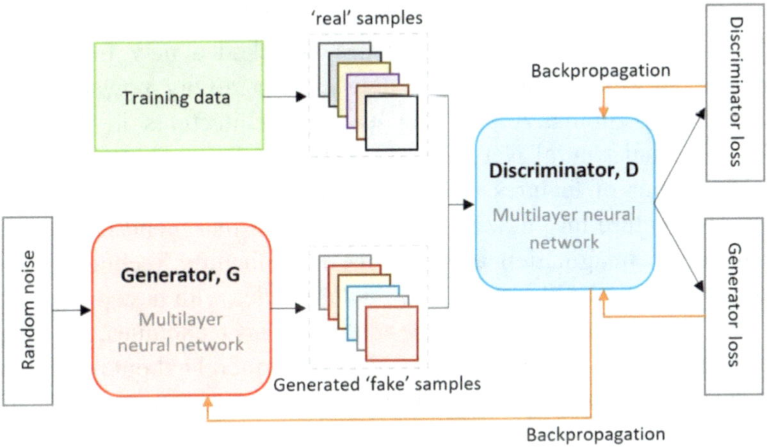

Figure 8.8. *Generative adversarial networks (GANs) architecture diagram.*

Source: https://www.presidio.com/wp-content/uploads/2024/05/1_gPaBNqy4YP-piQx_liRJ9Mw.webp.

This interaction creates a dynamic system as both networks improve continuously through a rigorous training process. Both networks' loss functions guide their learning trajectory, the generator attempting to reduce the likelihood that the discriminator successfully classifies false data and the discriminator trying to increase its classification accuracy. Such a configuration enables GANs to tap into massive volumes of training data to model intricate distributions successfully, thereby generating outputs increasingly similar to actual examples. The advancements made in GAN architecture recently have influenced the development of new models that help to enhance performance while minimizing mode collapse and issues of training instability. For instance, WGANs utilize the Wasserstein distance in order to measure the distance between the true and generated distributions, which leads to enhanced training convergence and stability. Conversely, models like Wasserstein Introspective Neural Networks (WINN) combine the generator and discriminator into a joint model and show the potential to significantly enhance generative modeling capability. These advancements reflect the versatility of GANs but also their ability to address multiple machine learning issues in a wide range of applications, from image generation to adversarial training methods for addressing model robustness enhancement, as discussed in recent studies (Brunton et al., 2020) and (Fan et al., 2018) (Figure 8.8).

8.3.2. Applications in Image Generation and Art

The development of neural networks has unlocked a new frontier for art and image generation, unleashing a deluge of creativity powered by high-performance algorithms. Among the leading architectures in this realm is the Convolutional Neural Networks (CNNs), which are famous for learning image hierarchies of features in space. This capacity has enabled artists and designers to venture into new forms of expression that blend the distinctions between human imagination and machine manufacture. Techniques such as style transfer allow for blending individual art styles with new pieces, making tools that enhance rather than replace traditional art techniques. As suggested by recent research, the application of CNNs is not merely about mimicking but also about generating fresh pieces from scratch that contain a combination of human imagination and the machine learning process. Real-world applications of neural networks in art create interesting debates on creativity and authorship in the age of technology. Painters making use of these technologies can create intricate designs, which would be challenging or impossible to manually create. Moreover, the computational expense of training these advanced architectures pushed the boundaries of hardware utilization. For instance, the application of parallel processing methods, such as CHAOS on Intel Xeon Phi coprocessors, significantly enhances CNN training efficiency with spectacular improvements in performance metrics over standard configurations. This not only accelerates the design phase so that rapid prototyping of creative ideas can be achieved but also facilitates access to sophisticated tools so that more people are able to contribute to art projects based on cutting-edge technology. With progressing machine learning algorithms, the significance for image generation in various industries, including remote sensing and environmental observation, becomes increasingly relevant. The fact that deep learning is now being applied across various other disciplines such as remote sensing is a testament to its applicability and potential for cross-disciplinary application. The challenge of handling monstrous amounts of data in real-time can be effectively overcome by advanced neural network designs, thereby making innovative solutions possible to terrifying global issues such as climate change and urbanization. By the facilitation of interdisciplinary collaboration between holders of expertise and machine learning experts, opportunities for powerful and creative use are endless. As the debate regarding the use of such technology grows, it is important to navigate the ethical dimensions and redefine creativity in the current rapidly evolving world of digital images and images creation (Fraundorfer et al., 2017; Pllana et al., 2015) (Figure 8.9).

Figure 8.9. *Generating modern art using generative adversarial network (GAN) on spell.*

Source: https://camo.githubusercontent.com/e7c1e212c22a582004858686ce778a437d08ad351952a2752913abde400f7785/68747470733a2f2f6d69726f2e6d656469756d2e636f6d2f6d61782f313136302f302a3170724f504d2d6b574f4a3274543231.

8.3.3. Ethical Considerations and Misuse of Generative Adversarial Networks (GANs)

The rapid advancement of GANs has brought about a new window of creative opportunities, but it has also given rise to significant ethical implications. GANs possess the capability to generate hyper-realistic images and deepfakes that can look very similar to real human beings, which gives rise to a wide range of ethical dilemmas. One of the most critical problems is misuse of these technologies for misleading purposes, such as creating counterfeit videos or altering photographs to create falsehoods. This manipulation provides fertile ground for disinformation, which poses serious threats to personal privacy as well as to civic trust. Moreover, the potential of GANs to produce realistic media poses legal systems to intellectual property and consent issues because the line between original and generated content is blurred, such that one wonders about ownership and accountability in the digital age. Moreover, the impact of GAN use extends beyond individual privacy issues to society. As increasingly large numbers of people gain access to GANs, malicious use is on the rise, resulting in vast risk across a wide variety of domains, from politics to individual safety. For instance, generating deepfakes for political ends or social manipulation can destabilize democratic institutions and result in public distrust of institutions. Besides, the use of content generated by GANs in identity theft strategies poses severe implications for human beings since they can have their likeliness boundaries manipulated against them without their will. Such a moral environment demands some overarching framework to regulate the development and deployment of GAN technologies, which should emphasize responsibility and accountability from developers and users alike. To fight these ethical challenges, policymakers and researchers must come together and formulate effective guidelines encompassing the design, deployment, and use of GANs.

Figure 8.10. *Ethical considerations of generative adversarial networks (GANs).*

Source: https://so-development.org/wp-content/uploads/2023/10/Ethical_Considerations-1024x576-1.jpg.

This includes formulating standards to ensure transparency while producing doctored content, thereby enabling viewers to understand what is real and what is manipulated. Educational campaigns also become important to make individuals aware of the potential risks of doctored GANs and the necessity of critical media literacy. As noted in the research on AI-driven solutions that aim towards fairness and reducing bias in recruitment, similar methods can be applied to the field of GANs for increasing ethical aspects in AI development (Shah et al., 2025). Through the establishment of an ethical awareness culture and proactivity, society can reap the potential of the change-making capability of GANs but also preclude the danger from their misuse (Pal et al., 2023) (Figure 8.10).

8.4. TRANSFORMER MODELS

The transformer models have been a milestone in the evolution of neural network architecture, particularly in the field of natural language processing (NLP). Originally brought forth in the revolutionary paper Attention is All You Need, the models utilize a method known as self-attention to assign weights to the contribution of individual words in a sentence irrespective of their locations. This capacity has placed transformers more capable of capturing long-distance dependencies in text compared to previous architectures like recurrent neural networks (RNNs) and convolutional neural networks (CNNs). Due to this, transformer models have set new state-of-the-art benchmarks across various NLP tasks, indicating their versatility and potency in human language processing and generation. Particularly, their ability to handle variable-length input sequences has made them incredibly versatile, leading to their ubiquitous deployment across numerous applications, from text summarization to machine translation. Adding yet another feather to transformer models' cap, recent work has shown their ability in expert tasks like entity matching (EM), a key aspect of data integration operations. Experiments reveal that transformer-based models, i.e., BERT, XLNet, RoBERTa, and DistilBERT, perform better than traditional deep learning methods in EM with an astounding 27.5% rate even in challenging datasets. The attention mechanism of the architecture enables such models to capture contextual similarities even in extremely long or dirty data samples, thus making entity matching very cost-effective. Such historical performance highlights not only the versatility of transformers but also their capacity to enhance precision and effectiveness in data-related operations within complex linguistic contexts. Through the evolution of time, employing transformers for specific applications could lead to new ways of managing and interpreting huge datasets. Although they have great advantages, the computational costs of transformer models pose heavy challenges, particularly in real-world applications where latency and resource requirements dominate. For instance, although deep pretrained transformer networks can excel in some applications, such as question answering and document ranking, their high computation expenses may render them impossible. To address this issue, techniques such as PreTTR (Precomputing Transformer Term Representations) were created, offering a speedup of up to 42x compared to query-time procedures. The method precomputes certain document term representations in advance during the indexing process, actually reducing real-time computing load. Additionally, compression techniques designed for the models can lessen storage requirements by up to 95% and enable one to use them practically with minimal loss of performance. Thus, as transformer models continue to progress, it will remain a continuously critical focus for practitioners and researchers to balance complexity and efficiency (Figure 8.11).

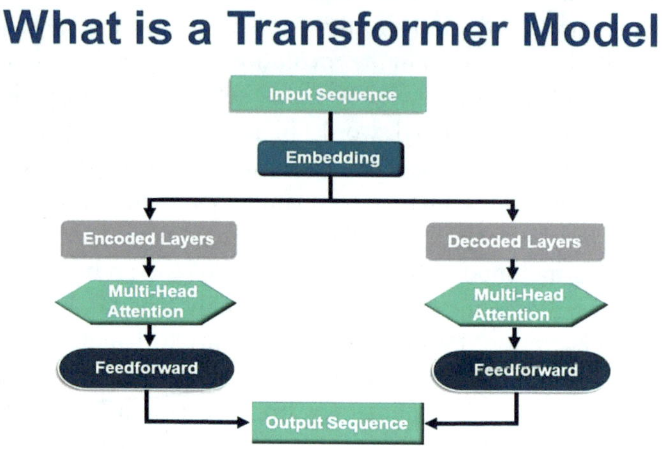

Figure 8.11. *Transformer models.*

Source: https://cdn.educba.com/academy/wp-content/uploads/2023/11/Transformer-Model.jpg.

8.4.1. Introduction to Transformer Architecture

The Transformer architecture is a milestone in the history of natural language processing (NLP) and neural network design. The model was introduced by Vaswani et al. in 2017, taking a departure from paradigms of recurrent and convolutional and utilizing the ability of self-attention mechanisms to process input sequences efficiently. Self-attention allows the model to weigh different words differently according to the relative importance of each word in a sentence regardless of their position, hence being able to learn long-range dependencies essential in linguistic settings. This new approach not only improved performance on numerous benchmarking tasks but also reduced training times by a great deal, clearing the path for subsequent breakthroughs in deep learning uses. The efficiency and efficacy of Transformers have motivated researchers to explore their application beyond standard NLP contexts, holding out for a broader potential for enhancing artificial intelligence systems. In the wake of the success of the first Transformer architecture, researchers have looked to further optimize its functionality, with several follow-ups and variations. One advancement that stands out is the use of pre-trained models, like BERT and GPT, which utilize the base architecture of Transformers for a particular application. Such models are pre-trained on huge datasets to understand context and language nuances and subsequently fine-tuned for purposes like question answering and sentiment analysis.

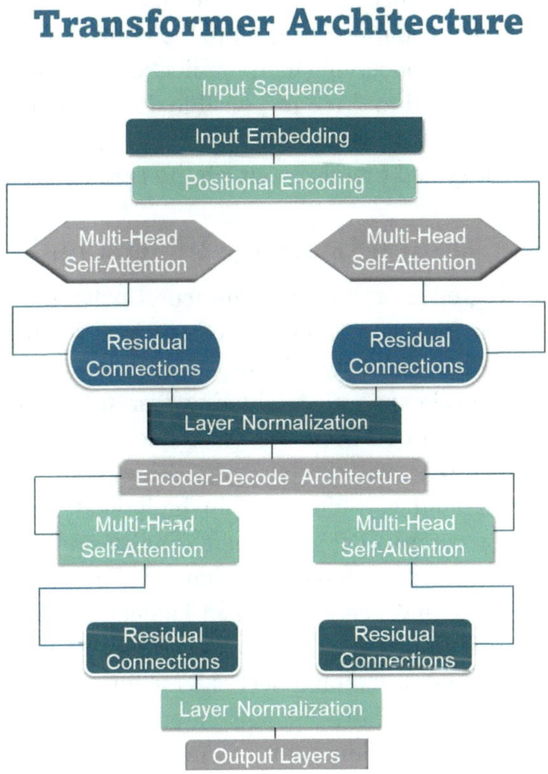

Figure 8.12. *Transformer architecture.*

Source: https://cdn.educba.com/academy/wp-content/uploads/2023/11/Transformer-Architecture.jpg.

The universal usage of pre-trained Transformer networks has not only proven their versatility but also exposed computational challenges, primarily in terms of query-time efficiency in actual deployment. As highlighted in recent studies, Optimizing the Transformer framework is crucial to avoiding bottlenecks in performance without compromising on accuracy, ushering in possibilities of practical real-world applications in industrially reliant real-time data processing (Frieder et al., 2020). Furthermore, as studies on Transformers continue, its security implications and ethical considerations have garnered quite a lot of attention. For instance, the ability of Transformer-based models to consume vast amounts of data rapidly creates new applications as well as potential threats, particularly in areas like surveillance and data privacy. The DeepKey project illustrates how novel neural architecture could potentially enable features such as image-based automatic key modeling and create ethical questions regarding the impact on society of this technology (Krizhevsky et al., 2018). As researchers continue to explore the multi-dimensional aspects of Transformers, arguments concerning their implications become more important. The ethical guidelines need to drive responsible development and deployment of these architectures so that innovations flow into society's good, balancing innovation with security and moral accountability (Figure 8.12).

8.4.2. Impact on Natural Language Understanding (NLU)

The advent of cutting-edge architectures in neural networks has significantly transformed NLU, an integral component of artificial intelligence. One such advancement is the development of high-end models that take advantage of complexity-based morphospaces, facilitating careful examination of the nature of intelligent systems. Theoretical modeling categorizes systems based on autonomous, cognitive, and social complexities, which gives insightful information to understand consciousness in biological as well as synthetic systems. Thus, such understanding is increasingly extrapolated directly to NLU by facilitating a better comprehension of the mechanism by which machines read, process, and generate human language, eventually translating into innovation that optimizes their responsiveness and situational awareness. This type of consciousness mapping serves as a foundation for constructing language models mirroring how humans interact, hence developing more interactive and intelligent machine-to-user interfaces (Arsiwalla et al., 2017). Further, research on Evolved Plastic Artificial Neural Networks (EPANNs) has heightened the contribution that neural architectures have to offer to NLU. EPANNs are very adaptive and evolve based on their surroundings, learning from experience, much like a human being. With such adaptive functionality, scientists can create models that not only understand language but also change their linguistic capacity based on context and user interaction. This plasticity enables machines to generate more complex and contextually appropriate responses, thereby increasing user satisfaction and comprehension. The scope of EPANNs is in advancing language translation, sentiment analysis, and conversational agents, essentially reshaping the usage of computers in everyday linguistic communication and thereby broadening machine-learning horizons in NLU (Abbott et al., 2018). With advancements in technology, the effects of such inventions in neural network architectures go deeper in natural language processing. With more computational power and emergent properties of intelligent systems, researchers will increasingly develop more intuitive and realistic systems for processing language. The systems not only form the cornerstone of better human-machine communication but also to address problems of linguistic diversity and nuances of communication. The ongoing research into complexity-driven systems and sophisticated neural models will most definitely be instrumental in further advancing algorithms that propel existing NLU systems towards more sophisticated artificial intelligence versions that engage human language meaningfully. The development will be capable of reshaping the way communication and interaction are understood and bring about a paradigm shift in computational linguistics (Abbott et al., 2018; Arsiwalla et al., 2017).

8.4.3. Comparison with Recurrent Neural Networks (RNNs) and Convolutional Neural Networks (CNNs)

The contrast between RNNs and CNNs indicates evident architectural merits tailored for other types of data and tasks. CNNs are particularly suited to handle spatial hierarchies in image data by leveraging local spatial relationships and weight sharing. This aspect enables CNNs to learn sophisticated features through multiple convolutional layers, making them very suitable for image classification and object detection. Models such as AlexNet and GoogLeNet achieved better performance on standard tests such as ImageNet by incorporating additional connections and loss layers that leverage the high-level features without sacrificing efficiency in computation. This illustrates the capacity of CNNs to merge low- and high-level contextual data, which is vital in improving classification precision (Afzal et al., 2017). Unlike the design of RNNs, which allows them to handle sequential input data, they thus remain the best bet for cases involving time series analysis or natural language processing. RNNs are unique as they can retain contextual information between various time steps and therefore are capable of modeling dependencies within sequences. This feature is particularly useful in speech recognition, say, where understanding the temporal dynamics of acoustic signals is essential. The delta network topology proposed here enhances standard RNNs by having neurons pass along their state only when there is a significant change and thereby minimizing redundant computation. This results in a dramatic reduction in memory access and computational cost, allowing more efficient models at the expense of accuracy

(Delbruck et al., 2016). On the TIDIGITS speech digit recognition benchmark, for example, the delta network demonstrates a stunning 9X reduction in operating costs with little loss of performance. These adjustments prove the versatility of RNNs, especially in systems with unstructured data inputs that vary over time. Further, the integration of RNN and CNN architectures is a recent development that tries to leverage the strengths of both models to tackle complex tasks. By combining the spatial feature extraction power of CNNs with the temporal feature extraction capabilities of RNNs, researchers hope to create hybrid models that are better in multi-modal tasks such as video analysis or sequential image synthesis. These designs leverage CNNs' hierarchical pattern recognition and apply RNNs' sequential memory capabilities, offering a profound improvement in accuracy and performance across a broad variety of applications. With improving machine learning platforms and further development, this conjunction of CNNs and RNNs is a fertile ground for investigation, breaching the boundaries of neural network performance and application. This convergence is also an indication of the continuing evolution of advanced neural architectures that support increasingly demanding datasets and task requirements.

8.5.HYBRIDNEURALNETWORKARCHITECTURES

Hybrid neural network architectures are a fundamental innovation in artificial intelligence system design and deployment. Hybrid architectures combine the benefits of multiple modeling paradigms, integrating physics-informed layers with traditional data-driven methods. This approach facilitates enhanced performance in complex tasks, where empirical data may be scant or untrustworthy. In predictive maintenance, for example, hybrid models can have the ability to leverage known physical principles and extrapolate data-based insights, thus providing better predictions of asset lifespan and performance. Through the convergence of multiple approaches, hybrid architectures provide greater flexibility and robustness, leading to successful applications across various sectors, including industrial maintenance and medical diagnosis. One of the applicable applications of hybrid neural networks is in the field of engineering asset prognosis. Bringing together recurrent neural network cells and physics-informed ones allows the simulation of processes such as cumulative damage accumulation in mechanical systems. This method, according to scientists, allows them to predict fatigue crack growth when normal data may be limited, such as in aerospace engineering applications. This capacity to leverage theoretical knowledge and empirical data proves the flexibility of hybrid architectures since they accommodate both well-defined and ill-defined system behaviors, increasing the predictability of outcomes with uncertain inputs (Nascimento et al., 2019). For medical imaging applications, hybrid neural networks similarly prove their usefulness by improving segmentation performance in radiographic images. These have highlighted the strengths of advanced U-Net architectures, which utilize pre-trained encoder weights to enhance segmentation accuracy in key anatomical structures. By using hybrid models that integrate fully convolutional networks with established loss functions, researchers have achieved impressive performance metrics, such as high values of Jaccard overlap in lung and cardiac segmentation on test sets. Such achievements underscore the importance of hybrid models in overcoming challenges in segmentation tasking, required for accurate computer-aided diagnostics (Novikov et al., 2018). As more research is conducted on hybrid models, implications on efficiency and accuracy in other fields of artificial intelligence also promise well.

8.5.1. Combining Different Neural Network Types

The blending of different kinds of neural networks has been the key strategy in seeking enhanced model performance and flexibility. Through mixing heterogeneous models, researchers have found that each kind of network can benefit from the strengths of other kinds, thereby offsetting respective limitations. For instance, convolutional neural networks (CNNs), which are commonly recognized for their spatial representation of data, can be directly paired with recurrent neural networks (RNNs), which are known to excel in sequential data processing. With this integration, intricate tasks such as video analysis, which requires both spatial and temporal features, are processed efficiently. One of the most significant advances in this area is introducing architectures that combine multiple methods while maintaining the same number of parameters and training effectiveness. As suggested in recent research, such models have demonstrated significant improvement across a number of benchmarks, indicating the success of this consolidated approach (Klakow et al., 2017). In considering the potential of hybridizing neural network forms, one new framework involves a double-layer design composed of a mixture layer and a feature layer. The feature layer derives unique features of different neural models, each designed to optimize specific attributes of the dataset. The mixture layer subsequently mixes the outputs, effectively integrating the features into a singular predictive framework. This new architecture not only enhances the overall capacity for learning by reducing the ambivalence pertaining to data processing but does so without imposing significantly enhanced computation load. This design can thereby prove particularly valuable in applications like natural language processing, where subtlety of comprehension is essential. Such advancements show how hybrids of different types of neural networks can yield paradigm-shifting optimization of complicated task processing (Klakow et al., 2017). Besides, the union of neuromorphic computing and hybrid neural network models points toward a paradigm revolution in processing. Neuromorphic processors, replicating the brain's functional and structural characteristics, represent an intriguing factor in supporting various neural configurations. Their ability to undertake massive parallel processing suits the demand of multiple neural models and better computational efficiency most aptly. With increasing sophistication in these brain-inspired architectures, new possibilities in bringing together dissimilar types of networks are possible, such as integrating deep neural networks with neurobiologically inspired models. The challenge in constructing such systems is substantial but is countered by strong methods that attempt to simulate the dynamic plasticity of biologic networks. Emphasizing these advancements is a critical step towards the actualization of neural architectures that extract the richness and diversity of human intelligence.

8.5.2. Benefits of Hybrid Approaches

The convergence of hybrid approaches in neural network architectures has led to unprecedented advancements in various fields, including medical imaging and wireless communication. By integrating methods from more than one paradigm, these approaches enhance model accuracy and performance, and they are particularly suited for difficult tasks. For instance, in the field of medical imaging, utilization of the altered designs like U-Net has proved to be exceptional in anatomical structures segmentation from chest radiographs. Most notably, one such model exploited pre-trained encoder weights and outperformed state-of-the-art methods by achieving Jaccard overlap rates of 96.1% for lung fields, illustrating the potential of hybrid architectures in taking the best aspects of various algorithms and removing their corresponding frailties (Novikov et al., 2018). Thus, hybrid approaches not only increase the technical success of neural networks but also add more flexibility to their use across a broad array of problems. In addition, hybrid approaches have applications beyond medical imaging to wireless communications, where machine learning (ML) techniques play a central role in developing efficient and resilient systems. The combining of innovative ML techniques with traditional network architecture has the ability to redefine the 6G wireless network infrastructure. By employing big data and massive computational power, hybrid models have the ability to solve significant challenges such as network optimization, resource allocation, and quality of service. For instance, ML-enabled zero-touch network optimization is a paradigm shift that offers automated and intelligent adjustments that respond to real-time data needs (Abbas et al., 2020). This adaptive learnability not only enhances network performance but also to the overall robustness of communication systems, highlighting the revolutionary impact of hybrid approaches. In addition to their functional enhancements, hybrid approaches provide a paradigm for interdisciplinarity, marrying insights from such disciplines as computer science, engineering, and application-specific knowledge. This blending of ideas forges innovation, which leads to more sophisticated architectures that can solve demanding and evolving problems. These partnerships are put into play for the construction of new models as well as improvements to existing ones. By combining conclusions from various disciplines, scientists can design neural network architectures that not only can perform well but also generalize sufficiently enough to be useful across various domains and types of data. The various benefits of hybrid approaches position them as a cornerstone in the evolution of the next generation of neural network architectures, driving theoretical advances and practical applications across numerous fields.

8.5.3. Case Studies of Successful Hybrid Models

Examples of successful hybrid approaches illustrate the performance benefits of combining various neural network architectures to enhance performance in numerous applications. Hybrid approaches are often able to leverage the strengths of convolutional neural networks (CNNs) and recurrent neural networks (RNNs) to extract better features and model sequences. For instance, in medical imaging, an architecture variation of the U-Net has significantly improved segmentation of anatomical structures in chest radiographs. This model employed pre-trained weights for the encoder and achieved tremendous Jaccard overlap scores on lung fields, heart, and clavicles, thus demonstrating the tremendous synergy between architectural modifications and transfer learning in enhancing diagnostic accuracy and efficiency (Novikov et al., 2018). These advancements are aimed at ensuring the ability of hybrid networks to not only enhance performance rates but also ease computational processes in the medical sector. The integration of new memory technologies into hybrid neural network models continues to bridge important gaps of traditional frameworks. Hybrid models will enhance computational effectiveness at the cost of reduced integration density as nanoscale non-volatile memory is becoming a reality. The unique characteristics of such memory technologies present solutions to the scalability issues typically found in CMOS-based architectures. In an in-depth examination of the communication requirements of large-scale neuromorphic architectures, it is apparent that hybrid models benefit from improved on-chip communication networks. These networks allow for large-fanout connectivity necessary for next-generation neuromorphic applications, thereby illustrating how hybrid architecture can grow and persist within the landscape of modern computational demands (Manohar et al., 2018). This correlation not only favors accelerated rates of processing but also emphasizes breaking communication barriers in the development of neural networks. In addition, effective utilization of hybrid models largely depends on competent pairings of reinforcement learning algorithms with conventional neural networks. This has been of great help in achieving great strides in complicated decision-making processes, such as robotics and real-time data processing. By leveraging the capability of reinforcement learning to learn optimal actions from feedback, and merging it with the visual recognition ability of CNNs, hybrid systems have demonstrated exemplary performance gains in measures and learning flexibility. For example, in autonomous driving systems, hybrid models can analyze visual inputs and change driving strategies in real time. This dynamic interaction between perception and decision-making processes highlights the richness and potential of hybrid structures in addressing multifaceted problems in the majority of fields, solidifying their place in the creation of advanced neural network models even more.

SUMMARY

In general, the development of neural network architecture has significantly transformed the art of artificial intelligence and machine learning. Deep learning architectures have always worked better in challenging tasks such as natural language processing and computer vision. While algorithms developed using conventional approaches such as Random Forests have been found to be reliable, particularly in virus classification, empirical data indicates that with the progress in computational power, the benefit of deep learning systems may increasingly dominate. This progress is accompanied by an ongoing evaluation of the trade-off between performance and computational cost, with a harmonious choice of models in practical applications (Rathore et al., 2018).

Studies of intricate architectures also provide the potential for an in-depth understanding of adaptive systems. Inspired by neural networks in biology, innovative architectures like Evolved Plastic Artificial Neural Networks (EPANNs) exhibit the potential of dynamically evolving models to model biological learning processes. These frameworks not only enhance computational power but also provide the potential for discovering new algorithms that can modify themselves based on varying environments. As the relationship between evolutionary processes and artificial intelligence becomes more robust, the boundaries of what is possible for neural networks become expansive, yielding new insights into technology as well as the nature of intelligence (Abbott et al., 2018). Finally, the future of neural networks lies in the union of artificial intelligence and biological insight. By integrating knowledge from evolutionary events, researchers can design increasingly sophisticated and adaptive neural network architectures that transcend traditional models. This technological potential is amplified by the possibility of systems that learn and adapt during operation, and thus are capable of handling unforeseen problems. As advances continue, the field stands at the threshold of revolutionary understanding, with implications that may redefine not only technological landscapes but also fundamental notions of learning and intelligence in artificial and natural systems equally. Continued research and development of these architectures are necessary to inform the creation of the next generation of intelligent systems (Abbott et al., 2018).

In the research into top-level architectures for neural networks, one of the most important achievements has been the integration of consistent frameworks that optimize working efficiency and interoperability. The frameworks are designed to coordinate procedures from data acquisition at the front-end to delivering conclusions at the user interface, paralleling the architectural vision given for the Deep Space Network (DSN) information system. This vision emphasizes open-systems standards enabling seamless communication between disparate components and calling attention to matters that are pivotal, such as data security and automated monitoring. As seen in the DSN architectural implementation, these technological advancements enable radical increases in processing speeds and error control that are vital in high-risk applications where real-time processing and precision are fundamental (Atkinson et al., 1992). The second critical domain in the progression of neural networks is predictive maintenance, particularly its use in engineering assets and fleet management. Companies increasingly utilize higher-level analytics and predictive modeling techniques to ensure efficient utilization of large fleets. The challenge lies in the precise capture of component lifespan complexity that is open to a spectrum of internal and external factors such as environmental conditions and usage demands.

The physics-informed neural network approach allows for the integration of data-driven insight into traditional physical models in order to tackle discrepancies between forecasted and actual performance previously unimaginable. Such confluence of methodologies not only enhances forecasting accuracy but also brings in valuable domain knowledge into machine learning procedures, thereby making them more potent (Nascimento et al., 2019). Also, the application of recurrent neural networks (RNNs) in this context shows how versatile neural architectures are in addressing practical problems. Using traditional RNNs and subsequently introducing aspects of cumulative damage modeling, researchers have proposed methods of predicting component failure, such as fatigue crack propagation in fleets of airplanes. This physics-informed and data-driven hybrid methodology allows engineers to leverage previous knowledge of material response while also adapting accordingly to cases not well studied for specific operational conditions. Their achievement in application with sparser observational data illustrates the potential of high-fidelity architectures to offer actionable insight, which drives innovation in various sectors based on complicated systems and predictive maintenance practices (Nascimento et al., 2019).

REFERENCES

1. Abbas, A., Andreopoulos, Y., Chadha, A., Jubran, B., et al. (2018). Rate-accuracy trade-off in video classification with deep convolutional neural networks. https://core.ac.uk/download/195315109.pdf (accessed on 25th September 2025).
2. Abbas, R., Ahmad, I., Ali, S., Amuru, S., et al. (2020). 6G white paper on machine learning in wireless communication networks. http://arxiv.org/abs/2004.13875 (accessed on 25th September 2025).
3. Abbott, A., Abraham, A., Allis, L., Alpaydin, E., Anderson, J., et al. (2018). Born to learn: The inspiration, progress, and future of evolved plastic artificial neural networks. https://core.ac.uk/download/162581731.pdf (accessed on 25th September 2025).
4. Afzal, M. Z., Kölsch, A., & Liwicki, M. (2017). Multilevel context representation for improving object recognition. http://arxiv.org/abs/1703.06408 (accessed on 25th September 2025).
5. Alienin, O., Gordienko, N., Gordienko, Y., Kochura, Y., et al. (2018). Batch size influence on performance of graphic and tensor processing units during training and inference phases. http://arxiv.org/abs/1812.11731 (accessed on 25th September 2025).
6. Alvarez-Melis, D., Bunne, C., Jegelka, S., Krause, A., et al. (2019). Learning generative models across incomparable spaces. http://arxiv.org/abs/1905.05461 (accessed on 25th September 2025).
7. Arsiwalla, X. D., Herreros, I., Moulin-Frier, C., Sanchez-Fibla, M., et al. (2017). The morphospace of consciousness. http://arxiv.org/abs/1705.11190 (accessed on 25th September 2025).
8. Ashcraft, N., Cook, M., Djerekarov, E., Luckow, A., et al. (2017). Deep learning in the automotive industry: Applications and tools. http://arxiv.org/abs/1705.00346 (accessed on 25th September 2025).
9. Atkinson, D. J., Beswick, C. A., Cooper, L. P., Crowe, T., et al. (1992). Deep space network information system architecture study. https://core.ac.uk/download/pdf/10438278.pdf (accessed on 25th September 2025).
10. Bagci, U., Han, W. W., Lee, J. S., Liberton, D., et al. (2019). Relational reasoning network (RRN) for anatomical landmarking. http://arxiv.org/abs/1904.04354 (accessed on 25th September 2025).
11. Banerjee, D. S., Barnett, M., Chu, C. H., Hoefler, T., Jia, Y., Liu, J., Mamidala, A. R., et al. (2017). Optimized broadcast for deep learning workloads on dense-GPU InfiniBand clusters: MPI or NCCL? http://arxiv.org/abs/1707.09414 (accessed on 25th September 2025).

12. Beck, A., He, K., Parikh, N., & Russakovsky, O. (2018). Data-driven sparse structure selection for deep neural networks. http://arxiv.org/abs/1707.01213 (accessed on 25th September 2025).
13. Bengs, M., Drömann, D., Ellebrecht, D. B., Gessert, N., et al. (2019). Deep transfer learning methods for colon cancer classification in confocal laser microscopy images. http://arxiv.org/abs/1905.07991 (accessed on 25th September 2025).
14. Brunner, U., & Stockinger, K. (2020). Entity matching with transformer architectures – A step forward in data integration. https://core.ac.uk/download/289121527.pdf (accessed on 25th September 2025).
15. Brunton, S., Koumoutsakos, P., & Noack, B. (2020). Machine learning for fluid mechanics. http://arxiv.org/abs/1905.11075 (accessed on 25th September 2025).
16. Cao, J., & Saxena, D. (2020). Generative adversarial networks (GANs): Challenges, solutions, and future directions. http://arxiv.org/abs/2005.00065 (accessed on 25th September 2025).
17. De Filippo De Grazia, M., Testolin, A., Zanella, A., Zorzi, M., et al. (2015). Cognition-based networks: A new perspective on network optimization using learning and distributed intelligence. https://core.ac.uk/download/53523614.pdf (accessed on 25th September 2025).
18. Delbruck, T., Lee, J. H., Liu, S. C., Neil, D., et al. (2016). Delta networks for optimized recurrent network computation. http://arxiv.org/abs/1612.05571 (accessed on 25th September 2025).
19. Fan, F., Lee, K., Tu, Z., Xu, C., et al. (2018). Wasserstein introspective neural networks. http://arxiv.org/abs/1711.08875 (accessed on 25th September 2025).
20. Fraundorfer, F., Mou, L., Tuia, D., Xia, G., et al. (2017). Deep learning in remote sensing: A review. https://core.ac.uk/download/147324205.pdf (accessed on 25th September 2025).
21. Frieder, O., Goharian, N., MacAvaney, S., Nardini, F. M., et al. (2020). Efficient document re-ranking for transformers by precomputing term representations. http://arxiv.org/abs/2004.14255 (accessed on 25th September 2025).
22. Gallego, G., Garcia, N., Loquercio, A., Maqueda, A. I., et al. (2018). Event-based vision meets deep learning on steering prediction for self-driving cars. http://arxiv.org/abs/1804.01310 (accessed on 25th September 2025).
23. Heittola, T., Huttunen, H., Parascandolo, G., Virtanen, T., et al. (2017). Convolutional recurrent neural networks for polyphonic sound event

detection. https://core.ac.uk/download/417848943.pdf (accessed on 25th September 2025).

24. Hui, S. C., Phan, M. C., Tay, Y., Tuan, L. A., et al. (2017). SkipFlow: Incorporating neural coherence features for end-to-end automatic text scoring. http://arxiv.org/abs/1711.04981 (accessed on 25th September 2025).
25. Indiveri, G., & Liu, S. C. (2015). Memory and information processing in neuromorphic systems. http://arxiv.org/abs/1506.03264 (accessed on 25th September 2025).
26. Jin, Z., Li, G., Liu, Y., Mou, L., et al. (2014). Building program vector representations for deep learning. http://arxiv.org/abs/1409.3358 (accessed on 25th September 2025).
27. Klakow, D., & Oualil, Y. (2017). A neural network approach for mixing language models. http://arxiv.org/abs/1708.06989 (accessed on 25th September 2025).
28. Koutník, J., Schmidhuber, J., Srivastava, R. K., Zilly, J. G., et al. (2017). Recurrent highway networks. http://arxiv.org/abs/1607.03474 (accessed on 25th September 2025).
29. Krizhevsky, A., & Krizhevsky, A. (2017). Large scale evolution of convolutional neural networks using volunteer computing. http://arxiv.org/abs/1703.05422 (accessed on 25th September 2025).
30. Krizhevsky, A., Adelson, E. H., Schmidhuber, J., He, K., & Ren, S. (2018). DeepKey: Towards end-to-end physical key replication from a single photograph. https://core.ac.uk/download/195283609.pdf (accessed on 25th September 2025).
31. Manohar, R., & Moradi, S. (2018). The impact of on-chip communication on memory technologies for neuromorphic systems. http://arxiv.org/abs/1809.06016 (accessed on 25th September 2025).
32. Nascimento, R. G., & Viana, F. A. C. (2019). Fleet prognosis with physics-informed recurrent neural networks. http://arxiv.org/abs/1901.05512 (accessed on 25th September 2025).
33. Novikov, A. A., Van Ginneken, B., Greenspan, H., Shiraishi, J., Chen, L. C., Ronneberger, O., Hwang, S., et al. (2018). Improving the segmentation of anatomical structures in chest radiographs using U-Net with an ImageNet pre-trained encoder. http://arxiv.org/abs/1810.02113 (accessed on 25th September 2025).
34. Pal, S. (2023). Deep Learning Architectures and Their Pivotal Role in Big Data Processing. https://core.ac.uk/download/618327730.pdf (accessed on 25th September 2025).

35. Pllana, S., & Viebke, A. (2015). The potential of the Intel Xeon Phi for supervised deep learning. http://arxiv.org/abs/1506.09067 (accessed on 25th September 2025).
36. Rathore, H., Sahay, S. K., & Sewak, M. (2018). Comparison of deep learning and the classical machine learning algorithm for the malware detection. http://arxiv.org/abs/1809.05889 (accessed on 25th September 2025).
37. Roig Marí, C. (2016). Deep learning architectures for computer vision. https://core.ac.uk/download/81572231.pdf (accessed on 25th September 2025).
38. Shah, K., Rana, M., & Pimple, T. (2025). Fair and transparent AI-driven resume screening: Enhancing recruitment with bias-aware machine learning. https://core.ac.uk/download/647975611.pdf (accessed on 25th September 2025).
39. Sun, A., Tay, Y., Yao, L., Zhang, L., et al. (2019). Deep learning-based recommender system: A survey and new perspectives. http://arxiv.org/abs/1707.07435 (accessed on 25th September 2025).

CHAPTER 9

NEURAL NETWORK FRAMEWORKS

Contents

INTRODUCTION

The artificial intelligence and machine learning environment has been revolutionized with the advent of the architectures of neural networks, which provide robust platforms for the analysis of complex data sets. Neural networks, inspired by the architecture of the brain, facilitate the processing of massive amounts of data using nodes that are networked to each other in order to identify patterns effectively. With the increasing demand for automation across different fields, from healthcare to smart technologies, there has been increased research and development of advanced neural networks. These models empower a range of applications, such as speech recognition, image processing, and predictive modeling, thus demonstrating the range and unmatched capability that they have in fueling innovation. As industries battle for more insightful solutions, understanding and use of such neural network architectures grow in significance to researchers and practitioners alike. Perhaps the most promising progeny of neural network architectures is the development of graph neural networks (GNNs), particularly in graph-structured data modeling of intricate relationships. GNNs have drawn considerable interest in medicine due to their ability to encode entity dependencies, making them suitable for applications like disease prediction and drug discovery. Nevertheless, despite the promise they offer, the literature evidences a lack of comprehensive reviews taking into account systematically GNN uses in medicine.

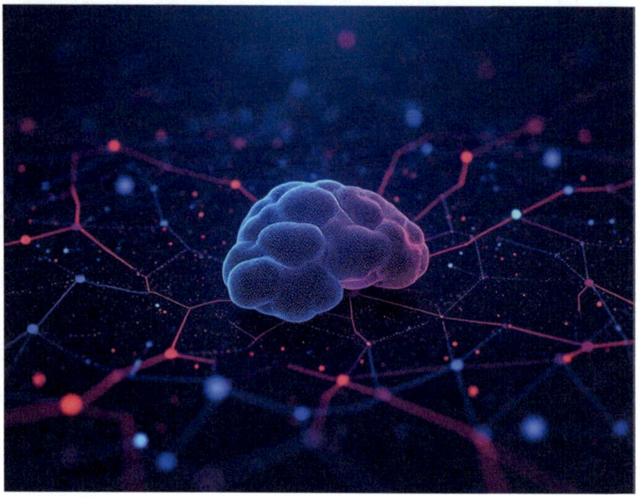

Figure 9.1. *Neural network frameworks.*

Source: https://quantumzeitgeist.com/wp-content/uploads/ANN.jpeg.

This audit places emphasis on the importance of conducting a robust investigation and review of prevailing research trends and limitations faced in the implementation of GNNs with a perspective to generating vital findings and strategic recommendations that will inform future research. Closing this gap can eventually aid in enhancing healthcare systems through the delivery of improved and efficient methodologies that leverage the promise of GNNs (Paul et al., 2024). In contrast to advancements in GNNs, architectures supporting edge computing-based applications, i.e., keyword spotting with a Small

Footprint (SF-KWS), are also major contributors to today's advancement in neural networks. Such architectures are particularly pertinent in an era where intelligent devices and the Internet of Things (IoT) dominate everything, and the demand for efficient and secure voice-controlled systems is on the rise. SF-KWS model deployment needs strongly optimized neural network structures that can perform suitably within the constraints of limited power and memory. Existing work has positioned techniques such as model compression and feature optimization, and some potential solutions have been found to enhance the performance of SF-KWS systems on edge devices. The understanding of these frameworks is vital in designing systems that meet real-world requirements without sacrificing acceptable levels of accuracy, thus the sophistication of neural network applications across different contexts (Garai et al., 2024) (Figure 9.1).

Definition of Neural Networks

The definition of neural networks is based on their structure and operation, and this is driven by biological systems, and specifically the human brain. A neural network is made up of nodes or neurons linked together, organized in layers: an input layer, some hidden layers, and an output layer. Each of the connections between the neurons has an associated weight with each that governs the amount of influence one neuron had over another. Through a process called training, neural networks' weights are adjusted by input information and output desired so that they can learn and improve their capability to predict. Adapting capability makes neural networks particularly valuable for many various uses, from image recognition to natural language processing. Neural networks have one of the primary characteristics as they can express complex, non-linear data relationships. Traditional algorithms stumble over high-dimensional data, whose interactions between features may be intricate. Neural networks, particularly deep learning architectures, have a ball here since they have several layers that are capable of learning hierarchical representations of data. In audiovisual speech processing, for instance, research identifies the groundbreaking work of deep learning architectures such as the bimodal recurrent neural network (BRNN), which can capture acoustic and visual features effectively. This modeling technique enhances systems like speech activity detection (SAD) to overcome challenges posed by noise in the surrounding environment, thus demonstrating the practical applicability of neural networks (Busso et al., 2018). The growing list of neural network architectures also demonstrates the flexibility and usability of the technology. Each architecture offers unique features that are suited to specific needs and performance requirements. Recent studies emphasize the importance of determining optimal combinations of neural network frameworks and models based on performance requirements such as accuracy, throughput, and energy efficiency. For example, benchmarking various frameworks and models across embedded systems can provide useful insights into their efficiencies and strengths. Flexibility of the selection process highlights the necessity for tailored solutions in using neural network solutions effectively, with the assurance that they are compatible to meet specific application needs, and considering the dynamic nature of the technology environment (Galán et al., 2018) (Figure 9.2).

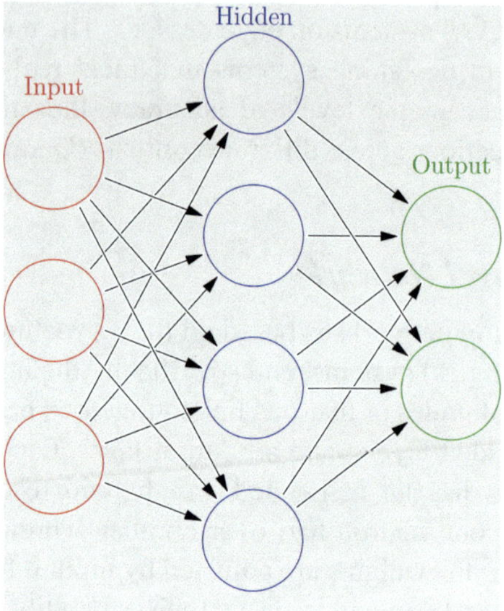

Figure 9.2. *Definition of neural networks.*

Source: https://i.ibb.co/DDnV50L/1200px-Colored-neural-network-svg.png.

Importance of Neural Network Frameworks

The importance of neural network architectures is that they enable the abstraction of sophisticated computations into forms that can be handled, making it possible to develop and deploy machine learning models. By abstracting, scientists and practitioners can concentrate on the design of the algorithm and optimization of performance without being weighed down by the complexity of low-level coding. Libraries such as TensorFlow and PyTorch enable a huge audience to experiment with deep learning techniques, leading to quicker innovation in the field. Moreover, modular components ensure easier reuse of code, making it simpler to move from prototype to production. This facilitates not just creativity but also better collaboration, as several members can work on individual components while progressing towards a common framework. As such, the development of the neural network frameworks significantly lowers the barrier to entry for new researchers in this fast-evolving category. Furthermore, the applicability of neural network frameworks in real-world settings also extends to performance efficiency. For instance, a recent publication discusses benchmarking various neural network models on various frameworks in an effort to identify the most suitable combination for a specific task. Through comparison of parameters such as throughput, power usage, and accuracy, the architects can select the optimal architecture for their applications (Galán et al., 2018). Following this methodological process guarantees efficient resource utilization, which is particularly true for application areas where computing performance and power are critical constraints, such as in embedded systems. The modularity of such frameworks allows for iterative optimization and scalability, and users can enhance model performance through ongoing tweaking and optimizations tailored to their operational environments. In the area of high-performance computing (HPC), neural network frameworks also have a significant role in ensuring efficient communication as well as resource management, particularly for multi-GPU designs. The availability of MPI+CUDA applications demonstrates how these frameworks have been tailored to address the tremendous data requirements of deep learning computations. For example, sophisticated communication schemes have been developed to take advantage of dense multi-GPU deployments with much higher efficiency in collective operations (Banerjee et al., 2017). These innovations not only enable greater performance in distributed training processes but also mirror the demands of workloads with high data volumes in today's era. With deep learning gaining more favor as a tool for addressing difficult tasks by numerous businesses, the role of neural network frameworks will only increase, driving research as well as actual application across a wide range of industries.

9.1. TYPES OF NEURAL NETWORK FRAMEWORKS

The landscape of neural network architectures is profoundly influenced by a variety of architectural shapes, each of which is optimal for specific computational processes and forms of data. Most elemental is the feedforward neural network, whose one-way flow of data has inputs pass through layers of neurons in a one-way path to finally reach an output layer. These networks work best for image recognition and light regression, where pattern recognition is paramount. Also, convolutional neural networks (CNNs) are a specialized architecture designed for grid-structured (chiefly image) data processing. CNNs effectively extract spatial hierarchies and local features using convolutional layers and therefore work best in image and object detection problems. The exact architectural structures employed therefore directly affect both data processing effectiveness and accuracy of result in machine learning (ML) processes. Conversely, recurrent neural networks (RNNs) introduce a temporal and dynamic dimension to neural networks, allowing sequential data such as language and time-series data to be processed. RNNs possess a hidden state that evolves over time, allowing storage of information from one time step to the next, which is crucial for speech recognition and natural language processing, among other applications. Variants of RNNs such as Long Short-Term Memory (LSTM) networks and Gated Recurrent Units (GRUs) have mechanisms to manage long-range dependencies better, overcoming the vanishing gradient problem that is common with basic RNNs. The use of these state-of-the-art RNN architectures allows deep learning practitioners to construct models that can learn from past data, stressing the significance of using the proper neural framework type according to the particular data features and requirements of the task. Latest developments also underscore breakthroughs in memory management mechanisms within neural network frameworks for further improved performance. For instance, support for runtime memory managers like vDNN enables smoother use of the available CPU and GPU memory, significantly reducing the constraints imposed by constrained GPU DRAM. By embracing methods that reduce peak memory utilization, vDNN demonstrates exponential enhancements, making deeper architectures like VGG-16 trainable even on systems with limited memory. Equally, technologies such as SuperNeurons highlight the evolution of dynamic GPU memory scheduling in order to support training beyond normal memory limits at the cost of sacrificing performance. These emerging frameworks are an ongoing attempt at enhancing the functionality of neural networks, providing a culture for researchers to craft deeper architectures without being victimized by hardware constraints, thus broadening the scope of machine learning research and practice (Abadi et al., 2018; Clemons et al., 2016).

9.1.1. Open-source Frameworks

The artificial intelligence scene has been revolutionized dramatically by the proliferation of open-source frameworks, particularly with regards to neural networks. These frameworks democratize access to advanced machine learning and deep learning technology and allow researchers and developers of different backgrounds to give back and take advantage of cutting-edge techniques. Open-source frameworks such as TensorFlow and PyTorch, besides allowing for the construction of advanced neural models, also facilitate global collaboration among researchers. As creators share their outputs, the majority of their advances result from the iterative nature of open-source collaboration, with the environment favorable to constant improvement. With open coding practices, the barriers to entry in machine learning are significantly reduced, and the door is opened for a broader base of talent to solve computational puzzles and advance the field. The utilization of open-source frameworks has also led to standardized practices in training and testing of neural networks. Specifically, noteworthy is the emergence of MLPerf Inference as a critical benchmark that helps identify the need for uniform tests across various hardware and software setups (Anderson et al., 2020). Having the ability to compare performances of different systems in a reproducible manner assists developers and researchers in finding the most efficient configurations for their own applications. Open-source platforms like TensorFlow also assist in this ecosystem by providing extensive documentation and assistance for deploying and optimizing neural networks on different environments. This availability not only makes the frameworks themselves more sound but also has the impact of enhancing the quality of products of research since practitioners can draw on transparently documented methodologies upon which to base replication and extension of previous work. In addition, open-source framework performance is constantly optimized through collective learning from various distributed training approaches. Empirical evidence shows that distributed training methods employed by TensorFlow can be very categorically divided into gRPC-based and No-gRPC design, and the performance results differ significantly between these designs (Awan et al., 2018). The experience gained from comparisons of these methods shows that No-gRPC designs outperform their gRPC counterparts, particularly in cases with high scalabilities. As the models are further developed, they employ these optimization techniques to deliver the best resource utilization while training the models. The continuous feedback loop between framework development and user experience enables an open dynamic system where bottlenecks on performance can be addressed by open-source communities, hence enhancing overall functionality and beauty of neural network frameworks in real-world use (Figure 9.3).

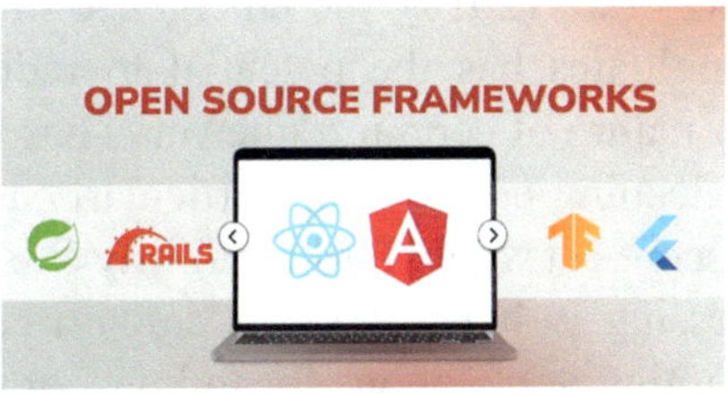

Figure 9.3. *Open-source frameworks.*

Source: https://www.orientsoftware.com/Themes/Content/Images/blog/2024-09-25/open-source-frameworks.webp.

9.1.2. Proprietary Frameworks

Proprietary frameworks have increasingly become a central feature in neural network development and deployment in various industries. These frameworks are typically created and sustained by private companies, which facilitates faster innovation at the expense of reliance on certain vendors. This kind of environment can build competitive strengths; for example, firms that build proprietary frameworks are able to inculcate optimizations that are customized to suit their specific hardware configurations, thus enhancing performance and efficiency. Yet, the utilization of proprietary systems might limit portability and flexibility, posing challenges for organizations looking to integrate multiple technologies. Hence, while proprietary frameworks make systems more operational and effective, vendor lock-in and problems about whether they can be utilized with open-source alternatives are still relevant topics within the discussion about neural network development. One of the most notable aspects of proprietary frameworks is their emphasis on user documentation and support, which greatly contributes to the learning curve for new developers and researchers.

Organizations that invest in proprietary frameworks tend to offer good support, generating a less complicated user experience. This has a tendency to result in a shorter period of onboarding, enabling teams to focus on application and research and not necessarily technical challenges. However, this systemic support system can lead to a dependency that suppresses innovation and thinking skills. Moreover, proprietary nature can lead to ossification if the structure is not periodically updated with cutting-edge features. Therefore, while the initial benefits of proprietary frameworks may appear beneficial, their long-term influence on the developer community must be scrutinized closely. Expanding the scope of neural networks through proprietary frameworks has broader implications for technological advancement and global competitiveness. As articulated by Horowitz et al. (2018), the emergence of artificial intelligence and its enabling technologies has the potential to redistribute international power. The proprietary nature of certain frameworks has the potential to create unbalanced access to leading-edge tools, particularly to smaller actors and poorer nations. This disconnect would further solidify existing power dynamics, as organizations possessing in-house systems enjoy a competitive advantage in terms of rapidly adapting applications for military or strategic purposes. In this case, the interplay between proprietary frameworks and the socio-political dynamics of technology adoption becomes increasingly complex, demanding a nuanced appreciation for how these frameworks influence individual innovations as well as broader societal patterns.

9.1.3. Specialized Frameworks for Specific Applications

The rampant proliferation of neural network technologies has necessitated the development of domain-specific frameworks for specific applications. These frameworks cater to the unique requirements of various fields, ranging from image recognition to natural language processing. To illustrate, TensorFlow and PyTorch are examples of frameworks that have been instrumental in streamlining it to become easier to design and deploy machine learning models effectively. As applications grow more complex, the need for frameworks that are capable of managing the complexity of different neural network architectures also increases. Specialization in such a manner guarantees not just that computational resources are optimized, but that model performance is enhanced as well, which means better results in different applications. The distinction of such frameworks emphasizes the worth of flexibility in machine learning platforms, providing developers with systems able to execute successfully across different tasks and hardware configurations, a quality crucial in the fluidity of neural network studies. To counter the wildly increasing demand for machine learning capability, a series of specialist inference systems has emerged. Over 100 firms are in the process of developing ML inference chips, whose performance and power consumption profiles are relatively variable. This hardware diversity poses special challenges at integration with existing software frameworks. As noted in recent research, the extensive range of ML hardware coupled with the enormous diversity of software combinations complicates the assessment of total system performance. Hence, initiatives like MLPerf Inference have been established to unify benchmarking so that ML systems can be compared in architecture-agnostic terms. By providing a systematic method of comparison, such initiatives allow for a more consistent understanding of the value proposition of custom frameworks, ultimately guiding practitioners into making more informed decisions in which tool to employ in their specific applications (Anderson et al., 2020). Advanced frameworks in machine learning applications also have simple challenges in data management and transfer. For instance, the maintenance of efficient distribution of huge quantities of datasets and resource optimization becomes more vital as the scale of applications increases. The comparison of the Apache-Hadoop model and high-performance computing illustrates the operational issues encountered by such frameworks. Each paradigm shares important architectural commonalities with its specific software implementations. This renders complexity in understanding standard workloads such as K-means clustering to evaluate performance on varied platforms appropriately. From the perspective of a "Big Data Ogres" framework, researchers may study the unique advantages and weaknesses of the paradigms systematically to better facilitate open integration of domain-specialized frameworks optimized for specific areas of applications (Fox et al., 2014). These efforts serve to underscore the vital function played by robust, elastic frameworks in meeting the broad challenge of data-intensive applications.

9.2. POPULAR NEURAL NETWORK FRAMEWORKS

The evolution of neural network frameworks has led to the development of various popular tools that can be used in supporting machine learning implementations. Among them, Google's TensorFlow is well-known because it is flexible and has a rich ecosystem for deep learning and machine learning operations. TensorFlow lets individuals develop complex neural network models because it has a scalable graph-based computational model. It not only simplify scalability in distributed systems but also supports smooth integration with hardware accelerators such as GPUs for performance acceleration. Moreover, its robust community support and rich library of pre-trained models make it a favorite choice among researchers as well as practitioners (MLPerf). H_2O.ai also offers a high-performance open-source platform that focuses on simplicity as well as performance optimization for various machine learning applications.

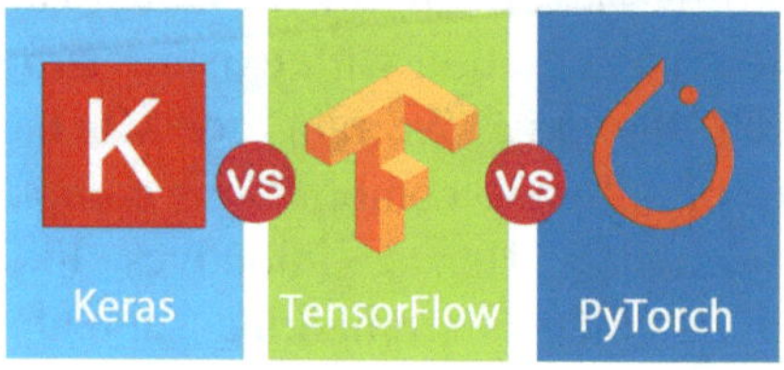

Figure 9.4. *Popular neural network frameworks.*

Source: https://cdn.educba.com/academy/wp-content/uploads/2020/05/Keras-vs-TensorFlow-vs-PyTorch.jpg.

Notably, H_2O provides optimized implementations of advanced algorithms, which are put at the disposal of users of various levels of expertise. Support for many data types is provided with the framework and with easy integration with popular statistical programming languages such as R and Python. Pre-existing dataset performance testing, like the MNIST dataset for handwritten digit recognition, has demonstrated the effectiveness of H_2O with user-controllable parameters and how blind parameter selection can decrease runtime substantially with little effect on accuracy (Alienin et al., 2017). This understanding explains why optimization is indispensable in machine learning operations. PyTorch is another well-known framework for use in neural network situations and is operated by Facebook's AI Research lab. PyTorch stands out due to its dynamic computational graph that allows the real-time modification during training, making easy debugging and quick experimentation feasible. This feature is particularly valuable to researchers testing out new algorithms, which has made PyTorch the academic favorite. The library also boasts an active community that includes libraries for specific use cases, e.g., torchvision for images. Apart from that, it provides strong hardware accelerators integration, which keeps the performance equal in many ML applications. As more demands are being placed on ML frameworks, their functionalities and architectures will be pivotal in defining the future of machine learning research and its usage (Anderson et al., 2020) (Figure 9.4).

9.2.1. TensorFlow

TensorFlow is one of the leading open-source deep learning development and deployment frameworks, exerting a powerful influence on a wide range of machine learning applications. Its architecture facilitates the development of complex neural network models in a computationally efficient way, with beneficial utilization of computing resources. TensorFlows adaptability allows developers to create a wide range of machine learning operations, e.g., image classification, natural language processing, etc. The flexibility of the frameworks to both CPU and GPU platforms enhances its performance, enabling researchers and engineers to experiment with different architectures and optimize models quickly. Moreover, TensorFlows large community support ensures constant improvement and complete access to resources, which enhances collaborative research and innovation in artificial intelligence. The application of deep learning algorithms by TensorFlow is most apparent in fields such as computer vision. The presence of support for convolutional neural networks (CNNs) within the frameworks facilitates breakthroughs in applications ranging from automated image analysis to real-time surveillance systems. For instance, TensorFlow can preprocess large datasets with effectiveness, a process that is an important milestone towards deep learning model training. As with the majority of automotive applications, approved labeled datasets are important components of this training process that has the tendency to make or break image recognition systems. The ability to construct and deal with such datasets within TensorFlow makes workflow easier, paving the way for higher accuracy in model results. Such ability in handling robust data validates the use of TensorFlows in current machine learning pursuits (Ashcraft et al., 2017). Additionally, the comparison of TensorFlow with other platforms shows major strengths and areas of enhancement. Recent research has put the performance metrics of TensorFlow to a test against other frameworks such as H_2O and Deep Learning4j (Alienin et al., 2017). While TensorFlow surpasses the others in scalability and ease of integration with current systems, there were some settings that could yield uneven processing times depending on model parameters. Precise calibration of the parameters can also influence runtime performance along with the quality of the output classifiers as seen through differing benchmarks for different neural network architectures. Understanding these processes can provide the best optimization possibilities when employing deep learning systems, pointing out the foundational position that TensorFlow occupies in enhancing neural network platforms in real-world applications (Figure 9.5).

Figure 9.5. *TensorFlow.*

Source: https://upload.wikimedia.org/wikipedia/commons/thumb/a/ab/TensorFlow_logo.svg/1200px-TensorFlow_logo.svg.png.

9.2.2. PyTorch

The advent of PyTorch as a leading neural network platform has significantly transformed the scenario of applications of deep learning. Competing with other platforms like TensorFlow, PyTorch has drawn eyeballs with its dynamic computation graph that allows for the creation and modification of neural networks dynamically. This flexibility is particularly helpful when trying out new ideas or making modifications to model architecture. The ease of use in the framework, which is created mainly for Python, ensures that researchers and programmers can implement complex algorithms with ease. This has made PyTorch extensively used in research as well as in industries, and developing leading-edge models becomes simpler. The shift towards effortless libraries such as PyTorch has popularized deep learning, allowing a larger number of individuals to handle these advanced technologies. The practical uses of PyTorch go beyond ease of use; they involve significant improvements in efficiency when it comes to training models. Research indicates the utilization of GPU resources through PyTorch resulting in drastically lowered running times compared to CPU utilization in deep neural networks. This efficiency is critical in light of increasing data size and complexity in modern machine learning projects. As suggested by work on time and memory consumption, the framework design benefits from optimal use of available hardware resources, and this results in improved model training using enormous datasets. For shallow networks as well, increased performance gains may not be apparent, but nonetheless, the framework provides a solid platform for exploration and optimization. This feature of PyTorch is in place to push research outcomes, speeding up the construction and deployment of sophisticated neural network models in a variety of domains (Gyawali et al., 2023). Aside from performance capabilities, PyTorch has built an ecosystem where rookies and experts can thrive. The framework design philosophy emphasizes simplicity and usability, addressing the core hindrance that often prevents non-experts from leveraging deep learning technologies. Notably, newer work has looked into the use of visual programming interfaces as secondary tools for those who are not so adept with traditional coding paradigms. The visual systems in which users can design deep learning models with drag-and-drop interfaces have been found to significantly reduce the entry barriers. This democratization of deep learning is consistent with PyTorch's goal of making advanced techniques accessible to more individuals and eventually contributing to innovation and cross-disciplinary collaboration in the artificial intelligence field (Aralikatte et al., 2019). The blend of usability and performance still makes PyTorch an appealing choice from among neural network frameworks (Figure 9.6).

PyTorch

Figure 9.6. *PyTorch.*

*Source: https://miro.medium.com/0*xXUYOs5MWWenxoNz.*

9.2.3. Keras

Keras has emerged as the trendy high-level neural network API for constructing and training deep learning models. It's simple-to-use interface allows researchers and developers to prototype and iterate their models rapidly, significantly improving productivity when using deep learning. Built atop lower-level frameworks such as TensorFlow and Theano, Keras abstracts out the underlying complexity of the aforementioned libraries to enable users to create models with little code. The seamless integration is so that traditional machine learning practitioners can easily transition to applying deep learning techniques without having to undergo the necessary steep learning curve. Furthermore, Keras has a collection of pre-configured layers and architectures so that individuals can experiment with many different neural network configurations, from convolution networks for image processing to recurrent networks for sequences. This diversity places Keras at the forefront of the ongoing evolution of neural network software. Perhaps the most valuable aspect of Keras is its scalability, particularly helpful in examples involving large datasets. According to the trend in deep learning, Keras supports the training of huge models over advanced hardware configurations like GPUs and cloud infrastructures. This scalability is critical, keeping in mind the performance metrics associated with deep learning tasks, as in various studies on image classification, natural language processing, and other computer vision tasks. Keras also makes it easy to integrate with cloud services, thereby opening doors to massive computational resources for training and testing models. How easily Keras enables exploration in terms of different architectures and training methods is perhaps the secret to inducing innovation in deep learning. As scientists aim to expand the boundaries of neural models, Keras is a framework that encourages rapid iterations and experimentation. The adaptability and versatility of applications of the framework can be both academic research and industrial. Healthcare to automotive technology and natural language processing, several types of projects have benefited with Keras providing outstanding performance. As introduced in present literature, Keras is optimally suited for developing applications across domains, as mentioned in studies on its use in computer vision tasks to natural language generation (Ashcraft et al., 2017). In addition, the ability of the framework to utilize abstract representations across domains provides additional avenues for investigation with users being able to implement successful generalization of trained models (Dethlefs et al., 2017). This capability not only reduces model tuning time for specific tasks but also enhances the frameworks real-world applicability in a wide variety of domains. Lastly, Kerass ease of use, scalability, and capacity to adjust secure its place as a cornerstone in modern neural network frameworks (Figure 9.7).

Figure 9.7. *Keras.*

Source: https://victorzhou.com/media/keras-posts/keras-nn.png.

9.3. KEY FEATURES OF NEURAL NETWORK FRAMEWORKS

One of the most prominent features of neural network frameworks is architectural flexibility, making users able to configure it to an incredibly heterogeneous set of configurations for various uses. Users can deploy sophisticated models through layers, activation units, and task-specific optimization algorithms through such frameworks. For instance, users can implement convolutional neural networks (CNNs) for image processing and recurrent neural networks (RNNs) for sequence-based data processing. This level of personalization is called for in fields such as computer vision and natural language, where specialized problems need to be addressed by specialized solutions. Furthermore, most modern frameworks are capable of being easily combined with other technologies to provide seamless interaction with other systems and data structures. Such versatility not only optimizes the performance of neural networks but also allows researchers and practitioners to build upon previously successful architectures more easily, thereby driving the field forward faster. One of the most important aspects distinguishing today's neural network frameworks is the integration of no-code paradigms, with the purpose of decreasing the entry threshold for novices.

Deep learning development in the traditional sense usually involves a deep understanding of programming and mathematical principles, which can discourage users from accessing these incredible tools. As noted in recent studies, the application of visual drag-and-drop interfaces greatly reduces model design to the point where users can create models intuitively without necessarily paying much attention to coding intricacies (Aralikatte et al., 2019). With the application of such user-friendly interfaces, frameworks enable more people to participate in the creation of neural networks, boosting innovation across diverse sectors and industries. This technology democratization not only increases availability but also refines the discipline by exposing it to input from individuals who are not necessarily classically technically qualified. Moreover, real-time monitoring and real-time adjustment is increasingly being considered a vital attribute within the architecture of neural networks. The integration of real-time data feeds allows models to respond incrementally to dynamic conditions, further qualifying them as predictors and responders. For instance, integrated systems can monitor environmental parameters in systems such as renewable energy control and make changes to output according to prevailing conditions (Frizziero et al., 2007). This flexibility is crucial in an era of constantly changing data and the ability to use real-time data has the potential to dramatically alter decision-making in many industries. With this, the ongoing improvement of frameworks that allow such dynamic interactions is central to the advancement of neural network applications, ultimately leading to more robust and valuable solutions in real-world applications.

9.3.1. Flexibility and Scalability

Flexibility and scalability are central attributes of neural network frameworks that play a significant role in their efficiency and usability. Flexibility allows researchers and developers to adapt frameworks to meet evolving computational needs so that they can experiment with new network structures and algorithms. Flexibility is important since the pace of developing machine learning algorithms would be quicker than existing frameworks can handle. One great bottleneck, however, is the limitation placed by hardware support, particularly more so with Graphics Processing Units (GPUs), such that memory utilization cannot be pushed to its limit. Where models need to be finely tuned for memory allocation to fit a GPUs DRAM capacity, it restricts the user from running different models and optimizations. This means that researchers may need to settle for less efficient architectures or divide the workload across multiple GPUs with the implication of losing efficiency and gaining complexity in managing resources (Clemons et al., 2016). Deployment of novel techniques can immensely improve the scalability of neural network architectures. Runtime memory management virtualizing use of deep neural networks (DNN) memory, for example, enables access to both GPU and CPU memory simultaneously. The process brings impressive reductions in use of memory, allowing such architectures as VGG-16, which are well-known for consuming a huge resource footprint, to be effectively trained using a single GPU. This virtualization functionality not only improves scalability by allowing broader models to run without hardware upgrades but also fosters cost-efficiency and power savings in machine learning research. By overcoming hardware constraints, this advanced technology provides a platform where flexibility can flourish, eventually driving the frontiers of neural network breakthroughs in the data-driven world of the future (Clemons et al., 2016). Furthermore, the paradigm shift in serverless computing highlights the other facet of flexibility and scalability in neural network architectures. Serverless architecture offers an event-driven platform that dynamically adjusts resource allocation as demanded, enabling varying workloads characteristic of neural network inference use cases. Even as scalability is inherent through this model by design, problems such as latency during cold starts must be addressed in order to maintain the efficiency and responsiveness of the frameworks' operations. Research comparing serverless platforms such as AWS Lambda emphasizes the feasibility of deploying large neural network models in these environments but cautions that service level agreements (SLAs) are compromised if natural latencies are not addressed.

Lastly, adoption of serverless computing demonstrates a direct move towards achieving dynamic resource management with an emphasis on maintaining continuous optimization to guarantee consistency in performance under neural network contexts.

9.3.2. Ease of Use and Accessibility

Ease of use and accessibility are significant in the adoption and effectiveness of neural network frameworks in academic and industry settings. Easy interface and clean design allow practitioners with varying skill levels to engage with these frameworks, thereby increasing audience access. Simpler deployment processes and readable documentation also enhance accessibility such that users with little programming skill can build, fine-tune, and deploy machine learning models. This democratization of technology provokes innovation, with users being able to draw on neural networks for a range of uses, from academic pursuits to commercial efforts. The usability of a framework ultimately leads to the quality and range of neural network projects created, with users tending to explore advanced methodologies if the point of entry is simplified. With the development of advanced neural networks, the demand for environments that not only streamline the process of creating models but also support varied hardware architectures is growing rapidly. For instance, fast model deployment on varied platforms is a major consideration towards gaining optimal performance. Environments with cross-platform support and abstraction of hardware complexity allow users to focus on model architecture rather than technical hurdles. By offering capabilities such as easily accessible pre-trained models and libraries, frameworks enhance user experience and encourage experimentation with deep learning paradigms. Deployment of these user-centered features also complements newer innovations; for instance, swTVM demonstrates how deep learning compilers can improve accessibility through code generation optimization on diverse devices, which is essential to users expecting the highest efficiency and productivity from their implementations (Gan et al., 2019). Moreover, social support cannot be overestimated in the provision of neural network frameworks. Live user forums, extensive tutorials, and readily found troubleshooting documentation augment a collective transfer of knowledge, enabling newcomers and gurus alike. When confronted with problems, the support offered by the frameworks community can illuminate solutions and facilitate learning. Besides, collaboration among researchers has been found to enhance the frameworks themselves, including the comparative analysis of predictive features in photometric redshift estimation that highlights the need to combine a large number of stakeholder inputs to make machine learning techniques better (Hoyle et al., 2015). This open-source culture of the community enhances not only the functionality of frameworks but also encourages more active participation, amplifying the scope and functionality effect of neural networks on various fields.

9.3.3. Community Support and Documentation

Support and documentation of the community are important in the rapidly evolving area of neural network frameworks to encourage collaboration and innovation among researchers and developers. With increasing investment in machine learning (ML) applications by more and more organizations, there is a growing need for robust frameworks that can accommodate heterogeneous software and hardware configurations. Unlike what is seen in conventional software paradigms, ML is very fragmented and features a range of tools and programming languages that require high interoperability. This complexity points to a need for community-oriented activities that provide not just detailed documentation but also areas of discussion for best practices, thus bridging gaps between technical backgrounds that are diverse. By participating in these common spaces, practitioners gain benefits from being able to tap into abundant resources to maximize their models and adapt them to different computational formats, as evidenced by the growth of MLPerf, which synchronizes performance benchmarks across architectures (Anderson et al., 2020). Furthermore, the value of proper documentation cannot be overemphasized, especially in a field where entrants have difficulty with sophisticated algorithms and systems. Properly documented frameworks are a valuable resource that guides users through the installation, setup, and utilization of neural network frameworks. Comprehensive manuals, tutorials, and demonstration projects allow the user to learn complex concepts in a short time and implement them successfully. In an environment where technologies and innovations are becoming increasingly prominent, documentation needs to be enhanced along with the frameworks, adopting the suggestions of the end-users and real implementations. This versatility not only enhances the scope of advanced ML methods but also enables community contribution, whereby users contribute back to the community, further enhancing support materials and networks available (de la Vega et al., 2017). Open-source collaborative feature extraction tool development also demonstrates the necessity for community support within the realm of neural network frameworks. As the tools get more common, they have varying interfaces, which are challenging to data scientists who must integrate them into cohesive workflows. The innovation of standardized platforms, such as the open-source package Pliers, addresses such challenges since users can carry out feature extraction from diverse types of data under a uniform interface. By facilitating annotation of different types of data with modular classes, Pliers illustrates how collective innovation can simplify complex processes, thereby making them more effective and increasing productivity. Such collaboration between documentation and support from the community is quite essential since it helps users bypass the complexity of machine learning application and develop more sophisticated models (de la Vega et al., 2017).

9.4. APPLICATIONS OF NEURAL NETWORK FRAMEWORKS

Applications of neural network frameworks go well beyond conventional domains, with significant interest in predictive maintenance and health monitoring. In industries that are dependent on sophisticated machinery, including manufacturing and aerospace, the capability to estimate the remaining useful life of equipment can translate into substantial cost savings and enhanced reliability. As outlined by the research, many system degradation prediction techniques have been developed, leading to more accurate predictive models. Notably, monitoring continuously enables firms to pursue condition-based maintenance strategies, more effectively utilizing resources and preventing unplanned failures, underlining the frameworks importance in technical prognosis. Ongoing evolution of the field underlines the importance of precision and responsiveness of implemented methods, as observed in recent discourse on predictive methods (Krupa et al., 2012). Neural network designs also facilitate advancements in automatic differentiation (AD), maximizing the effectiveness of model training and derivative computation in machine learning. AD techniques have typically been inadequately developed in the machine learning arena, uncovering a potential lost for performance gain in computing tasks. By integrating automatic differentiation with neural networks, practitioners are in a position to leverage improved gradient computation, which is important for effective optimization of the model. Integration unlocks high-end applications in engineering design and computational fluid dynamics. Additionally, the transition towards dynamic computational graphs and differentiable programming is a major milestone that allows for a deeper understanding of what happens internally in neural network models (Baydin et al., 2018). Therefore, the interaction between AD and neural networks provides an impetus for more advanced computational solutions. The intersection of neural network paradigms and their applications continues to flourish as researchers venture into newer methodologies and cross-disciplinary interactions. Fields of finance, medicine, and environmental science increasingly utilize neural networks to make forecasts and analyze data of complexity, boosting predictivity in scenario modeling and outcome forecasting. Neural networks, for instance, are used in finance to implement automated trading strategies as historical pattern performance, whereas in medicine they aid in diagnostic imaging, identifying anomalies at very high levels of accuracy. The learning capacity and flexibility of neural networks make them vital tools for resolving intricate issues, ultimately maximizing efficiency and effectiveness across numerous fields. Increasing the application of the tools further ensures unleashing new possibilities and enhanced problem-solving skills, further making the role of neural network structures significant in modern technology platforms (Figure 9.8).

Figure 9.8. *Real-life applications of neural networks.*

Source: https://www.smartsheet.com/sites/default/files/ic-og-NeuralNetworks-FacebookLinkedIn.jpg.

9.4.1. Image and Video Processing

The advancement of image and video processing has been significantly accelerated by the innovation of neural network architectures. Such architectures have enabled scientists and engineers to design algorithms capable of processing and reformatting visual information with degrees of accuracy and velocity previously unforeseen. Underlying the advancement is the use of convolutional neural networks (CNNs), which have become standard fare for image classification, object detection, and depth estimation for other uses. CNNs leverage spatial hierarchies in images and learn features via consecutive layers, thereby facilitating highly efficient data processing. With increasing uses of image processing across all aspects of life, ranging from healthcare to automobile and entertainment, the demand for complex neural network architecture increases, portraying the role of robust frameworks in this multi-disciplinary approach. Applications in the automotive sector have witnessed deep learning techniques emerging as indispensible tools for real-time image processing. For instance, Image and Video Processing in autonomous vehicles is contingent upon machine vision capabilities provided by neural networks. CNNs are utilized by the systems to convert visual data, which enables object detection and lane detection to drive safely. Multispectral data processing capacity of advanced neural networks allows depth information required for environmental mapping and obstacle detection to be integrated. As described by Karaman et al. (2019), focus on the optimization of such architectures on embedded platforms emphasizes achieving high rates of processing without compromising accuracy.

Thus, evolution of such lightweight and scalable network designs like FastDepth demonstrates the progress towards real-time image analysis to satisfy the growing need for automation and intelligent systems. Further, the practical utility of deep learning in image and video processing is emphasized by the creation of large datasets used to train high-capacity models. The availability of well-prepared, labeled datasets is one important factor in enhancing the performance of neural network structures. Some sources reference difficulties in gathering exhaustive datasets, particularly in nearby fields such as manufacturing and social media analysis (Ashcraft et al., 2017). The development of domain-specific datasets, such as auto-specific datasets, facilitates feature learning and enhanced classifier performance. The application of cloud infrastructures and mobile applications in gathering data also facilitates the image processing process to be effective, resulting in easy conversion from raw data to meaningful insights. This systematic and holistic approach to image and video processing reflects the profound impact of neural network architectures on modern technological innovation (Figure 9.9).

Figure 9.9. *Image and video processing.*

Source: https://blog.geetauniversity.edu.in/wp-content/uploads/2023/12/ffg.jpg.

9.4.2. Natural Language Processing (NLP)

The development of NLP has considerably been influenced by the evolution of neural network architectures, which now allow us to comprehend and create human language. Previous rule-based systems were not dynamic enough to cope with the functionality of natural language, and that generally translated into falling short in precision and performance. However, with the advent of deep learning models that utilized recurrent neural networks (RNNs) and transformers, NLP applications have improved considerably. Not only do such frameworks allow for processing complex patterns within huge datasets, but they also enhance the processing capacity of the model to understand language contextually and semantically. Besides, the transition towards utilizing neural networks has created new avenues for creative applications, ranging from machine translation to sentiment analysis, thereby revolutionizing the field and expanding its applications across multiple fields. Although the performance of NLP models today is robust, domain adaptation issues remain pervasive. Stochastic natural language generation models tend to generalize poorly when trained only on domain-specific data, resulting in limited applicability across several contexts.

Thus, most learned models restrict their applicability to individual uses, presenting an important limitation in real-world applications. Researchers have sought to counter this problem by increasing the focus on domain adaptation methods, which utilize prior knowledge from a given domain in order to enhance performance within another. Through the use of abstract meaning representations, models can bridge these gaps, as it allows the complex patterns learned in one domain to be effectively transferred to new linguistic landscapes. This technique takes advantage of the ability of neural network paradigms to induce NLP tasks with flexibility and responsiveness. Use of neural network paradigms has also brought to the forefront the importance of high-quality training data in the success of NLP systems. Availability and variety of quality training data are on the foundation upon which data must be exhaustive in sets, as well as there must be efficient ways of training and fine-tuning such models. Today's trends in deep learning methods point towards the application of cloud and on-premises infrastructures to accelerate training. Empirical experimentation with the architectures reveals that hybrid approaches can significantly reduce training time while providing optimal classifier accuracy. Classifiers trained using these perform well in real-world scenarios, showing the applicability of deep learning to research and real-world applications. By maximizing training techniques, NLP can further enhance its functionalities, ultimately leading to more powerful and interactive human-machine interactions (Ashcraft et al., 2017; Dethlefs et al., 2017) (Figure 9.10).

Figure 9.10. *Unlocking the potential of natural language processing (NLP).*

Source: https://www.innovationnewsnetwork.com/wp-content/uploads/ 2023/04/% C2%A9-shutterstockPeachShutterStock_1928145566-696x392.jpg.

9.4.3. Autonomous Systems and Robotics

The growth of robotics and autonomous systems has largely been spurred on by the creation of neural network designs, on which most machine learning is based. The surging demand for machine learning inference hardware and software systems, fueled by their applicability in an immense array of industries, has prompted exponential growth in the generation of heterogeneous inference systems. With more than 100 firms currently engaged in creating machine learning inference chips, there is a broad range of capabilities that support a variety of power consumption and performance needs. The interconnectedness of these systems creates a demand for standardization in the methods of benchmarking to properly account for performance across architectures. Tools such as MLPerf Inference support this requirement with solid evaluation criteria in place to allow comparisons and comprehension of autonomous systems' performance across the myriad frameworks competing in the market (Anderson et al., 2020). As deep learning techniques continue to advance, their impact in autonomous systems and robotics becomes increasingly evident, particularly in the domain of computer vision. Deep learning methods, especially convolutional neural networks, have proven to be highly useful resources for applications that demand high levels of accuracy, such as object recognition and detection, that are critical to the operational effectiveness of autonomous vehicles and robots. Incorporating deep learning into these applications not only enhances their ability to process visual data but also leads to more intelligent decision-making processes. Moreover, in order to efficiently train such neural networks, quality-crafted and large datasets are required. The process of obtaining large, labeled datasets is confronted with the problem of how to find innovative workarounds for this challenge, as illustrated by the establishment of dedicated automotive databases that enable systems to learn and detect various vehicle features within real-world contexts (Ashcraft et al., 2017).

The real-world implementation of such technology displays the potential to revolutionize neural network architectures within autonomous systems. For instance, the application of mobile applications in data gathering in factories demonstrates how natively deep learning can be integrated into existing workflows. Mobile applications are capable of analyzing and processing data in real-time, thus helping various production stages and quality assurance. Cloud-based infrastructures that support data storage and training of deep neural networks allow industries to use computational resources to enhance the accuracy of models and reduce training time. Besides, successful implementation in real-world applications guarantees the sustainability of these developments, as reflected through the utilization of trained classifiers to streamline manufacturing processes and promote operational efficiency. With continued advancements in autonomous systems, the involvement of complex neural network architectures and real-world applications will undoubtedly shape the future of robotics (Ashcraft et al., 2017) (Figure 9.11).

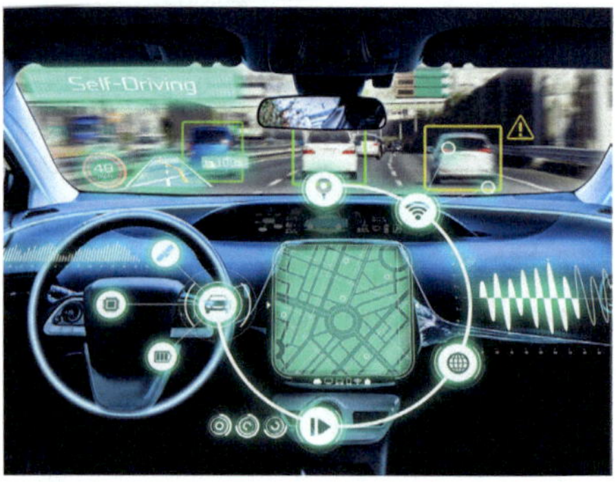

Figure 9.11. *Recurrent Neural Network in Autonomous Vehicles*

*Source: https://miro.medium.com/v2/1*1H-HIn-bpUHU_wVj1Nl8ug.jpeg.*

9.5. CHALLENGES IN USING NEURAL NETWORK FRAMEWORKS

The use of neural network structures is usually hampered by a range of problems, particularly that of access to large, high-quality data sets. Neural networks adore well-parametrized data for training, but such data sets are generally difficult to find, especially in niche domains. A case in point is in the instance of application to motor vehicle usage, where finding an over-arching data set that encompasses broad-spectrum vehicle characteristics is a monumental exercise. As explained in the deep learning discussion, the process of data collection and labelling plays a critical role in making the model training process effective. A lack of sufficient sets of varied data can make it susceptible to overfitting, such that the model performs well when being trained but fails when encountering new data, which will ultimately reduce its reliability in real life (Ashcraft et al., 2017). This issue calls for more studies on even more powerful data gathering methods. This is another primary challenge with the application of neural network frameworks since the discipline is noted with complex tools and architectures. Various neural network frameworks present varied functionalities and performance metrics, which tend to be daunting to practitioners, particularly to newcomers in machine learning. The need to select an appropriate architecture is then compounded by the intricacies that go into hyperparameter tuning, for which small differences can lead to considerably different results. Researchers then face considerable challenges in determining the models, such as convolutional neural networks for image tasks, to use based on their respective application domains. For example, satellite imagery analysis is burdened with the sheer volume of pixels it has to contend with, with vast computational loads and sophisticated algorithms to detect small objects correctly (Etten et al., 2018). Addressing all these issues correctly is the way forward to appropriate application and deployment. Finally, computational needs present a huge hindrance in the deployment of neural network models. With increased data size and model complexity, the need for effective Computational resources becomes apparent. Models like those presented in the SIMRDWN pipeline underscore the need for employing scalable infrastructure that can effectively process arbitrarily sized satellite images. The mismatch between computational resources being utilized and the computing power needed by the process to effectively train and infer in models poses a serious threat to institutions. In addition, the choice between on-premises versus cloud-based implementations provides another level of complexity, as companies will have to weigh cost-effectiveness, throughput, and interactivity for successful implementations. In the end, resolution of these computational challenges is required in order to maximize performance and deployment of neural network architectures across applications (Etten et al., 2018).

9.5.1. Computational Resource Requirements

The computational resource requirements of neural network architectures are a critical consideration in developing and deploying machine learning systems. The more complex the networks, such as Convolutional Neural Networks (CNNs), the higher the computational and memory requirement. Such networks are inclined to use hardware such as Graphics Processing Units (GPUs) and Central Processing Units (CPUs) to meet their computational needs. New hardware has emerged in the form of reconfigurable hardware, such as Field Programmable Gate Arrays (FPGAs), which presents a thrilling alternative. FPGAs are able to provide a customized balance between performance and power consumption, thereby enabling scientists to tightly manage their systems to achieve their maximum output. Such adaptability can significantly enhance the performance of CNN implementations, particularly for applications requiring fast processing of large data, as seen in studies of CNN-to-FPGA toolflows providing insightful information about the architectural choices needed for efficient deployment (Bouganis et al., 2018).

Optimizing the computational resources in cloud settings for neural networks increases the complexity. Conventional resource allocation methods tend to struggle with the dynamic demands that advanced neural structures present. The high-dimensional state and action spaces complicate these standard methods from being effective, and more sophisticated methods like DRL have to be used. Hierarchical virtual machine (VM) resource allocation and power management framework demonstrates the necessity for a dynamic distribution of resources that maximizes power consumption while maintaining system performance. The two-level approach of this framework indicates how neural networks can leverage top-level management algorithms to dynamically optimize GPU and CPU allocations to maximize the usage of computational resources without sacrificing system reliability or increasing operating costs (Li et al., 2017). Moreover, the effect of computational resource management carries across the spectrum of applications of neural network structures from cloud to edge computing.

The demand for effective dynamic power administration arises as the need for computational resources scales with the growing sophistication of neural networks. It is possible that an integrated VM resource allocator and power manager can facilitate the general objectives of system reliability enhancement and cost savings. As the application of neural networks grows, optimized methods of resource management will be imperative. More advanced strategies, including the integration of autoencoders with DRL techniques, can help to streamline the processing of large state space dimensions and enhance convergence rates. That focus on adaptive resource management is imperative to ensuring the performance and efficiency of neural network models under more demanding computational environments.

9.5.2. Overfitting and Generalization Issues

Overfitting is the most significant drawback to the design and construction of neural network architectures. As models become more sophisticated with increasing depth and parameters, they tend to memorize training data rather than capture the salient patterns that govern the form of the data. This impact not only deteriorates the performance of the models on new data but can even impact its interpretability, in such a way that it becomes difficult for researchers to identify why decisions are being made. Overfitting is often exacerbated by having access to large datasets providing rich features, which means that models are very specific to single training instances rather than generalized decision boundaries usable in a broad range of situations. Gupta et al. (2025) deems it necessary to apply regularization techniques in order to prevent overfitting because these techniques are crucial in optimizing generalization capacities. Regularization techniques like dropout, L1/L2 regularization, and batch normalization are crucial in preventing overfitting of deep learning models. Dropout, for example, is utilized to preventively deactivate at training time randomly a subarray of neurons, thereby compelling the model to learn more robust features and less reliant on any particular pathway. Similarly, L1 and L2 regularization penalize the loss function and avoid over-complex models by lowering the magnitude of the weights. By incorporating these methods, practitioners are able to make their networks more generalizable and improve them on unseen data. Aside from this, adaptive learning rate optimizers and other techniques aimed at improving the training process aid in making models more stable, thus the learning trajectory is optimal even as difficulties arise. Use of such techniques not only aids in combating overfitting but also aids in fostering model construction that is both effective and resilient in diverse applications. The study of generalization issues transcends traditional regularization methods; it also uncovers new solutions with new approaches such as neural architecture search (NAS) and transfer learning. NAS offers automation in the design of neural network architectures, optimizing them for specific tasks and preventing overfitting through the discovery of suitable complexities of models suited to datasets. Transfer learning also increases generalization by using pre-trained models, making it possible for frameworks to start from where previous knowledge is already established and not from scratch. This approach can easily shorten training time and curb the problems of overfitting, especially in areas with minimal availability of data. Additionally, the advances in score matching as outlined in Han et al. (2024) provide a mathematical groundwork for generalizability improvement through kernel regression tasks combination during training, thereby offering an integrated approach to tackling the issue of overfitting in neural networks (Figure 9.12).

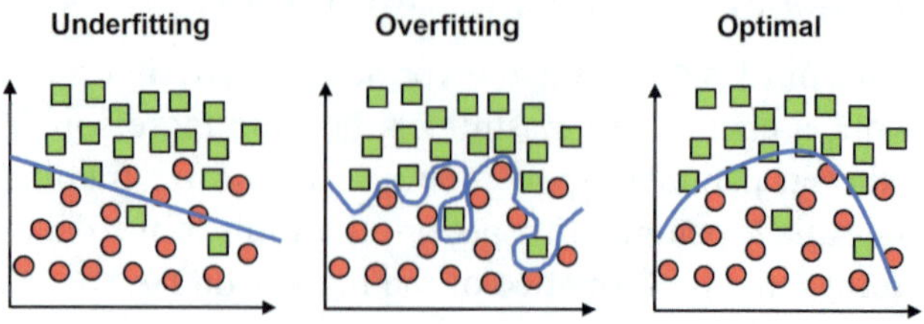

Figure 9.12. *Popular techniques to prevent the overfitting in a neural networks.*

Source: https://media5.datahacker.rs/2021/11/Picture3-1536x522.jpg.

9.5.3. Interpretability and Transparency

In the broader context of neural network designs, its tenants of interpretability and transparency are better established as foundational pillars of sound artificial intelligence implementation. As more sophisticated machine learning solutions have emerged, understanding what transpires behind their decision-making has become increasingly important. The gaming industry, for instance, has begun applying complex algorithms to predict potentially harmful behaviors, introducing the era of data-driven means to minimize risk. But unless the workings of these models are understood clearly, stakeholders may not accept the adoption of these innovations. Researchers have found that adopting techniques such as the TREPAN algorithm may make complex models easier to interpret by recognizing decision trees that give more understandable explanations of model predictions. This evolution exists to highlight the ongoing necessity of preserving predictive accuracy against comprehensible output as a way of increasing trust between users and governing bodies (Dragicevic et al., 2016). In addition, transparency lack in black-box models presents massive challenges in maintaining effective decision-making processes. Numerous techniques have been developed to describe artificial intelligence that respond to this query, yet most of them are specialized in nature and provide very general descriptions that fail to serve the varied information needs of all interested stakeholders. LIMEtree, a locally-interpretable technique, is a new method being developed to make neural networks more understandable. Unlike traditional models with fixed explanations, LIMEtree allows the user to customize their questions regarding model performance and thus produce a range of customized explanations. By adopting such innovative methods, the discipline can be placed more strongly within the frameworks of transparency and accountability of AI applications, thus enhancing user trust and facilitating increased adoption of neural networks as a decision-support tool (Flach et al., 2020). Lastly, the infusion of interpretability and transparency into neural network platforms not only anchors the ethical foundations of artificial intelligence but also supports smarter and more effective use. The transformational potential of these platforms can be better harnessed when stakeholders comprehend the mechanisms behind which AI systems operate. As indicated by the growing emphasis on methods like TREPAN and LIMEtree, the path to more interpretable models is possible and necessary for data-driven businesses. By prioritizing these qualities, businesses can address the dilemmas of model governance while creating strategies consistent with the values and expectations of society. Against this backdrop, ongoing research on explanatory models remains a major area of research that can bridge the gap between state-of-the-art AI technologies and their human users (Dragicevic et al., 2016; Flach et al., 2020).

SUMMARY

In conclusion, the advancement in neural network structures has revolutionized the artificial intelligence and machine learning field significantly. These architectures have enabled phenomenal breakthroughs in numerous applications, such as computer vision, natural language processing, and so on. Relying on architectures such as CNNs, scientists have been able to tackle tough issues previously believed to be inaccessible. The development of sophisticated models, that have the ability to learn intricate patterns within vast data sets, illustrates the ability of these systems to not only drive performance statistics higher but also facilitate greater comprehension of underlying data frameworks. As research continues, further investigation will most certainly discover increasingly more effective means of distributing neural networks to different and beneficial contexts outside of current paradigms. In addition, the collaboration between different architectures within neural networks has proven to be viable towards optimizing overall performance. For instance, the coupling of more than one discourse annotation framework enables the improvement of implicit discourse relation classification, such as evidenced by new approaches based on multi-task learning systems (Li et al., 2016). By the integration of multiple relevant tasks, researchers can take advantage of unique and shared features across sets, thus improving the performance of neural networks in real-world applications. These cross-disciplinary efforts highlight the need to develop frameworks that update and revise, further bridging theory-practice distances. This adaptability is necessary to sustain momentum built within the field and ensure neural network uses endure in different industries. Ultimately, the future of neural network frameworks relies on a commitment to continued innovation and cross-disciplinary collaboration. With the evolving technology, it will be required to surpass the limitations of conventional frameworks and create new paradigms that embrace new methods, such as Dense Neural Patterns, that enable object detection by providing dense local features based on CNNs (Lin et al., 2014). The potential to usher such integration implies a future direction of neural networks wherein efficiency and accuracy can complement each other. Overall, the development of neural network architectures will continue to be vital to the growth of artificial intelligence, offering the tools to deal with nuanced data sets and make valuable contributions to a changing technological world.

Looking at the neural network architectures, of particular importance is how the models have developed to address nuanced system behaviors. One such interesting development is the use of structural rigidity theory in a network framework to help analyze the combinatorial rigidity of different biological systems, most notably proteins. It helps in understanding the structure dynamics, which can then be used to inform the design of neural networks that are inspired by biology, pointing to a balance between functional flexibility and rigidity. This insight broadens the platform for building neural network models to better anticipate and optimize interactions such as protein-protein interactions and metabolic pathways, thereby enhancing their use in a broad spectrum of applications in computational biology and artificial intelligence (Almaas et al., 2012). Further, integrating deep learning into mobile devices signifies an important step towards the utilization of neural network frameworks in practical applications. With growing demand for real-time features like image recognition and chat applications, understanding the computational complexities is essential. Mobile apps rely on trained deep learning models, which in the past needed to be executed in the cloud due to the computational limit of mobile phones. However, the improvements in on-device inference techniques will overcome these constraints, provide quicker response times, and improve usability in network-constrained situations. The reality of such architecture demands continuous performance bottleneck monitoring, as the empirical study unfolds to identify the necessity for mobile-optimized CNNs (Guo et al., 2018). Another essential element of summarizing takeaways in neural network models is their diverse utilization and inherent constraints. As researchers explore multiple architectures, one must comprehend the trade-offs between computational efficiency, accuracy, and practical use. The transition to on-device processing, though promising, is not without its disadvantages in terms of increased energy consumption and slower response times in certain cases. Such a comparison of cloud-based and on-device inference is a referral to the ever-evolving nature of deep learning utilization, hence the need for ongoing research and optimization. In summary, the discovery of these basic elements within neural network architectures will not only guide future development but also advise practitioners how to apply these technologies to best effect across various fields (Guo et al., 2018).

REFERENCES

1. Abadi, M., Coates, A., Collobert, R., Dean, J., Krizhevsky, A., LeCun, Y., Szegedy, C., et al. (2018). SuperNeurons: Dynamic GPU memory management for training deep neural networks. http://arxiv.org/abs/1801.04380 (accessed on 25th September 2025).
2. Alienin, O., Gordienko, Y., Kochura, Y., Novotarskiy, A., et al. (2017). Performance analysis of open-source machine learning frameworks for various parameters in single-threaded and multi-threaded modes. http://arxiv.org/abs/1708.08670 (accessed on 25th September 2025).
3. Almaas, E., Andrusier, N., Atilgan, A. R., Barabasi, A. L., Bateson, M., Bergman, C. M., Bhalla, U. S., Iyengar, R., et al. (2012). Rigidity and flexibility of biological networks. http://arxiv.org/abs/1204.6389 (accessed on 25th September 2025).
4. Anderson, B., Breughc, M., Charlebois, M., Cheng, C., et al. (2020). MLPerf inference benchmark. http://arxiv.org/abs/1911.02549 (accessed on 25th September 2025).
5. Aralikatte, R., Khare, S., Mani, S., Panwar, N., et al. (2019). A visual programming paradigm for abstract deep learning model development. http://arxiv.org/abs/1905.02486 (accessed on 25th September 2025).
6. Ashcraft, N., Cook, M., Djerekarov, E., Luckow, A., et al. (2017). Deep learning in the automotive industry: Applications and tools. http://arxiv.org/abs/1705.00346 (accessed on 25th September 2025).
7. Awan, A. A., Bedorf, J., Chu, C. H., Panda, D. K., et al. (2018). Scalable distributed DNN training using TensorFlow and CUDA-aware MPI: Characterization, designs, and performance evaluation. http://arxiv.org/abs/1810.11112 (accessed on 25th September 2025).
8. Banerjee, D. S., Barnett, M., Chu, C. H., Hoefler, T., Jia, Y., Liu, J., Mamidala, A. R., et al. (2017). Optimized broadcast for deep learning workloads on dense-GPU InfiniBand clusters: MPI or NCCL? http://arxiv.org/abs/1707.09414 (accessed on 25th September 2025).
9. Baydin, A. G., Pearlmutter, B. A., Radul, A. A., Siskind, J. M., et al. (2018). Automatic differentiation in machine learning: A survey. https://core.ac.uk/download/297029995.pdf (accessed on 25th September 2025).
10. Bouganis, C. S., Kouris, A., & Venieris, S. I. (2018). Tool flows for mapping convolutional neural networks on FPGAs: A survey and future directions. https://core.ac.uk/download/189837587.pdf (accessed on 25th September 2025).

11. Busso, C., & Tao, F. (2018). End-to-end audiovisual speech activity detection with bimodal recurrent neural models. http://arxiv.org/abs/1809.04553 (accessed on 25th September 2025).
12. Carmona Galán, R., Fernández Berni, J., Rodríguez Vázquez, Á. B., Velasco Montero, D., et al. (2018). Optimum selection of DNN model and framework for edge inference. https://core.ac.uk/download/225123778.pdf (accessed on 25th September 2025).
13. Clemons, J., Gimelshein, N., Keckler, S. W., Rhu, M., et al. (2016). vDNN: Virtualized deep neural networks for scalable, memory-efficient neural network design. http://arxiv.org/abs/1602.08124 (accessed on 25th September 2025).
14. de la Vega, A., McNamara, Q., & Yarkoni, T. (2017). Developing a comprehensive framework for multimodal feature extraction. http://arxiv.org/abs/1702.06151 (accessed on 25th September 2025).
15. Dethlefs, N. (2017). Domain transfer for deep natural language generation from abstract meaning representations. https://core.ac.uk/download/151162093.pdf (accessed on 25th September 2025).
16. Dragicevic, S., Garcez, A., Percy, C., Sarkar, S., et al. (2016). Accuracy and interpretability trade-offs in machine learning applied to safer gambling. https://core.ac.uk/download/77603866.pdf (accessed on 25th September 2025).
17. Flach, P., & Sokol, K. (2020). LIMEtree: Interactively customizable explanations based on local surrogate multi-output regression trees. https://core.ac.uk/download/389422028.pdf (accessed on 25th September 2025).
18. Fox, G. C., Jha, S., Luckow, A., Mantha, P., et al. (2014). A tale of two data-intensive paradigms: Applications, abstractions, and architectures. http://arxiv.org/abs/1403.1528 (accessed on 25th September 2025).
19. Frizziero, E., Hobson, P. R., Huang, C., Irving, D., et al. (2007). Grid computing technologies for renewable electricity generator monitoring and control. https://core.ac.uk/download/1440905.pdf (accessed on 25th September 2025).
20. Gan, L., Liu, C., Luan, Z., Qian, X., et al. (2019). swTVM: Exploring the automated compilation for deep learning on Sunway architecture. http://arxiv.org/abs/1904.07404 (accessed on 25th September 2025).
21. Garai, S., & Samui, S. (2024). Exploring TinyML frameworks for small-footprint keyword spotting: A concise overview. 2024 International Conference on Signal Processing and Communications (SPCOM). https://www.semanticscholar.org/paper/

edb7d2f7f39a014634ea67e74ac0aeeb818906c8 (accessed on 25th September 2025).

22. Guo, T. (2018). Cloud-based or on-device: An empirical study of mobile deep inference. http://arxiv.org/abs/1707.04610 (accessed on 25th September 2025).
23. Gupta, R., & Jindal, R. (2025). Impact of too many neural network layers on overfitting. International Journal of Computer Science and Mobile Computing. https://www.semanticscholar.org/paper/4380f0fdfa652b05f7824d946162e397fcfaf067 (accessed on 25th September 2025).
24. Gyawali, D. (2023). Comparative analysis of CPU and GPU profiling for deep learning models. http://arxiv.org/abs/2309.02521 (accessed on 25th September 2025).
25. Han, Y., Razaviyayn, M., & Xu, R. (2024). Neural network-based score estimation in diffusion models: Optimization and generalization. abs/2401.15604. https://www.semanticscholar.org/paper/1805e1f17787afa50b4784760aba518608bfc51b (accessed on 25th September 2025).
26. Horowitz, M. C. (2018). Artificial intelligence, international competition, and the balance of power (May 2018). https://core.ac.uk/download/211333744.pdf (accessed on 25th September 2025).
27. Hoyle, B., Rau, M. M., Seitz, S., Weller, J., et al. (2015). Feature importance for machine learning redshifts applied to SDSS galaxies. http://arxiv.org/abs/1410.4696 (accessed on 25th September 2025).
28. Ishakian, V., Muthusamy, V., & Slominski, A. (2018). Serving deep learning models in a serverless platform. http://arxiv.org/abs/1710.08460 (accessed on 25th September 2025).
29. Karaman, S., Ma, F., Sze, V., Wofk, D., et al. (2019). FastDepth: Fast monocular depth estimation on embedded systems. http://arxiv.org/abs/1903.03273 (accessed on 25th September 2025).
30. Krupa, M. (2012). Methods of technical prognostics applicable to embedded systems. https://core.ac.uk/download/30311032.pdf (accessed on 25th September 2025).
31. Li, S., Liu, Y., Sui, Z., Zhang, X., et al. (2016). Implicit discourse relation classification via multi-task neural networks. http://arxiv.org/abs/1603.02776 (accessed on 25th September 2025).
32. Li, Z., Lin, S., Liu, N., Qiu, J., et al. (2017). A hierarchical framework of cloud resource allocation and power management using deep reinforcement learning. http://arxiv.org/abs/1703.04221 (accessed on 25th September 2025).

33. Lin, Y., Sun, M., Wang, X., Zou, Y., et al. (2014). Generic object detection with dense neural patterns and regionlets. http://arxiv.org/abs/1404.4316 (accessed on 25th September 2025).

34. Paul, S. G., Saha, A., Hasan, M. Z., Noori, S. R. H., & Moustafa, A. (2024). A systematic review of graph neural network in healthcare-based applications: Recent advances, trends, and future directions. IEEE Access, 12, 15145–15170. https://www.semanticscholar.org/paper/30027db6420ab5438dfd6e492e4e765928f5e52e (accessed on 25th September 2025).

35. Van Etten, A. (2018). Satellite imagery multiscale rapid detection with windowed networks. http://arxiv.org/abs/1809.09978 (accessed on 25th September 2025).

CHAPTER 10

FUTURE TRENDS IN NEURAL NETWORKS

Contents

INTRODUCTION

Recent years have witnessed the history of neural networks being marked by spectacular advances that have the potential to change the future in myriad applications. While computations are increasing, the necessity to optimize the efficiency and effectiveness of neural networks has become an imperative. The discovery of new architectures—such as dynamic graph neural networks—has opened up new research and application fronts. These networks enable the description of complex, time-varying systems, which can both structure and temporal patterns observed in dynamic data environments. These developments not only reaffirm the universality of neural networks to the many disciplines but also indicate the necessity for an integrated explanation of dynamic network ideas, as indicated in the ongoing debate by the research community (Gabrys et al., 2021). This very first step is the key towards constructing a unified framework that will manage the affluent richness of modern data. As we navigate through the intricacies of next-generation neural network paradigms, it is crucial that we acknowledge the multidisciplinary push of the field. Scientists are now integrating concepts from various fields, including computer science, engineering, and social sciences, to push the performance of neural networks. This cross-disciplinary area is leading the investigation of novel methods, such as multiple linear regression (MLR) and principle component analysis (PCA), to further develop neural network performance. For instance, MLR has been effectively employed for estimation of equipment expenditures in mines for validating the usefulness of established statistical methods in neural network output refinement. Such an interdisciplinary framework not only broadens the horizon of neural networks but also facilitates holistic assessment of new models so that they are flexible regarding real-world implementation (Lashgari et al., 2011).

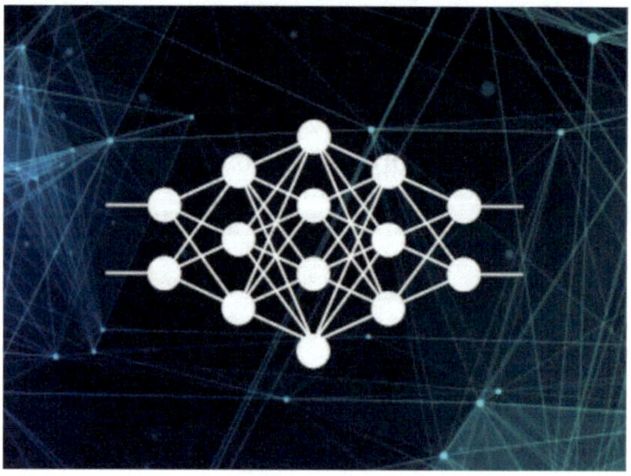

Figure 10.1. *Future trends in neural networks.*

*Source: https://miro.medium.com/v2/resize:fit:640/format:webp/1*R4y1DzsgcF-7Ho3hAD7b4Q.jpeg.*

This phenomenon represents a shift toward a more synthesized development and application framework. Overall, neural network development is directly associated with developments in dynamic modeling and interdisciplinary approaches. As future trends develop, the foundation in dynamic network systems and the groundwork lexicon will be crucial to researchers and practitioners. By embracing a multi-layered paradigm of these innovations, the field can better accommodate the demands of practical needs, advancing innovation from healthcare to finance. Most significantly, growing interest in graph neural networks and the capacity to process dynamic networks sets the stage for more intricate and dynamic systems. On-going research into such methods marks not only a technical revolution but also an open invitation to cross-disciplinary groupings, portending a rosy future for neural networks and their revolutionary impacts on society (Figure 10.1).

Definition of Neural Networks

Neural networks, an artificial intelligence discipline, have evolved to play very fundamental roles in modeling very intricate patterns and behaviors across numerous applications. In their nature, these computational models are designed with architecture in the form of an attempt to replicate the way biological neural networks within the human brain function so that systems can process information in an organized, layered manner. This organization is typically an input layer, some hidden layers, and an output layer, each of which consists of connected nodes, or neurons. The nodes are in contact with each other by weighted links, and in the process of learning, the weights are adjusted, or trained. This recurrent learning process enables neural networks to recognize patterns and make choices based on input data, illustrating their use in tasks ranging from image recognition to natural language processing. Consequently, a proper comprehension of the origin definition of neural networks is critical when addressing their future trends and uses. As advancements in neural networks enhance, so do the issues in integrating them and their efficiency in real-world applications. Issues of interpretability, overfitting, and the requirement of large datasets are common, complicating their deployment in high-stakes domains such as medicine or autonomous vehicles. Increasing numbers of researchers are investigating the neural basis for such issues, emphasizing the contextuality of cognitive processes. For example, studies highlight the differential intervention responses to environmental and genetic influences and emphasize that behaviors like those in autism spectrum disorder can be due to complex neural mechanisms. Most importantly, genetic mutations and environmental influences have been discovered to significantly impact cognitive and neurodevelopmental outcomes, thus reframing our understanding of neural networks and helping us develop more robust models that account for such factors (Bryson et al., 2014). Furthermore, the integration of ideas from cognitive science in the development of neural networks would help drive the development of more human-like systems to understand and process. The weak central coherence theory, which describes a preference in individuals with autism to treat information piecemeal rather than as a general gestalt, illustrates the way in which some neural groupings can affect thinking (Boucher et al., 2002). Through investigation of the tailored neural interactions and considering the operation of processes such as temporal binding, which deals with how networks collaborate in processing information, researchers may be able to optimize current neural network designs. Better models would not only be able to improve prediction accuracy for predictive tasks but also enable these systems to perform contextual reasoning. As such, the future direction of neural networks will likely depend on cross-disciplinary research that marries neuroscience and artificial intelligence in an effort to transform how machines react to and process complex stimuli.

Importance of Neural Networks in Modern Technology

Their role in modern technology spans various industries, a reflection of their extensive impact on life itself and economic paradigms. One such pivotal use is their integration with Big Data analytics, already becoming an essential necessity for the development of smart cities. With the use of computational intelligence strategies, neural networks facilitate processing of massive data generated in city living. This synergy of Big Data and neural networks not only enhances urban planning but also offsets the issues embedded in mobility and resource management in urban settings. In efforts to implement smart solutions, the adaptive capabilities of neural networks allow for real-time decision making that further results in sustainable ways of life in cities (Doctor et al., 2020). Therefore, the importance of these technologies is underscored in their ability to innovate and transform how modern societies operate. In practical usage, neural networks play a pivotal role in energy management systems, as demonstrated by their applicability to building heating and cooling load forecasting. Since energy used from buildings accounts for approximately 40% of total energy use, accurate forecasts are paramount both during design and operational management. By applying artificial neural network models, engineers can process datasets of various building characteristics, such as relative compactness and surface area, in order to achieve precise energy load prediction. Not only do these advancements lead to optimized design, but also improved energy efficiency, as evident from models with validation accuracies of up to 99.60% (Abu-Naser et al., 2019). This is a reflection of the way neural networks heavily impact key industries, propelling innovation towards clean energy alternatives. Additionally, neural networks' flexibility puts them at the cutting-edge of artificial intelligence developments. Neural networks play a key role in machine learning operations, wherein they use intricate algorithms to learn from large amounts of data and become more accurate with time. This learning procedure has far-reaching implications, particularly in fields such as healthcare and finance, where real-time data analysis can inform critical decision-making processes. For instance, neural networks enable diagnostic procedures in medical imaging to perform early disease diagnosis, and in the financial sector, they enable the prediction of market trends and risk mitigation. As scientists continue to explore newer neural network architectures and training processes, the potential applications seem virtually boundless, ensuring that these systems will remain at the forefront of technological advancements in the coming future. Continued advancement in neural networks underscores their inherent relevance to shaping upcoming technologies (Figure 10.2).

Figure 10.2. *Importance of neural networks.*

Source: https://miro.medium.com/v2/resize:fit:1100/format:webp/0 f5oHQZEi-IqF4kDFm.*

Overview of Future Trends

As neural networks advance, the application of advanced techniques to optimize their scalability and performance is a dominant trend. One area that has come under focus is applying improved clustering algorithms, such as the Stochastic Block Model (SBM), to inspect effectively citation networks in research and patent data. This approach is able to identify more accurately technology growth potential so that corporate managers and investors can make appropriate decisions based on the technology cluster life cycle. Using Long Short-Term Memory (LSTM) networks to predict future citations, researchers have exhibited dramatic accuracy improvement, with outcomes indicating a direction accuracy in excess of 50%. Thus, application of these advanced clustering methods can significantly improve the forecasting capability of neural networks to facilitate innovation and strategic planning in various fields of technology (Carreón et al., 2019). The increasing complexity of operational problems also increases the trend towards adopting artificial intelligence techniques into neural network models. The application of AIs in operations management has been extensive, with applications ranging from design to scheduling, process planning and control, and quality maintenance. Research, after reviewing over 1,200 published papers, shows growing reliance on diverse AI techniques, such as genetic algorithms and fuzzy logic, for the resolution of multi-dimensional problems. This is a trend that marks a turning point in neural networks towards hybrids that combine a number of methods, giving rise to more robust and resilient systems capable of handling dynamic environments. Thus, the future for neural networks is more varied, highlighting their application in solving complex operational issues in many areas (Kobbacy et al., 2007). Another trend gaining momentum is emphasis on fair AI and the moral use of neural networks in society. As these technologies permeate more and more into daily life, considerations regarding fairness, transparency, and accountability are at the forefront of discussion. The potential for bias in neural network algorithms makes it critical to develop ways of generating fair outcomes across various populations of users. Scientists are now advocating for initiatives that foster ethical practice in AI adoption, including fairness audits and good auditing processes. This greater focus on ethics will shape future advances in neural networks, affecting technical innovation as well as the effects on society. Therefore, with ever-evolving neural networks, emphasis on the ethical will be a cornerstone for their future sustainable and dignified development.

10.1. ADVANCEMENTS IN DEEP LEARNING

The major innovations in deep learning have had a great influence in many fields, particularly in the field of technology-enriched instruction. Advances lately have leveraged the power of deep neural networks, enabling intelligent tutoring systems and language training software that learn the unique requirements of an individual learner. Such systems take advantage of sophisticated algorithms that scan user interactions and adapt instruction, providing real-time feedback. As argued within research communities, current advances pinpoint the need for models like the Future TELL Model that highlight the importance of recognizing emerging technologies in language acquisition. The ability of deep learning to create more engaging and interactive learning environments means that ongoing investigation into these models can lead to better learning outcomes, ultimately changing teaching practices in an electronic world (Zou et al., 2018). Additionally, serverless computing has also been an efficient model for deployment of deep learning models with the extra advantage of managing computational resources. With this model, the developers are able to focus on application development without worrying about server management, which aligns very well with scalability demands of deep learning applications. Recent research has indicated that serverless platforms, such as AWS Lambda, have the right environment for deep neural network models to be inferred. However, challenges still lie in wait, particularly regarding latency due to cold starts, which need careful planning in order to meet stringent service level agreements (SLAs). This intersection of serverless and deep learning reveals the significant upcoming trend where flexibility and efficiency are prioritized, with the potential for enhanced deployment tactics which are adapted to the evolving demands of AI applications (Ishakian et al., 2018). As deep learning advances, the intersection of multidisciplinary solutions becomes more critical. Future advancements indicate that interdisciplinary research from various fields, such as cognitive science, neuroscience, and computer science, will be held accountable for developing more sophisticated neural network architectures. These multidisciplinary collaborations could enhance the performance and interpretability of deep learning models, addressing some of the ethical challenges surrounding AI. Secondly, studies on new algorithms that benefit from human cognitive knowledge can trigger breakthroughs in the way information is interpreted and processed by machines. With work towards building more intelligent and competent neural networks, the intersection of cognitive ideas with deep learning techniques is likely to characterize the future of artificial intelligence as a milestone in technological advancement (Zou et al., 2018) (Figure 10.3).

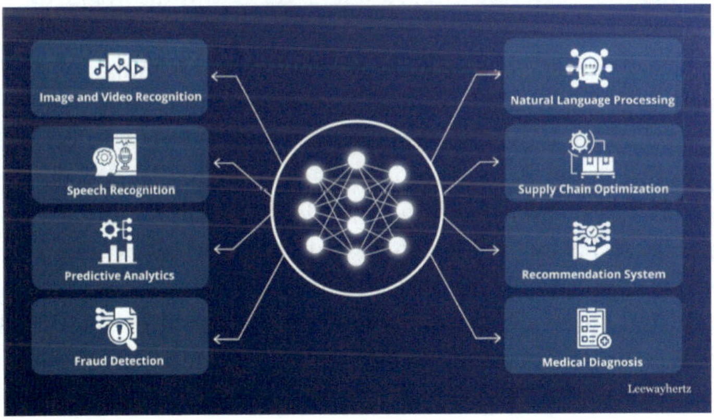

Figure 10.3. *Advancements in deep learning.*

Source: https://media.licdn.com/dms/image/v2/D5612AQGpjLwZ0_Gwuw/article-cover_image-shrink_600_2000/B56ZVqu2cnHQAQ-/0/1741252426865?e=2147483647&v=beta&t=RiPFKgnmmUhUlMJCY1mWN3qKz8322WOPEjz2_9jqmnw.

10.1.1. Enhanced Architectures and Models

Recent developments in neural network models are having a significant impact on machine learning program design, particularly in diagnostic and medical image applications. New architectures, such as Convolutional Neural Networks (CNNs), have demonstrated exceptional performance in classifying complex image information. For instance, CNNs were successfully utilized in detecting tissues while conducting colorectal cancer evaluations using confocal laser microscopy. By employing several transfer learning techniques, researchers were highly successful, with an area under the curve (AUC) of 97.1 in peritoneal metastases classification, showing how improved architectures can optimize real-time imaging in clinical use. This adaptability highlights the ongoing shift towards modern neural network models' inclusion to facilitate real-time feedback for intraoperative decision-making, and it highlights one of the prevalent trends in applying state-of-the-art neural architectures in high-risk environments like surgery and medicine (Bengs et al., 2019). The development of advanced architectures extends beyond the field of medical applications and shifts to others like single image super-resolution (SISR). Traditionally, SISR has proven to be a hard challenge to solve due to its ill-posed nature. Deep learning in recent years, however, has introduced extremely powerful algorithms that augment performance significantly. The models are categorized based on their contribution to good neural network design and optimization techniques, and play a key role in the overcoming of baseline limits. Through critical analysis of such architectures, researchers can optimize ways of addressing significant issues such as artifacts and detail loss. Continued developments in SISR are evidence of the potential of developments in neural networks to bridge conventional boundaries and pave the way for future innovation in image processing and restoration techniques (Liao et al., 2019). With increasingly advanced architectures extending into various fields, the way forward for neural networks is clearer. With being able to fine-tune models for specific tasks, there must be an understanding of the mechanics and requirements behind various applications. For instance, the optimal transfer learning strategy must be adjusted based on whether the dataset is large or small and the type of classification that is being carried out, as in recent research into colorectal cancer tissue classification. Moreover, continuous architecture innovation will place efficiency, scalability, and resilience as the key drivers to enable a broad spectrum of operating conditions. Neural network futures will be shaped by the present momentum in building and refining more effective architectures to address the high-performance requirements of applications across industries, with adaptability and task-oriented design playing key roles in compelling the creation of artificial intelligence tools.

10.1.2. Transfer Learning and Its Implications

The landscape of artificial intelligence is evolving at a fast rate, with transfer learning playing a pivotal role in neural network development. Transfer learning enables one to use the knowledge gained in a field and apply it in another, making model training more efficient and effective in low-data environments. The ability to apply pre-trained models to new tasks has the potential to significantly accelerate the development phase of machine learning projects, and hence it emerges as a handy tool in fields such as computer vision and natural language processing. Curiously, the growing popularity of transfer learning is due to its potential to render the historically resource-hungry training phases of deep learning less burdensome, and therefore accessible to more visionary models capable of learning how to easily adapt to various applications, as stipulated by the general categorization of TL methods apparent in the literature (Alexandre et al., 2017).

In the past years, the power of transfer learning has extended beyond adapting models, uncovering novel artificial neural network paradigms. Evolved Plastic Artificial Neural Networks (EPANNs), for instance, utilize biological intelligence and learning paradigms, where networks will dynamically change over time to adapt to new information. This is mimicking the human brains ability to transfer knowledge between various tasks and environments, ultimately leading to the creation of more robust and adaptive network architectures. With EPANNs potential for generating novel learning algorithms independently, scientists are tasked with finding systems that can overcome the constraints of traditional fixed networks. This ongoing research is critical, as it does not just give an opening for emerging trends in neural network technology but also proves holes into the brittleness of conventional design methods (Abbott et al., 2018). The importance of transfer learning cannot be overstated, particularly considering its applicability to the future directions of neural networks.

By accelerating the model training and enabling generalization, transfer learning makes it possible to create intelligent systems capable of performing on different applications. As researchers are continually perfecting transfer learning methods and bridging knowledge gaps across different domains, the possibilities for phenomenon-altering AI breakthroughs grow by orders of magnitude. The ongoing evolution of this field, with the inclusion of new methods such as EPANNs, augurs well for a future when neural networks are not just efficient but also smart and adaptive learners. As we move into this new era, it is imperative to utilize the knowledge achieved from transfer learning to drive further research and knowledge in neural networks (Abbott et al., 2018; Alexandre et al., 2017) (Figure 10.4).

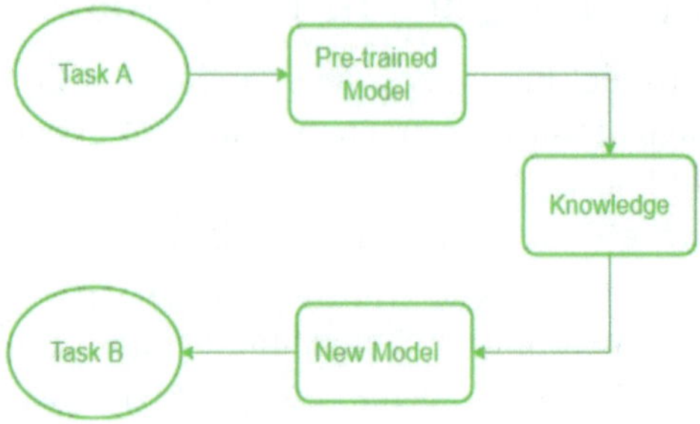

Figure 10.4. *Transfer learning.*

Source: https://media.geeksforgeeks.org/wp-content/uploads/20191027085246/Untitled-Diagram57.jpg.

10.1.3. Integration of Reinforcement Learning (RL)

The addition of RL to neural network architectures represents a significant breakthrough to enhance autonomous decision-making capacities in various domains. By using RL algorithms, neural networks can learn the best strategies through trial and error, improving their performance based on feedback from their surroundings. This incorporation upgrades classical supervised learning paradigms by enabling systems to modify and improve their behaviors in real time, making RL especially relevant for robotics and autonomous system applications. Worthily, advances in deep RL have attracted considerable attention, as evidenced by the growth in research on deep artificial neural networks within robotic systems, representing a coordinated effort to make such technologies more sophisticated for more complex real-world tasks (Gashler et al., 2017). The future of RL lies beyond robotics and tends towards wireless communications, where its coupling with neural networks can redefine connectivity technologies. While 6G wireless networks are on the horizon, the need for sophisticated machine learning (ML) methods becomes an imperative to deal with the increasing complexities of handling connectivity for enormous devices. RL can give zero-touch optimization, which enables networks to adapt and manage themselves dynamically on the basis of real-time data and user needs. This new system, in addition to being useful in optimizing protocol efficiency of the network, can also help design systems with high resilience that are capable of giving solutions to issues in different layers of communication architecture (Abbas et al., 2020). Thus, the synergy between reinforcement learning and neural networks presents an exciting way to create the next-generation communication systems. Briefly, the future path for neural networks largely hinges on the robust integration of reinforcement learning, combining adaptive learning capabilities with sophisticated modeling. As industries find themselves more and more in need of adaptive remedies to cope with changing conditions, e.g., robotics and wireless networks, the place of RL becomes further accentuated. With its ability to learn from experienced failures and successes, RL rounds out neural networks to produce applications that need high levels of interaction and responsiveness. This innovation is not only important for technology adoption but also for addressing pressing issues within society, paving the way for smart systems that can seamlessly be integrated into everyday life. Thus, strengthening the collaborative potential of these disciplines puts us in a position to investigate new frontiers in technology (Abbas et al., 2020; Gashler et al., 2017) (Figure 10.5).

Figure 10.5. *Reinforcement learning (RL).*

Source: https://indianai.in/wp-content/uploads/2021/05/Reinforcement-Learning.jpg.

10.2. EXPLAINABLE AI (XAI)

The development of XAI is a significant point in the history of neural networks, particularly in higher-order systems with deep learning. With increasing complexity, models start to resemble black boxes wherein internal workings are not available to users. This lack of transparency causes trust, responsibility, and ethical issues, particularly in high-risk applications like healthcare. Through the use of XAI methods, scientists aim to demystify such intricate algorithms so that their conclusions and outputs are more comprehensible. This is especially necessary in situations where human life and well-being come into play, with a requirement for a guarantee that AI systems are not only efficient but also explainable in their decision-making processes. The future of neural networks will indeed be guided by the evolution of XAI, which will engage people and manage to bridge the gap between technical success and ethical responsibility. The role of XAI becomes even more important in medical imaging, where accurate diagnoses that come from complicated algorithms can have life-changing effects on patient health. As noted in current research, the demand for AI solutions is high and, in addition to providing precise outcomes, also explain the reasons behind them. For instance, in diabetic retinopathy screening, convolutional neural networks (CNNs) are able to provide astounding classification accuracy as evidenced by achieving a 91% accuracy level (Pete et al., 2023). But the application of such models must have a robust interpretability framework to ensure that clinicians will be able to trust the AIs judgment. With the application of XAI techniques like LIME, such systems can give explanations of key features in images employed for making diagnoses, fostering users confidence and allowing for informed decision-making in clinical care. In more complex applications, XAI has the potential to transform not just healthcare technology but also a wide variety of industries based on neural networks.

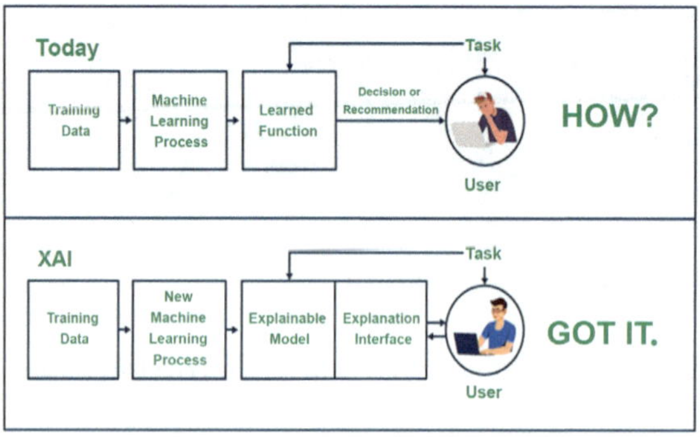

Figure 10.6. *Explainable artificial intelligence (XAI) concept.*

Source: https://media.geeksforgeeks.org/wp-content/uploads/20231201153509/Explainable-AI-Concept-1-660.png.

The importance of interpretability resonates in finance, self-driving cars, and criminal justice, where AI system decision-making must be explained for ethical and legal reasons. Therefore, XAI facilitates a new paradigm of multi-disciplinary collaboration that is required for creating and implementing reliable AI systems. Research in this area today is not only seeking to better refine techniques but also to grapple with the ethical implications of decision-making systems. Through anticipation and mitigation of biases in AI suggestions, practitioners are able to deploy neural networks that uphold social values while confronting challenges of modern technology. The integration of XAI will have a constitutive function in forming the responsible deployment of neural networks across diverse applications, with a synergy-based approach to innovation along with ethicality (Figure 10.6).

10.2.1. Need for Transparency in Neural Networks

With neural networks becoming increasingly integrated into diverse applications—ranging from autonomous vehicles to stock market prediction—there is an exigent requirement for transparency into their operations. This transparency is a result of the complexity and mystery that tend to encompass these models, giving rise to distrust and reluctance among users and stakeholders. One of the important elements of this transparency is a description of how these algorithms arrive at specific decisions or predictions. Through providing more knowledge of the workings of neural networks, developers are able to foster user confidence and promote wider use of AI technologies. This transparency matters not only to professionals but also to non-professionals who may be confronting analogous systems within social or commercial environments. Ultimately, rendering neural networks transparent will serve as a counterbalance to the in-built threats of algorithmic prejudice and error, fostering equity and accountability in their utilization. The ethical consequences of neural networks also reiterate the need for transparency, particularly in areas like healthcare, finance, and law enforcement, where the stakes are considerably higher. When neural networks are employed for making life-critical decisions affecting human lives, awareness of the inputs to data and procedures is essential. For example, biases introduced during the training data may generate unequal outcomes, which may not be realized in the absence of sufficient transparency. This problem is echoed in SIS debates, where the ethical concerns come to the forefront in predictive risk intelligence (Jiya et al., 2019). Addressing such ethical concerns is not just about the identification of potential bias but about mechanisms to ensure data is being used responsibly. Transparency facilitates easier riding over these ethical waves and encourages a sense of responsibility in using neural networks. Moreover, the dynamic nature of neural networks places an ongoing strain on maintaining transparency in the long term. As the systems are updated and optimized in a recurring manner, documenting and communicating the changes to their decision-making functions must be done. Stakeholders like researchers, developers, and the general public must be able to trace changes to the algorithms or underlying data that could affect outputs. This approach echoes the need for a collaborative discourse on AI's ontology and ethical considerations, as outlined in contemporary discourse about the nature of AI itself (Hawley et al., 2019). Failure to establish clear guidelines and frameworks for transparency can lead to a loss of trust among users, eventually stalling the innovation and growth of neural network applications. So, imposing transparency is not only a prophylactic measure against ethical fallacies but also triggers long-term innovation in the field of neural networks (Figure 10.7).

Figure 10.7. *Transparency and explainability of artificial intelligence (AI).*

Source: https://www.persistent.com/wp-content/uploads/2019/08/blog-banner-Thoughts-on-Transparency-and-Explainability-of-AI-scaled.jpg.

10.2.2. Techniques for Improving Interpretability

Increasing the interpretability of neural networks is becoming even more important since these models are going to be used across numerous high-risk applications, such as healthcare and finance. Methods for enhancing interpretability have the potential to make much more trusted and understandable neural model predictions for users. One notable method includes controlled manipulation of input data to examine how various elements contribute to the performance of the models and, as such, which features are most important. Conferences such as EMNLP 2018's BlackboxNLP featured this technique, demonstrating how altered input can expose the internal workings of neural architectures. By understanding the connection between some inputs and outputs, researchers can build models not only more accurate but also simpler, thereby ultimately aligning model behavior with user expectations (Alishahi et al., 2019). Another means of advancing interpretability is by examining the internal representations produced by neural networks directly. For instance, examining intermediate layers would be able to decrypt data obtained by such models. Recent work has proved that changes in neural architectures enhance interpretability since they render states of knowledge and network outputs within neural states more comprehensible. Researchers apply ways to demystify intricacies embedded in layers within neural networks to shed insight into decision-making states at different levels of processing. These kinds of changes also matter, as they simplify each layer's contribution and role towards end predictions, thereby serving as an important tool for more responsible AI use (Alishahi et al., 2019). The development of methodologies for interpreting some types of neural networks, such as recurrent neural networks (RNNs), has also yielded significant success in the context of enhancing interpretability. Recent studies have proposed systematic pipelines to comprehend single neuron dynamics in models like long short-term memory (LSTM) networks. By analyzing single cell contributions and responses, researchers can construct a deeper understanding of the contribution of individual components to the end output. The methods not only indicate the contribution of individual neurons but also identify the quantitative relationship between their dynamics and predictive accuracy of the models. With evolving methods, they provide more information on how network capacity influences dynamic behavior, which reinforces the call for interpretability in the broader conversation of future trends in neural networks.

10.2.3. Impact on Trust and Adoption in Industries

In the conversation of future trends in neural networks, the impact on trust and adoption across industries cannot be overstated. As firms continue to adopt sophisticated neural network technologies, the resulting improvement in operational efficiency and service quality are important drivers in shaping consumer mindsets. Customers base their trust on the degree of enhancement of such technologies in their own experiences. For instance, in areas such as tourism and hospitality, information technology has played an important role in offering personalized services and streamlining processes. The literature review reveals that IT is becoming more and more fundamental in customer relationship management and marketing, and productive IT applications can enhance significantly the trust consumers place and invite widespread usage across the industry (Buhalis et al., 2009). Hence, the creation of neural networks complements the industry's need for digitalization, establishing synergy between technological innovation and consumer trust. As business firms grow with the introduction of neural networks, implications go beyond just business development; they also encompass ethical concerns that have a significant impact on trust. Data usage transparency and algorithms hold pivotal positions in deciding public acceptance. Business firms must establish ethical operations, where data privacy is upheld while introducing the benefits of neural networks. This is particularly applicable in sectors such as healthcare and finance, where technology has to be relied upon. Consumers will embrace systems that present not only obvious advantages but also protect their interests. By fully describing how neural networks enhance decision-making, companies can overcome fears of automation and data security and provide greater uptake and acceptance of such technologies (Adams et al., 2019). The success of neural networks' integrity to gain consumer trust depends on this fine line between responsibility and morality. In addition, stakeholder engagement appears as a critical factor in establishing confidence and enabling neural networks to be embraced across industries. Engaging stakeholders, including customers, employees, and regulatory bodies, in the development process can build increased trust in the technology. Moreover, collaboration can foster a diverser innovation strategy, adapting to different needs and phobias of embracement of neural networks. By shared labor, sectors may create environments in which potential issues are openly discussed and resolved, generating well-educated consumption. This strategy is especially true for sectors that are highly influenced by public opinions, such as the tourism and hospitality sector, whose commercial prosperity depends directly on consumers' confidence. Therefore, strategic integration of stakeholder perspectives is essential in developing neural networks that not only develop technology but also enhance community trust and confidence (Buhalis et al., 2009).

10.3. NEURAL NETWORK OPTIMIZATION TECHNIQUES

The ongoing development of neural networks depends significantly on developing and using optimization methods. As neural architectures increase in size and complexity, efficient optimization methods become overwhelmingly paramount. Classic optimization approaches, such as gradient descent, typically fail to perform when applied to large data sets or deep networks. Various other alternative approaches, e.g., genetic algorithms and swarm optimization, have been researched as a substitute, and they can explore vast search spaces more effectively. Genetic algorithms, in particular, mimic natural mechanisms for evolution and provide a general framework to find optimal parameters for neural networks and thus enable rapid convergence and improved model performance. These advances illustrate a significant future direction for neural network research, showing how new approaches can overcome present constraints with conventional optimization paradigms (Kobbacy et al., 2007). Swarm optimization provides another novel trend for neural network optimization, simplifying the transition toward more nuanced and accurate predictive models. Drawing on a decentralized search approach, swarm optimization harnesses the aggregate behavior of agents to conduct comprehensive explorations of potential solutions. This approach has proven to be most effective in hyperparameter optimization of deep learning models, leading to predictive accuracy as well as computational efficiency enhancement. The combination of an ensemble neural network with swarm optimization can detect sophisticated patterns from sophisticated datasets, further solidifying its place in upcoming neural network approach. This integration accentuates the possibility of interdisciplinary approaches to harness the strength of various optimization paradigms to bring about a new age of model accuracy and performance (N et al., 2023). While neural networks continue to be widely used in domains as varied as finance, healthcare, and autonomous systems, the requirement for advanced optimization techniques will be mounting. Optimization breakthroughs will not only make existing neural frameworks better but will also provide the foundation for new paradigms to solve emerging issues. The mix of advanced techniques will enable better generalization, faster training, and enhanced problem-solving. As industries are increasingly dependent on AI-based solutions for decision-making, mastering and applying these optimization methods will be critical. As such, scientists must be careful to track trends and create methods that will enable neural networks to function within dynamic and complex systems so that they can continue to be relevant and effective in practical use (Kobbacy et al., 2007).

10.3.1. Evolution of Training Algorithms

Training algorithm development has been a cornerstone of the advancement of neural networks, significantly enhancing their efficiency and effectiveness. Early training algorithms such as backpropagation lay the ground by allowing networks to adjust weights based on error feedback. However, with increasing task and structure complexities, traditional methods were challenged, particularly for deep learning structures. This gave rise to the creation of contemporary algorithms that implement adaptive learning rates and optimization procedures, significantly boosting convergence speed and accuracy. Advances such as Adam and RMSprop are a reflection of this trend, offering adaptive methods that adjust learning rates dynamically. These advances enable training of algorithms that better deal with the intricacies of the data landscape, expanding the field of computer vision, natural language processing, and numerous other fields. Advances continued to drive the quest for biologically inspired training approaches that simulate natural learning to better train neural networks. The concept of Evolved Plastic Artificial Neural Networks (EPANNs) embodies such a phenomenon by using simulated evolution in order to build networks capable of evolving to adapt to their surroundings. Through the interplay of evolution, development, and lifelong learning, these systems have the ability to automatically deduce adaptive algorithms, giving insight into artificial as well as biologic mechanisms of learning. The remarkable advancement witnessed in EPANNs during the last two decades is an indication of the urgent demand for more versatile solutions that break the constraints imposed by hand-crafted networks. With further development of these algorithms, new approaches for designing neural architectures that allow not only increased efficiency but also flexibility for responding to new situations will be unlocked, as is essential for future applications of neural networks (Abbott et al., 2018). Another prevailing trend in the design of training algorithms continues to be their incorporation into emerging wireless communication networks, particularly with the anticipated rollout of 6G technology. Machine learning (ML) has the potential to revolutionize wireless systems by maximizing network operation based on advanced training algorithms. ML's ability to process high volumes of data enables it to learn and adapt to dynamic network conditions in real time. Zero-touch optimization is a concept where training algorithms powered by ML autotune network parameters such that they yield robust performance over a broad set of applications. This transition is significant as the demand for connectivity rises, and ML becomes a significant solution to challenges in complex communication layers ranging from physical to application layers. With such advancements, the future of neural networks intricately intertwines with enhanced training algorithms for enabling smooth connectivity and intelligence (Abbas et al., 2020).

10.3.2. Use of Genetic Algorithms (GAs) and Evolutionary Strategies (ES)

The union of GAs and ES is a milestone in the context of neural networks, particularly when considering the future directions. These methods take inspiration from natural selection mechanisms by using mechanisms such as mutation, crossover, and selection to optimize artificial neural network (ANN) architectures. This kind of *in silico* simulation of evolutionary processes enables researchers to search over an extremely broad space of network architectures that may outperform static, hand-tuned architectures better. This approach has not only shown new solutions for obscure challenges but has also highlighted the promise of GAs and ES in generating adaptive networks that evolve over time, paving the way for future AI advancements. Accordingly, with continued advances in computational power, the role of these evolutionary techniques in the development of neural networks is poised for exponential growth, ushering in a new era of smart systems. Particularly, the arrival of Evolved Plastic Artificial Neural Networks (EPANNs) showcases the profound potential in the merging of evolutionary techniques and neural network design. EPANNs adapt their function and architecture in real time relative to the environment, as they emulate the fabulous resilience of biological organisms. This resilience enables the creation of new algorithms that enhance learning processes, which in turn results in systems able to learn independently in real-world settings. As indicated by recent breakthroughs, continued development of EPANNs can potentially enable networks that not only adapt to experience but also autonomously propose adaptive approaches, resonating with the complexities of human-like intelligence. Incorporating such evolved concepts into neural networks is a promising path to follow in developing more advanced artificial intelligence systems that mirror real-life issues (Abbott et al., 2018). Moreover, the application of natural computing techniques, including GAs and ES, has expanded to many fields beyond typical computational problems, providing insights into environmental problems. With these nature-inspired algorithms, researchers can model and analyze complex dynamics of nature systems. Due to the flexibility of these techniques, efficient solutions for environmental informatics issues are obtained, demonstrating that these techniques can also be applied to broader issues such as climate change and resource management. The advantages of evolutionary strategy use derive from their ability to search across vast solution spaces as well as incrementally enhance outcomes through environmental feedback, thereby providing useful information that could transform sustainability and conservation practices. As the potential of such natural computing methodologies becomes better known and understood, they can play an important role in shaping future neural network applications and encourage innovative solutions for the most difficult global challenges (Kamilaris et al., 2018).

10.3.3. Hardware Acceleration and Its Benefits

The coming of hardware acceleration is a paradigm shift for the field of neural networks that will enable unprecedented performance improvements. Subspecialized electronics such as Field Programmable Gate Arrays (FPGAs) and Graphics Processing Units (GPUs) play a crucial role in speeding up convoluted computations typical of deep learning operations. By facilitating parallelism in processing, the devices reduce training as well as inference times significantly, enabling real-time use which was otherwise not possible. In particular, FPGAs' application in image recognition and particle physics simulation has shown enhancement of latency and throughput, as an example of hardware acceleration's role in simplifying existing neural network architectures. According to the presentation in recent reports, these enhanced improvements not only make operations more efficient but also allow for a greater exploration of machine learning algorithms, which pushes innovation in numerous fields like healthcare, finance, and autonomous systems. Besides speed enhancements, the benefits of hardware acceleration extend to energy efficiency and cost reduction as well. Both performance enhancement and significant power saving are attained by the deep neural network algorithm-hardware co-optimization framework, and both are most important for green computing. Excellent reductions in both computational complexity from O(n^2) to O(n log n) and storage complexity from O(n^2) to O(n), during training as well as inference, have been achieved by researchers using block-circulant matrices. These innovations not only ease the deployment of neural networks but also tackle the increasing requirement for energy-conscious solutions for applications in machine learning. Experimental results reported in research show that quicker systems are able to achieve impressive improvements in energy efficiency—up to 71X over traditional hardware, which is essential for scaling up neural networks in practical applications. As we look ahead, the coming together of hardware acceleration and advanced neural network techniques holds out a new era of functionality in artificial intelligence. FPGAs' flexibility to allow real-time processing, as evidenced by their application in a variety of domains ranging from particle physics to autonomous vehicles, brings into focus the potential for broader applications and economies of scale for these technologies. Higher throughput now enables large-scale data processing, opening the door to more sophisticated AI models reliant on big data sets and quick computation speed. In addition, existing research indicates that deploying these technologies as cloud or edge services not only enables their widespread high performance but also allows accessibility through platforms. As the future of machine learning continues to evolve, so will that of hardware acceleration, necessarily assuming a more and more pivotal position, solidifying itself as an element of neural network creation and societal use.

10.4. APPLICATIONS IN HEALTHCARE

Applications of neural networks in healthcare become increasingly revolutionary, particularly by machine learning technology such as Human Action Recognition (HAR). HAR uses deep learning systems to track gestures, movements, and activity and provides immense benefits in areas such as eldercare and support for disabled patients. By the application of sensors such as accelerometers and vision systems, neural networks can tag human actions with breathtaking accuracy. This capability is particularly important within healthcare settings where monitoring patient activities is critically necessary for prompt interventions. Architectures like Convolutional Neural Networks (CNNs) and Recurrent Neural Networks (RNNs) facilitate the design of powerful models that enhance action recognition. By resolving problems on the basis of data purity as well as the unbalanced distribution among classifications, researchers can design robust systems that improve the quality of life for vulnerable populations, which renders HAR an upcoming field in future research and development across healthcare applications (Valli et al., 2025). Another popular application of neural networks across healthcare is the integration of Convolutional Neural Networks (CNNs) for medical imaging diagnosis. CNNs have significantly enhanced the speed and accuracy of image analysis across various medical specialties, including oncology and cardiology. Being able to process large volumes of imaging data makes it possible to detect disease at an earlier stage and hence improve patient outcomes. Transfer learning and self-supervised learning methodologies also avoid the common pitfall of limited labeled datasets in medical use. With the use of pre-trained models, clinicians can perform with better diagnostics even under conditions of limited data. However, challenges still abound with regards to model interpretability and generalizability, particularly to diverse patient populations. The study should, therefore, still focus on enhancing data availability and establishing explainable AI paradigms in a way that CNN-based models can be seamlessly integrated into the clinic and ultimately end up improving patient care (Durgaraju et al., 2025).

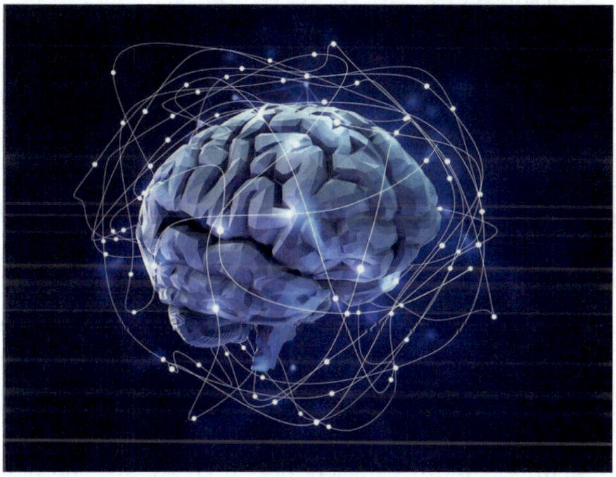

Figure 10.8. *Neural networks in healthcare.*

Source: https://miro.medium.com/v2/resize:fit:4800/format:webp/1 R3aNVhBi-H1TxBy3e_StWZQ.jpeg.*

In the years to come, the future of neural networks in medicine looks rosy, powered by continuous innovation in boosting diagnostic performance and personalizing treatment. Model design in federated learning can potentially bring inter-institutional cooperation to building comprehensive datasets without compromising patient confidentiality. In addition, endeavors towards leaner neural network architectures can enable real-time analysis on mobile devices and embedded systems, paving the way for healthcare applications in low-resource settings. The convergence of behavior testing through HAR and advanced imaging diagnostics through CNNs implies a cultural model of healthcare that intersects technology with empathetic delivery of healthcare. However, as neural networks find their way into ever more clinicians' hands, it is essential to address ethical issues and ensure equal access to these technologies. This balanced focus on technological advancement and ethical responsibility will shape a robust future environment for applications of neural networks in healthcare (Durgaraju et al., 2025; Valli et al., 2025) (Figure 10.8).

10.4.1. Diagnostic Tools and Predictive Analytics

The convergence of diagnostic tools and predictive analytics is going to redefine the future of many industries, courtesy of advances in neural networks. With companies accumulating immense amounts of data in regular activities, the necessity to convert this data into actionable insights ranks highest. This is a procedure of applying complex algorithms that can sort trends and patterns within complex datasets. The concept of rich data and poor information is handled precisely through the application of machine learning techniques, which maximize the extraction of valuable insights from collective pools of data (Koronis et al., 2018). With the capability of offering real-time monitoring and analysis, such tools allow organizations to make informed decisions on asset management and operational efficiencies in a bid to enhance overall productivity and performance. In addition, the application of predictive analytics with the use of neural networks has a significant influence on industries like building management and energy consumption. Recent studies have demonstrated how machine learning can be applied to improve many aspects of building performance, from design through use (Hong et al., 2020). By using neural networks to analyze patterns of energy consumption and predict occupancy, businesses can achieve significant energy savings and increased occupant comfort. However, despite success with initial applications, concerns remain regarding the transferability of models between systems and environments. Without huge datasets to learn on, many prediction models will collapse, and it only accentuates the need for complete datasets and good validation methodologies to guarantee reliability in use. Foreseeing the future of neural networks, the role of diagnostic tools and predictive analytics will increasingly become indispensable in most industries. The combination of big data analytics and IoT presents a remarkable opportunity to transform asset management activities by providing insights previously difficult to obtain. Through the victory over data administration complexity, organizations stand at an excellent position to leverage these technologies in developing more intelligent plans for future operations. Additional studies on the efficiency of neural networks for these applications will continue to produce revolutionary results, paving the way for innovations to maximize the utilization of resources and enhance decision-making processes, ultimately ensuring enhanced operational resilience and flexibility in a progressively changing world (Hong et al., 2020; Koronis et al., 2018) (Figure 10.9).

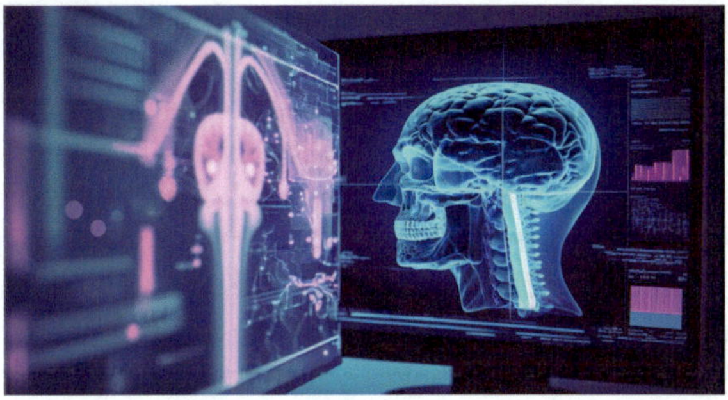

Figure 10.9. *Diagnostic tools.*

Source: https://www.talkerian.com/wp-content/uploads/2023/08/neural-networks.webp.

10.4.2. Personalized Medicine and Treatment Plans

The basis of personalized medicine is rapidly evolving through the assistance of developments in the field of neural networks, which are central to personalizing treatment regimens to the uniqueness of a patient. As medicine increasingly relies on evidence-based approaches, personalized medicine promises improved outcomes by using extremely large data sets to create personalized treatments. Central to this is the ability of neural networks to decipher complex biological information and identify patterns that would be otherwise undetectable. With the utilization of these technological tools, health professionals are able to offer therapies that are aligned with the genetic susceptibility, lifestyle, and preferences of every individual patient. This change of course has the potential for enhanced treatment options, minimizing side effects and optimizing therapeutic efficacy, ultimately leading to better patient satisfaction and outcome. However, the use of personalized medicine through neural networks is faced with gigantic challenges of patient privacy and accountability of algorithmic decisions. Utilizing vast databases implies dealing with sensitive patient information, raising the issue of data protection and data privacy breaches. As research data, the success of black-box medicine, in which the use of machine learning diagnoses and heals diseases, depends on being able to solve these issues. Major steps must be undertaken to ensure that data are collected, implemented, and disseminated ethically, as patient confidentiality must be safeguarded while developing algorithms for personalized medicine (Ford et al., 2016). Thus, a delicate balance must be struck between using big data for health improvement and the protection of patients' rights, which remains a key consideration as this field progresses. Besides ethical considerations, deep learning method construction offers novel paradigms for the optimization of treatment planning in personalized medicine. Emerging evidence has demonstrated the efficacy of using deep feature selection methods, particularly with stacked auto-encoders, to discover relevant biomarkers driving health outcomes. For instance, investigations into the determinants of hypertension in African-Americans utilized deep learning to assess and compare these determinants, providing insightful findings on left ventricular mass and heart health consequences (Levy et al., 2017). Such technologies continue to evolve and are a revolutionary means of disease diagnosis and treatment with even greater accuracy, paving the way ultimately towards broader ends of personalized medicine. This blending of technological innovation and health care delivery represents the dynamic future envisioned for neural networks in individualized treatment protocols (Figure 10.10).

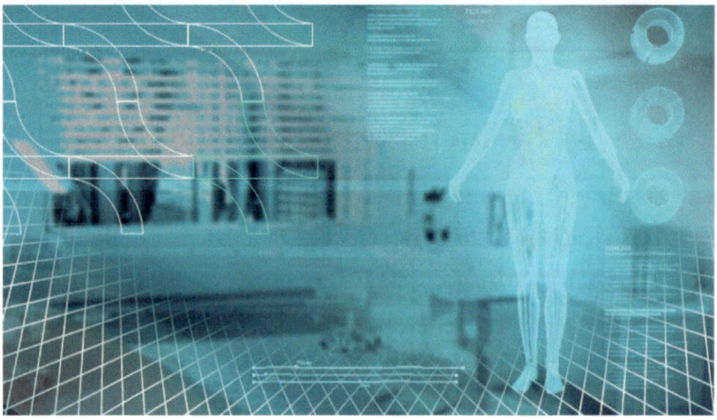

Figure 10.10. *Understanding personalized medicine.*

Source: https://www.bgosoftware.com/blog/wp-content/uploads/2024/01/bgo-software-blog_post-in-article-simple-img-%E2%80%93-Understanding-personalized-medicine.png.

10.4.3. Ethical Considerations in Medical Artificial Intelligence (AI)

As AI makes more inroads into the health sector, ethical issues have become more crucial. The application of AI systems within hospitals is accompanied by critical concerns regarding patient privacy, informed consent, and data security. These are eclipsed by the technological innovation of the potential of AI. Ethical standards, however, must guide the incorporation of AI to ensure that the welfare of the patient is always paramount. The aggregation and utilization of personal healthcare data require robust safeguards to safeguard patient privacy. This concern is particularly important in that AI algorithms require a gigantic amount of data to perform well, opening the potential for misuse of data. Ethical expectations call for healthcare practitioners to be concerned not merely with efficiency but with transparent practices that establish patient trust, enabling a more humane technological culture for medical AI. Contributing to ethical consideration are implications for AI decision-making in treatment and diagnosis. As autonomous AI becomes more widespread, accountability issues ensue.

Figure 10.11. *Ethical considerations in artificial intelligence (AI) for healthcare.*

Source: https://media.licdn.com/dms/image/v2/D5612AQFhROXsxCjLHw/article-cover_image-shrink_720_1280/article-cover_image-shrink_720_1280/0/1720037320836?e=2147483647&v=beta&t=C0uuuZDfJwSUiNDrtUms9hjuqsh8kkn_aP-KkYwJ_vSI.

If a machine makes an incorrect diagnosis or recommendation, attributing fault is problematic. Such vagueness will also be reflected in medical professionals' hesitation to fully embrace AI tools. Ethical systems will need to establish clear boundaries of responsibility that enable both human and machine operations, where roles are distinguished and marked clearly. In addition, the threat of bias in AI algorithms represents additional risk; training data may unintentionally reflect societal biases, promoting discriminatory health care delivery. This is an ethical issue which necessitates the active engagement of developers, clinicians, and ethicists to monitor and offset biases regularly, eschewing discriminatory behavior patterns that could damage the very fabric of fair care. Lastly, the dynamic conception of consciousness and emotional intelligence in AI systems is useful in further accentuating the necessity of ethical intervention. As referenced in books, the quest for artificial consciousness yields profound implications for the development and implementation of medical AI. Machine learning algorithms have the ability to mimic human-like responses but lack true emotional engagement or empathy, which play crucial roles in patient care. While AI facilitates clinical decision-making, it can never replicate contextual understanding human caregivers provide. This gap underlines the necessity of maintaining human control in medicine AI. Ethical consideration must also address the potential simulation of emotional response by AI without real comprehension, even misleading patients seeking genuine human compassion. As technologies advance, it is now essential to construct ethics that accept such limitations while enabling responsible incorporation of AI in healthcare settings, ultimately welcoming innovation specific to patient-centric care (Figure 10.11).

10.5. NEURAL NETWORKS IN AUTONOMOUS SYSTEMS

The evolution of neural networks has served to greatly ease the construction of autonomous systems, offering a powerful tool with which decision-making processes can be enhanced. With autonomous systems rapidly becoming an industry norm, the ability of neural networks to process massive volumes of data in real time has been invaluable. Such networks utilize techniques such as deep learning to analyze sensory information, enabling vehicles, drones, and robots to perceive the world around them and respond appropriately. Applications of such systems could range from transport to medicine, demonstrating their wealth in the area of applications. As indicated by recent research, the connection between operations management and artificial intelligence (AI) has produced new solutions to complex issues, further highlighting the central role that is played by neural networks in operational performance (Kobbacy et al., 2007). In coming times, we can anticipate the launch of increasingly sophisticated autonomous systems. The use of machine learning in wireless networks is poised to transform the autonomous systems paradigm, particularly as predicted on the horizon is the emergence of 6G technologies. The impetus for this transformation is that it makes transparent connectivity essential for facilitating real-time interactions between autonomous systems and their surroundings. As defined in recent research, machine learning techniques have a central role to play in the improvement of network performance, assisting in the development of self-driving vehicles and other autonomous systems (Abbas et al., 2020).

The utilization of ample computational resources and large datasets makes it simple to train complex neural models, which dynamically adapt to new problems encountered while navigating autonomously and communicating. Consequently, the integration of wireless technologies and neural networks not only enhances capabilities in operation but also provides the basis for the future developments in autonomous systems. Future directions with neural networks portend a paradigm shift in the performance and implementation of autonomous systems in the long term. As the sophistication of neural designs continues to grow, so will the capacity of these systems to understand advanced situations and make independent decisions. The direction that the future takes is towards hybrid models, which combine traditional algorithms with neural networks in an attempt to create increased reliability and explainability in decision-making. As businesses look to tap into the advantages of AI, it is imperative to listen to ethics and the inherent problems that accompany the deployment of these technologies. The debate on how AI ought to be used responsibly will be instrumental in ensuring that neural network development benefits society while ensuring safety and accountability concerns are handled. The trajectory of innovations thus promises a wiser, more networked world, in which autonomous technologies can elegantly become part of daily life (Figure 10.12).

Figure 10.12. *Revolutionizing autonomous vehicles with neural networks.*

Source: https://thedailyplaniot.com/wp-content/uploads/2019/03/Self-driving-neural-networks.png.

10.5.1. Role in Self-Driving Vehicles

Self-driving car development is a significant benchmark in the history of transport systems, heavily reliant on innovation in the field of neural network technologies. These vehicles use sophisticated algorithms to translate sensor data in real-time, cameras, and LiDAR inputs to navigate autonomously in crowded spaces. Neural networks drive perception layers in such systems, transforming sensory data into usable information. Road signs, pedestrians, and other hazards are recognized by image recognition algorithms, for instance, and decision-making models balance out likely risks to allow vehicles to make safe navigation choices. This dynamic interaction of neural networks not only enhances the operational effectiveness of autonomous vehicles but also their ability to react to diverse driving conditions, both of which are critical factors in the wider adoption of autonomous driving technology. Moreover, neuromorphic computing integration heads the way in maximizing self-driving vehicle systems.

By mimicking the structure and function of the human brain, neuromorphic implementations offer higher processing rates and reduced energy consumption, both needed for real-time vehicle operation. The systems are capable of handling massive amounts of data with event-based dynamic vision sensors to capture data as it occurs in the environment rather than operating off a stream of continuous frames. Therefore, autonomous vehicles have improved perception and quicker responsiveness, which are required to cope with urban environments or highways. The connection between neural networks and neuromorphic computing is a pivotal trend shaping the future of autonomous systems and their functional potential, representing an efficient complement to conventional computing models, which could result in additional robotics and mobile agent applications as emphasized by current contributions (Marchisio et al., 2025). Aside from efficiency and safety, the role of machine learning algorithms in autonomous vehicles also encompasses more advanced things such as path planning and obstacle avoidance. Reinforcement learning-based approaches enable vehicles to plan optimal routes while dynamically adapting to unforeseen circumstances, such as roadblocks or changes in traffic lights. Application of neural networks for control and navigation facilitates advanced decision-making, allowing the vehicle to operate smoothly in dynamic scenarios that are continuously changing. As detailed in recent research, application of these advanced methods is more superior compared to traditional control approaches since it eliminates limitations created by fixed programming techniques (Kumar et al., 2025). Besides, anticipating future developments in artificial intelligence allows developing more resilient and adaptable systems, to better optimize not just performance but also ethics and trustworthiness for autonomous driving solutions. All of them hold the promise of reshaping the transportation industry, leading it to a future of intelligent, responsive, and sustainable mobility (Figure 10.13).

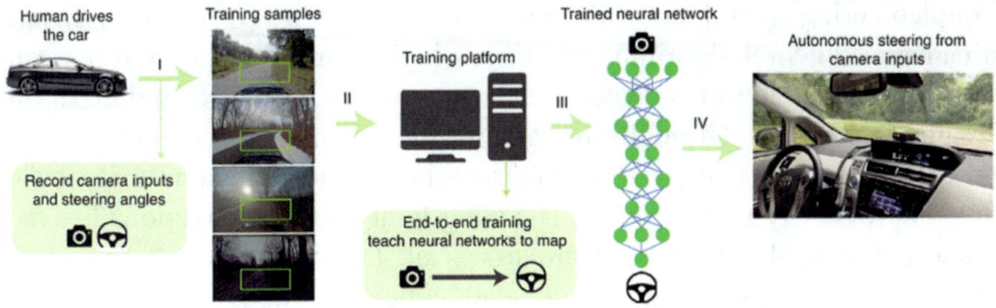

Figure 10.13. *End-to-end representation of a self-driving algorithm.*

*Source: https://cdn-images-1.medium.com/max/880/1*YQg4IKxIFVZmdsSyDblwuw.png.*

10.5.2. Applications in Robotics and Drones

As neural network advancements grow, their applications in robots and drones are becoming more revolutionary. Neural networks provide greater machine learning capabilities, and robots and drones are able to sense, comprehend, and respond to their surroundings more effectively. For instance, autonomous drones employing real-time processing can do complex operations like precision agriculture and surveillance autonomously. This ability significantly enhances performance, reduces costs, and increases efficiency in many industries. In addition, neural networks enhance decision-making for robotics, allowing machines to learn from experience and adapt their behaviors accordingly. As a result, we have the emergence of more intelligent and advanced robots capable of doing tasks in ambiguous environments, which is essential in operations such as disaster relief or search and rescue missions. The use of neural networks in drones is a culmination of those that exceed sheer functionality; they have an impact on global politics as well. Military establishments, especially those of China and the U.S., are increasingly studying the functions that AI-based systems, such as drones, can perform in warfare and spywork. Horowitz et al. (2018) highlights how the present artificial intelligence revolution is reshaping military power and describing how advanced AI technologies could lead to revolutionary changes in global security frameworks. With drone technology moving at a breakneck speed, the capability of drones to conduct high-risk missions from reconnaissance to precision attacks underlines the necessity for robust regulatory frameworks. The convergence of AI, robotics, and the use by the military demands careful assessment of ethical implications and international competition to ensure that these technologies do not fall into wrong hands or result in inacceptable consequences. Furthermore, the environmental importance of implementing neural networks on drones cannot be overlooked. Drones with advanced neural algorithms are increasingly employed for environmental surveillance, assisting in endeavors such as monitoring wildlife and observing ecological changes. Through the application of natural computing-based methods, researchers can make use of drones in order to gather and analyze data that was previously unachievable, shedding light on the interactions between human and natural activities. Kamilaris et al. (2018) looks at some of the nature-inspired methods that enhance data collection, modeling, and analysis for environmental informatics. Consequently, the emerging synergy between neural networks and unmanned aerial vehicle (drone) technology not only fuels robotics development but also significantly contributes to sustainability efforts. A well-informed understanding of these uses will be vital to informing future development that not only is ethically sound but also green (Figure 10.14).

Figure 10.14. *Drones.*

Source: https://www.avnet.com/wcm/connect/3f17233a-12d4-4d48-9ee9-f64d-3de0e880/drone-768x432.jpg?MOD=AJPERES&CACHEID=ROOTWORKSPACE-3f17233a-12d4-4d48-9ee9-f64d3de0e880-paijYkP.

10.5.3. Challenges and Safety Concerns

As the growth of neural networks continues, so do the challenges and concerns that must be resolved to make them effective and reliable. The primary concern is transparency in neural network decision-making, more familiarly referred to as the black box problem. This obscurity creates the problem of understanding how exactly the systems arrive at certain decisions, which creates trust and verification problems. Stakeholders, such as end-users, regulatory bodies, and developers, are looking for higher transparency and accountability, particularly in high-stakes applications like autonomous driving or healthcare. The ongoing quest for tenable traceability in uses of neural networks is now helping to bring such issues into relief because the capability to provide robust connections between inputs, decisions, and output is important for building trust and supporting safe release in safety-critical systems (Antoniol et al., 2017). Safety concerns are also heightened by the need for neural networks to operate in dynamically changing environments. Given that these systems are being deployed in real-world applications, they are confronted with unforeseen variables and adversarial conditions. Compelling these systems to be robust and safe requires rigorous testing and validation protocols capable of simulating a wide variety of circumstances and edge cases that can reveal vulnerabilities. The calls for greater measures of assurance in the sector are informed by research work aimed at identifying gaps in existing safety protocols.

Figure 10.15. *How to guarantee the safety of autonomous vehicles.*

Source: https://media.wired.com/photos/65bd5ee7960589665dfbad00/3:2/w_1920,c_limit/AutonomousSystems-bySenorSalme-Lede-Quanta-Science.jpg.

For instance, the Tigar's project finds it essential to integrate assurance methods such as formal verification and dynamic testing to enhance the safety and reliability of autonomous vehicles and other forms of automated systems in which neural networks are applied (Bloomfield et al., 2020). In addition, the use of neural networks in safety-related areas raises ethical and legislative issues that must be met with care. As the technologies spread into society, the impact of decisions made by neural networks can have serious consequences for human life and social systems. Defining standards and guidelines that govern the deployment of neural networks is therefore paramount in controlling risks and promoting ethical use. More focus is currently being placed on involving a wide range of stakeholders from ethicists and engineers to public policy experts in the debate regarding the safety of neural networks. This multi-stakeholder interaction can result in the development of comprehensive frameworks for solving the technological and societal challenges posed by these advanced systems and thereby make them more reliable and efficient (Antoniol et al., 2017) (Figure 10.15).

10.6. INTEGRATION WITH OTHER TECHNOLOGIES

Integration of neural networks with other cutting-edge technologies has the ability to transform numerous different fields, enhancing capabilities and efficiencies in numerous different applications. Integrating neural networks with Internet of Things (IoT) devices, for instance, results in decidedly more intricate real-time data processing and decision-making. Neural networks can analyze data collected from heterogeneous sensors in real-time to make smarter choices in intelligent homes, healthcare monitoring, and process control. Such synergy notwithstanding, it also provides an environment in which predictive maintenance and anomaly detection can thrive, leading to improved operations longevity and cost savings. As businesses search for more innovative solutions, their integration with IoT technology is a classic example of a necessary trend that demonstrates their capability to transform operating models and enhance efficiency. Moreover, the combination of neural networks with bioinformatics provides the serious implications for medicine and healthcare. As reviewed recently, unraveling complex biological systems, such as disease, requires the integration of diverse types of data across multiple dimensions of genome, transcriptome, and microbiome profiles. Neural networks are a strong tool to integrate these disparate data sets that offer a holistic systems perspective hard for traditional methods to achieve. Through the use of machine learning, researchers can now identify important biomarkers, predict disease prognosis, and even tailor treatments to a patient based on a wealth of genetic and phenotypic data. This combined approach not only facilitates enhanced diagnostic accuracy but also propels the development of personalized medicine, and underscores the key role that neural networks play in the future of biotechnology and health sciences, as argued at more length in Goldenberg et al. (2018). Lastly, efficiency in engineering tasks by way of integration with neural networks clarifies yet another aspect of technological progress. The theoretical foundation presented in attempts to enhance sustainability in engineering projects focuses on the interaction between machine learning practices and traditional engineering practice. With the use of neural networks for the processing and optimization of information about materials, processes, and the environmental impact, engineers have the potential to significantly enhance their ability to create sustainable solutions. It is a multi-faceted method—spanning from application design to the actual machine learning practices used—designed to balance operational performance with environmental needs. With industries increasingly focusing on sustainability, integrating neural networks into engineering systems becomes essential in driving innovation to support environmental stewardship, which is the future of neural networks in facilitating sustainable technological development, as presented in García de Vinuesa et al. (2020).

10.6.1. Synergy with Internet of Things (IoT)

The convergence of neural networks and the IoT is a revolutionary change in processing and using real-time information through different applications. Through the use of neural networks, IoT devices will be able to process huge volumes of data collected through sensors, which will result in more sophisticated decision-making. For example, in the healthcare sector, the use of IoT and neural networks can improve predictive analytics so that interventions can occur in a timely manner and patient outcomes will be enhanced from Jung et al. (2017), it is possible to explain and understand the multifactorial nature of health-related events using such synergy, with a focus on the critical need to merge physiological information with contextual information derived from IoT sensors. Such synergy not only improves the accuracy of the predictions but also ensures an improved grasp of the factors causing an impact on health status, resulting in preventive healthcare strategies. Also, the development of Building Information Modeling (BIM) reflects the significance of IoT in encouraging efficiency within architectural and engineering settings. The effective utilization of BIM has improved alongside the development of IoT technologies, which encourages an integrated and sustainable environment within the building construction industry, as specified by Aish et al. (2019). The harmony between neural networks and IoT delivers data-driven information that translates into efficient energy usage and resource usage. For example, neural networks can incorporate occupancy and environmental information collected by IoT sensors, producing smart design modifications that optimize energy efficiency. This also increases working-in-sustainability and drives innovation in building practice as a significant step toward future-proofed infrastructure planning. As the intersection of neural networks with IoT advances further, it is crucial to address the problems associated with this technology. Data privacy and protection become paramount concerns, particularly in cases where personal data—such as health metrics or behavior patterns—is being collected and transmitted through. Ensuring robust data protection mechanisms will be critical to maintaining user trust and compliance with standards. Additionally, establishing seamless interface interaction points between users and IoT systems will be critical to enhancing user experience and engagement. Moving beyond such complexities, as observed by Jung et al. (2017), but utilizing the capability of prediction by neural networks in IoT environments simultaneously, will ensure future applications not only become innovative but also secure and user-friendly (Figure 10.16).

10.6.2. Collaboration with Quantum Computing

A combination of quantum computing and neural networks has high potential for enhancing computational power in artificial intelligence. As neural networks improve, adding quantum computing might make them more efficient at processing complex sets of data and optimizing complex problem-solving operations. Quantum computation's ability to process superposition and entanglement allows for the parallel execution of many calculations, potentially speeding up neural network training and improving it on tasks involving large-scale data processing. For instance, recent developments have demonstrated that machine learning can effectively address challenging quantum many-body problems by utilizing architectures like restricted Boltzmann machines (RBMs). By employing these tools within the quantum realm, researchers are constructing innovative bridges that deepen our understanding of both disciplines, ultimately contributing to a more robust framework for future neural network applications (Deng et al., 2017). Moreover, the alignment of neural networks and quantum computing exposes one to the possibility of creating hybrid systems that would leverage the strengths of both domains. As algorithms become more sophisticated in quantum computing, one can utilize them to specialize in enhancing neural network learning procedures, particularly in identifying high-level representations and features from complex input data. These advancements also have the potential to create superior machine learning paradigms to traditional methods through the leverage of the high-dimensional spaces present in quantum information. In addition, human computation progress highlights further the relevance of this synergy. By leveraging human cognition combined with quantum-enhanced capabilities, it is possible to create systems which process information with an unprecedented degree of precision and effectiveness. Such an integrated approach not only boosts each's computational capacity but creates a synergistic environment where human and machine intellect support one another (Clark et al., 2015). The implications of merging quantum computing and neural networks extend beyond the research community into real-world applications that would address many of society's most vital concerns. For example, future developments in predictive modeling driven by these collaborative platforms can lead to breakthroughs in various disciplines like healthcare, climatology, and finance analytics. Such predictions would be supported by high accuracy possible with quantum-augmented neural networks, allowing for more knowledgeable decision-making protocols. With the advancement of skills in such hybrid platforms, they could potentially integrate into robust, multi-modal platforms with the capability to tackle complex socio-technical issues. These systems can very well become the backbone of a collective intelligence, allowing human acknowledgment of a potential to enhance our capability to deal with an increasingly complex world and solve the wicked problems currently driving the world agenda. The marriage of neural networks and quantum computing will therefore dictate future technological avenues (Clark et al., 2015).

10.6.3. Impact on Cybersecurity Measures

With neural networks advancing further, their integration into security mechanisms has attracted significant attention due to their two-way capability of strengthening defenses as well as making sophisticated attacks easier. Artificial intelligence, in the form of neural networks, enhances detection and reaction to threats, allowing organizations to process massive amounts of data quickly and identify anomalies that are indicative of potential threats. By doing so, security mechanisms become proactive instead of reactive. Yet this same technology also poses risks since cyber attackers increasingly employ neural networks to develop adaptive attacks, enhance malware capabilities, and generate evasive actions. The knowledge that AI may build cyber offense as effectively as it fortifies defense sparks an imperative burden on security systems, highlighting the value of concerted efforts based on intelligence from diverse actors in the industry (Diep et al., 2020). The intersection of cybersecurity and AI has been the source of initiatives like the Centre for European Policy Studies Task Force, which exemplifies the growing recognition of AIs role in cybersecurity settings. This group of stakeholders aims to address the technical, ethical, and governance challenges posed by the use of AIs in cybersecurity. Their discourse is focused on the urgent need for threat intelligence sharing, especially concerning vulnerabilities enabled by AI. With neural networks at the forefront of their deployment for cybersecurity, this cross-functional approach is critical to understanding the offensive and defensive capabilities of AI technologies. Moreover, the Task Forces investigation of policy experimentation and the need for rigorous assessment guidelines for Trustworthy AI indicates a commitment to managing the complexity imposed by these technologies (Fantin et al., 2020). With neural networks being universally accepted by companies, their implications on cybersecurity need to be considered from a very general perspective. It is incumbent upon trustworthy AI architectures and ethical codes of practice to make sure that such technology is responsibly utilized. The new ecosystem calls for an architecture that not only protects against misuse of AI but also makes developers and users accountable. Meeting the requirements of prevailing law while conforming to the distinct challenges faced by AI necessitates a creative approach to implementing cybersecurity interventions. Through a culture of ongoing evolution through policy change and participation by stakeholders, the sector is able to ease the risks associated with AI-based cybersecurity solutions. Lastly, the two-pronged function of neural networks as both a means of attack and defense calls for a system-wide response to addressing the emergent trends of modern-day cybersecurity (Diep et al., 2020; Fantin et al., 2020).

SUMMARY

The finding of this research into future developments in neural networks highlights the monumental advancements and potential that lie ahead for this rapidly developing field. As artificial intelligence is being incorporated increasingly into industries, developing neural networks will play a key role in resolving complex, large-scale problems. Advances such as improved architectures and the use of new algorithms signal a trend toward more efficient and responsive systems. These developments not only enhance the capacity of neural networks to process vast amounts of data but also provide for more sensitive interactions with users and environments, thus paving the way for unprecedented applications spanning industries from medicine to autonomous systems. Something that is most critical to consider going forward is how to provide better means of measuring the potential of emerging technologies, particularly in the context of neural networks. The citation network analysis, as outlined in recent research, emphasizes the understanding of the development patterns of various technology clusters. One primary contribution of this research is the application of the Stochastic Block Model as a robust methodology for patent citation clustering.

This approach can also provide company executives and investors with knowledge of the life cycle of the technology, making strategic investments in future developments of neural network innovation, particularly because such technologies are diversifying and coming of age (Carreón et al., 2019). Furthermore, operational management using AI methods, although solving increasingly complex problems, suggests future trends that will determine the development trajectory of neural networks. A wide-ranging review of artificial intelligence applications illustrates the range of approaches and their evolution during the past decades, highlighting major areas such as design, scheduling, and quality control. As neural networks become increasingly complex, exploration of hybrid approaches blending genetic algorithms with traditional techniques will establish further innovation. The ability to integrate varying AI techniques to solve operating issues reinforces the need for continued research and investment in adaptive and dynamic neural networks that adjust to changing demands and technologies (Kobbacy et al., 2007).

The neural network environment is changing rapidly, closely following advances in AI and machine learning. Among the top trends is the growing usage and implementation of AI technologies across various sectors, primarily in human resources (HR). According to research, it has been established that even though the majority of organizations acknowledge the significant role AI will play, only 31% are prepared to utilize it within their HR processes. Specifically, recruitment and hiring top AI applications, whereby 49% of organizations apply these systems for talent sourcing. This trend emphasizes the necessity for organizations to optimize efficiency and improve decision-making in HR practices. Refusal on the part of companies to adopt full-scale AI points to a more general challenge in aligning technological advancement with organizational readiness, ultimately determining the course of neural network adoption across industries (Joh et al., 2018). Apart from the field of HR, another established direction in the future of neural networks is the development of Evolved Plastic Artificial Neural Networks (EPANNs). EPANNs are inspired biologically, with a degree of computation performance optimized through evolutionary processes.

Owing to progress in the domain, EPANNs have been able to develop adaptive algorithms autonomously, revolutionizing the artificial intelligence world. The flexibility embedded in such networks allows for the disruption of traditional hand-crafted limitations, and what emerges is new and innovative solutions that can adapt in a given environment. This is a significant development that highlights the capacity of EPANNs to simulate biological adaptation as well as the application of simulated evolution in expanding the paradigms of artificial neural networks (Abbott et al., 2018). Along with the advancements in neural networks is the increasing focus on ethical considerations and implications of AI technologies. With more organizations relying on AI-based solutions, there is a greater need to address the potential for bias in datasets and algorithms. Integrating equitable and accountable AI methods is required to establish trust and acceptability by stakeholders. This crossing of technology development with ethical standards will significantly influence the destiny of neural networks. Researchers and organizations are faced with making transparency, accountability, and inclusivity their primary focus as they tackle the challenges of AI deployment. The crossing of state-of-the-art neural network techniques with ethics is, therefore, important in ensuring that AI is developing responsibly in various areas, towards a more sustainable future in technology.

REFERENCES

1. Abbas, R., Ahmad, I., Ali, S., Amuru, S., et al. (2020). 6G white paper on machine learning in wireless communication networks. http://arxiv.org/abs/2004.13875 (accessed on 25th September 2025).
2. Abbott, A., Abraham, A., Allis, L., Alpaydin, E., Anderson, J., et al. (2018). Born to learn: The inspiration, progress, and future of evolved plastic artificial neural networks. https://core.ac.uk/download/162581731.pdf (accessed on 25th September 2025).
3. Abu-Naser, S. S., Abu-Nasser, B. S., Barhoom, A. M., Khalil, M., et al. (2019). Energy efficiency prediction using artificial neural network. https://core.ac.uk/download/237182408.pdf (accessed on 25th September 2025).
4. Adams, R., Amafabia, D., Barker, T., Beka, G., et al. (2019). Proceedings of Abstracts Engineering and Computer Science Research Conference 2019. https://core.ac.uk/download/287582059.pdf (accessed on 25th September 2025).
5. Aish, C., Crawley, D., Eastman, C., Engelbart, D., Salmerón-Manzano, E., et al. (2019). Bibliometric maps of BIM and BIM in universities: A comparative analysis. https://core.ac.uk/download/286590556.pdf (accessed on 25th September 2025).
6. Alexandre, L. A., de Sá, J. M., Santos, J. M., Silva, M. J., et al. (2017). Distribution-based categorization of classifier transfer learning. https://core.ac.uk/download/304001828.pdf (accessed on 25th September 2025).
7. Alishahi, A., Chrupała, G., & Linzen, T. (2019). Analyzing and interpreting neural networks for NLP: A report on the first BlackboxNLP workshop. http://arxiv.org/abs/1904.04063 (accessed on 25th September 2025).
8. Amini, A., Grosu, R., Hasani, R. M., Lechner, M., et al. (2018). Response characterization for auditing cell dynamics in long short-term memory networks. http://arxiv.org/abs/1809.03864 (accessed on 25th September 2025).
9. Antoniol, G., Cleland-Huang, J., Hayes, J. H., Vierhauser, M., et al. (2017). Grand challenges of traceability: The next ten years. http://arxiv.org/abs/1710.03129 (accessed on 25th September 2025).
10. Arsiwalla, X. D., Herreros, I., Moulin-Frier, C., Sanchez-Fibla, M., et al. (2017). The morpho space of consciousness. http://arxiv.org/abs/1705.11190 (accessed on 25th September 2025).
11. Bengs, M., Drömann, D., Ellebrecht, D. B., et al. (2019). Deep transfer learning methods for colon cancer classification in confocal laser

microscopy images. http://arxiv.org/abs/1905.07991 (accessed on 25th September 2025).

12. Bloomfield, R. E., Fletcher, G., Imai, K., et al. (2020). Towards identifying and closing gaps in assurance of autonomous road vehicles–A collection of technical notes Part 1. https://core.ac.uk/download/305120054.pdf (accessed on 25th September 2025).
13. Boucher, J., Brock, J., Brown, C. C., et al. (2002). The temporal binding deficit hypothesis of autism. https://core.ac.uk/download/48714.pdf (accessed on 25th September 2025).
14. Bryson, S. E., Clahsen, H., D'Souza, D., Gopnik, M., Guiraud, J. A., Karmiloff-Smith, A., Pinker, S., et al. (2014). Environmental and genetic influences on neurocognitive development: The importance of multiple methodologies and time-dependent intervention. https://core.ac.uk/download/20117923.pdf (accessed on 25th September 2025).
15. Buhalis, D., Law, R., & Leung, R. (2009). Information technology applications in hospitality and tourism: A review of publications from 2005 to 2007. https://core.ac.uk/download/75017.pdf (accessed on 25th September 2025).
16. Carreón, E. C. A., Hentona, A., Hiraoka, T., et al. (2019). Community detection and growth potential prediction using the stochastic block model and the long short-term memory from patent citation networks. http://arxiv.org/abs/1904.12986 (accessed on 25th September 2025).
17. Clark, A., Dugas, A. F., Westphal, A. J., Woolley, A. W., Resch, B., Cardamone, C., Martin, C. C., et al. (2015). Human computation and convergence. http://arxiv.org/abs/1503.05959 (accessed on 25th September 2025).
18. de las Heras García de Vinuesa, A., Luque Sendra, A., Zamora-Polo, F., Ávila al. (2020). ADAPTS: An intelligent sustainable conceptual framework for engineering projects. https://core.ac.uk/download/322844241.pdf (accessed on 25th September 2025).
19. Deepa, N., & Devi, T. (2023). Unveiling future trends for predicting online smart market stock prices using ensemble neural network. https://core.ac.uk/download/618248282.pdf (accessed on 25th September 2025).
20. Deng, D. L. (2017). Machine learning Bell nonlocality in quantum many-body systems. http://arxiv.org/abs/1710.04226 (accessed on 25th September 2025).
21. Di Zou, Wang, F. L., & Xie, H. (2018). Future trends and research issues of technology-enhanced language learning: A technological perspective.

https://core.ac.uk/download/201668357.pdf (accessed on 25th September 2025).

22. Diep, Q. B., Truong, T. C., & Zelinka, I. (2020). Artificial intelligence in the cyber domain: Offense and defense. https://core.ac.uk/download/323112801.pdf (accessed on 25th September 2025).
23. Ding, C., Li, Z., Liao, S., et al. (2018). Towards ultra-high performance and energy efficiency of deep learning systems: An algorithm-hardware co-optimization framework. http://arxiv.org/abs/1802.06402 (accessed on 25th September 2025).
24. Doctor, F., Iqbal, R., Mahmud, S., et al. (2020). Big data analytics: Computational intelligence techniques and application areas. https://core.ac.uk/download/228156656.pdf (accessed on 25th September 2025).
25. Duarte, J., Harris, P., Hauck, S., et al. (2019). FPGA-accelerated machine learning inference as a service for particle physics computing. http://arxiv.org/abs/1904.08986 (accessed on 25th September 2025).
26. Fantin, S., Ferreira, A., & Pupillo, L. (2020). CEPS Task Force on Artificial Intelligence and Cybersecurity Technology, Governance and Policy Challenges: Task Force Evaluation of the HLEG Trustworthy AI Assessment List (Pilot Version). CEPS Task Force Report, 22 January 2020. https://core.ac.uk/download/287647893.pdf (accessed on 25th September 2025).
27. Ford, R. A., & Price, W. N., II. (2016). Privacy and accountability in black-box medicine. https://core.ac.uk/download/84123604.pdf (accessed on 25th September 2025).
28. Gabrys, B., Musial, K., & Skarding, J. (2021). Foundations and modelling of dynamic networks using dynamic graph neural networks: A survey. http://arxiv.org/abs/2005.07496 (accessed on 25th September 2025).
29. Gashler, M. S., & Pierson, H. A. (2017). Deep learning in robotics: A review of recent research. http://arxiv.org/abs/1707.07217 (accessed on 25th September 2025).
30. Goldenberg, A., Hoffman, M. M., Leskovec, J., et al. (2018). Machine learning for integrating data in biology and medicine: Principles, practice, and opportunities. http://arxiv.org/abs/1807.00123 (accessed on 25th September 2025).
31. Haladjian, H. H., & Montemayor, C. (2016). Artificial consciousness and the consciousness-attention dissociation. https://core.ac.uk/download/131210570.pdf (accessed on 25th September 2025).

32. Hawley, S. H. (2019). Challenges for an ontology of artificial intelligence. https://core.ac.uk/download/187718197.pdf (accessed on 25th September 2025).

33. Hong, T., Luo, X., Wang, Z., et al. (2020). State-of-the-art on research and applications of machine learning in the building life cycle. https://core.ac.uk/download/288432582.pdf (accessed on 25th September 2025).

34. Horowitz, M. C. (2018). Artificial intelligence, international competition, and the balance of power (May 2018). https://core.ac.uk/download/211333744.pdf (accessed on 25th September 2025).

35. Ishakian, V., Muthusamy, V., & Slominski, A. (2018). Serving deep learning models in a serverless platform. http://arxiv.org/abs/1710.08460 (accessed on 25th September 2025).

36. Jiya, T. (2019). Ethical implications of predictive risk intelligence. https://core.ac.uk/download/228181605.pdf (accessed on 25th September 2025).

37. Joh, E. E., & White, W. B. (2018). How we can apply AI and deep learning to our HR functional transformation and core talent processes? https://core.ac.uk/download/219377041.pdf (accessed on 25th September 2025).

38. Jung, T. P., Litvan, I., & Rajagopalan, R. (2017). Fall prediction and prevention systems: Recent trends, challenges, and future research directions. https://core.ac.uk/download/323065612.pdf (accessed on 25th September 2025).

39. Kamilaris, A. (2018). A review on the application of natural computing in environmental informatics. https://core.ac.uk/download/572206900.pdf (accessed on 25th September 2025).

40. Koronis, A., Zhou, C., Tamilselvan, P., Khuntia, S. R., Khuntia, S. R., Khatri, V., & Peng, X. (2018). Smart asset management for electric utilities: Big data and future. http://arxiv.org/abs/1706.09711 (accessed on 25th September 2025).

41. Kumar, Y., & Thakar, V. (2025). The review of control and navigation using ML and AI techniques. Journal of Information Systems Engineering and Management. https://www.semanticscholar.org/paper/c26dfdf5cde6e75082a65fbb5c016981d644352b (accessed on 25th September 2025).

42. Lashgari, A., Oraee, B., & Sayadi, A. R. (2011). Estimation of capital and operation costs of backhoe loaders.

43. Levy, P., Li, X., Nezhad, M. Z., et al. (2017). SAFS: A deep feature selection approach for precision medicine. http://arxiv.org/abs/1704.05960 (accessed on 25th September 2025).

44. Liao, Q., Tian, Y., Wang, W., et al. (2019). Deep learning for single image super-resolution: A brief review. https://core.ac.uk/download/227336600.pdf (accessed on 25th September 2025).
45. Marchisio, A., & Shafique, M. (2025). Neuromorphic computing for embodied intelligence in autonomous systems: Current trends, challenges, and future directions. https://www.semanticscholar.org/paper/e78dac7a8830f52a12e2c63cbc6195cc0076c322 (accessed on 25th September 2025).
46. Parmar, J., Parmar, J., Sahatiya, P., Tulsani, et al. (2023). XAI applications in medical imaging: A survey of methods and challenges. https://core.ac.uk/download/591405083.pdf (accessed on 25th September 2025).
47. Pete, V. S. (2023). XAI-driven CNN for diabetic retinopathy detection. https://core.ac.uk/download/596330875.pdf (accessed on 25th September 2025).
48. Sairam Durgaraju, D. V. T. V., & Harikrishna Madathala. (2025). Transforming healthcare diagnostics: A comprehensive review of convolutional neural networks in medical imaging and disease prediction. 2025 6th International Conference on Mobile Computing and Sustainable Informatics (ICMCSI). https://www.semanticscholar.org/paper/cb4203e0ddc48722ea81dec6d658cf908b098d39 (accessed on 25th September 2025).
49. Valli, C., & Amutha, R. (2025). Neural networks in human activity recognition: Trends, challenges, and future directions. 2025 3rd International Conference on Intelligent Data Communication Technologies and Internet of Things (IDCIoT). https://www.semanticscholar.org/paper/2507609c048b7d2f8c6d05c1ad0e458ee9ff189f (accessed on 25th September 2025).

INDEX

P

Q

R

S